UNVEILING *the* MUSE

UNVEILING *the* MUSE

The Lost History of Gay Carnival in New Orleans

HOWARD
PHILIPS SMITH

Foreword by
Henri Schindler

University Press of Mississippi / Jackson

www.upress.state.ms.us

Support for this publication has been generously provided
by the John Burton Harter Foundation. Additional funding
also provided by the LGBT+ Archives Project of Louisiana.

LGBT+ ARCHIVES PROJECT of LOUISIANA

The University Press of Mississippi is a member of the
Association of American University Presses.

First printing 2017
∞

Library of Congress Cataloging-in-Publication Data

Names: Smith, Howard Philips, author.
Title: Unveiling the muse : the lost history of gay carnival
    in New Orleans / Howard Philips Smith ; foreword by
    Henri Schindler.
Description: Jackson : University Press of Mississippi,
    2017. | Includes bibliographical references and index. |
    Description based on print version record and CIP data
    provided by publisher; resource not viewed.
Identifiers: LCCN 2017015271 (print) | LCCN 2017017382
    (ebook) | ISBN 9781496814029 (epub single) |
    ISBN 9781496814036 (epub institutional) | ISBN
    9781496814043 (pdf single) | ISBN 9781496814050
    (pdf institutional) | ISBN 9781496814012 (cloth : alk.
    paper) | ISBN 9781496814067 (mobi)
Subjects: LCSH: Carnival—Louisiana—New Orleans—
    History. | Gays—Louisiana—New Orleans—Social life
    and customs. | Lesbians—Louisiana—New Orleans—
    Social life and customs.
Classification: LCC GT4211.N4 (ebook) | LCC GT4211.N4
    S65 2017 (print) | DDC 394.2509763/35—dc23
LC record available at https://lccn.loc.gov/2017015271

British Library Cataloging-in-Publication Data available

For Michael Joseph Bonnet

The joyous, chaotic Carnival season distinguishes New Orleans from all other American cities and particularly those with gay communities. New Orleans gays use this time of year to show the rest of America just how wondrous their city can be. Although bedlam and wholesale cavorting are reserved for Mardi Gras day, the true glory of Carnival is represented in the more than two hundred balls that take place between Epiphany and Shrove Tuesday. Some balls are considered low class; others are highly exclusive. The gay balls of New Orleans are even more elite than those given in straight society. It is not unusual to see a member of Comus go begging for a ticket to a gay tableau. Whereas some straight krewes have more than two hundred members, gay carnival organizations are small—under fifty members—and limit the number of guests to fewer than a thousand. The preparations are more arduous, the costumes more fanciful and refined, and the tableau more imaginative for the gay balls, where themes and decorations are jealously kept secrets.

The special experience of going to a gay Mardi Gras ball, it is said, is only exceeded by actually participating in one.

—*Impact Magazine*, Carnival Supplement, March 1979

CONTENTS

Meanwhile, welcome joy and feast,
midnight shout and revelry, tipsy
dance and jollity.

—John Milton, *Comus, a Mask*

Cross-dressing, older than Carnival itself, has always been an integral part of the great festival. In the early 1830s, the earliest written newspaper account of Mardi Gras in New Orleans offered witty descriptions of several maskers: "In the procession were several carriages superbly ornamented—bands of music, horses richly caparisoned—personations of knights, cavaliers, and Punchinellos, all mounted. Many of them were dressed in female attire, and acted the lady with no small degree of grace."

On Gallatin Street, the raucous sailor district, most of the women were dressed as men and the men as women. "One we noticed as particularly good. It seemed to be a boy of about sixteen, with a female countenance, who was rigged up in fashionable female attire. The skirts of his, or her dress, were hooped out so extravagantly that the whole sidewalk was covered, and the bonnet was so wonderfully small that it covered but a small portion of the back of the head, leaving a flood of ringlets free to flutter as they pleased."

In the following century, the soirées of gay men were no doubt enjoyed, but no written accounts of them have survived. The first attempts to form organizations of gay men in the 1950s were greeted with police hostility, harassment, and arrests. Howard Smith's new book, *Unveiling the Muse: The Lost History of Gay Carnival in New Orleans*, is an important and long overdue history that documents the evolution of gay Carnival from oppression to glory. Smith's thorough and smartly written chronicle begins with details of police raids of the first krewe and traces the eventual formation of major organizations and their wide acceptance by the public. Back in the streets on Shrove Tuesday, the annual competition of the Bourbon Street Awards, now more than fifty years old, is considered

Drag pioneer Harvey Goodwin performing as his alter ego, Harvey Lee, at the Club My-O-My on the Lakefront, 1950s. Female impersonators sang live at the club, entertaining tourists as well as prominent figures such as Al Capone and Tallulah Bankhead. Courtesy of the University of Arkansas at Little Rock Center for Arkansas History and Culture.

by many a highlight of the day by the hundreds of viewers who struggle for a view of the flamboyant costumes, many taken directly from the gay balls.

Smith's delightful panorama is also the first to name names, from Miss Dixie's Bar of Music, which was the center of the universe for gay men and women on Mardi Gras afternoons, to the forgotten founders of the gay krewes and the all-important role of Elmo Avet. A full chapter is devoted to Avet, a legendary antiquarian whose role in gay Carnival was as pivotal as his fabulous costume creations. It's all there and more in *Unveiling the Muse*, a splendid collection of colorful tales and previously unseen ephemera.

—HENRI SCHINDLER
November 1, 2015
New Orleans

Great Babylon is come up before me. Oh, the wickedness, the idolatry of this place, and the unspeakable riches and splendor!

—Rachel Jackson, Wife of General Andrew Jackson

Gardette-LePrêtre House, corner of Dauphine and Royal Streets, 1938. The ubiquitous ironwork balconies of the Vieux Carré can appear incongruous to first-time visitors, like an old Hollywood movie set. Photograph by Frances Benjamin Johnston. Courtesy of the Louisiana State Museum, New Orleans, Accession No. 1981.132.059.

Tennessee Williams, as he recounted in his personal *Notebooks*, first landed in New Orleans in December 1938 in a haze of anticipation and excitement. For gay men in the South especially, New Orleans was a mecca, a sacred city mentioned in hushed tones and awe even among those Southern Baptists who despised its blatant hedonism. The city became known as New Babylon, and for those who sought an alternative way of living, it was the first stop after the closet door was finally unbolted. With it came the promise of a different life, one that could barely have been imagined elsewhere. Williams wrote, "I am delighted with this glamorous, fabulous old town. I've been here about three hours but have already wandered about the Vieux Carré and noted many exciting possibilities. Here surely is the place that I was made for, if any place on this funny old world." For many, it was also a revelation, for here in the center of the city was a movie-set world of fantasy and history, filled with openly gay men and women living a parallel existence out in plain view. This amazing and unique island came into focus slowly and inexorably and by the 1950s had blossomed into a

Bourbon Street in the French Quarter, early 1950s. Home to jazz and strip clubs, female impersonators, and cocktail bars, none of which ever closed. Bourbon Street was where native New Orleanians, travelers, and transplants felt welcome and uninhibited. The area became the center of the city's small gay community, allowing members to be themselves and experience an existence quite different from the one in the outside world. Photograph by Jack Robinson. Courtesy of the Jack Robinson Archive, Memphis.

Tennessee Williams, 1940s. Photograph by Vandamm Studios. Courtesy of the New York Public Library, Theater Division, NYPL for the Performing Arts.

Jack Robinson, early 1950s. Courtesy of the Jack Robinson Archive, Memphis.

Gabriel, Robinson's partner, early 1950s. Photograph by Jack Robinson. Courtesy of the Jack Robinson Archive, Memphis.

rich and expressive center of gay culture caught up in the high rituals of Carnival and its grand centuries of excess.

The French Quarter had long held the reputation of a Bohemian ghetto, a rundown, forgotten part of the city where artists and writers congregated. This not-so-subtle code was also readily understood as homosexual. But where others avoided the area, many found an unlikely haven and refuge, such as writer and preservationist Lyle Saxon, a well-known gay figure who hosted an international salon in his French Quarter apartment. Eventually, many bars were catering to a gay clientele—the St. James, Mack's, the Rendezvous, the Starlet Lounge, Jean's, the Powder Puff, the Bourbon House Restaurant and Bar, Café Lafitte, and the extraordinary Dixie's Bar of Music. Bourbon Street became a nexus for all things gay, and friendships formed and bonds were strengthened over cocktails and gossip during endless, carefree nights. These were more than occasional get-togethers, and a real sense of community began to develop among the natives and transplants, all sympathetic souls caught up in the slowed-down pace and insistent air of decadence.

However, New Orleans was an exception to the rule as the country fell under the spell of a madman in the 1950s. Senator Joseph McCarthy appeared as a growing menace, and his hearings to find and oust communists and their sympathizers from the government struck fear across the nation. This so-called Red Scare permeated the media, and searches for subversives and deviants became a national obsession. Little known during this period was McCarthy's other agenda, his Lavender Scare, a concerted attempt to ferret out homosexuals and use them as scapegoats for the growing Cold War. Despite the harsh repression that resulted from these witch hunts, the gay scene in New Orleans enjoyed an openness and exuberance that seemed to defy the national postwar atmosphere of suppression. A raid on several bars in 1953, including the Goldenrod Inn on Frenchmen Street with its straight façade up front and lesbian bar in the rear, became a momentary harassment by the police, but few were charged. Gay bars in the French Quarter were allowed to prosper as long as they made their payoffs to the police and the mob. During the year, masking in public was forbidden, courtesy of laws that initially sought to control slaves and subsequently constituted a feeble attempt to thwart the power of the Reconstruction-era Ku Klux Klan. On Shrove Tuesday, however, the most flamboyant and creative costumes could be seen parading around the narrow streets of the Old Quarter. Jack Robinson, a recent arrival from Clarksdale, Mississippi, photographed his friends in the streets and in Miss Dixie's courtyard, celebrating the day in costume, drinking and socializing, and not only recording a visible and defiant gay culture but to a great extent capturing a sense of self-awareness that permeated the day. Not content with ordinary masks or costumes, gay men in particular channeled camp figures from the depths of history and idolized stage and screen actresses and even exotic characters from fiction, exhibiting an abandon and creativity unique to an established gay culture. Another series of Robinson photographs from this period reveals gay men in their apartments, artists at work in their studios, and a general gay café society at ease in New Orleans and comfortable enough to allow itself to be recorded for posterity. Lee Bailey, Robinson's friend and confidant, urged Robinson to pursue his growing photographic talent. A native of Louisiana, Bailey subsequently accompanied Robinson and his partner, Gabriel, to the East Coast and become famous himself as an author of a series of cookbooks revered by many as great examples of American cuisine.

Toward the end of the decade, the French Quarter changed dramatically. Both the district attorney and the mayor wanted to clean up its so-called moral corruption to appease complaints from locals and cater to a growing tourist trade. Gay men were targeted, and signs of effeminacy—pants with zippers on the side, makeup, flamboyant scarves, high heels, or simple gestures—could result in arrest. Undercover policemen came into bars and vigorously entrapped patrons. Even Tulane fraternity brothers created a sport out of gay bashing—a sort of initiation and rite of passage. One dramatic incident in October 1958 not only caught the attention of the city but struck fear in the gay community. Fernando Rios died after three Tulane students accosted him in the French Quarter. All three were found innocent of the charges, much to the dismay and horror of Rios's friends. Instead of remaining visible targets, gay costume parties moved to private homes, where participants felt safer from harassment. Many have speculated that the Rios incident galvanized the gay population and directly influenced the formation of a gay Carnival krewe. This was not the case, as the Krewe of Yuga, the first gay krewe, predated the attack. The general atmosphere of repression and danger, especially for any sort of visibility, prompted the move out of the inner city to areas where things could be kept more hidden and relatively safe. Recalled John Henry Bogie, the last captain of the Krewe of Yuga, "We had already had our first costume ball Uptown. The French Quarter was dangerous and violent. When the Rios incident happened, we decided to stay away and have our balls elsewhere."

Lee Bailey, early 1950s. Photograph by Jack Robinson. Courtesy of the Jack Robinson Archive, Memphis.

What did it mean to be gay during the 1950s in New Orleans? It meant being different, developing a subterranean culture with its own jargon and gestures, and mostly hiding this new persona from the general population. Assimilation was not an option, and secret codes and quotations from revered figures, such as Oscar Wilde and Mae West, in both literature and on the silver screen were memorized and idolized. Coming out was a slow process, a cautious coming-of-age repeated over and over again. Gay culture in New Orleans was itself unique but exhibited the general trend among gay men and women at the time: a transformation into an exaggerated personality to fit into these narrow niches. Particularly expressive was the coded use of camp talk. In "Inverted Histories: 1885–1979," Richard Meyer notes that it was "a parlance in which femininity may be assigned to and possessed by men as well as women." Even today, the debate continues within the broader gay community whether camp and flamboyance are now passé, no longer needed as clandestine points of reference. But in the early days of gay consciousness and liberation, to be gay was to connect with an already established way of speaking, acting, and reacting, and this discrete lexicon served to create bonds and connections where there was safety in community and ultimately acceptance.

John Kennedy Toole explores this depiction of the gay sensibility with Dorian Greene, a character in Toole's *A Confederacy of Dunces*. Hearkening back to a similar characterization found in Oscar Wilde's *The Picture of Dorian Gray*, Toole's Dorian is effeminate and flamboyant, catty and wildly witty, wearing a "bottle-green velvet jacket" from his vintage clothing store in the French Quarter and drinking frozen daiquiris that looked like "pineapple snowballs." Even though this portrayal was somewhat clichéd, Toole allows these gay characters enough space to be themselves in the relative shelter of the Old Quarter. His main character, Ignatius J. Reilly, describes all homosexuals as "degenerate" and their lives as a "surreptitious form of living" but not as something to be avoided. Here Toole uses Greene as a solution to warfare, in itself an extremely camp solution. Even Dorian, trapped in the fictitious Night of Joy bar on Bourbon Street in a downpour, declares, "I think I'm in the wrong bar anyway."

This early gay male persona was embodied in Eloi Bordelon, the quintessential queen, and he flaunted this Otherness with charisma and charm, tempered with equal doses of venom and vitriol. Coupled with a razor-sharp sense of aesthetics, a lethal tongue was a survival strategy. Born into an old Algiers family across the river, Eloi had become a fixture in the French Quarter demimonde, living on St. Ann Street across from the Caverns, a notorious gay hustler bar now known as the Bourbon Pub. Bordelon guided Tennessee Williams through the intricate labyrinths of this new world when he first came to the city. Williams had found someone unapologetic and confident about being seen as gay and at the same time tedious and moody. Their relationship quickly blossomed into a sexual one. He looked upon Bordelon and his group of friends, however, with awe and respect and allowed himself to surrender to this overpowering force, swirling like a juggernaut around this newfound gay universe behind the looking glass. In a September 1941 letter, Williams admitted, "I got reckless and invested half of my current checque in a membership at this rather exclusive club [the New Orleans Athletic Club], but it is worth it as there is a marvelous salt water pool, Turkish bath and the prettiest Creole belles in town. I am already well-established in their circles and my particular intimate is Eloi Bordelon." However, this liaison was not to outlast the autumn. "I had a violent and rather bloody matrimonial break-up with the Bordelon, and as she is the queen bee of the bitch society there, it would be unpleasant for me to remain during her displeasure." Williams briefly moved back to St. Louis, as he never seemed to stay in one place for very long. Bordelon later moved to New York City and found success as an interior designer of distinction, specializing in trompe l'oeil effects. Having studied at Tulane University, he found Manhattan a good fit and lived comfortably with his partner, Paul Uihlein. In 1984, shortly before his death, Bordelon garnered the Arthur Ross Award, a prestigious honor from the Institute of Classical Architecture and Art. His departure from his native city however left a considerable vacuum, one that was quickly and readily filled.

Elmo Delacroix Avet arrived in New Orleans as a young man from Plaquemine, a small town upriver, but did not stay very long. Born in the 1890s, he traveled to Los Angeles after a stint in the U.S. Navy during World War I and later worked in the Metro-Goldwyn-Mayer art department, where he met famous actors and actresses and schmoozed with the gay Hollywood elite, including Cedric Gibbons and George Cukor. Legend surrounded this sojourn in Los Angeles and placed Avet on the sound stages of *The Wizard of Oz* beside Gibbons, creating some of the most memorable sets of the movie. During World War II, he settled in Manhattan, where his social circle still included actors and theater people. However, Avet's interest in decor and antiques led him back to New Orleans, where he established a series of Flea Market Antique Shoppes (continuing to operate one in Manhattan). By the early 1950s, he had firmly placed himself at the center of a gay underground in the French Quarter, surrounded by a growing coterie of young men hungry for tales of his travels. Central to this group was Dixie's Bar of Music on Bourbon Street, owned by Yvonne Fasnacht. The annual Carnival season, with its parades and costumed balls, only added creative fuel to the fire. The French Quarter formed the epicenter of a growing band of restless celebrants that included such early gay luminaries as John Dodt, Douglas Jones, and the ill-fated

Clay Shaw. They became caught in the whirlpool of Carnival in a city where it was not only welcomed but worshiped like a god.

Traditional Carnival in New Orleans had its origins in Europe and Catholicism, celebrating the flesh before the penitence of the Lenten season and the rebirth of Easter. The Mistick Krewe of Comus first paraded in the streets of the city in 1857 and held its first tableau ball at the elegant Gaiety Theatre. Several men from Mobile had wanted to continue their Carnival traditions in a more structured manner rather than the random street clashes of New Orleans and formed this first krewe, named after the masque written by John Milton. Other Carnival clubs, or krewes, were soon formed—Rex, Proteus, and Momus—and the procession of krewes with their elaborate balls took hold over the city, which came to expect ever-more-extravagant displays and lavish presentations. These traditions became inviolate, as only elite families filled the ranks of these organizations, and their daughters' debut in society served as a highlight of these highly ritualized *soirées dansantes*. However rigid the old-line krewes appeared on the surface, beneath it all was a spirit of play and mockery, even a nod to pagan mythology and themes that titillated and entertained the populace. Other marginal groups in the early 1900s had formed their own mock-royalty krewes, such as the African American Zulu Social Aid and Pleasure Club, and by the mid-1950s, the well-attended gay costume parties thrown every year in Uptown naturally and as a matter of course were transformed, perhaps in jest, into the first gay krewe, the irrepressible Krewe of Yuga.

The Yuga balls became larger every year, and by the time the fifth ball was held in Metairie, the police arrived in full force to put a stop to a supposedly lewd party. All those in attendance were in costume, some in drag, and the mounted police easily arrested almost everyone and threw them in jail. The atmosphere of the French Quarter had forced the krewe to find other venues for their balls, but the overall police clampdown on so-called deviants continued at a breakneck pace. Tragedy somehow seemed unavoidable. Miss Dixie, a staunch supporter of her gay clientele and a lesbian herself, put up bail money from her own bar. This dramatic turn of events spelled doom for the Krewe of Yuga, but the Krewe of Petronius, formed a year earlier by a younger, more adventuresome group of gay men, dealt with this catastrophe with surprising ingenuity. Petronius regrouped and secured a state charter as a legitimate Carnival organization and held tableau balls much in the manner of the old-line krewes. With guests required to attend in formal wear and all costumes presented on stage, there was little chance of raids. No other costumes were allowed, and members ensured that the audience included plenty of women, especially mothers, sisters, and friends of the krewe.

This formula was a grand success, and other krewes soon followed suit, among them Amon-Ra, Ganymede, Armeinius, Apollo, Olympus, Lords of Leather, and Celestial Knights, among many others. By the mid-1980s, gay Carnival enjoyed a much-deserved Golden Age, where brilliant tableaux graced the stages of the city with flair and flamboyance. Still maintaining an air of mystery and sophistication, these balls were described by audience members as some of the most daring ever witnessed. Tickets, which from the beginning were always gratis, suddenly became extremely desirable and were meted out with such exactitude and vengeance that only those deemed worthy were granted this privilege. Kevin Flot and his husband Steve Rutledge, who attended many of the Golden Age balls, commented that "when a spectacular costume came on stage the packed audience would collectively gasp in amazement." The cachet of the gay krewes grew

Artists in the French Quarter during the early 1950s. The gay community had a strong presence here even during the McCarthy witch hunts. Photographs by Jack Robinson. Courtesy of the Jack Robinson Archive, Memphis.

in prestige until there seemed no bounds to their creativity. Yet few gay krewes survived the decades to come, and even fewer recalled their mysterious origins or the names of those who had worked so tirelessly to make it all happen.

The history of gay Carnival must stand alongside that of traditional Carnival as one of its many manifestations and is recounted in all its glorious detail and nuance in this first complete study. New Orleans, a haven for many a lost soul, has survived despite all the tempests and tantrums yet possesses an infectious esprit that remains indefatigable, a hunger that remains insatiable. This spirit of revelry and impertinence that permeates the atmospheres of this most European of cities inevitably abides. Once thought lost and irretrievable, the history of gay Carnival has been salvaged from the maw of time and triumphantly declares itself in bold legitimacy.

Toward the end of his life, Tennessee Williams came to long for New Orleans and its charm. His pied-à-terre at 1014 Dumaine Street beckoned him to return to the bosom of his beloved city. He became a fixture at the side bar of Marti's Restaurant across the street and happily attended gay balls during the festive weeks of Carnival when he could. On February 9, 1980, Williams attended the Krewe of Amon-Ra's Omicron ball, whose theme was the *Bluebird of Happiness*, an appropriate title for Williams, who always seemed to search for this elusive creature. He danced the night away with several friends at the ball and was once again among the Creole belles of New Orleans.

UNVEILING *the* MUSE

Dixie's Bar of Music, 701 Bourbon Street, early 1950s. Photograph by Jack Robinson. Courtesy of the Jack Robinson Archive, Memphis.

Prancing down the streets of the Vieux Carré on Fat Tuesday, early 1950s. Photograph by Jack Robinson. Courtesy of the Jack Robinson Archive, Memphis.

THE ROYAL
KREWE OF
YUGA AND
THE BIRTH OF
GAY CARNIVAL

In our society most of us wear protective
masks of various kinds, and for various
reasons. Very often, the end result is
that the mask grows to us, displacing
our original characters with our assumed
characters.

—Clarence John Laughlin, New Orleans Writer and Photographer

In the Beginning

The first gay Carnival krewe was the fantastic Krewe of Yuga. A mock ball was
held in 1958 at the Uptown home of Douglas Jones, located at 1120 South Carrollton Avenue. Over the years, Jones had thrown parties to celebrate Carnival
and view the Krewe of Carrollton parade, whose ranks included friends from
the French Quarter. However, the great leap of faith that occurred at this auspi-
cious moment was a shift from a loose-knit party to a more formalized costumed
ball with a captain, queen and king, maids, and debutantes, mimicking and at
the same time mocking the traditional old-line krewes and their presentation of
royalty. By creating a krewe in a similar vein, the members of this group made
evident their grand intentions in response to the great spirit of Carnival unique
to New Orleans.

The early part of the decade had seen the blossoming of a vibrant gay community in the French Quarter. Gay men and their friends gathered at various bars
sprinkled throughout the old section of the city to gossip, drink, and socialize. At
Dixie's Bar of Music, all were welcome. Everyone knew each other and recognized
kindred spirits with the same sensibilities and cultural references. They enjoyed a
protective environment where they could be themselves, and within this rarefied
society, gay men especially thrived and became more visible. On Shrove Tuesday,
the laws against masking in public were waived, providing a call to arms, to leave
behind all restrictions. The French Quarter came alive with the sound of these
celebrations and was further colored by elaborate and surprising costumes, full of
flair and camp.

Krewe of Yuga ball at the Rambler Room dance studio,
Metairie, 1961. Left to right: Douglas Jones (green
costume), Bradley Lysholm (white dress), William
McKenzie (Indian), Carlos Rodriguez (gold face), Miss
Frog (yellow hat), James Schexnayder (blue hat), JoJo
Landry (holding small ball), Otto Stierle (Indian chief),
and George Roth (red dress in front). Courtesy of Tim
Wolff and George Roth.

View from the balcony down into the courtyard of Dixie's Bar of Music, Fat Tuesday, early 1950s. In the center is Elmo Avet in his Captured Mermaid costume with a mannequin of a sailor attached behind. Photograph by Jack Robinson. Courtesy of the Jack Robinson Archive, Memphis.

Clay Shaw as Socrates, Dixie's Bar of Music, Fat Tuesday, early 1950s. Photograph by Jack Robinson. Courtesy of the Jack Robinson Archive, Memphis.

JoJo Landry as Lady Godiva astride her "steed" with Clay Shaw looking on, Fat Tuesday, early 1950s. Photograph by Jack Robinson. Courtesy of the Jack Robinson Archive, Memphis.

Douglas Jones, as Pierrot, and mates, out and about in the streets, Fat Tuesday, early 1950s. Photograph by Jack Robinson. Courtesy of the Jack Robinson Archive, Memphis.

Dixie's Bar of Music

Jack Uther Robinson Jr., who lived in the French Quarter in the early 1950s and later became an important fashion photographer in New York City, began to take photographs of his friends as they celebrated Mardi Gras in the French Quarter. The future founders of gay Carnival were already something of a legend within this community, and here he captured in exciting detail the relaxed atmosphere on the sidewalks and inside Miss Dixie's back courtyard, whose side entrance had a sign, *For Male Bachelors Only.* Elmo Avet, the last Queen of Yuga, appeared, sipping a cocktail in his mermaid costume with a strategically attached sailor. Clay Shaw, a local preservationist, an impresario, and later a target in the Kennedy assassination investigation, was costumed as Socrates, with a false beard and a toga, standing completely at ease, chatting with friends. JoJo Landry as Lady Godiva paraded around the streets with an abandon only possible during Carnival, and Douglas Jones, sporting a fashionable Pierrot guise, sipped whiskey from a flask. Society's rigid mores were loosened somewhat, allowing a larger space for gay expression. These incredibly candid photographs presaged the creative force and drive that soon came together to form the first gay Carnival krewe in New Orleans.

In the French Quarter, the members of this close-knit society were already frequenting Miss Dixie's, the Bourbon House, and other gay bars along Bourbon Street. These clubs existed despite the harsh laws against homosexuality because of payoffs and backdoor deals. Most clubs in the Old Quarter knew the drill and not only survived but prospered. Tennessee Williams wrote about the gay scene in his *Notebooks.* He duly noted his day-to-day friendships, bar hopping, and liaisons with a candor that underscored the openness of the period. He mentioned several bars, among them the Starlet Lounge, Mack's, the Rendezvous, and Miss Dixie's, and described how effortlessly he moved within this group of intimate friends. Similarly, John Rechy devoted a large portion of his seminal *City of Night* to gay Carnival in New Orleans, mentioning the old Bourbon House and a gay bar nearby with a side courtyard, fictionalized as the Rocking Times bar. Rechy's book follows the exploits of a gay hustler, based on Rechy himself, as he visits various cities, including New Orleans.

Despite the intolerance of McCarthyism, with homosexuals depicted as a threat to national security, gay culture in its myriad forms found a way to thrive, simmering beneath the surface and at times boiling over into plain view. Robinson illustrated this openness with another series of stark photographs depicting gay couples in their apartments and artists in their studios, a strong collection of subtle portraits that revealed a decidedly gay world within the confines of the

Fantastically draped reveler in front of the Bourbon House Restaurant and Bar, across from Miss Dixie's, early 1950s. Photograph by Jack Robinson. Courtesy of the Jack Robinson Archive, Memphis.

Gay couple, early 1950s. Photograph by Jack Robinson. Courtesy of the Jack Robinson Archive, Memphis.

French Quarter. However, by the end of the 1950s, police harassment and entrapment became rampant. Mayor deLesseps Story Morrison and district attorney Richard Dowling wanted to clean up the moral corruption for the tourists, and a crackdown ensued. Hundreds of gay men were arrested, and a sense of danger replaced the relative security that had previously existed. Undercover cops were numerous, and even a simple gesture could result in an arrest. Bashing became a sport, and after several publicized incidents, gay men became more cautious than ever. The Los Angeles–based *ONE Magazine*, the first national gay publication,

KREWE OF CARROLLTON
PRESENTS
THE GLITTERING FESTIVAL

The Auditorium
Sunday, February 9, 1958

Program for the Krewe of Carrollton's *Glittering Festival* ball, 1958. Courtesy of Loyola University New Orleans, Arthur Hardy Mardi Gras Collection, Special Collections and Archives, J. Edgar and Louise Monroe Library.

reported in September 1958 the stepped-up harassment under the headline "New Orleans Witchhunt." One councilman complained that he had seen great numbers of "men with blondined hair and awful looking people all day and all night in the French Quarter."

The First Yuga Ball, 1958

Robinson's circle of acquaintances included Douglas Jones, who continued to frequent Dixie's Bar of Music on Bourbon Street, along with Elmo Avet, John Dodt, Jim Schexnayder, Jerry Gilley, Tracy Hendrix, Otto Stierle, Carlos Rodriguez, William Woolley, John Henry Bogie, and JoJo Landry, among others. As these friendships developed, the idea of a gay krewe was mentioned, possibly in jest. Since its founding in 1953, the Steamboat Club, an exclusive gay social organization, had celebrated Carnival with private parties and dinners. Some of its members also frequented the French Quarter bars. Not wanting to create scenes in the bars or on the streets, private homes replaced public places by the time the Mardi Gras parties grew into elaborately costumed affairs. Jones and his clique merely transformed their annual costume party into a Carnival ball. As the Krewe of Carrollton's *Glittering Festival* floats passed along Carrollton Avenue during the 1958 Carnival season, the Krewe of Yuga and its costumed revelers celebrated the day, and as the last strokes of midnight sounded, the new queen stepped forth in a glittering gown of golden sequins and jewels. "All hail Queen Yuga the First, the fabulous Yuga Regina!"

Douglas Jones

Douglas Jones knew that Carnival in New Orleans had never pretended to be anything but excessive and extravagant. With inspiration from ancient mythologies and strange histories, the gods of ancient Rome and Egypt, the decadent tales of William Beckford and Gustave Flaubert, and the wonders of the Hindu ages were transformed by the Krewes of Comus, Proteus, Rex, and Momus into marvels that rode on magical floats for the populace to see and adore before the long days of atonement during the Lenten season. Such flirtations of the flesh paved the way for the spirit to seek pardon for all its excesses. As Elmo Avet, perhaps the most important figure behind gay Carnival, often said, "After all, you have to have sinned in the first place to seek forgiveness. Lord knows, I've had my share of forgiveness."

Jones, who knew and revered Avet, had grown up in New Orleans and knew Carnival history as well as any fairy tale or nursery rhyme. Each year was anticipated with intense excitement, and costuming was a very serious matter. In addition, his family had ties with the Krewe of Proteus that stretched back to the nineteenth century and the Golden Age of Carnival. One parade in particular, the amazing *Hindoo Heavens*, presented by Proteus as the Narayana in 1889, caught his interest. Jones and his friends chose to name themselves the Krewe of Yuga, after the Kali Yuga of Hindu mythology. They also jokingly referred to the new gay krewe as KY, and thus the gods of Carnival were appeased with a touch of humor and the requisite homage to a beloved pagan past. Some even have hinted that the word *Yuga* is a play on the phrase *(Are) you gay?* Such wordplay is prevalent in Carnival parlance, and it might well have concealed a coded question to determine if someone were gay, trustworthy, or a potential date.

The Second Yuga Ball, 1959

The second Yuga ball was another huge success, with more than two hundred revelers vying for spots in the cramped parlors and on the balcony overlooking Carrollton Avenue. Otto Stierle, one of the original members of Yuga, noted that "everyone arriving at the house had to be in costume and climb a large staircase in front of the house to reach the second-floor entrance, a spectacle for an otherwise quiet neighborhood." The surrounding neighbors indeed became irate, and by the time of the appearance of the Yuga Regina at midnight, it had become apparent that another venue would be needed for the next ball.

Invitation to the Krewe of Proteus's *Hindoo Heavens* ball, 1889, an important touchstone and inspiration for the Krewe of Yuga. Courtesy of The Historic New Orleans Collection, Williams Research Center, New Orleans, Accession No. 1977.40.9a.b. Gift of Richard C. Plater.

Getting ready for the second Yuga ball, 1959. *Left to right:* James Keyes, John Henry Bogie, and JoJo Landry. This is the earliest extant photograph documenting the gay Carnival balls. Courtesy of Tim Wolff.

Program for the Krewe of Carrollton's *Fantasyland* ball, 1959. Courtesy of Loyola University New Orleans, Arthur Hardy Mardi Gras Collection, Special Collections and Archives, J. Edgar and Louise Monroe Library.

Krewe of Carrollton

Presents

Fantasyland

The Auditorium
Sunday, February 1st, 1959

Mama Lou's camp on Lake Pontchartrain, early 1960s.
Courtesy of the Hogan Jazz Archive, Tulane University,
New Orleans.

The Third Yuga Ball, 1960

Mama Lou's camp on the shoreline of Lake Pontchartrain was a popular jazz club, sitting astride huge wooden beams. Such camps were outside the city's reach, moored on the lake like permanent cruise ships, and every weekend they were filled to capacity with people drinking and dancing. Mama Lou's was a perfect location for the 1960 Yuga ball, complete with cocktails and a young Pete Fountain playing the clarinet in the popular Assunto Brothers Band. The long, boarded walkway that stretched from the shore to the camp, however, proved an almost insurmountable obstacle for all the girls in their high heels. The next day found the camp in complete disarray, and Mama Lou, the longtime owner and a jazz musician, was not happy.

The Fourth and Fifth Yuga Balls, 1961–1962

One of the krewe members worked for a day care facility in Metairie, off Veterans Boulevard behind the giant Schwegmann's grocery. The school had a large dance studio, the Rambler Room, and was chosen as the site for the next Krewe of Yuga ball. At night, the hall was empty, and the neighborhood, surrounded by a wooded area toward the lake, was relatively quiet. The 3800 block of Edenborn Avenue seemed a perfect hideaway for another even more opulent ball. Personalized invitations soon appeared, and the returning queen of Yuga and her court promised an extravaganza never before seen. So successful was the 1961 ball that the Rambler Room once again hosted the 1962 ball. The newly formed Krewe of Petronius, made up of friends and a few members of the Krewe of Yuga, also held its first ball at the same location a week earlier. The invitation for the 1962 Yuga ball was a masterpiece of draftsmanship by Stewart Gahn Jr., a member of the krewe. Its elaborate drawing depicted a coat of arms and spoke to a type of pseudoroyalty inherited from the old-line krewes, strongly resembling those forgotten invitations by the Twelfth Night Revelers. The invitation came from the reigning Yuga Regina herself, Claude M. Davis Jr., requesting the presence of her loyal subjects. However, police, alerted to an out-of-control party, came out with the K-9 division and mounted policemen. What followed became a story cloaked in as much legend as actual fact.

The Police Raid

Elmo Avet, well-known antiquarian and aging dowager of the cufflink set, as Miss Dixie fondly called her boys, sat poised to receive his rightful crown as the fifth Yuga Regina. His stark costume as Mary, Queen of Scots, had been reworked and resequined, but it was replaced by a more glamorous and opulent costume, more worthy of royalty. The Jefferson Parish Police arrived in full force and began arresting everyone for what was later dubbed a "lewd stag party." Hearing the tumult, Avet fled out the back, as other frightened queens jumped from windows and fled into the forest. Most were apprehended by mounted policemen as they fled, while others were spotted by the K-9 division and their snarling attack dogs. According to legend, Carlos Rodriguez, who the preceding week had been crowned the first queen of the Krewe of Petronius, was arrested after his sequined bathing suit sparkled in the glare of the police lights: "It was like a thousand sparklers had gone off when the flashlights hit those sequins," summed up Albert Carey of the Krewe of Armeinius. "Almost one hundred were arrested, cuffed, fingerprinted, and held for bail. This had been the most glamorous and extravagant Yuga ball the world had ever seen—and its last."

Alvin Payne, future Queen of Petronius, had been invited to attend the last Yuga ball along with his partner, Ray Cronk, another Queen of Petronius, but they had been out of town visiting relatives. Recalled Payne, "Yuga was a closed group of mostly well-established older men, many from the mysterious Steamboat Club. Clay Shaw was a member, but no one would admit it. You had to be part of Miss Dixie's group to even receive an invitation. Mostly wealthy Uptown queens for sure. We were too young, I suppose, to become members at that time. But the raid was a catastrophe for our friends. Everyone was petrified to show their faces in public for months."

A Call to Arms

News of the raid spread quickly as escapees reached the French Quarter. Miss Dixie, especially incensed, leapt into action. She called her lawyer and grabbed money from the bar's cash registers to help bail out her boys. Yvonne Fasnacht, aka Miss Dixie, and her sister, Irma, had become pillars of strength in the gay community, and she boasted that her political savvy and connections with the police meant that her bar had never been raided or threatened. However, she could not prevent the names of all those arrested from appearing in the newspapers during the weeks that followed. Most lost their jobs. Recalled Tracy Hendrix more than fifty years later, "My name was printed in all the newspapers along with the rest. It was a terrifying experience I'll never forget. It was all over before we had a chance to really get going."

William Woolley and Elmo Avet sat dishing the dirt the next morning as the usual coffee klatch gathered at the Bourbon House Restaurant and Bar across from Miss Dixie's. Both men had escaped the dragnet. According to Carey, Woolley "came up to a neighboring house of an elderly half-blind lady and asked to use her phone. Still in drag and covered in mud, Woolley explained that his date had gotten fresh. What else could she do under the circumstances but help a gal in need?" Jerry Gilley, later an important captain in the Krewe of Amon-Ra, sat in silence as the story unfolded between gasps and sighs. "I had not attended the ball, my lover fearing that his job as a high school principal would be compromised, but I was very much frightened by all the accounts. Simply terrifying," said Gilley. "No one wanted to attend any balls for a long time." Avet vowed vengeance, while John Dodt nursed his black eye. Douglas Jones, JoJo Landry, and Tracy Hendrix appeared the next day in a state, having suffered the crowded pens adjacent to the Jefferson Parish Police Station since the cells could not hold all those arrested. "I was in my Mariachi costume with my tasseled hat and tight matador pants. You couldn't even go to the restroom," lamented Hendrix. But instead of abandoning their dreams for gay Carnival, everyone pulled together and continued the tradition with the Krewe of Petronius. Petronius eventually changed the format of its balls and obtained a state charter. As a legitimate Carnival club, guests would have to attend in formal wear. Only the members of the krewe would appear in costume on stage, performing a spectacular tableau to amuse and entertain friends.

Candy Lee

Other legends persisted regarding the Krewe of Yuga. The most tantalizing of stories, which came out during that morning's many tales, concerned a female impersonator professionally known as Candy Lee who had gotten her start at the Club My-O-My on the Lakefront. A part-time bartender at the infamous Tony Bacino's bar, she lived on Decatur Street and knew Tennessee Williams when he returned to New Orleans in the late 1950s for inspiration. Williams became caught up in Candy Lee's life story, which some say inspired his 1958 short play, *And Tell Sad Stories of the Death of Queens*. This play was unique in that it was unapologetically set in a gay milieu with gay characters. It was never performed during his lifetime but now enjoys a wide circulation. Set in the French Quarter, the play tells the story of Candy, abandoned by her older lover at a turning point in her life that was to prove her undoing. The real Candy Lee, already notorious as a raunchy French-speaking Cajun drag queen, had blamed all too loudly those she thought had caused her 1958 arrest at Bacino's. She and the other bartenders were constantly harassed by the police, and she was arrested five times. One of the tight-knit group of gay men who had begun the first gay krewes, by the early 1960s Candy Lee had fallen from grace and had been banned from all balls. Even Tune, a well-known black doorman at the bar, once admitted Candy's role in the whole affair. Never one to confess any of her shortcomings, she instead sought revenge against those who she felt had betrayed her. Douglas Jones avowed that he believed the tale, and thus her fate was sealed when she called the police on the night of the fifth Yuga ball to complain about a disorderly and chaotic party. Thus, the story survived, and the tale of the police raid held onto its air of mystery and intrigue.

Clay Shaw

Clay Shaw, or Madame Queen, as his friends affectionately called him, was a likely participant in the revels of the first gay krewe. Already having a certain celebrity as the managing director of the International Trade Mart, he knew or had a hand in almost everything that happened within the French Quarter gay scene. He greeted his friends by name at Miss Dixie's, where everyone congregated on weekends. A fixture in the revitalization of the French Quarter, he felt at ease enough to be himself with his friends. And Shaw was a devout follower of all things Carnival. During his trial for conspiring to assassinate President John F. Kennedy, another attack from his archenemy, district attorney Jim Garrison, several friends testified that Shaw had all sorts of lavish and flamboyant costumes hidden away in his apartment closet—strange and wonderful costumes of every creation imaginable. Someone with such a collection would indeed seem likely to have taken part in these early gay Carnival parties and to have had a hand in the formation of the first gay Carnival krewe. Some say he was a member of the mysterious Steamboat Club, and several attendees remember him at the meetings. At the very least, he, along with many other denizens of Miss Dixie's, attended the first Yuga costume balls.

The Designer Gowns

And finally, there was the tale of the designer gowns from the haute couture section of Gus Mayer. Several regulars at the Bourbon House worked for this Canal Street department store, and William Woolley was the head window dresser. According to Jerry Gilley, "Woolley and fellow window dressers had access to all gowns, jewelry, and furs for their windows. They simply borrowed what they needed for the Yuga ball. Although many attendees wore costumes, there was a contingent that wanted to arrive in drop-dead drag, drenched with jewels and sables and high fashion originals. It took a long time to pay all that back. His date was an Indian wearing only a loincloth."

The Demise of the Krewe of Yuga

And with that, the Krewe of Yuga, having blazed a trail like a shooting star, faded into darkness. The legacy of the ill-fated krewe subsequently became obscured as the years passed by. Yet those who had suffered the most emerged from the disaster fiercely determined. The Krewe of Yuga's last two balls had constituted superbly crafted spectacles, and a creative lightning bolt had been unleashed. Many of those arrested carried high the torch of gay Carnival. The Krewe of Petronius, which included some former Yuga members, pulled together to continue

Dixie's Bar of Music, 701 Bourbon Street, early 1950s. Photograph by Jack Robinson. Courtesy of the Jack Robinson Archive, Memphis.

Bayou Pom Pom Grocery, 701 Bourbon Street, late 1930s. Photograph by Frances Benjamin Johnston, 1938. Courtesy of the Louisiana State Museum, New Orleans, Accession No. 1981.011.

Miss Dixie and Dorothy Sloop, Dixie's Bar of Music, late 1940s. Miss Sloop was the inspiration for the song "Hang On, Sloopy." The jazz mural by Xavier Gonzalez on the wall in the background is preserved today at the Louisiana State Museum. Courtesy of Brett Ruland.

this tradition, encouraged by Elmo Avet, the enigmatic provocateur and one of the original forces behind gay Carnival. Despite their arrests, Carlos Rodriguez, who just a week earlier had been crowned the first queen of Petronius, and Otto Stierle, who went on to become its sixth queen, remained undaunted. Minor legend JoJo Landry also made her mark within the Krewe of Petronius. William Woolley, who narrowly escaped capture, went on to great acclaim within Petronius and later founded the Mystic Krewe of Celestial Knights. Another one of those arrested, Jim Schexnayder, regrouped and helped form the third gay Carnival club, the Krewe of Amon-Ra. Tracy Hendrix was among the founders of the Krewe of Armeinius several years later. "

The Aftermath

By the mid-1980s more than a dozen gay krewes had been formed, and most of them held their balls at the old Saint Bernard Civic Auditorium downriver in Chalmette, famous as the site of the Battle of New Orleans in 1815. Each year, these krewes sought to outperform one another with ever more dazzling tableaux and ever more sensational costumes, sets, music, and special effects. During these years, the krewes were at their finest and never disappointed. Balls were free but tickets were hard to come by, which only made them more desirable and sought after. Formal wear was de rigueur, and many who did not heed this rigid requirement were turned away. Even Uptown matrons fought among themselves for tickets from their hairdressers. But by this time, few could recall those who had set everything in motion. But the legacy of the first krewe, the fabulous Krewe of Yuga, continued, not only in the creative excellence on these stages around town but also in the determination to continue despite the obstacles, which soon included AIDS. The New Orleans community retained its steadfast resolve to avoid letting the great work of gay Carnival fall into the darkness of the past. Undaunted, gay krewes continue to hold tableau balls each year, and the community now recognizes the Krewe of Yuga's rightful place in history.

Krewe of Yuga (1958)

1958–59

The Krewe of Yuga, the first gay Carnival krewe, gave
its premier ball in 1958, when it had only a few dozen
members. Invited friends gathered in the home of
Douglas Jones at 1120 South Carrollton Avenue to
watch the Krewe of Carrollton parade, as was the tradition. An invitation-only party was held and everyone
arriving had to be in costume. During the ball, a krewe
captain emerged and presented the first Yuga Regina.
There was a repeat performance the next year, much to
the delight and amusement of the more than two hundred costumed merrymakers in attendance. But the
costume ball had grown too large for a private home.
The neighbors complained, and a new, more protected
venue was sought for the next *bal masqué*. Police
harassment had escalated in the French Quarter, and
an atmosphere of fear generally prevailed.

1960

The third Krewe of Yuga ball was held at Mama Lou's
camp in Little Woods on the Lakefront. Camps were
tin-roofed wooden buildings built over Lake Pontchartrain. They had screen porches and rested on large
pilings sunk deep into the lake, beyond the reach of
certain restrictions. These were restaurants and jazz
halls, and every camp had a wooden walkway running
from the shore out to the camp. A costume ball was
held there with the appearance of the krewe captain
and the returning queen, and at the ball's conclusion,
the reigning queen came forth to hold court at the
stroke of midnight.

1961–62

The fourth ball was held in 1961 at the Rambler Room,
a dance studio for a Metairie day care center and
school off Veterans Boulevard, hidden behind a large
Schwegmann's grocery store. This venue proved very
successful, and in 1962 the krewe held its fifth and
final ball there. Police raided the ball, tipped off either
by a complaining neighbor or by another queen, and
arrested nearly one hundred people on charges of
disturbing the peace at a very lewd party (supposedly featuring a band and several completely naked
people). Local newspapers published the names of all
those arrested, completing the demise of the fantastic
Krewe of Yuga.

Krewe of Yuga Ball (1962)	
Arrestees Who Later Went on to Become Important Contributors to Gay Carnival	
Joseph Barcellona	Petronius
John H. Bogie	Yuga
Claude M. Davis Jr.	Yuga
Don J. Fitzpatrick	Petronius
Stewart K. Gahn Jr.	Yuga
Tracy M. Hendrix	Yuga and Armeinius
Douglas Jones	Yuga
Joseph E. "JoJo" Landry Jr.	Petronius and Ganymede
Bradley R. Lysholm	Petronius and Amon-Ra
Carlos M. Rodriguez	Petronius and Celestial Knights
James H. Schexnayder	Yuga and Amon-Ra
Otto Stierle Jr.	Petronius and Celestial Knights
Attendees Who Escaped Arrest and Went on to Become Important Contributors to Gay Carnival	
Elmo Delacroix Avet	Yuga and Petronius
John Dodt	Yuga and Petronius
William McKenzie	Petronius and Celestial Knights
William M. Woolley	Petronius and Celestial Knights

Invitation from the Twelfth Night Revelers, 1870. A traditional krewe, the Twelfth
Night Revelers may have inspired the Krewe of Yuga. Courtesy of Tulane University,
Louisiana Research Collection, Howard-Tilton Memorial Library, New Orleans.

Handmade invitation, 1961. Courtesy of The Historic New Orleans Collection, Williams Research Center, New Orleans, Accession No. 1980.178.59. Gift of Tracy Hendrix.

YOU HAVE A CALL OUT

Call-out card, 1962. In keeping with the tradition followed by debutantes at the old-line balls, drag debutantes at the Krewe of Yuga balls were presented with small call-out cards for dancing. Courtesy of Tulane University, Louisiana Research Collection, Howard-Tilton Memorial Library, New Orleans, Otto Stierle Collection, Manuscripts Collection 902.

Invitation, 1962. Design by Stewart K. Gahn Jr. Courtesy of The Historic New Orleans Collection, Williams Research Center, New Orleans, Accession No. 1980.178.71. Gift of Tracy Hendrix.

THE MYSTIC KREWE OF
CELESTIAL KNIGHTS

presents

PERFUMES

A MARDI GRAS EXTRAVAGANZA
1978

MURPHY

THE CHILDREN OF YUGA AND A GLORIOUS GOLDEN AGE

New Orleans is a city that dwells within its own aura, and that aura is one of mystery and uniqueness.

—Jon Newlin, New Orleans Writer

The Classic Pantheon

In the wake of the demise of the Krewe of Yuga, a variety of new krewes formed. Some have subsequently dissolved, the Krewes of Petronius (1962), Amon-Ra (1966), Armeinius (1969), and the Lords of Leather (1984) are the only early New Orleans gay krewes that still hold balls. There were two tiers of krewes: the major krewes, which held lavish tableaux and presented amazing costumes at their annual balls, and the minor ones, which held costume parties, celebrated the day on a balcony or in a bar, or paraded on foot around the French Quarter. Petronius, Amon-Ra, Armeinius, and the Lords of Leather were among the best of the major krewes, along with the defunct Ganymede, Apollo, Memphis, Celestial Knights, Ishtar, and Polyphemus. The Krewe of Memphis formed a sister krewe in Lafayette. The Krewe of Olympus still holds balls but moved to Houston in 1991. The Mystic Krewe of Apollo's founder, Roland Dobson, promoted various franchise krewes in other cities. Important new organizations that still present tableau balls include the Krewe of Mwindo, the Mystic Krewe of Satyricon, the Krewe of Narcissus, and the Krewe of Stars.

The minor krewes, including Tequemen, Jason, Frollicking Krewe of PO, Satin and Sequins, Désimé, Phoenix, Snow White, Dionysus, Kancellation, Tragoidia, Dirtie Dottie, Trash, Perseus, David, Eros, Cerci, Somnus, Vesta, and possibly Aeolus, rarely presented tableaux and usually confined their celebration to Mardi Gras weekend or Fat Tuesday. However, these krewes still occupy a legitimate place in the history of gay Carnival for their extravagance and visibility, if nothing else.

Mystic Krewe of Celestial Knights, *Perfumes* ball, 1978. This masterpiece of gay Carnival artistry depicts the lady's boudoir as she performs her toilette and douses herself with exotic fragrances. Design by Michael Murphy. Courtesy of the Louisiana State Museum, New Orleans, Accession No. 1995.010.054.

THE CLASSIC PANTHEON
Gay Carnival Krewes in New Orleans from 1958 to the Present, with the Year of the First Ball and Longevity, if Known

1958–62	KREWE OF YUGA
1962–	KREWE OF PETRONIUS*
1966–	KREWE OF AMON-RA*
1968–74	KREWE OF GANYMEDE
1969–	KREWE OF ARMEINIUS*
1970–86	MYSTIC KREWE OF APOLLO ¶#
1970	KREWE OF FIDDLER'S FUCK**
1971–90	KREWE OF OLYMPUS§
1972–73	KREWE OF TEQUEMEN
1973–	MYSTIC KREWE OF PHOENIX**
1975–77	LA KREWE MYSTIQUE DE DÉSIMÉ (DAISY MAE)
1975–	KREWE OF JASON**#
1976–83	KREWE OF MEMPHIS
1977–92	MYSTIC KREWE OF CELESTIAL KNIGHTS
1977–	FROLLICKING KREWE OF PO**
1977–	KREWE OF SATIN & SEQUINS**
1977–82	KREWE OF DIRTIE DOTTIE
1978–86	KREWE OF SNOW WHITE
1979–	KREWE OF DIONYSUS**
1979–80	KREWE OF KANCELLATION
1981–86	KREWE OF ISHTAR
1981	KREWE OF SOMNUS**
1983–92	KREWE OF POLYPHEMUS
1983–	KREWE OF VESTA**
1984–88	KREWE OF PERSEUS
1984–86	KREWE OF DAVID
1984–	LORDS OF LEATHER*
1984–	KREWE OF TRASH**
1984	MYSTIC KREWE OF TRAGOIDIA**
1985–86	KREWE OF CERCI
1987–	KREWE OF EROS**#
1987–	KREWE OF QUEENATEENAS*
1999–	KREWE OF MWINDO*
2000–2003	KREWE OF LA CAGE AUX FOLLES
2001–	KREWE OF ANUBIS**#
2003–	MYSTIC KREWE OF SATYRICON*
2014–	MISTIK KREWE DU RUE ROYALE REVELERS*
2015–	KREWE OF NARCISSUS*
2017–	KREWE OF STARS*

* Gay krewes still active in Carnival each year
** Gay krewes no longer active, last year of ball not known or no ball
¶ Other franchise Mystic Krewes of Apollo established outside of New Orleans include Baton Rouge, Birmingham, Dallas, Lafayette, and Shreveport
§ Krewe of Olympus moved to Houston in 1991 and still holds balls
# Also the name of a straight krewe at one time

It may never be possible to construct a complete list of gay Carnival krewes and their fantastic tableau balls. However, this master compilation, which borrows the phrase the *Classic Pantheon* from the 1858 Mistick Krewe of Comus parade, brings together the names of all known gay krewes compiled from various sources, especially invitations and posters produced by the krewes themselves. Groups that did not define themselves as krewes or present similar tableau presentations in New Orleans are not included in this definitive list.

A Long-Awaited Renaissance

Many observers see a resurgence of interest in the gay krewes. Some even speak of a renaissance, as gay krewes hold more lavish balls, recalling the opulence of the fabled Golden Age of the early 1980s. During this time, representatives from all the krewes attended the annual Uniboard meeting to share information, discuss the upcoming Carnival season, and strategize about fund-raising. More important, these yearly meetings of representatives from all the gay krewes helped coordinate the scheduling of fund-raisers, dinners, and other events throughout the year as well as Carnival balls. The Uniboard was an integral part of gay Carnival planning from roughly 1982 to 1999. As the AIDS epidemic took its toll, gay krewes shifted their focus to fighting the disease, and the united group disappeared toward the late 1990s. Further difficulties arose after Hurricane Katrina devastated New Orleans and caused many residents to leave the city permanently. Yet Carnival, and especially gay Carnival, have persevered. In 2015, when financial difficulties prevented the Krewe of Petronius from presenting a formal ball, the group held the Banquet of Trimalchio with the theme *Divined by the Stars*. The krewe again held balls in 2016 and 2017.

The so-called return to grandeur for gay krewes also recalled another interesting facet of gay Carnival itself. The gay krewes originally mocked the traditional elite Carnival krewes, with their sacrosanct rituals and rigid ceremonies, but subsequently turned to delivering dazzling spectacles—serious tableau balls with professional-quality costumes, music, and sets. They combined camp and satire with serious artistry, to startling effect. The gay krewes developed their own unique take on Carnival.

A shining example of this renaissance came with the Krewe of Armeinius's 2016 *Beauty and the Beast* ball, which featured first-class costumes. According to Wayne Phillips of the Louisiana State Museum, "The Armeinius ball was by far the best of the year. The *Beauty and the Beast* theme was well carried out, and most of the costumes were actually pairs: the Phantom of the Opera and Christine, Little Miss Muffet and the Spider, Apollo and Daphne, and many others. My friends Scott Pivey and John Peifer made a nice king and queen. The whole krewe invested a lot of creativity and money in the ball, and it showed."

Inaugural Gay Parade

In May 2015, several gay krewes broke through another barrier to parade down the streets of the French Quarter. Prior to the early 2000s, gay krewes generally did not even attempt to parade, deterred by high costs and especially fear of police reprisals. In 2003, the Krewe of La Cage aux Folles tried and failed to secure a parade permit.

Twelve years later, the Gay Krewe of Krewes parade included the Krewes of Amon-Ra, Queenateenas, and Satyricon as well as the Lords of Leather. Marching bands accompanied the floats, and some walking clubs participated as well. Organized by Larry Bagneris Jr., longtime liaison between the gay community and the mayor's office, this parade proudly processed down Bourbon Street in the French Quarter and reflects the remarkable societal changes over the past decade and a half.

Other Mardi Gras Clubs

Other gay groups are linked to gay Carnival but do not necessarily constitute krewes per se. The Fat Monday Luncheon is the city's oldest organized gay celebration of Carnival. It got its start in 1949, when Bob Demmons hosted a small group of gay men for lunch at Brennan's Restaurant on the day before Mardi Gras. A queen was crowned with a tiara and covered in bouquets of flowers, which were then liberally tossed at passersby in the street. The group grew larger every year, and when Demmons died, his friend, Jim Wynne, took over as Master of the Revels. In grand Carnival tradition, the luncheon soon became too rowdy for Brennan's and moved to Restaurant Jonathan, Menefee's, and Café Sbisa over the following years before finally finding a permanent home at Arnaud's in 1984. Hosted by Bill Bryan and David Hood, the luncheon features many members of gay krewes as well as others. For example,

Poster for the Gay Krewe of Krewes, First Annual Parade, 2015. Courtesy of the Louisiana State Museum, New Orleans, Accession No. 2015.021.1.

in recent years the Krewes of Amon-Ra, Armeinius, and the Lords of Leather have maintained a presence. Women are also welcome and have often been named as royalty.

In 1953 (or perhaps earlier), Leon Zany formed the Steamboat Club, an exclusive group of a dozen mostly older and influential gay men. The club celebrates the beginning of each Carnival season with a New Year's Eve celebration. Patterned after New Orleans's elite Boston Club, formed in the 1850s, the club also holds private parties throughout the months leading up to Shrove Tuesday. Several members of the group were involved in the founding of the Krewe of Yuga. Known

Invitation to the Fat Monday Luncheon, Arnaud's, 2013. First held in 1949 at Brennan's Restaurant, this private, invitation-only luncheon is New Orleans's oldest gay celebration of Carnival. Courtesy of the Louisiana State Museum, New Orleans, Accession No. 2013.014.8.

A behind-the-scenes look at the Fat Monday Luncheon, Arnaud's, 2014. Photographs by Zachary Mason Krevitt. Courtesy of Zachary Mason Krevitt.

for its secrecy as much as its revels, the Steamboat Club rarely reveals itself even to friends in the gay krewes, but many of its members also participate in the Fat Monday Luncheon. The boundary lines between these groups appear to fluctuate and are as fluid as the various members would wish.

Other groups with mixed memberships of note who celebrate Carnival are the Société de Ste. Anne, a Shrove Tuesday walking club, and La Scuola Vecchia, which presented a tableau ball each year but did not consider itself a krewe. Formed in 1969 by Henri Schindler, Paul Poché, and Jon Newlin, La Société de

Invitation to a Steamboat Club party at 920 St. Louis Street, the home of John Dodt, 1986. One of the earliest gay groups to celebrate Carnival, the Steamboat Club patterned itself after more traditional Carnival groups that cloaked themselves in mystery and kept their membership secret. The Steamboat Club worked behind the scenes to mold gay Carnival. Courtesy of the Louisiana State Museum, New Orleans, Accession No. 1995.010.141.

Invitations to Société de Ste. Anne *bals masqués*, Napoleon House, Chartres Street. January 6 (also known as Twelfth Night or Epiphany) is the traditional start of the New Orleans Carnival season. Designs by Rembert Donelson. Courtesy of the John C. Kelly and Michael J. Rosa Collection, Earl K. Long Library, University of New Orleans.

La Société de Ste. Anne, Shrove Tuesday walking parade, 2006. Costumes for the walking parade are always some of the most striking of Carnival, demonstrating the event's importance to participants. Also depicted is the sprinkling of deceased friends' ashes into the Mississippi River on Shrove Tuesday, after the midday Rex Parade. Photographs ©Nell Campbell. (bottom right) Photograph by Syndey Byrd.

Ste. Anne's main event was a parade of walking costumes, which began in Bywater early on Shrove Tuesday and became larger and more colorful as the troupe made its way to Canal Street to view the Rex Parade around noon. Anyone could participate—the only requirement was knowing when to join the entourage. For many years, the group then proceeded down to the Mississippi River, where dearly departed friends had instructed that their ashes be rendered to the muddy waters. Inspiration for the name came from Ste. Anne, the mother of the Virgin Mary. The society at times also hosted an invitation-only masked ball on the Eve of Epiphany (January 6) or later on during the season, such as the Saturday before Shrove Tuesday.

La Scuola Vecchia was a Mardi Gras group with both gay and straight members who enjoyed the older, more baroque aspects of Carnival and went on to produce some extraordinary balls. Formed by Rembert Donelson, André de la Barre, and Louise Coleman, La Scuola Vecchia's star burned brightly for several years until Donelson, who designed many of the group's superb invitations and balls, left the city for Memphis. Henri Schindler described him as "a dear friend who was the moving spirit behind the group." Schindler, who was also involved with La Scuola Vecchia for many years, explained, "I designed and built the sets for La Scuola Vecchia. That hellish invitation for our 1994 ball was re-created as an eight-foot tablet. It had many gay invitees, and two of the three founders were gay, but the ball was also attended by a large number of straight couples in fine costumes. The balls were great fun but only lasted a few years, maybe five or six."

The Friday Night Before Mardi Gras club presents the Masquerade Ball Extravaganza each year on the Friday before Fat Tuesday. The celebration began

Invitation to La Scuola Vecchia's *Lost Empire* ball, 1993. The Quadroon Ballroom takes its name from the quadroon (i.e., one-quarter black) mistresses commonly kept by white men in antebellum New Orleans. Design by Rembert Donelson. Courtesy of the John C. Kelly and Michael J. Rosa Collection, Earl K. Long Library, University of New Orleans.

modestly in 1985 at the home of Ivan Sherman and David Wood, where guests were invited to attend in wigs and costumes. By 1999, the party had grown to include more than 350 attendees in outrageous costumes. The following year's Friday Night before Mardi Gras party became a fund-raiser for HIV/AIDS charities and the newly christened Extravaganza I Gala took place at the Carrollton and was overseen by an event committee. Carl Ricketts, from the Krewe of Amon-Ra, was among the initial members of the club, which was spearheaded by Billy Henry and Ed Portratz. According to its mission statement, the group "celebrates Carnival and the well-being of the gay community of New Orleans."

Finally, the Radical Faeries have celebrated Carnival since 1990 and for many years have presented an annual St. Brigid Ball with its Imperial Coronation ceremony. Carl Mack of the Krewe of Stars was one of the chapter founders. The Radical Faerie movement began in the 1970s. It rejects

Invitation to La Scuola Vecchia's *Gente Lasciate Ogni Speranza Voi Ch'Entrate* ball, 1994. The phrase comes from Dante's *Inferno* and translates as "Abandon All Hope, Ye Who Enter Here." Design by Rembert Donelson. Courtesy of the John C. Kelly and Michael J. Rosa Collection, Earl K. Long Library, University of New Orleans.

Empress Keith, Clowns-Only Luau, Radical Faeries Brigid Ball, AllWays Lounge and Theatre, Faubourg Marigny, 2010. Photograph © Pat Jolly 2017.

Radical Faeries' Brigid Ball, *Legends of the Wood: A Faerie Ball*, 2011. The Royal Court included Lady in Waiting Myron, Empress XXII Clay, and Page of Honor Rebecca Rae. The Panorama Jazz Band played for the festivities. Photograph © Pat Jolly 2017.

hetero-imitation, emphasizes pagan spirituality and queer consciousness, and has spread around the world. The group continues its traditions through a distinctly New Orleans lens.

During the long history of traditional Carnival in New Orleans, gay men and lesbians were often part of the straight krewes, but necessity dictated that they remain hidden. Recently, however, as society has begun to applaud diversity and equality, gay men have risen to prominence in several krewes. For its 2016 ball, Metairie's Krewe of Argus named an out gay man as its king. Other straight krewes have gay contingents. For example, the Knights of King Arthur, which calls itself the "most diverse Mardi Gras krewe," has a gay man as its permanent captain. The krewe was founded in 1977 by Philip Fricano and Carl Scivicque, and Fricano is today one of the longest-tenured krewe captains and has actively recruited gay members, who have "really had a big part in helping grow the krewe to its current 975 members," Fricano explained. The diversity of traditional Carnival is likely to continue increasing in the future.

THE KREWE OF PETRONIUS

The Grande Dame of Gay Carnival

Petronius comes in on a cloud so beautiful to behold and so exquisitely conceived that only the less fortunate could say nay to him. We bring you the beauty of pageantry, the excitement of Bacchus. May our bacchanale please you and this night be something to remember.

—JoJo Landry, Krewe of Petronius

Half a Century and Counting

Queen Petronius XXXII, Mickey Gil, *Straight from the Heart* ball, 1993. Photograph by Syndey Byrd.

The Krewe of Petronius, the oldest active gay Carnival krewe, celebrated its fifty-sixth anniversary in 2017. Petronius not only constitutes a major contributor to the history of Carnival in New Orleans but also represents a milestone in gay history. Taking its name from the chronicler of decadent Rome, Gaius Petronius Arbiter, the Krewe of Petronius continued a long line of gay krewes that celebrated the often hidden world of gay themes and icons. Formed in 1961, the Krewe of Petronius gave its first ball on Saturday, February 17, 1962, at the Rambler Room, a dance studio located in a Metairie day care off Veterans Boulevard, a week before the police raided the Yuga ball. Important founding members were Clyde Webb, Ray Cronk, William Woolley, William McKenzie, Charles Ulfers, and JoJo Landry. As first captain, Landry produced the first real gay tableau ball.

Recalled Woolley, "Yuga was definitely the older set, heavily influenced by the Steamboat Club, very elitist. We were younger. For God's sake, I was only in my early twenties. We were all having coffee at the Bourbon House and started talking about a new krewe. We wanted to try out our own ideas, something more risqué and fun. More drag and fantastic costumes. At our first meeting we elected our first president, Charles J. Ulfers, and it all took off like a rocket. JoJo Landry really crafted Petronius, molding the group into a cohesive unit. We had our work cut out for us after the Yuga raid, but we carried on nonetheless."

Queen Petronius I, Carlos Rodriguez, *Broadway* ball, 1962. Rodriguez was arrested along with almost a hundred others when the police raided the Krewe of Yuga's ball a week later. This photo has appeared in many ball programs. Courtesy of Howard Philips Smith.

Queen Petronius VI, John Casper Dodt III, *The Wizard of Oz* ball, 1966. Dodt's costume featured a small-scale beglittered rendition of the fabled Emerald City mounted as a headpiece. Courtesy of the Louisiana State Museum.

Survival Strategies

Despite harsh laws that targeted gays and lesbians, early gay krewes took up the spirit of Carnival and parody and celebrated with larger-than-life costume parties. A king and queen reigned at these presentations along with a captain and ball lieutenant. Police harassment was common in the early 1960s, and it was a risk even to attend a ball. Carlos Rodriguez, the first queen of the Krewe of Petronius, attended the ill-fated Krewe of Yuga ball and was arrested along with other members during the police raid. Three important members of the Krewe of Petronius somehow escaped the raid. William Woolley, John Dodt, and Elmo Avet represented the future of gay Carnival, exhibiting unflinching defiance coupled with inexhaustible creativity. Under their guidance, the Krewe of Petronius obtained a state charter and became incorporated as a legitimate Carnival group in 1966.

Obtaining a state charter for a gay krewe was more than clever move: it was a survival strategy. In Woolley's words, "We knew that we had to become more legitimate in order to survive. We had to get smart, work within the system to our advantage. Having a costume party was a risk in itself, but a real tableau ball—that was what we really wanted, and it served to inspire us to submit paperwork for a state krewe charter. We were an all-male group, which at the time was above reproach, since many of the straight krewes were all-male. They simply could not refuse us. Once we had the charter, we had to rethink our presentations." Working behind the scenes to obtain the charter was Douglas Jones, a former member of the Krewe of Yuga and a member of the secretive Steamboat Club.

The krewe wisely changed the format of its balls. All guests were required to wear formal tuxedoes and gowns, and only those who received invitations could attend. Members of the krewe would present costumed tableaux on stage for the amusement of their guests, who now included Uptown ladies as well as mothers and sisters of the krewe members. This nod to traditional Carnival served Petronius well, and this custom continues on today. Over the next five decades, the krewe's diverse and grandiose balls helped define a uniquely gay culture in New Orleans.

The Great Leap in Creativity

Woolley reigned as Queen Petronius III for the 1965 *Wicked Bitches of History* ball, with Brad Lysholm serving as captain. For *The Wizard of Oz* ball in 1966, John Dodt stunned the audience by wearing a re-creation of the entire Emerald City in glorious shades of green as a headpiece. Dodt had settled in New Orleans in the mid-1950s and soon became one of the regulars at Dixie's Bar of Music, along with Avet and Woolley. With his inheritance, Dodt bought a beautiful house at 920 St. Louis Street in the French Quarter not far from the bar. The old Edmund J. Forstall House, built in 1857 by James Gallier Jr. and Richard Esterbrook and once the gem of the French Quarter with its exotic garden and conservatories, had fallen into ruin. Dodt brought the house back to glory as a showplace. A member of the ill-fated Krewe of Yuga, Dodt had been present at the last ball and barely escaped the police raid with a black eye. Not only was he active in gay Carnival, in Petronius, and in the Steamboat Club, but he also served on the Louisiana State Museum's Board of Managers (now the Board of Directors) from 1961 to 1963. However, by the time of the *Petronius Salutes Royalty* ball in 1991, when past queens were invited back to parade about for the Grand

March, Dodt had gone through most of his money. Dodt chalked his misfortune up to fate, even when he fell and broke his hip at the ball. Many considered Dodt the "Old Lady" of the gay krewes, after Avet. By 1992, he considered himself and his friends "war-weary veterans" of so many Carnival seasons. But his coup de grâce that year was a brilliant group costume with a series of seven Whistler's Mothers—all with chairs—based on the famous painting, cavorting about the French Quarter on Fat Tuesday. He hoped that the balls would survive the devastation wrought by AIDS and remain an important segment of New Orleans history. From 1995 until his death in 2010, he lived in Mandeville, across Lake Pontchartrain.

Woolley remembered Dodt at "Pioneers of Gay Carnival: A Conversation with the Legends," an April 2016 panel discussion held at the Louisiana State Museum: "Miss Dodt was known for her parties. One party in particular stands out, and that was the Opera Party in the mid-1960s. Everyone was to come wearing their favorite mask referencing an opera. I wore a bat mask for *Die Fledermaus*. Miss JoJo Landry, always the cheeky bitch, just glued three pennies to her forehead. I thought that one was the best. Also at the party was Rudolf Nureyev, who was performing in town. Those were the exciting early days, which are now gone forever."

Woolley oversaw some of Petronius's most spectacular balls. For *Shangri-La* (1968), Captain Woolley took his cue from *Around the World with Auntie Mame—It's Sheer Camp*, in which Elmo Avet and John Dodt presented famous and exotic women in history. Woolley and Millard Wilson, who worked together as window dressers, conceived another batch of even more extravagant showgirl costumes for *Shangri-La*, but Avet stole the show with his appearance as Scarlett O'Hara.

Returning Queen Petronius IV, William Wooley, on the street on Shrove Tuesday, 1966. Courtesy of the Louisiana State Museum, New Orleans, Accession No. 2016.026.03.

According to Woolley, "At first Elmo did not want to become part of Petronius after the disastrous turn of events with Yuga. And I can't blame him, really. He wasn't like the other ball queens. I kept badgering him at his Flea Market shoppe until one day he called me back and barked something about what he should wear. I told him the theme was *Shangri-La*, but his only response was that he would wear something antebellum. Now how in the world could you get something antebellum out of *Shangri-La*? But we made it work. Elmo was a difficult, opinionated, bitchy genius. I miss him so much till this day."

A Milestone Achieved

Elmo Avet was behind the glamorous 1967 *It's Sheer Camp* ball, which took its theme from the Auntie Mame sequel, *Around the World with Auntie Mame*. The captain was JoJo Landry, while Otto Stierle was Auntie Mame. On the second Sunday before Mardi Gras 1969, the krewe presented its eighth ball, *The Glorification of the American Girl*, at the International Longshoremen's Association Hall on Claiborne Avenue. This extravagant tour-de-force tableau solidified the krewe's place in

Glorifying the American Girl movie poster, 1929.

Cleopatra movie poster, 1934.

The Story of Vernon and Irene Castle movie poster, 1939.

the history of gay Carnival. The ball captain was Lewis "Jamie" Greenleaf III, and he used his experience as well as knowledge gained from Avet, who had previously worked on Hollywood movie sets, to steer the krewe into using film and theater as inspiration, much as the old-line krewes had used pagan mythologies and strange literatures. The Ziegfeld Follies movie of 1929, *Glorifying the American Girl*, was transformed into a daring fashion extravaganza. Lavish costumes worthy of the court of Louis XIV graced the stage, the culmination of months of elaborate planning and hard work from the krewe members, who created and paid for the costumes themselves. The film's finale included a fashion sequence in full color, "Loveland," but the sensational and surreal costumes of the Petronius ball outdid the film that inspired it.

Six blond showgirls in pink tights with enormous pink feathery fans (A Potpourri of Plucked Plumage Perfection) formed a screen and parted way to reveal a series of increasingly extravagant costumes. Greenleaf appeared as a Beaded

Extravaganza of Shimmering Boa. Bill Woolley stopped the show with his Golden Vision, a dazzling gold lamé costume spouting long curvy tendrils and gold discs. Elmo Avet followed, covered from head to toe in live flowers, A Floral Tribute to the Flower Child. The returning king was King Plumus of the Realm Bicepticus (Millard Wilson), and his returning queen was Queen Irrisistabus of the Realm Pootius and Impedimenta (Clyde Webb). Both, costumed in high–Hollywood Roman attire, looked like they had stepped off the set of Claudette Colbert's classic movie *Cleopatra*. Other magnificent costumes included the Fluttering Fulfillment of the Magnificent Moth of Desire, a Gushing Geyser of Gorgeous Glitter, and a Lustrous Lavishness of Lemon Loveliness. At many gay balls, the entertainment was served up with a twist. A simple dance number could become an exercise in gender-bending politics. A film, *The Story of Vernon and Irene Castle*, in which Fred Astaire and Ginger Rogers portrayed the famous ballroom dance team, inspired a dance number at the ball, The Castles and Then Some. A man and a woman danced across the stage. Midway through the number, they tugged at their clothes and transformed themselves into their gender opposites. The finale of the ball was the entrance of Queen Petronius VIII as Marie Antoinette. Her ensemble and piled-high wig were a perfection, revealing a heaving fake bosom, and the audience members screamed with delight and waved their programs, which were pink feathery fans. Ray Cronk, krewe member and later queen, remembered, "I had to glue all those damn pink feathers on the programs. Now talk about torture! It took days. I never thought I would finish in time."

George Wilson, who had recently moved to New Orleans from San Diego, had been recruited for the krewe by Bill Woolley. Wilson and his lover, Nick Donovan, ran the Finale Bar on Royal Street, which featured an upstairs restaurant where the krewe held its fund-raisers. Wilson's debut on stage was the Melodic Mimsy of Musical Motion, a fantastic candy-striped costume with chimes and bells. He became close friends with Greenleaf and helped Avet with his Mermaid costume, an annual camp classic at Carnival. The wig had become ratty over the years, and Wilson, who worked for Greenleaf and his lover, Harvey Hysell, in their studio in the Marigny, rewove the wig into a presentable state. Avet was so touched that he gave Wilson a special pair of earrings. According to Wilson, "Those earrings were a sight to behold! They were clips but they had wirework that came over and surrounded the front of the ear, and then the huge pink pendant jewels were the campiest thing ever."

2069: A Space Oddity

David Bowie's ode to space travel, "Space Oddity," was a global hit in 1969, building on the wave of excitement from the moon landing and the avant-garde science fiction film, *2001: A Space Odyssey* (1968). One of the creators of the nascent "glam rock" trend in music, Bowie wore makeup and glitter onstage, inspiring young gay men with his androgynous and often provocative costumes. Millard Wilson, captain for the 1970 ball, took the title of Bowie's song and ran with it into the drag realms of outer space, where future extraterrestrials wore high heels. Using a limited palette of greens and oranges highlighted with silver and a few flourishes of magenta, Millard created an extraordinary tableau, using many unconventional materials such as clear plastics and other synthetics. Millard himself was Dazzling in Moon Rays, and other camp and strange costumes pranced about the stage. Lady

Poodiva, Moonstone in Motion, and Our Dizzy Darling Moon-Child sought to outdo Rounds of Brilliants and Our Radiant Saturnian, but the Duchess Diamanté from the Sea of Pootius and Her Hairdresser, a Gilded Globolink, stole the show. A rather risqué ball poster by Calvert had the letters of *Petronius* interweaved with green and blue stripper aliens.

Taking a Break

Bickering and creative differences had arisen during the *Glorification* ball of 1969, and according to Woolley, several of the krewe members decided that they would be "taking a break." In George Wilson's account, however, "When we approached Jamie Greenleaf to join our new Krewe of Olympus in 1970, formed after the Petronius ball, we discussed the tensions we had experienced within the Krewe of Petronius and that he would consider joining Olympus." These tensions were not to be dismissed, and certainly Woolley was involved, since Greenleaf had been captain. Woolley and several other Petronius members, including Carlos Rodriguez, Charles Ulfers, Bill Sumter, Jimmy Keyes, and George South, then decided to form yet another krewe. The Krewe of Fiddler's Fuck was a jab at the older krewe and a resounding declaration that its members were bucking the template of a gay ball. After a single fund-raising event, however, the effort died: "The energy just wasn't there," explained Woolley. "You either have it or you don't, and it was really tough to get things going in Fiddler's. That's the troublesome thing about a group of queens. You just never know what's going to work. We never even had a ball." After Greenleaf's departure to Olympus, Petronius invited its wayward members back into the fold, and they all were back on board for the 1972 season.

The Wedding Legend of Maheo

For the 1972 tableau ball, captain Joey Barcellona brought to life the Cherokee legend of Maheo (the Creator God). Often known in English as Great Medicine or Great One, Maheo was a divine spirit without human form or attributes and was rarely personified in Cherokee folklore. According to legend, a tribe living in the Valley of the Sun was suffering from a great drought. In desperation, the people danced in hopes that Maheo would let his son, Onoco, shower the earth with tears. However, Maheo was so moved that he appeared among them. If one of their fairest maidens was found worthy of being his bride, he would bring forth rain. Eventually, the daughter of Chief White Eagle was chosen, and Maheo sent the rain. Petronius's splendid tableau referenced Native American costumes, with copious amounts of feathers. Ray Cronk portrayed the daughter, while the king, Hank Ranna, played her father and William Woolley played the campy and sinister Medicine Woman.

Signs of the Zodiac

Seeking to create another over-the-top tableau for 1973, captain William Woolley designed costumes for all twelve signs of the zodiac, while the invitation promised that the thirteenth sign would be revealed at the close of the ball. Alvin Payne served as the queen, and Jerry Morgan was the king. Woolley came out as the astrologer, with four attendants in thongs pulling his tiered platform on wheels. The attendants—one of whom was Ray Cronk—held hoops and danced around Woolley. Each zodiac sign was represented with a specific color and mood.

During this time, the gay community was becoming more visible, and candidates for city office often quietly met with krewe members. According to Woolley, "Harry Connick, when he was running for district attorney, actively sought the gay vote, attending balls and coming to fund-raisers. I personally canvased the French Quarter for him. I lived on Dumaine Street near Marti's Restaurant, where Tennessee Williams had his house, in a back apartment, and I distributed flyers for weeks. For the gay community, Connick was a piece of candy."

As captain of the *Zodiac* (1973) and *Circus* (1975) balls, Woolley expanded into even more grandiose territory. But for Petronius's fifteenth anniversary ball, *Memories* (1976), he paused to review the earlier themes and costumes and envisioned a new type of tableau in which all aspects of the arts would coalesce for an even more elaborate and cohesive presentation.

The Great Schism

No Carnival group was immune to strong personalities, power plays, and rivalries. Petronius and the other gay krewes were no exception. The Krewe of Amon-Ra was born in 1965 with former members of the Krewes of Petronius and Yuga. In 1970, Jamie Greenleaf broke away from the Krewe of Petronius and became captain of the Krewe of Olympus. The following year, the new group held its first ball in the Saint Bernard Civic Auditorium. Very few venues were now willing to rent to gay krewes, so other places had to be found that not only could accommodate the growing guest list but also preserve the anonymity of krewe members. Thus began the long-running tradition of holding gay balls in Chalmette, which gave the krewes more room for their tableaux and seating for hundreds of guests. Special guests sat at elegant tables in front of the stage, enabling costumed krewe members to come right down from the stage and engage their audience. The tables were then removed to make room for dancing. In 1976, after Petronius's fifteenth-anniversary ball, William Woolley split off and formed the Mystic Krewe of Celestial Knights, composed mainly of window dressers and dancers. His first ball, *Heavenly Bodies* (1977), sought to steal the spotlight from the aging dowager. But the Queen of Petronius would not be outshone by her children. In her *Fantasie de la Mer* ball, Rolando "Cha Cha" Afre reigned as queen, and at the end of the ball she appeared in a gloriously sequined green octopus gown with tentacles spreading out to cover the entire stage. Captain Millard "Pooh" Wilson had saved the krewe and helped retain its luster, at least for the moment.

The Satyricon Feast

Faced with rising costs, gay krewes found several ways to bring in money for the balls. In 1970, the Krewe of Petronius had begun the tradition of holding a fall fund-raiser, the Satyricon, a camp party of feasting and entertaining that recalled the excesses of ancient Rome. Attendees had to wear togas and threw food liberally onto the floor. Originally held at the Sir Thomas Hall on Burgundy Street, the feast moved by the mid-1980s to the Country Club, in the Bywater neighborhood. Rummage sales, drag competitions, cabaret acts, and bingo nights throughout the year also helped bring in money. Inspiration for the feast came from Petronius Arbiter's *Satyricon*, published around the first or second century A.D., which contains ribald tales regarding the travels of two former lovers who traipse across the ancient landscape with young boys, transvestites, and slaves.

A Splendid Golden Age

Millard "Pooh" Wilson, a strong force within the krewe for many years, returned as ball captain for both the *Valentine* (1971) and the *Clowns* (1981) anniversary balls, which featured large posters designed by George Dureau and Charles Kerbs, legendary gay artists of New Orleans. Gay krewes often commissioned posters for their balls, along with doubloons (fake coins minted with the theme of the ball) and sometimes necklaces. These krewes took their balls seriously, and their ambition continued to grow in proportion to members' creativity and their desire to outdo their sister krewes. Many observers consider the balls in the mid-1980s the height of gay Carnival, with eager audiences amazed and dazzled by the creativity displayed by the krewes. More than a dozen krewes were active during that time—Cerci, David, Apollo, Armeinius, Lords of Leather, Ishtar, Polyphemus, Amon-Ra, Celestial Knights, Olympus, Snow White, and Perseus—and all were the offspring of Petronius, after the demise of Yuga.

For the 1985 *Petronius Goes to Hell* ball, Rowena, famous drag legend, was the captain, and the theme once again explored the devil and fire-breathing dragons. The Bourbon Street Awards that year returned to their original location in front of Café Lafitte in Exile, the sponsor, with Miss Blanche and Pickle from the Golden Lantern as cohosts. The Petronius Dragon, portrayed by Garron Lenaz, was awarded Overall Best Costume. The daring costume swirled ten feet above Lenaz's head and was crowned with a fanged creature so realistic that many gasped when he mounted onto the stage in the middle of the street. Edd Smith, who usually was the emcee for the awards, was stationed above the LaunDryTeria and coaxed Miss Blanche with his usual banter via walkie-talkies. Writing in *Ambush Magazine*, Wally Sherwood declared, "By presenting a true bal masqué, Petronius is always one of the more pleasurable functions to attend and usually excels in exceptional individualized costumes. This treatment continued the tradition for 1985 with the magnificent smoking dragon and the introduction of the royalty."

A Swath of Destruction

With AIDS decimating the ranks of the gay krewes, especially Petronius, gay Carnival faced extinction by the late 1980s. But a renaissance came along with the arrival of Mickey Gil and his partner, George Patterson, a native of New Orleans. Born in Israel, Gil met Patterson in New York, and they returned to Patterson's home city around this time. Patterson was already well versed in set design, having worked at the Gallery Circle Theatre on Madison Street prior to departing for New York. His 1967 production of *Gypsy* employed Jamie Greenleaf and Harvey Hysell and gave Becky Allen, diva and local favorite, her start in the theater. She later reigned over the newly formed Mystic Krewe of Satyricon as Queen Satyricon I.

A Return to Glory

Mickey Gil's exuberance and creative style reinvigorated the ailing Krewe of Petronius. In 1987, he became ball captain, and his *The Diva in Me* ball returned the krewe to grandeur. Gil's larger-than-life personality and charisma served him well, enticing Wendell Stipelcovich, a founder of the Krewe of Armeinius, to join Petronius. Stipelcovich's Flying Dutchman costume featured the entire haunted vessel and won the Best Costume award that year at the Academy of the Golden Goddess Inc. (AGGI) Awards, gay Carnival's version of the Oscars. Along with George Patterson's genius for set design and costumes, Gil's tongue-in-cheek themes, often self-referential and witty, brought a welcome return to frivolity and whimsy in the face of such catastrophic loss. *Petronius Gets Culcha* (1990), a camp play on New Orleanian pronunciation of the word *culture*, and *Petronius Punctures Pomposity* (1994) were highly successful and elaborate balls in the 1990s. However, the situation changed dramatically when Jamie Greenleaf moved back to the city.

For the 1992 *Fairy Tales* ball, Gil had recruited Greenleaf to construct one of the major costumes of the tableau, the Queen of the Faeries. Not content with a static costume, Greenleaf installed movable parts and lights serviced from underneath by batteries and computers. The queen's costume as the consummate fairy was an unparalleled masterpiece. In the words of Petronius member Errol Rizzuto, "The costume was an awesome creation for Paul Gehardt, Queen Petronius XXXI. Everything was mounted on a framework of lightweight aluminum with eight casters, which were so sensitive the entire structure moved effortlessly when he moved. Onto the aluminum superstructure was a layer of plywood sprayed white, onto which was added countless strings of tubed chaser lights covering the entire surface. On top of the plywood was layer upon layer of white opalescent sheer fabric, creating the queen's gown. The butterflies were animated, as well as the large pair of wings on the queen's back. He also had tiny pecan-sized bees and butterflies, which were on transparent wires coming off of his bodice and shoulders. His crown was of crystals, and it, too, lit up. The entire costume was run by three computers tucked underneath the gown on a platform. Under the gown the queen wore blue jeans with belt loops, and the gown portion of the costume was attached by eight spring-latch key rings. Watching this costume move across the floor was like watching a cloud, because the chaser lights gave the illusion of a real cloud. The cost for it all was over seven thousand dollars, but it was a perfection." Rizzuto himself was Jack Frost, with a costume that was seventeen feet wide and seventeen and a half feet tall. It looked like a lighted weeping willow with Jack Frost in the middle, and it was covered with opalescent crackle and mirrors. Recalled Rizzuto, "When I came out on stage, it was totally blacked out, with only my weeping willow with thousands of minilights illuminating the stage. Looked like an enchanted tree standing in the midst of the dark, murky swamp of the stage set. When I turned around, the audience went crazy. On Mardi Gras day, I walked Bourbon Street with this costume, and when the sun hit the mirrors, my costume lit up homes for blocks as if I were a mirror ball! I won Best of Show that year for the Bourbon Street Awards."

Gil himself appeared as the Sorcerer, and his ball lieutenant was the Sorcerer's Apprentice, but the trick was "to avoid the Disney look," according to Ron Aschenbach, who designed most of the costumes. "We were trying for a European turn-of-the-century look." Other costumes included Mother Goose, Red Riding Hood, Rapunzel, the Mad Hatter, Jack Frost, Turandot, Morgan le Fay, Scheherazade, and

Queen Petronius XXXIII, Mickey Gil, *Straight from the Heart* ball, 1993. Photograph by Syndey Byrd.

Aladdin. Aladdin was hunched over a magic lamp with a huge purple genie attached behind "like a sort of incubus."

As Scheherazade, Richard Egyud wore a huge spiral headdress atop a luxuriously sequined gown. However, the showstopper was the cape, which had thousands and thousands of sequins on the back and an underside carpeted with the eyes of hundreds of blue and green peacock feathers.

The Petronius balls of the early 1990s were so successful because Gil was adept at finding the right people to realize his visions. He relinquished his role as captain for only one year, 1993, when he became Queen of Petronius and Jamie Greenleaf served as captain. This combination, too, produced sensational results.

In addition to captaining Petronius in 1969 and the Krewe of Olympus, Greenleaf had previously designed costumes for the 1971 Rex Parade and for opera companies across the country. During the 1980s, he lived in Anchorage, Alaska, and designed sets for the Alaska Repertory Theatre and gowns for the Imperial Court of All Alaska, part of the International Imperial Court System, which sponsors Gala Coronations to raise money for charitable causes. In 1993, however, Greenleaf returned to New Orleans and focused all of his wizardry and expertise on Gil, who gave a bombastic performance in the *Straight from the Heart* ball, all red and pink in honor of Valentine's Day. Even Gil's face was a luminous patchwork of lipstick and powder, courtesy of Harvey Hysell, who seemed never too far away from his former partner. As Patterson described that night at the Municipal Auditorium, "The fan-shaped curtain rose slowly at the very end of the ball to reveal Mickey as Queen Petronius XXXII, dressed in a flaming red bodysuit with its flames curving up, flying wildly all around him. Jamie had embedded hundreds of small lights in the costume to great effect. As Mickey came forward with scepter in hand, the audience went wild, with wave after wave of applause. Suddenly a white Bentley rolled out on stage and out popped Mickey's king, Larry Branch, in a white tuxedo. Branch had to change quickly from his tableau costume, but he did not have enough time to switch out his flaming orange pumps. It was a sight to behold, something I'll never forget in all my life."

Petronius Punctures Pomposity

In the brilliant *Petronius Punctures Pomposity* ball of 1994, Gil took on the powers that be and held up a mirror that revealed a bit more than they wanted to see. The early 1990s saw bitter controversy over an antidiscrimination ordinance that threatened the annual parades and Carnival itself. Dorothy Mae Taylor, the first African American woman to serve in the Louisiana House of Representatives, was determined to desegregate Mardi Gras organizations. On the New Orleans City Council, she sought to end discrimination in the traditional Mardi Gras krewes by rescinding parade permits for any krewe that refused to modify their policies of exclusion and elitism. Some krewes responded by refusing to parade—the Mistick Krewe of Comus, for example, has never returned to the streets. In this climate, *Petronius Punctures Pomposity* featured a tableau involving parodies of New Orleans mayor Sidney Barthelemy (Sidney Barthology) and Georgia senator Sam Nunn (in drag for the first time). Such political satire has always been part of the spirit of Carnival: Comus, for example, satirized Reconstruction-era carpetbaggers with *The Missing Links to Darwin's Origin of Species* (1873). As Henri Schindler described the tableau, "Invitations to this ball offered no suggestion of the ingenious theme, but the program was profusely illustrated with tableaux groupings of the [Charles] Briton caricatures, which depicted members of the carpet-bag regime as all manner of strange creatures," among them Ulysses Grant as a grub worm. More than a century later Gil's satire, spared no one, including Blaine Kern, who designed most of the Carnival floats every year, and the Pentagon.

Forty Years of Petronius

In 2001, Gil enlisted designer and author Henri Schindler to create the poster for Petronius's fortieth anniversary ball, *Color Me Red*. The artwork featured Elmo Avet dressed in high-camp drag from 1926 and referenced the history of gay Carnival with a nod to the Krewe of Yuga. As Gil noted in the program, "This year's ball will also honor the memory of Miss Fly, Lee Featherston, one of the krewe's most beloved members, who died in December only two months before he would have been featured in the 40th ball as the returning Queen Petronius XXXIX."

Gabe Nassar, who joined the Krewe of Petronius after the demise of the Mystic Krewe of Celestial Knights, participated in many of Gil's balls and remembered that "Mickey was an amazing person to work with. Even though I had been a member of Petronius for only a couple years, he took me under his wing and allowed me to develop and create my own costumes, according to each theme, of course. But he wasn't someone who had to control everything. As long as your costume was fantastic and well done and represented the ball theme, he was a hands-off captain. An amazing and creative mind, and a very supportive captain."

Several years later Gil broke from the Krewe of Petronius to form the Mystic Krewe of Satyricon. Wally McLaughlin, who had served as captain in the Krewe of

Commemorative poster for the Krewe of Petronius's *Color Me Red* ball, 2001. Design by Henri Schindler based on a photograph of Elmo Avet in costume from 1926. Courtesy of the Louisiana State Museum, New Orleans, Accession No. 2001.105.3; Courtesy of Henri Schindler.

Krewe of Petronius (1962)

Armeinius for many years, had moved to Petronius. After several of his friends followed over the next couple of years, he won the election to become captain, displacing Gil, who had always held this title. In response, Gil left and formed the new krewe.

The New Renaissance

The Krewe of Petronius subsequently strengthened its ranks with younger members and presented such balls as *Let It Be*, a Beatles-themed ball; *The Mirror Has Two Faces*; and *Fill in the Blank*. In 2015, however, the krewe, faced with financial problems and a dwindling membership, decided not to have a tableau ball and instead had a presentation at its Banquet of Trimalchio dinner.

Daryl Dunaway, former captain of Petronius, summed up the situation: "We were encouraged in recent years by gaining new members who had never been part of a krewe before, but the overall trend for gay Carnival organizations has been downward as the general population becomes more accepting of gay culture. Groups like Petronius need to find new ways to be relevant and get the kind of active participation required to keep a krewe running."

Even though many observers believe that gay Carnival has rebounded, certain circumstances remain worrisome. In the past, gay krewes were especially protective of their work, and ball themes and costumes were closely guarded secrets. Memberships seldom overlapped, guaranteeing a constant state of healthy competition that fueled the creative fires. Now however, many krewes have begun pooling their resources, with members sitting on the boards of two or three krewes. In addition, krewes have begun collaborating on fund-raising and costumes. Petronius in particular faced the real possibility that its creative energies would dissipate as a consequence of the lack of competition.

In Dunaway's view, "Many krewe members believe they have to concentrate on supporting each other and then sort out the details later. Not presenting a ball, as was the case for Petronius in 2015, is a symptom of this general trend and must be addressed. But I have absolute faith in our ability to succeed. We came back strong in 2016, and the future will be even better."

Dunaway and other relatively new members represent an emboldened and reinvigorated spirit. They, along with the members of such new krewes as Narcissus and Satyricon, are continuing the move into the next phase of gay Carnival history, overcoming the setbacks not only of AIDS but also of Hurricane Katrina. With *Gay, Glitz, and Glamour*, the Krewe of Petronius not only returned to the stage by presenting a ball in 2016 but resumed its place as the premier gay Carnival krewe.

The year 2017 marked an even greater burst of creative energy. John Zeringue, former captain of the Krewe of Amon-Ra, was captain and his adept talent at designing costumes, which he does professionally, came to the fore with the masterful *Seven Deadly Sins* ball. Zeringue elaborated, "All the pieces are in place for the success of this incredible krewe. In my heart I know there will always be a need for a safe place for creative expression for all of our LGBT community. You may have committed one or two sins; tonight we commit all seven, and a few more!" On board for the commemorative poster was nationally know artist Michael Meads, who produced a mesmerizing cornucopia of sins upon sins in his original artwork. The future path for the Krewe of Petronius has been paved with gold enough to last for many a year to come.

Krewe of Petronius Tableau Balls List	
1962	BROADWAY
1963	ROARING TWENTIES
1964	THIRD ANNUAL BALL
1965	THE WICKED BITCHES OF HISTORY
1966	THE WIZARD OF OZ
1967	AROUND THE WORLD WITH AUNTIE MAME—IT'S SHEER CAMP
1968	SHANGRI-LA
1969	GLORIFICATION OF THE AMERICAN GIRL
1970	2069: A SPACE ODDITY
1971	AN EVENING OF LOVE (TENTH ANNIVERSARY)
1972	THE WEDDING LEGEND OF MAHEO
1973	SIGNS OF THE ZODIAC
1974	WHERE THE WILD THINGS ARE!
1975	CIRCUS INTERNATIONAL
1976	MEMORIES (FIFTEENTH ANNIVERSARY)
1977	FANTAISIE DE LA MER—SEA BALL
1978	SPACE BALL—ALBEDO 0.39
1979	FANTAISIE DE LA TÊTE—DREAM FANTASY
1980	LE VOYAGE ENCHANTÉ—ENCHANTED VOYAGE
1981	CLOWNS (TWENTIETH ANNIVERSARY)
1982	LOVE IS BOTH BEAUTY AND BEAST
1983	LOST CIVILIZATIONS OF THE AMERICAS
1984	CONNECT WITH PETRONIUS
1985	PETRONIUS GOES TO HELL
1986	JEWELS—TWENTY-FIVE YEARS OF SELF ADORNMENT (TWENTY-FIFTH ANNIVERSARY)
1987	THE DIVA IN ME
1988	HOLIDAY GALA
1989	INVITATION TO THE DANCE
1990	PETRONIUS GETS CULCHA
1991	PETRONIUS SALUTES ROYALTY (THIRTIETH ANNIVERSARY)
1992	FAIRY TALES
1993	STRAIGHT FROM THE HEART
1994	PETRONIUS PUNCTURES POMPOSITY
1995	L'AMOUR BLEU
1996	STAR WHORES (THIRTY-FIFTH ANNIVERSARY)
1997	(COCKTAIL RECEPTION—NO BALL)
1998	DRESSINGS
1999	RAGTIME
2000	CARNIVAL IN VENICE
2001	COLOR ME RED (FORTIETH ANNIVERSARY)
2002	COME FLY WITH ME
2003	THE KILLER BALL
2004	—
2005	DECADENCE AND DECAY (GODS AND GODDESSES)
2006	TEENIE WEENIE BALL*
2007	TEENIE WEENIE BALL II*
2008	POSTCARD FROM THE EDGE OF EXTINCTION
2009	THE CAN BALL
2010	OUT OF THE FRAME AND OFF THE WALL

1980s

The Krewe of Petronius presented some of the most brilliant balls of gay Carnival during its Golden Age. But the krewe was hit hard by AIDS, and membership dwindled in the late 1980s. The krewe's survival appeared imperiled.

1990s

Mickey Gil joined the krewe in the late 1980s and oversaw a renaissance by the Krewe of Petronius, with presentations featuring frivolity and camp. In 1993, Jamie Greenleaf returned as captain to enable Gil to reign supreme as Queen Petronius XXXII.

2000s

Mickey Gil left in 2002 to form the Mystic Krewe of Satyricon. The 2003 *Killer* ball proved that Petronius could still hold its own under its new captain, Wally McLaughlin. The following year's Carnival season ushered in another difficult period, but the krewe held on, reaching a milestone in the history of gay Carnival: its fiftieth anniversary ball in 2011.

2015

Petronius did not host a complete tableau ball but instead presented the Banquet of Trimalchio to show that it was still active.

2016–17

The *Gay, Glitz, and Glamour* (2016) ball marked Petronius's return to grandeur under the exuberant leadership of captain Randall Brown. Kitty d'Litter reigned as Queen Petronius LV. For the next year's ball, the *Seven Deadly Sins*, Kayla Starr was chosen as queen with John Zeringue III as captain.

2011	GOLDEN JUBILEE BAL MASQUÉ (FIFTIETH ANNIVERSARY)
2012	LET IT BE / BEATLES
2013	THE MIRROR HAS TWO FACES
2014	FILL IN THE BLANK
2015	DIVINED BY THE STARS**
2016	GAY, GLITZ, AND GLAMOUR
2017	SEVEN DEADLY SINS
2018	DRAG'ON
	. . .
1970–86	SATYRICON FUND-RAISER FALL FEAST

*Costume party rather than a tableau ball in wake of Hurricane Katrina
**In lieu of a tableau ball, the Banquet of Trimalchio was held with the theme *Divined by the Stars*

Krewe of Petronius Royalty List			
YEAR OF TABLEAU BALL	**CAPTAIN**	**QUEEN**	**KING**
1962	Joseph E. "JoJo" Landry Jr.	Carlos Rodriguez	—
1963	William Woolley	Bradley Lysholm	—
1964	William Woolley	William McKenzie	Roeling Mace
1965	Bradley Lysholm	William Woolley	Joseph Barcellona
1966	Joseph Barcellona	John Dodt III	Andy Cracciola
1967	Joseph E. "JoJo" Landry Jr.	Otto Stierle	Aaron Swanson
1968	William Woolley	Millard Wilson	Clyde Webb
1969	Lewis "Jamie" Greenleaf III	Joseph Barcellona	Don Fitzpatrick
1970	Millard Wilson	Glenn Fusilier	Joseph Barcellona
1971	Millard Wilson	Clyde Webb	André Picou
1972	Joseph Barcellona	Ray Cronk	Hank Ranna
1973	William Woolley	Alvin Payne	Jerry Morgan
1974	Glenn Fusilier	Philip Torres	Ed Forsyth/Garron Lenaz
1975	William Woolley	René Garza	Richard Jones
1976	William Woolley/ James Weaver	James Keyes	Garron Lenaz
1977	Millard Wilson	Rolando "Cha Cha" Afre	Helmut Stuhlmann
1978	John Hebert	Jimmy Cappel	Garron Lenaz
1979	Glenn Fusilier	Helmut Stuhlmann	Russell Howard
1980	Jimmy Cappel	George South	Myrt Beeler
1981	Millard Wilson	David Baldwin	Dick Kale
1982	(Group)	Garron Lenaz	Jack Easton
1983	Roy Hermann (Rowena)	Chet Robin	Bobby Jones
1984	Bruce Gauthier	Millard Wilson	Hal Faulkner
1985	Roy Hermann (Rowena)	John Berry	Jason Alexander
1986	Garron Lenaz	Jack Easton	Tom Douglas
1987	Mickey Gil	George South	Easton Lala
1988	Millard Wilson	Kenny Petit	George Harry
1989	Mickey Gil	Paul Arnoli	Kenny Plaisance
1990	Mickey Gil	Robin Malta	Dick Egyud
1991	Mickey Gil	Hoyle Byrd	Doug Smith
1992	Mickey Gil	Paul Gehardt	Robert Dunlap

YEAR OF TABLEAU BALL	**CAPTAIN**	**QUEEN**	**KING**
1993	Lewis "Jamie" Greenleaf III	Mickey Gil	Larry Branch
1994	Mickey Gil	Randy Patterson (Phyllis Denmark)	Bill Shraberg
1995	Mickey Gil	Dick Egyud	Paul Bordelon
1996	Mickey Gil	Wess Hughes	Hoyle Byrd
1997	Mickey Gil	Wess Hughes*	Hoyle Byrd*
1998	Mickey Gil	Steve Peacock	Al Kohner/Joe Brooks
1999	Mickey Gil	Tom Conners	Wally McLaughlin
2000	Mickey Gil	Lee Featherston (Miss Fly)	Romnie Leleux
2001	Mickey Gil	Robert Dunlap	James Forde
2002	Mickey Gil	Tim Symsek	Jerry Meis
2003	Wally McLaughlin	Toni Pizanie	Bill Brandon
2004	—		
2005	Joseph Marrione	Romnie Leleux	Craig Schexnayder
2006	Romnie Leleux/Craig Schexnayder	Wally McLaughlin	Mae Falgout
2007	Romnie Leleux/Craig Schexnayder	Wally McLaughlin	Mae Falgout
2008	William McCarthy (Bootsie DeVille)	Dawn Falgout-Loebig**	Charles Turberville
2009	William McCarthy (Bootsie DeVille)	Fredrick Guess	Arthur Alacorn
2010	William McCarthy (Bootsie DeVille)	Randy Chauvin (Natasha Sinclair)	Lee Briggs
2011	Randy Chauvin (Natasha Sinclair)	William McCarthy (Bootsie DeVille)	Jimmy deBlanc
2012	William McCarthy (Bootsie DeVille)/ Chad Brickley (Dragzilla)	Ray Anderson	Les Falgout
2013	William McCarthy (Bootsie DeVille)/ Chad Brickley (Dragzilla)	Larry Anderson	Lee Worrells
2014	Daryl Dunaway Jr. (Countess C. Alice)	Theresa Braggs	Eunice Evans
2015	Brian Plauché	Theresa Braggs***	Eunice Evans***
2016	Randall Brown	Kevin Thomas (Kitty d'Litter)	Nick Olivares
2017	John S. Zeringue III	Kayla Starr	Starr Alexander
2018	John S. Zeringue III	Deanna Ninneman	Jake Thomas

*In 1997 Petronius only had a cocktail reception, retaining the two royals from the previous year. In the 1998 program, captain Mickey Gil explained that a "grand party" had been held in 1997 instead of a ball, which "immediately set some people to speculating whether Petronius was a thing of the past."

**First straight woman to reign as Queen Petronius. Her daughter, a lesbian, had served as king in 2006 and 2007.

***An African American lesbian couple.

Broadway 1962

Invitation to the *Broadway* ball, 1962. Courtesy of The Historic New Orleans Collection, Williams Research Center, New Orleans, Accession No. 1980.178.70. Gift of Tracy Hendrix.

William Woolley en route to the *Broadway* ball, 1962. Woolley, who served as one of the queen's maids, wore a costume that recalled Texas Guinan. Courtesy of the Louisiana State Museum, New Orleans, Accession No. 2016.026.01.

Third Annual Presentation 1964

Invitation to the third tableau ball, 1964. The Italian Union Hall on Esplanade Avenue was one of the few venues willing to rent to gay krewes at the time. Courtesy of the Louisiana State Museum, New Orleans, Accession No. 2013.014.1.

The Wicked Bitches of History 1965

Queen Petronius IV, William Woolley, as Turandot, 1965. Courtesy of the Louisiana State Museum, New Orleans, Accession No. 2016.026.02.

Returning Queen Petronius III, Bill McKenzie (*seated*) and captain, Brad Lysholm (*on stage*), 1965. Courtesy of the Louisiana State Museum, New Orleans, Accession No. 2016.026.02.5.

Captain Brad Lysholm as Mae West, 1965. Courtesy of the Louisiana State Museum, New Orleans, Accession No. 2016.026.02.2.

Around the World with Auntie Mame—It's Sheer Camp 1967

Program, 1967. Design by Elmo Avet. Courtesy of Tulane University, Louisiana Research Collection, Howard-Tilton Memorial Library, New Orleans, Otto Stierle Collection, Manuscripts Collection 902.

Inside reads: *Tableau 1967. Petronius presents the world's greatest camp Mame to tell you of some of the ancient cities she has visited and a few of the people she has met. She first met the Empress Messalina in Italy. The city the whole world loves Paris (Ball Captain). Then she hopped over to Peking and had dinner with the Empress (Ball Lieutenant). And over to Athens, Greece (1st Maid). A mad flight to Pompeii (2nd Maid). As no surprise, she found the lost city of Atlantis (3rd Maid). She also had to visit Alexandria to meet Cleopatra (4th Maid). Then a mad dash to Bangkok (5th Maid). Mame loved flowers, so to the Hanging Gardens of Babylon (6th Maid). She couldn't possibly forget Sodom and Gomorrah (7th and 8th Maids) the Captain found the King, then all Hell broke loose. Rome was burning (Queen Petronius VI).*

Invitation, 1967. Design by Claire Evangelista. Courtesy of the Louisiana State Museum, New Orleans, Accession No. 2016.010.01.

Shangri-La 1968

Program, 1968. Design by William Woolley. Courtesy of The Historic New Orleans Collection, Williams Research Center, New Orleans, Accession No. 1980.178.141. Gift of Tracy Hendrix.

Queen Petronius VII, Millard Wilson, and King Petronius VII, Clyde Webb, on Shrove Tuesday in the French Quarter, 1968. Courtesy of the Louisiana State Museum, New Orleans, Accession No. 2016.026.04.4.

Elmo Avet as Scarlett O'Hara, 1968. Courtesy of the Louisiana State Museum, New Orleans, Accession No. 2016.026.04.3.

Glorification of the American Girl 1969

Commemorative poster, 1969. Design by Lewis S. Greenleaf III. Courtesy of the Louisiana State Museum, New Orleans, Accession No. 1995.010.101.

Tableau 1969
King Plumus of the Realm Bicepticus
Queen Irrisistabus of the Realm Pootius and Imped-
    imenta
A Potpourri of Plucked Plumage Perfection
The Captain as a Beaded Extravaganza of Shimmering
    Boa
The Golden Vision
A Patriotic Pledge of Our Star Spangled States
A Floral Tribute to the Flower Child
The Castles and Then Some
The Fluttering Fulfillment of the Magnificent Moth of
    Desire
A Gushing Geyser of Gorgeous Glitter
A Melodic Mimsy of Musical Motion
A Tribute for the Birds
The Bedazzling Beauteous Blob of Glup
A Lustrous Lavishness of Lemon Loveliness
Heiress Presumptive to the Throne—The Former
    Princess Ruby Plush de Glitzendress
Heir to the Crown—The Semi-Precious Prince de
    Studzenshine

Captain Jamie Greenleaf as a Beaded Extravaganza of Shimmering Boa, 1969. Courtesy of the Louisiana State Museum, New Orleans, Accession No. 2016.026.05.1.

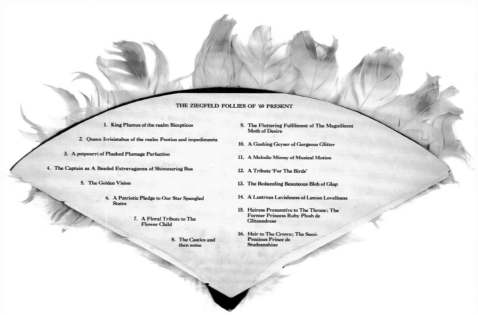

THE ZIEGFELD FOLLIES OF '69 PRESENT

1. King Plumus of the realm Bicepticus
2. Queen Irrisistabus of the realm Pootius and impedimenta
3. A potpourri of Plucked Plumage Perfection
4. The Captain as A Beaded Extravaganza of Shimmering Boa
5. The Golden Vision
6. A Patriotic Pledge to Our Star Spangled States
7. A Floral Tribute to The Flower Child
8. The Castles and then some
9. The Fluttering Fulfilment of The Magnificent Moth of Desire
10. A Gushing Geyser of Gorgeous Glitter
11. A Melodic Mimsy of Musical Motion
12. A Tribute 'For The Birds'
13. The Bedazzling Beauteous Blob of Glup
14. A Lustrous Lavishness of Lemon Loveliness
15. Heiress Presumtive to The Throne; The Former Princess Ruby Plush de Glitzendress
16. Heir to The Crown; The Semi-Precious Prince de Studzenshine

Program, 1969. Courtesy of the Louisiana State Museum, New Orleans, Accession No. 1995.010.102.

William Woolley as the Golden Vision, 1969. Courtesy of the Louisiana State Museum, New Orleans, Accession No. 2016.026.05.3.

One of the Potpourri of Plucked Plumage Perfection, a group of six showgirls who parted their fans for the entrance of each costume, 1969. Courtesy of the Louisiana State Museum, New Orleans, Accession No. 2016.026.05.6.

Joey Barcellona as Queen Marie Antoinette, the Former Princess Ruby Plush de Glitzendress, Heiress Presumptive to the Throne, 1969. Courtesy of the Louisiana State Museum, New Orleans, Accession No. 2016.026.05.2.

2069: A Space Oddity 1970

Captain Millard Wilson as Dazzling in Moon Rays, 1970. According to various sources, Wilson was rather inebriated when he came out in costume and continued to circle the stage over and over again. Though the audience booed him, he thought they were yelling his nickname, *Pooh*, and mistook their catcalls for encouragement. Courtesy of the Louisiana State Museum, New Orleans, Accession No. 2016.026.07.1.

Commemorative poster, 1970. Design by Calvert. Courtesy of The Historic New Orleans Collection, Williams Research Center, New Orleans, Accession No. 1980.178.219. Gift of Tracy Hendrix.

Tableau 1970
Flight of Fantasy—King Cardinale
A Night Flying Bird—Queen Fleur-de-Lis
Dazzling in Moon Rays—The Captain
Gleaming and Glistening—Pieces of Eight
From Jupiter—A Frosted Flower
Rounds of Brilliants—Our Radiant Saturnian
Lady Podia—Moonstone in Motion
Fire-Light—It Flies, It Leaps, It Roars, It Rolls—A Kick Baby!
Our Dizzy Darling Moon-Child
From the Sea of Pootius—The Duchess Diamanté
Her Maid—A Blazing Belle
Her Hairdresser—A Gilded Globolink
Her Chef—A Faceted Reflecting Gem
A Gyrating Minotaur
Heiress to the Throne—Queen Petronius IX
Heir to the Crown—King Petronius IX

Her Hairdresser—A Gilded Globolink, 1970. Courtesy of the Louisiana State Museum, New Orleans, Accession No. 2016.026.07.8.

From Jupiter—A Frosted Flower, 1970. Courtesy of the Louisiana State Museum, New Orleans, Accession No. 2016.026.07.3.

Rounds of Brilliants—Our Radiant Saturnian, 1970. Courtesy of the Louisiana State Museum, New Orleans, Accession No. 2016.026.07.5.

From the Sea of Pootius—The Duchess Diamanté, 1970. Courtesy of the Louisiana State Museum, New Orleans, Accession No. 2016.026.07.4.

An Evening of Love 1971

Poster, 1971. Design by George Dureau. Courtesy of
the Louisiana State Museum, New Orleans, Accession
No. 1995.010.123.

William Woolley as Queen Antares of Realm Pootius,
1971. Courtesy of the Louisiana State Museum, New
Orleans, Accession No. 2016.026.08.1.

Tableau 1971
King Gamma Ray of Planet Pootius
Queen Antares of Realm Pootius
The Captain as an Amorous Valentine
Ten Sparkly Candles of Stunning Seductiveness
Our Gift for You All, Gilded and Glossed, a Love Bird
Parfum, Our Special Fragrance for You Alone
Salute to Past Queens, Our Funny Valentines:
    Dorothy Lamour
    Sonja Henie
    Theda Bara
    Bette Davis
    Mae West
Heiress to the Throne—Queen Petronius X
Heir to the Crown—King Petronius X

The Wedding Legend of Maheo 1972

Queen Petronius XI, Ray Cronk, 1972. Courtesy of the Louisiana State Museum, New Orleans, Accession No. 2016.026.09.1.

Returning queen Clyde Webb, 1972. Courtesy of the Louisiana State Museum, New Orleans, Accession No. 2016.026.09.4.

Invitation, 1972. Courtesy of the Louisiana State Museum, New Orleans, Accession No. 1995.010.104.

Inside reads: *Centuries ago, long before the landing of Columbus on North American shores, began a legend still handed down from generation to generation, of the North American Indians, now known as the Cherokees. It is an exciting and beautiful one. The legend tells of worship and belief, ceremony and dance, beauty and splendor. Finally, it tells of love and marriage. In the valley of the sun, in the year of the great drought, lived the Salta Lamachias, a tribe feared throughout the mountains and plains for the valor of its warriors, envied for the beauty of its women. Eleven moons have passed since Onoco, the rain God, showered the Salta Lamachias with his blessings. The ground in their village has turned to dust, their crops have withered, and the once plentiful game animals are gone. In desperation, they dance in honor of Maheo, the All Spirit, and implore him to intercede with Onoco, his seventh son, to bless them with his tears, and save them from the dry death. So touched is Maheo that he transcends the boundaries of heaven and earth, amidst fire and smoke, thunder and lightning and takes human form to appear among them. He tells them, that if among their fairest maidens, there is one, worthy of being his bride, he will have his son bring the rains. After great preparation, the squaws of the village ready their daughters for the approval of Maheo, and the Medicini chants her most powerful spells. Eight of their most desirable daughters are presented, and eight are rejected. Finally, the daughter of White Eagle, chief of the Salta Lamachias, is brought forth. So taken is Maheo with her virtue and fair beauty, that he takes her as his bride, and carries her off to the great teepee, beyond the mountains and the waters, and sends Onoco to quench the parched land of the Salta Lamachias. Come with us now, and witness the previously unseen splendor and ceremony of the Wedding Legend of Maheo.*

Tableau 1972
The Braves Dance
Love Call
Wild Horse
Maheo—The Captain
The Squaws of the Village
Medicine Woman
The Daughters
Minni Few Curls
Theresa Tom-Toms
Patsy Papoose
Clarissa Canoe
Samantha Smoke Signals
Brenda Beads
Betsy Bear Claw
Frieda Firebird
Wanda Whitecloud, the Chosen of Mateo—Queen Petronius XI
Wanda Eagle, Father of Whitecloud—King Petronius XI

Signs of the Zodiac 1973

Commemorative poster, 1973. Design by Smith. Courtesy of The Historic New Orleans Collection, Williams Research Center, New Orleans, Accession No. 1980.178.316. Gift of Tracy Hendrix.

Where the Wild Things Are! 1974

Invitation, 1974. Courtesy of the Louisiana State Museum, New Orleans, Accession No. 1995.010.109.

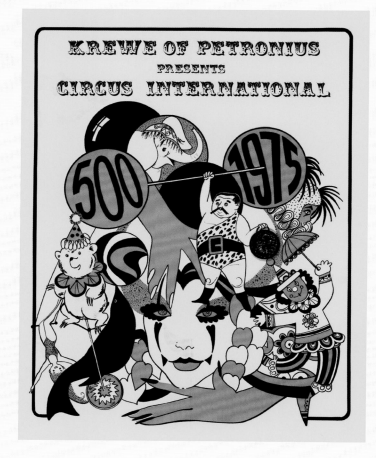

Circus International 1975

Commemorative poster, 1975. The stage was set up as a circus tent. Captain William Woolley came out on a miniature white animatronic elephant. Other animatronics appeared onstage, including a bear with a ball and a zebra. They had previously appeared in the display windows of the D. H. Holmes department store on Canal Street and had been borrowed for the ball. Courtesy of the Louisiana State Museum, New Orleans, Accession No. T0016.2001.731.

Memories—Fifteenth Anniversary Ball 1976

Commemorative poster, 1976. Design by James Keyes. Courtesy of the Louisiana State Museum, New Orleans, Accession No. 1995.010.112.

Cocaptain William Woolley, 1976. Courtesy of the Louisiana State Museum, New Orleans, Accession No. 2016.011.02.02.

Cocaptain James Weaver, 1976. Courtesy of the Louisiana State Museum, New Orleans, Accession No. 2016.011.02.06.

Queen Petronius XV, James Keyes, and King Petronius XV, Garron Lenaz, 1976. Courtesy of the Louisiana State Museum, New Orleans, Accession No. 2016.011.02.07.

Fantasie de la Mer 1977

Original artwork, 1977. Design by Charles Kerbs. Pen and ink on tracing paper. Courtesy of Randy Chauvin and James deBlanc.

Invitation, 1977. Design by Charles Kerbs. Courtesy of the Louisiana State Museum, New Orleans, Accession No. T0016.2001.939.

Space Ball—Albedo 0.39 1978

Commemorative poster, 1978. Design by Charles Kerbs. The following year, the Krewe of Olympus borrowed the idea of a poster in the form of a comic strip. Courtesy of The Historic New Orleans Collection, Williams Research Center, New Orleans, Accession No. 1980.178.480. Gift of Tracy Hendrix.

Fantasie de la Tête 1979

Le Voyage Enchanté 1980

Commemorative poster, 1979. Design by Charles Kerbs. Courtesy of Randy Chauvin and James DeBlanc.

Commemorative poster, 1980. Design by Charles Kerbs. Courtesy of The Historic New Orleans Collection, Williams Research Center, New Orleans, Accession No. 1981.178.537. Gift of Tracy Hendrix.

Clowns—Twentieth Anniversary Ball 1981

Love Is Both Beauty and Beast 1982

Invitation, 1982. Design by Charles Kerbs. Courtesy of The Historic New Orleans Collection, Williams Research Center, New Orleans, Accession No. 1982.251.34. Gift of Tracy Hendrix.

Commemorative poster, 1980. Design by Charles Kerbs. Courtesy of The Historic New Orleans Collection, Williams Research Center, New Orleans, Accession No. 1981.178.537. Gift of Tracy Hendrix.

Rowena (Roy Hermann) in costume, 1982. Courtesy of Jack Jones.

Lost Civilizations of the Americas 1983

Invitation, 1983. Invitation, costume, and set design by Norman McDole Millis. Courtesy of the Louisiana State Museum, New Orleans, Accession No. 1995.010.117.

Connect with Petronius 1984

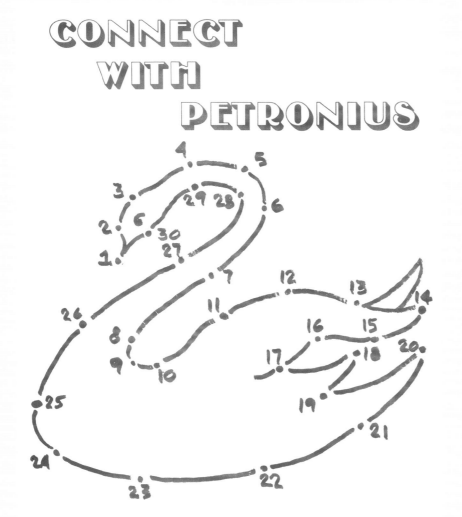

Program, 1984. Courtesy of The Historic New Orleans Collection, Williams Research Center, New Orleans, Accession No. 1984.170.25. Gift of Tracy Hendrix.

Petronius Goes to Hell 1985

Poster, 1985. Courtesy of Randy Chauvin and James DeBlanc.

Jack Jones as Medusa, 1985. Courtesy of Jack Jones.

Jewels—Twenty-Five Years of Self-Adornment 1986

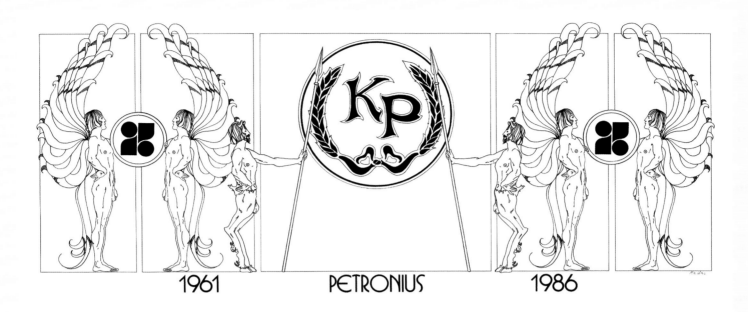

Program, 1986. Design by R. Mullins. Courtesy of The Historic New Orleans Collection, Williams Research Center, New Orleans, Accession No. 1986.30.2.

Tableau 1986
National Anthem
Petronius Theme
Dedication
A Salute to the First Captain and to Previous Royalty
The First Ball Captain (JoJo Landry)
Co-King Petronius XIII (Garron Lenaz)
　　Also King Petronius XVII
　　Also Queen Petronius XXI
And Now Captain Petronius of This the Twenty-Fifth Year 1986
THE TWENTY-FIFTH YEAR 1986
Dali's Soft Watches
Inca Gold
Emeralds
Queen Petronius V (John Dodt)
Opal
Dragon Fly
Scarab
Moonstone
Platinum
Canning Brooch
Jade and Pearls
Queen Petronius XIII (Philip Torres)
Pearl
Queen Petronius XVI (Rolando Afre)
Sapphire
Matching Accessories
Buckle
Diamonds
Queen Petronius VII and XXIII (Millard Wilson)
Jade
A Feathered Divertissement for Royalty
Fairies
Queen Petronius XXII (Chet Robin)
Queen Petronius XXV (Jack Easton)
King Petronius XXV (Tom Douglas)
Toasts
Grand March
Presentations

The Diva in Me 1987

Commemorative poster, 1987. Design by Charles Kerbs. Courtesy of Randy Chauvin and James DeBlanc.

Invitation, 1987. Design by Charles Kerbs. Courtesy of The Historic New Orleans Collection, Williams Research Center, New Orleans, Accession No. 1988.179.48. Gift of Tracy Hendrix.

Wendell Stipelcovich as the Flying Dutchman, 1987. This costume won the Best Costume at the AGGI Awards. Courtesy of the Louisiana State Museum, New Orleans, Jake and Kevin Thomas Collection, Accession No. SC2015.06.06.

Holiday Gala 1988

Invitation, 1988. Design by Charles Kerbs. Courtesy of The Historic New Orleans Collection, Williams Research Center, New Orleans, Accession No. 1981.179.51. Gift of Tracy Hendrix.

⚜

Tableau 1988
National Anthem
Musical Overture
Mother's Day Corsage—Ball Captain
Mother's Day Corsage of a Different Kind—Ball Lieutenant
Spring
Spring Fiesta
Atomic Bomb
Hot Peppers
Jambalaya
Summer
Top Cat Holiday
Bastille Day—La Cage aux Folles
Love Bird
Cuckoo Bird
Old Crow
Autumn
Thanksgiving
Turkey
American Indian
Tall Indian
Winter
Christmas
Queen Petronius XXVII
Coronation of King Petronius XXVII
Finale
Recognition

Invitation to the Dance 1989

Invitation, 1989. Design by James Keyes. The Queen personified the Red Shoes, based on the famous movie. The costumes and sets were designed by George Patterson, partner of captain Mickey Gil. Courtesy of The Historic New Orleans Collection, Williams Research Center, New Orleans, Accession No. 2000.34.71.

⚜

Tableau 1989
Dance Master—Captain
National Anthem
Mardi Gras Balls
Viennese Waltz
Belly Dance
African Dance
Argentinian Tango
Kabuki
Hula
Cha Cha Cha
Tap Dance
Inexpensive Dancing
Dirty Dancing
Jitterbug
Star of a Chorus Line
The Twist
Purple People Eater
Charleston
Busby Berkeley Girl
Sugar Plum Fairy
The Red Shoes—Queen Petronius XXVIII
Search for Her Dance Partner—King Petronius XXVIII
Grand Tableau
Guests and Krewe Representatives

Petronius Gets Culcha 1990

Invitation, 1990. Courtesy of The Historic New Orleans Collection, Williams Research Center, New Orleans, Accession No. 2000.34.82.

Tableau 1990
National Anthem
Returning King Petronius XXVIII
Miss NOLA—Captain
Anna Mae and Rosemary—Emcees
Ruthy the Duck Girl—Lieutenant
Presentations of 1990 Debutramps
Count and Countess Pontalba
The Burning Cabildo
The Historic New Orleans Collection Germaine Wells Fashion Show
    Easter Outfit
    Swimwear
    Summer Frock
    Symphony
    City Park Swans
    Marie Laveau
The Vampire Lestat
Cemeteries
Madame LaLaurie
Schwegmann Girls
The Patroness of New Orleans—La Dame de Bon Secours
Jazz Fest
Mardi Gras Fountain
Longue Vue Gardens
Zoo to Do
Fireworks on the River
Mardi Gras Balls
The Aquarium—Queen Petronius XXIX
Search for her King—King Petronius XXIX
Grand March
Guests and Krewe Representatives

Fairy Tales 1992

Queen Petronius XXXI Paul Gehardt, 1992. Mickey Gil produced an extraordinary ball composed of various fairies, genies, and strange creatures. Jamie Greenleaf created the queen's costume, which was covered with animatronic butterfly wings. Courtesy of the Louisiana State Museum, New Orleans, Jake and Kevin Thomas Collection, Accession No. 2015.046.10.1.

Straight from the Heart 1993

Invitation, 1993. Courtesy of The Historic New Orleans Collection, Williams Research Center, New Orleans, Accession No. 2000.34.80.

Tableau 1993
Return Appearance of King and Queen Petronius XXXI
God Bless America—Varla Jean Merman
Piano Overture—Harry Mayronne Jr.
Florenz Ziegfeld's Revelation—Captain Jamie Greenleaf
Flo and Girls
Frustration; or, the Kiss That Couldn't
Male Bonding
A Viennese Jewish Princess at the Folies-Bergère
I Only Have Eyes for You
Animal Magnetism
Could I Leave You?—Ron Brister
Miss Ziegfeld 1933
By a Waterfall
Intermission
I Can't Be Bothered
Is There Anyone Here for Love?
What We Do to Others' Hearts; or, I Wouldn't Do It to a Dog
Turn Around Is Fair Play
Love Land
Beautiful Girls
This Is the Moment
Her Most Exquisiteness—Queen Petronius XXXII (Mickey Gil)
His Regal Proudness—King Petronius XXXII
Guests and Krewe Representatives
Open Court

Petronius Punctures Pomposity 1994

Program, 1994. Design by James Keyes. Courtesy of the Louisiana State Museum, New Orleans, Accession No. 2014.005.46.

Tableau 1994
National Anthem
Returning King and Queen Petronius XXXII
Captain
Presentation of 1994 Debutramps
Krewe of City Hall
City Council—Dorothy Mae
Miss Peggy and Mayor Sidney
Krewe of Justice—The Singing D.A.
Krewe of Greed
Cynthia Owen and Harry Mayronne Jr.
Krewe de Vieux Carré Commission
Krewe of Floats—Chris, Mickey, and Blaine
Krewe of Chicken
    Fried—Miss Becks (Becky Allen)
    Raw—Michael, aka Jacko
Krewe of Toxins
Giving Something Back—Jim Bob
Krewe of Zoo—The Insectarium—Ronald
Krewe of Bigots—The Pentagon
Komenka Dance Group
Sam Nunn—In Drag for the First Time
Her Royal Highness, Queen Petronius XXXIII
Search and Coronation of King Petronius XXXII
Guests and Sister Krewes
Open Court

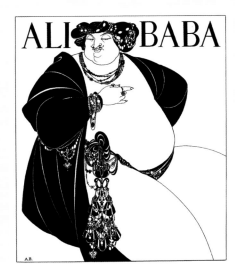

Aubrey Beardsley, *Ali Baba* (cover design for "The Forty Thieves"), 1897. Courtesy of the Harvard Art Museums/Fogg Museum, Bequest of Grenville L. Winthrop, 1943.647.t.

L'Amour Bleu 1995

Invitation, 1995. Design by James Keyes. Courtesy of The Historic New Orleans Collection, Williams Research Center, New Orleans, Accession No. 2000.34.97a.

Tableau 1995
National Anthem
Returning King and Queen Petronius XXXIII
Blue Angel—Captain
Main Herr—Four Skins
Presentations—1995 Debutramps
Ganymede
Alexander the Great—Lieutenant
Marquis de Sade
Susan B. Anthony
Harry Mayronne Jr. and Zelda Rose
Florence Nightingale
Thomas Mann
Tchaikovsky—Four Skins
Stephen Foster
Liberace
Valentino—Steve Lott and Janis Hornsby
Oscar Wilde
Gertrude and Alice
Salon d'Erté—La Soirée, Les Étoiles, L'Oiseau de la Nuit, Minuet, La Lune, La Brume du Matin, L'Aube
Georgia O'Keeffe
Legends
Divine
Josephine Baker
Agnes Moorehead
Harry Mayronne Jr. and Zelda Rose Sing Sondheim
Elton John
Michael Bennet—Komenka Dance Group
Tony Kushner—*Angels in America*—Queen Petronius XXXIV
Search and Coronation of King Petronius XXXIV
Guests and Sister Krewes
Open Court

Star Whores 1996

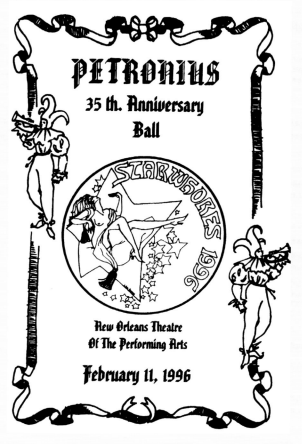

Invitation, 1996. Design by James Keyes. Courtesy of Howard Philips Smith.

Tableau 1996
Returning King and Queen Petronius XXXIV
Invasion of the Stars
Star Captain
Broadway Star
Debutramp
Starting Here, Starting Now
Gigantic Star
A Recording Star
When You Wish upon a Star
Star Gate
Divine Star
N.O. Star
Uranus
An Aging Star
Platinum Star
Sucker Star
A Star Is Born
Male Opera Stars
Female Opera Star
Country Star
Stars Fell on Alabama
Silent Movie Star
A Beautiful Dead Star
A Hungry Star
Material Star
Stars and Stripes Forever
The Biggest Star of All—Queen Petronius XXXV
Search and Coronation of Star King Petronius XXXV
Guests and Sister Krewes
Open Court

Commemorative poster, 2000. Design by Charles Kerbs. Courtesy of the Louisiana State Museum, New Orleans, Accession No. 2001.105.2.

February 27, 2000
Municipal Auditorium
New Orleans, Louisiana

Program, 2000. Design by Charles Kerbs. Courtesy of the John C. Kelly and Michael J. Rosa Collection, Earl K. Long Library, University of New Orleans.

Tableau 2000
National Anthem (Cynthia Owen and Harry Mayronne Jr.)
Returning King and Queen Petronius XXXVIII
The Doge of Venice—Captain
Presentation of Debutramps
Lucretia Borgia—Lieutenant Captain
The Winged Lion of Venice
Marco Polo
Kublai Khan
Mrs. Khan
The Pirate
Tarantella—The Komenka Song and Dance Ensemble
Grand Canal
Barcarolle (*Tales of Hoffmann*)
Death in Venice (Lyle Guidroz and Company)
Cardinal of Venice in Santa Maggiore
Italian Medley (Cynthia Owen and Harry Mayronne Jr.)
Vivaldi's *Four Seasons* (Winter, Spring, Summer, and Fall)
Casanova—Lieutenant Captain
Venetian Bougainvillea
Othello
Columbine (Commedia dell'Arte)
Bellini's Venus
St. Theodore and the Monster
The Beauty Spot—Queen Petronius XXXIX
Crowning of King Petronius XXXIX
Guests and Sister Krewes
Open Court

Color Me Red 2001

Invitation, 2001. Courtesy of Howard Philips Smith.

Tableau 2001
Salute to America by Miss Varla Jean Merman
Remembering Queen Petronius XXXIX—Lee Featherson
Returning King Petronius XXXIX—Romnie Leleux
Captain from the Red Planet—Queen Petronius XXXII
Acknowledgment of Past Royalty
The Only Red Haired Geisha—King Petronius XXXVII
Debutramps
Red Fish and Red Lobster
Red Velvet Cake—King Petronius XXXVIII
Red Strawberries—King Petronius XXXVII
Red Wine
Red Rose
Red Hot Peppers
Red Lady Bug—Queen Petronius XXXVIII
Red Devil—King Petronius XXIX and Queen Petronius XXXIV
Red Flaming Queen
Red Cloud
Red Witch Doctor
Divertissement No. 1—Miss Varla Jean Merman
Red Baron—Ball Lieutenant
Red Sox—With Lyle Guidroz Dancers
Red Ants—With Lyle Guidroz Dancers
Red Light District—Queen Petronius XXX and King Petronius XXXVI
Red Square—With Lyle Guidroz Dancers
Red China—With Lyle Guidroz Dancers
Divertissement No. 2—Miss Varla Jean Merman
Queen Petronius XXXX and Red Rubies (King Petronius XXXI)
Search for and Crowning of King Petronius XXXX
Guests and Sister Krewes
Open Court

Fly with Us 2002

Program, 2002. Courtesy of the Louisiana State Museum, New Orleans, Accession No. 2014.005.52.

Tableau 2002
National Anthem
King and Queen Petronius XXXX
The Maharajah and Maharani of India
Flight Stewardess
Flight Captain
Debutramp #41
Almost Flying in the Air
The Duprees and Group
Hot Air Balloon
Beach Balls Flying in the Air
Remember Ms. Fly (Lee Featherson)
Tinker Bell
Cupid
Flying Dragon, Crouching Tiger
Bar Fly
Venus Fly Trap
Flamingos Flew to South Beach
We Fly
The Birds
The Duprees in the Air
Wicked Witch of the West
Flying Space Ship
Dance on Air
Lunar Moth
Spanish Fly
Griffin
Phoenix
Music in the Air
Gay Monarch Butterfly—Queen Petronius XXXXI
Search for and Crowning of King Petronius XXXXI
Goodbye to King and Queen Petronius XXXX
Guests and Sister Krewes
Open Court

The Killer Ball 2003

KREWE OF PETRONIUS
41ST BAL MASQUE

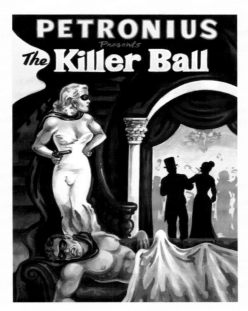

FEBRUARY 3, 2002
MUNICIPAL AUDITORIUM
NEW ORLEANS, LOUISIANA

Commemorative poster, 2002. Design by James Keyes. Courtesy of the Louisiana State Museum, New Orleans, Jake and Kevin Thomas Collection, Accession No. 2015.046.10.3. According to Wally Sherwood, "Another masterful bit of type-casting dominated the Petronius ball when Jerry Meis was revealed as the new King. Presented as a magnificent Phoenix during the tableau, Jerry is vice president of the Knights d'Orleans, a leather club that has the Phoenix as their home bar. Krewe captain Mickey Gil, who served as flight captain for the *Fly With Us* journey, paid special tribute in both the program and from the podium, to his partner of 28 years, George Patterson, news editor and theatre critic of *Ambush Magazine*. The return of the King, as the Maharajah of India, on a huge white elephant was stunning, but only set the stage for more delights until Queen Petronius XLI emerged as a Gay Monarch Butterfly. A blazing UFO highlighted the many special effects, but the cleverest presentation has to be Goldfinger, or 'The Bird,' a large hand well equipped to give the audience 'The Royal Bird.'"

Commemorative poster, 2003. Wally Sherwood called this ball "the most inspired, and by far, the most cerebral of all themes." Poster design by Henri Schindler; artwork by Manuel Ponce. Costume designs by James Keyes. Courtesy of the Louisiana State Museum, New Orleans, Accession No. 2013.014.2.

⚜

Tableau 2003
The Return of King Petronius XLI
Killers from the Sea—Captain
Man-Made Killers—Cars, Planes, and Trains
Time
Lead
Words
Blacks
Microscopic Killers
Chorea
Sin Nombre
The Spanish Lady
Acts of God
Earth, Wind, and Fire
Sins
Unnatural Killers
Poison
Natural Killers
Insects—The Killers
NaCL
Man
Insects—The Carriers
Sunlight
Queen Petronius XLII
Crowning of King Petronius XLII
Guests and Sister Krewes
Open Court

James Keyes, costume sketch for African Killer Bee, 2003. Courtesy of the Louisiana State Museum, New Orleans, Accession No. SC2015.06.20.

James Keyes, costume sketch for Black Balls, 2003. Courtesy of the Louisiana State Museum, New Orleans, Jake and Kevin Thomas Collection, Accession No. SC2015.06.14.

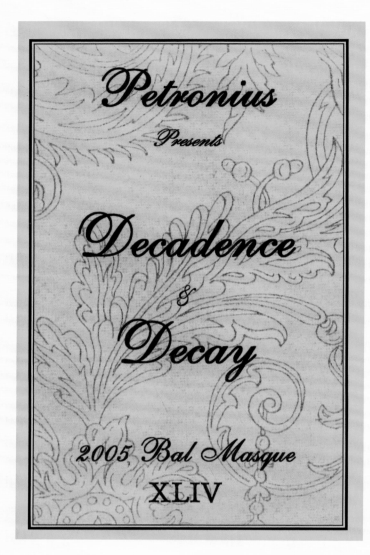

Program, 2005. Courtesy of Wayne Phillips.

Tableau 2005
National Anthem
President's Address
Introduction of the Mistress of Ceremony
Returning of Queen Petronius XLII as Anyareen Portunus
Texcatlipoca
Tribute to Aphrodite
Heracles
Bast
Pandora
Hare Krishna
Kane
Hrungnir
Captain Petronius XLIV as Yu-Huang, the Jade Emperor
King and Queen Petronius XLIV—God of All Gods
Presentation of Special Guest
Presentation of Visiting Royalty
Open Court

James Keyes, costume sketch for Aztec—Tezcatlipoca—
God of Smoking Mirror (Cocaine), 2005. Courtesy of
the Louisiana State Museum, New Orleans, Accession
No. 2013.014.3.

Teenie Weenie Ball 2006

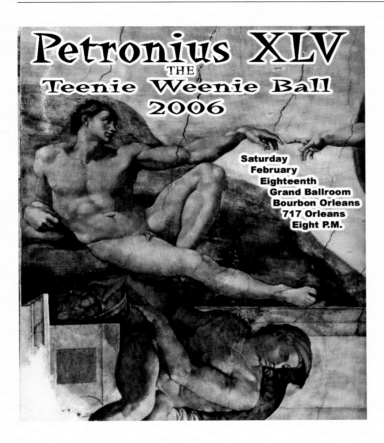

Program, 2006. Courtesy of Howard Philips Smith.

Golden Jubilee Bal Masqué 2011

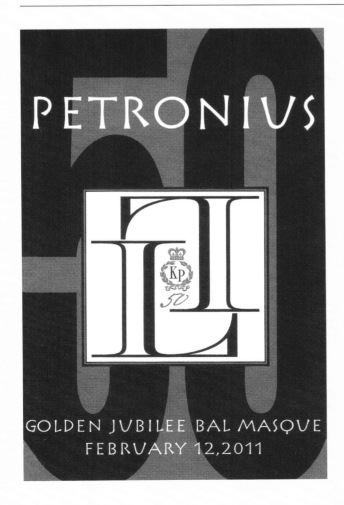

Program, 2011. Courtesy of Wayne Phillips.

Let It Be 2012

Program, 2012. Courtesy of Wayne Phillips.

The Mirror Has Two Faces 2013

Fill in the Blank 2014

Program, 2013. Courtesy of Wayne Phillips.

Program, 2014. Courtesy of Wayne Phillips.

Gay, Glitz, and Glamour 2016

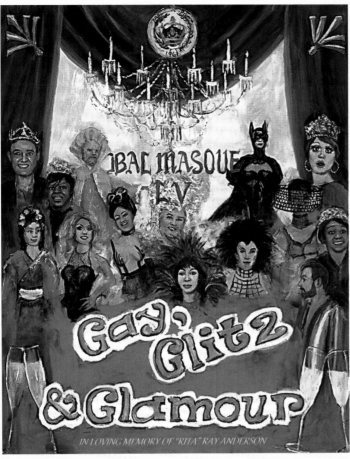

Program, 2016. Design by Fredrick Guess. Courtesy of Wayne Phillips. According to Wayne Phillips of the Louisiana State Museum, "Kitty d'Litter made a fabulous queen. . . . The captain, Randall Brown, came out in half drag, sort of Elton John–ish in knee breeches and high heels and tall wig with a ship mounted in it à la Marie Antoinette, and Jake Thomas, the krewe's president, did wear a male costume, but everyone else was in drag. The costumes were not huge and elaborate, but most of the drag queens did lip-sync numbers instead of just walking out and walking back."

Commemorative artwork, 2016. Queen Kitty d'Litter (Kevin Thomas) appears in the center of the panel, surrounded by her loyal subjects. Design by Michael Meads. Courtesy of Michael Meads.

King Petronius LV, Nick Olivares, and Queen Petronius LV, Kitty d'Litter (Kevin Thomas), during the Think Pink finale, 2016. Photograph by Barrett DeLong-Church. Courtesy of Barrett DeLong-Church.

Captain Randall Brown as Queen of England (Elton John), 2016. Photograph by Barrett DeLong-Church. Courtesy of Barrett DeLong-Church.

Satyricon Fund-Raiser

Invitation to Satyricon III, 1972. Courtesy of Tulane University, Louisiana Research Collection, Howard-Tilton Memorial Library, New Orleans, Otto Stierle Collection, Manuscripts Collection 902.

Aubrey Beardsley, *A Snare of Vintage*, 1894. The graphic for the Satyricon V invitation (1974) was taken from this illustration for Lucian of Samosata's *True History*, considered the first science fiction story. Courtesy of Tulane University, Louisiana Research Collection, Howard-Tilton Memorial Library, New Orleans, Otto Stierle Collection, Manuscripts Collection 902.

Invitation to Satyricon XIII, 1982. Courtesy of Jack Jones.

Invitation to Satyricon XVII, 1986. Design by Norman Millis. Courtesy of the Louisiana State Museum, New Orleans, Accession No. 1995.010.120.

Jack Jones at Satyricon XVII, 1986. Courtesy of Jack Jones.

Nothing compares to being on that stage
and transforming reality into a realm of
fantasy, even if it is only for one night.

—Jerry Gilley, Krewe of Amon-Ra

The Birth of Brilliance

During the 2015 Carnival season, the Krewe of Amon-Ra celebrated its fiftieth anniversary, marking a half century in which the krewe had presented some of New Orleans's most innovative and dazzling balls. One of the earliest gay Carnival krewes, Amon-Ra was founded in 1965 by five members of the Krewe of Petronius (Scott Hoy, Roeling Mace, Vic Scalise, Vincent Indovina, and Sidney Barrios) and one member of the Krewe of Yuga (James Schexnayder). Hoy served as captain when Amon-Ra held its first ball in 1966, and Mace, who had been King Petronius III in 1964, became king of Amon-Ra in 1970 and queen three years later. Schexnayder was among those arrested in the police raid on the Krewe of Yuga's ball in Metairie and served as captain of Amon-Ra in 1978, King Amon-Ra III and Queen Amon-Ra XVI. He again held the post of ball captain in 1989 and became known for his artwork. His seahorse costumes for the 1992 *Fantasylands* ball have become part of the permanent collection of the Louisiana State Museum.

The Krewe of Amon-Ra took its name from the king of the Egyptian gods. Traditional Carnival krewes had similarly chosen names from pagan literatures and ancient mythologies as a way to cloak their group in mystery, such as the Krewes of Thoth, Cleopatra, Osiris, and Isis. Many old-line krewes used Egyptian themes for their tableaux, such as the High Priests of Mithras in 1922. Delving into Egyptian history seemed only natural since it also mentioned the first male couple, Khnumhotep and Niankhkhnum, who were depicted together in wall carvings in their joint tomb and shared the title of overseers in the palace of King

Original artwork for a commemorative poster, Krewe of Amon-Ra, *Picnic Fantasy* ball, 1985. The poem along the border is William Rose's "The Butterfly's Ball, and the Grasshopper's Feast" (1807). Design by Earl Woodard. Restoration by Howard Philips Smith. Courtesy of the Louisiana State Museum.

Egyptian god Thoth depicted on an invitation to High Priests of Mithras ball, 1922. Design by Anne McKinne Robertson. Courtesy of The Historic New Orleans Collection, Williams Research Center, New Orleans, Accession No. 1993.125.11.

Charles Briton, costume design for Ammon Kneph, Krewe of Proteus's *Ancient Egyptian Theology* ball, 1882. Courtesy of Tulane University, Louisiana Research Collection, Howard-Tilton Memorial Library, New Orleans.

John C. Scheffler, costume sketch for the Krewe of Anubis, 1965. Courtesy of the Louisiana State Museum, New Orleans, Accession No. 2014.032.024.56.

Niuserre during the Egyptian Fifth Dynasty. The magic of ancient Egyptian art created a unique and enduring spirit for the krewe.

Many members of gay Carnival krewes were also involved with traditional krewes either as members who attended balls or as designers of costumes. Carter Church, an early member of Amon-Ra, did both. His grandfather had been a member of Rex, and Church was well acquainted with the grand history of Carnival. In fact, when he reigned as queen in 1972, he wore the Queen of Rex's mantle as part of his royal costume. He also designed costumes for such straight krewes as Iris, Sparta, Carrollton, and Dorians. He was captain of the Krewe of Amon-Ra in 1970 and 1975, queen in 1972, and king in 1980, and he was a key figure in the Krewe of Armeinius as well. However, Mike Moreau, also known as Opal Masters, led the krewe during the AIDS crisis. Moreau was a close friend of Church's who joined the krewe at its first meeting.

The First Balls

The theme of the first Amon-Ra ball was *A Night in Old New Orleans*, and the costumes depicted famous French Quarter streets and corners—Bourbon Street (Millard Wilson) as a stripper; the Canal Street Ferry (Mike Moreau) as a fairy; Basin Street (James Keyes) as Madame LuLu White, the infamous brothel proprietor from Storyville; and Clyde Ladner as Queen Amon-Ra I. The ball was held at the International Longshoremen's Association hall on Claiborne Avenue, which was home to Local 1419, a black group, and was one of the few venues to welcome gay krewes.

Moreau and Church Lead the Way

Moreau served as captain for the 1971 *Louisiana on Parade* ball. The poster for the event featured a pharaoh and his retinue taken from *Déscription de l'Égypte* (1809), a volume featuring images crafted by artists from the court of Napoléon, emperor of France, after his campaign in Egypt. Moreau was crowned queen at Amon-Ra's tenth anniversary ball, *Enchantment* (1975), with Church serving as the captain. The poster for this ball was designed by Jim Schexnayder and was a gem of art nouveau brilliance. Church and Moreau again turned to the pageantry of Egypt to inspire their artwork for the invitation to the 1980 *Bluebird of Happiness* ball.

Cocktails for Two

In 1982, captain Mike Moreau produced the glamorous *Cocktails for Two* ball. Each costume represented a well-known cocktail, a key part of life in the Crescent City. His costume as the Leilani Volcano cocktail was a masterpiece featuring red and orange feathers. Other drinks showcased included the Manhattan, the Shirley Temple, the Silver Cocktail, the Singapore Sling, the Scarlett O'Hara, the Potted Parrot, the Bloody Mary, Strawberry and Pineapple Daiquiris, the Roman Candle, the Pink Lady, the Black Magic, and the Black Russian, but Moreau's sensational burlesque costume outshone all the others.

Competition during this era became so fierce that the krewes closely guarded information regarding their themes, costumes, music, and staging, with even close friends keeping secrets from one another to avoid spoiling the great reveal on the night of the ball. For the *Cocktails for Two* ball, Robert Breaux, who was crowned the queen of Amon-Ra, had worked in secret with his friend, Daniel de Beau-Maltbie, on a Black Russian costume that featured a gorgeous black gown, as wide as it was long, covered in thousands of white sequins. A headdress shaped like the dome of a Greek Orthodox church completed the ensemble. A talented artist, de Beau-Maltbie also created the invitation and poster for the ball, which depicted a Victorian lady standing at a rather ornate bar ordering a cocktail and became legendary for its naughty details. But de Beau-Maltbie did not know that Breaux was slated to become the reigning queen of Amon-Ra and was surprised when he came out on stage for the finale.

According to Carl Ricketts, a former captain, king, and queen of the krewe, however, just twenty-four hours before the ball, the gorgeous costume was unfinished. Ricketts and his partner, Henry Tebbe, stayed up all night, attaching thousands of white sequins: "It was a dire emergency, and one we took up immediately, without really thinking about it. That's how it worked back then. We all made sure that the costumes were finished by the night of the ball, come hell or high water. That was the kind of commitment we had to our Carnival."

In an *Ambush Magazine* column, Frank Perez described the queen's entrance: "Queen Bob Breaux was lowered by a lift and descended upon the stage in a ten-foot-wide dress as the Black Russian. The crowd went wild." Breaux rewarded both de Beau-Maltbie and Ricketts for their help, and de Beau-Maltbie recalled, "I still have the gift the Queen gave me that night, as I was called up on stage to greet her majesty. A night I won't ever forget. I was totally surprised, caught off guard, but ecstatic nonetheless. All of it was gone in an instant, though, all that work, all that time. But it was worth it, a thousand times over."

De Beau-Maltbie had also created the invitation for the 1984 *Signs of the Zodiac* ball, at which Arthur Wallace was chosen king and Ron Ellis became queen. According to Jerry Gilley, another longtime member of the krewe, after Wallace learned "that he would be the returning king for the ball, he appeared sad and anxious and told everyone that his mother had died and that he needed hundreds of dollars for the funeral. Of course, we all chipped in, and he ended up with almost a thousand dollars. Come to find out his mother hadn't died at all, but Arthur did have a spectacular costume. I only found out about it serendipitously, and Arthur never knew that I had found out." Wallace was a very exuberant man with lots of charisma who died in 1995. Gilley kept the secret for nearly three decades.

The Picnic Fantasy

The early and mid-1980s are frequently regarded as the Golden Age of Gay Carnival, with the dozen or so gay krewes producing extremely lavish and elaborate balls. Memberships swelled, and guests clamored to attend the presentations. In 1985—arguably the last great gay Carnival year before AIDS laid siege to the community—the Krewe of Amon-Ra hosted its *Picnic Fantasy* ball, which took the spectacle to new heights. Many krewe members had expressed concerns regarding the mounting cost of costumes, and captain Jerry Gilley solved the problem by suggesting, "Let's make our costumes for the picnic out of foam rubber, painted with sizzling Day-Glo colors. Let's craft simple costumes at a minimum cost but with maximum impact." He succeeded, and even thirty years later, the ball remains among the most memorable. An exterminator by day, Gilley called on his knowledge of the insect world for ideas for a wonderland of strange and quixotic creatures. He appeared as the Cricket Captain in a dazzling white tuxedo.

When asked which ball he remembered best, Jack Sullivan, prominent lawyer and adviser to the John Burton Harter Foundation, which works to empower "awareness of visual and queer arts," answered, "Definitely the *Picnic* ball. You had to have been there to appreciate the surprise and wonder as those giant spiders, ants, snails and butterflies, love bugs and scorpions, and tasty treats moved about the stage and out into the audience. That's what Carnival is all about. It was creepy and inventive and something I'll never forget, especially the appearance of the queen. Queen Amon-Ra XX deserves her place in the history books. An unqualified masterpiece, that's for sure!"

The penultimate costume to appear was a long colorful segmented caterpillar, like a cavorting Chinese dragon. As the creature crossed the stage for the last time, the segments came apart, and each one became a brilliantly colored butterfly, manned by a krewe member. The audience then heard an announcement: "The queen is dead." As the onlookers gasped, an inert figure resembling a mummified body was carried aloft by members of the Gay Men's Chorus as they sang Handel's *Hallelujah Chorus*. After a long pause, the newborn queen burst forth as a glittering black moth and began to rise from the stage, lifted by hydraulics. As she rose, gigantic, rainbow-colored wings unfurled behind her, eventually covering the entire stage.

The queen was Douglas "Buddy" Rasmussen, a Houston native who had joined the U.S. Air Force to escape an abusive stepfather and eventually found a welcoming home in New Orleans. One of the survivors of the terrible fire at the Up Stairs Lounge, a gay bar torched in 1973, Rasmussen had already become a local hero for saving dozens from the flames. His Dark Queen costume also featured a long black gown with a black feather collar and a small feather headdress and sparkling gemstones. His whiteface makeup appeared almost sinister, a portent of a dark future. He held a silver scepter with a small white mask at its end, and when Rasmussen held up this mask to his own face, he resembled a terrible specter. His tight gown made him seem to glide in front of the attendees, but his demeanor remained unchanged.

Gilley recalled that night as filled with magic, wonder, and panic: "We had rehearsed the finale and the appearance of the queen many times over. She was to hit her mark behind the stage right before the chorus carried out the dead caterpillar in a cocoon. I went back to escort the queen to her place on stage when the announcement was made, but there was nothing. When I rushed to the dressing room, Buddy was still in his underwear and his attendant bolted out the door. Sensing a catastrophe and some last minute hanky-panky, I hastily stuffed the queen into her black dress and pushed her out on the stage. Luckily the audience only became more excited with the lengthy delay, and the final effect, I must admit, was near flawless. But if you look closely at the video tape, you will see the Queen not in her black pumps but her stocking feet!"

The AGGI Awards

At the year's annual Academy of the Golden Goddess Inc. (AGGI) Awards, the Krewe of Amon-Ra received trophies for Best Ball Theme, Best Set Design, and Best Costume Design as well as the most coveted prize, Best Reigning Queen, beating out the Krewes of Armeinius and Polyphemus. Confessed one of the AGGI judges, "Truth be told, Amon-Ra would have won all the awards that year, but we just couldn't give them all to just one krewe. We had to be realistic!"

A Thousand and One Nights

For Amon-Ra's 1989 ball, *A Thousand and One Nights*, captain Jim Schexnayder envisioned a story worthy of Scheherazade. The captain began the ball in a black cloak but after some smoke-filled magic, he was revealed as the scimitar-wielding narrator of the ball. "The queen was in repose, traveling incognito," he explained, "until the finale at the end of the ball, when she would be joined with her betrothed." Envoys from the far corners of the world came to pay homage to her, bearing exotic gifts and performing amazing feats of magic. African Zulus competed with Oriental mystics to gain the queen's favor, while other foreign dignitaries presented tame ostriches and sword dances for her entertainment. One of the more striking numbers was the Pearl Divers. Situated on planks affixed atop black-painted ladders on shopping cart wheels, divers in white wet suits seemed

Krewe of Amon-Ra (1966)

1966

The Krewe of Amon-Ra held its first Carnival ball at the International Longshoremen's Association Hall on Claiborne Avenue, following in the footsteps of the Krewe of Petronius. The first ball theme was *A Night in Old New Orleans*.

1970

For the *Circus* ball, the krewe secured the use of the Labor Union Hall on Tchoupitoulas Street. Very few venues would rent to gay krewes, but these black labor union halls were the exception.

1976

By 1976, the krewe had already begun holding its annual ball at the Saint Bernard Civic Auditorium, as did many other gay krewes. This large venue could hold more than three hundred people and had ample room for staging balls and for setting up tables in front with space for the Grand Procession. Amon-Ra's membership included both men and women, but only men were selected as queen.

1980

The Miss America Pageant summer fund-raiser had become a grand success, attracting contestants from other krewes. Awards were given not only for Miss America (best drag) but also for Mr. America (best muscle).

1982

The *Cocktails for Two* ball held on February 13, 1982, represented a milestone in the history of gay Carnival. Mike Moreau (Opal Masters) was the captain and produced a ball many observers have hailed as one of the best. The costumes were famous cocktails.

1985

For the *Picnic Fantasy* ball, captain Jerry Gilley created a memorable ball with surreal insects attacking a children's picnic.

1990s

At the beginning of the decade, the krewe celebrated its twenty-fifth anniversary. Over the next few years, however, Michael Moreau led the krewe in shifting its focus to fund-raising for AIDS organizations and supporting the gay community in other ways.

1995

With Amon-Ra having lost so many members to the AIDS epidemic, *Pictures from Our Past* cast a different light on all the krewe had accomplished and looked toward the future with renewed vigor.

2015

For the fiftieth anniversary ball, the krewe selected two of its most notable members as king and queen. Queen Mike Moreau, who had been in the krewe for fifty years, and his husband, King Darwin Reed, another longtime member, represented the essence of gay Carnival as they processed in front of their audience.

2016

Mike Moreau and Darwin Reed were designated as Empress and Emperor Amon-Ra I.

to float when the black lights were illuminated. Along side were brightly colored schools of fish held up by black poles. The effect, with half a dozen divers surrounded by glowing fish, was mesmerizing, and the audience saw quite the spectacle. John East had worked for months with Schexnayder on the king's headpiece, with East unaware that he was working on his own crown. As he recalled, "It was one of those moments I'll remember forever. I dared not hope that Jim would pick me as king, but when he approached me at the end of the ball with the headpiece, I just knew. When I processed in front of the crowds with the queen, I was in tears. Nothing would ever compare to a moment like that. Nothing."

Surviving the AIDS Crisis

By 1993, AIDS had slashed its way through New Orleans's gay community, leaving only four krewes—Petronius, Amon-Ra, Armeinius, and the Lords of Leather—to present balls. Soon thereafter, the Krewe of Amon-Ra, led by Mike Moreau (Opal Masters), began to focus its fund-raising efforts on AIDS organizations, working to support the gay community through charitable donations to Project Lazarus, Belle Reve, Buzzy's Boys and Girls, Odyssey House, and St. Anna's Episcopal Church. Two decades later, Amon-Ra and its supporters continue to participate in the NO/AIDS Walk and raise donations for the NO/AIDS Task Force, and the group is an Annual Gold Sponsor for the Gay Easter Parade down Bourbon Street, benefiting the Food for Friends and the NO/AIDS Task Force. The shift from looking inward to rallying support for the gay community brought a new kind of focus to the krewe.

Return to Opulence

In 2015, John S. Zeringue III, costume designer and captain of the krewe, reflected on Amon-Ra's extraordinary history: "The Krewe of Amon-Ra was one of the few gay krewes to present a ball after Hurricane Katrina. . . . We owe our longevity to our valued supporters for helping us to continue our Mardi Gras traditions and our members for pulling together to make all of our functions leading to our Mardi Gras Ball a huge success!"

The Heart of Amon-Ra

Mike Moreau (Opal Masters) has been involved with the Krewe of Amon-Ra from the beginning, and his partner, Darwin Reed, has been in the krewe for more than forty years. As Zeringue wrote in the 2015 program for the *Weighing of the Heart* ball, "Together, Moreau and Reed have been the heart of Amon-Ra." Moreau came to New Orleans by way of Opelousas in 1963 and began working with founding krewe member Carter Church. Church had established a costume business that catered to the traditional Uptown krewes, and Moreau worked with him for many years before striking out on his own with a costume business, Originals by Mr. Mike. He has designed for many traditional Carnival krewes, among them Diana, Gemini, and the Slidellians. In addition, Moreau and Church cofounded a Slidell krewe, Troy. Reed and Moreau were crowned king and queen of Amon-Ra L in

2015 and Emperor and Empress Amon-Ra I the following year, honors befitting their status as true gay Carnival royalty.

Recognition from City Hall

The Krewe of Amon-Ra has the distinction of being one of the few gay krewes to have both men and women among its members. "We wanted to be more open, more inclusive," explained Jerry Gilley. "There's more room for creativity that way." Carmen Huffer was selected King Amon-Ra in 1976 for the *Midsummer Night's Scream* ball, although the queenship has always been reserved for a man. Zeringue has committed himself to continuing Amon-Ra's long tradition of inclusiveness, and during his tenure, the New Orleans City Council presented the krewe with a proclamation honoring its fiftieth anniversary and acknowledging gay Carnival's contributions to the city.

Krewe of Amon-Ra Tableau Balls List	
1966	A NIGHT IN OLD NEW ORLEANS
1967	AROUND THE WORLD
1968	EVERYTHING'S COMING UP ROSES
1969	SEA CRUISE
1970	CIRCUS
1971	LOUISIANA ON PARADE
1972	MUSIC MAESTRO, PLEASE!
1973	MOONLIGHT MUSIC
1974	ALICE'S ADVENTURES IN WONDERLAND AND THROUGH THE LOOKING GLASS
1975	ENCHANTMENT (TENTH ANNIVERSARY)
1976	A MIDSUMMER NIGHT'S SCREAM
1977	ALL THAT GLITTERS
1978	SUPERSTITION (FRIDAY THE 13TH)
1979	IN THE BEGINNING
1980	BLUEBIRD OF HAPPINESS
1981	SOMEWHERE OVER THE RAINBOW
1982	COCKTAILS FOR TWO
1983	THAT'S ENTERTAINMENT
1984	SIGNS OF THE ZODIAC
1985	A PICNIC FANTASY (TWENTIETH ANNIVERSARY)
1986	BEST OF BROADWAY
1987	KALEIDOSCOPE
1988	THE OUTER WORLDS
1989	THOUSAND AND ONE NIGHTS
1990	COMMAND PERFORMANCE (TWENTY-FIFTH ANNIVERSARY)
1991	VIVA MEXICO!
1992	FANTASYLANDS
1993	MOVIES MAGIC MOMENTS
1994	SING! SING A SONG!
1995	PICTURES FROM OUR PAST
1996	A NIGHT AT THE ZIEGFELD FOLLIES
1997	IT'S PARTY TIME
1998	ARE YOU A FRIEND OF DOROTHY?
1999	ANY DREAM WILL DO
2000	OPENING THE TIME CAPSULE
2001	ALL ABOARD: ESCAPADES ON THE ORIENT EXPRESS
2002	HISTORY OF THE WORLD ACCORDING TO AMON-RA
2003	GAMES PEOPLE PLAY
2004	FICTION: MAKE-UP BETWEEN THE COVERS
2005	AMON-RA SALUTES THE CIRCUS
2006	A LITTLE BIT OF COUNTRY
2007	WHO DO THAT VOODOO YOU DO SO WELL?
2008	MY FAVORITE THINGS
2009	AMON-RA EXPRESS
2010	LOVE IS IN THE AIR
2011	MYTHS AND LEGENDS
2012	CARNIVALE: TWILIGHT IN THE JUNGLE
2013	DREAMS AND FANTASIES
2014	A YEAR THROUGH THE EYE OF AMON-RA
2015	THE WEIGHING OF THE HEART (THE FINAL JUDGMENT)
2016	ALL THAT GLITTERS ISN'T GOLD
2017	A NIGHT AT THE OPERA . . . AHH . . . OPRY
2018	EXPRESS YOURSELF

YEAR OF TABLEAU BALL	CAPTAIN	QUEEN	KING
1966	Scott Hoy	Clyde Ladner	Sidney Barrios
1967	Scott Hoy	Vic Scalise	Vincent Indovina
1968	Jim "Peaches" Gillon	Lee Oubre	Jim Schexnayder
1969	Pat O'Rourke	Bill Fleming	Errol D'Angelo
1970	Carter Church	Justin Bailey	Roeling Mace
1971	Mike Moreau (Opal Masters)	Corky Irwin	Pat O'Rourke
1972	Tommy Schneider	Carter Church	Don Gautreaux
1973	Vic Scalise	Roeling Mace	Timmy Henderson
1974	Derek Maenza	Bill Louvier	Roy Young
1975	Carter Church	Mike Moreau (Opal Masters)	Carl Ricketts
1976	Woody Cavalier	Bill Porter	Carmen Huffer
1977	Roy Young	Woody Cavalier	Derek Maenza
1978	Jim Schexnayder	Pat O'Rourke	Bill Fleming
1979	Vic Scalise	Roy Young	Mike Devidts
1980	Woody Cavalier	Carl Ricketts	Carter Church
1981	Doug Militz	Jim Schexnayder	Jerry Gilley
1982	Mike Moreau (Opal Masters)	Bob Breaux	Glen Guidroz
1983	Carl Ricketts	Dennis Hall	Woody Cavalier
1984	Michael Edwards	Ron Ellis	Arthur Wallace
1985	Jerry Gilley	Buddy Rasmussen	El Day
1986	Richard Mendoza	Richard Powell	Glenn Richmond
1987	Carl Ricketts	Michael Edwards	Mike Moreau (Opal Masters)
1988	Michael "Fish" Hickerson	Arthur Wallace	Gene Lee
1989	Jim Schexnayder	Jesse Houidobre	John East
1990	Mike Moreau (Opal Masters)	Michael Strong	Darwin Reed
1991	Woody Cavalier	Doug Gautreaux	Ron Issler
1992	Derek Maenza	Kenny Walker	Conway Horn
1993	Derek Maenza	Jim "Peaches" Gillon	Barbara Price
1994	Mike Moreau (Opal Masters)	Richard Mendoza	Gar Williams
1995	Danny Smith	Sam Jones	Nelson Savoie
1996	Gar Williams	Nat Cazeaux	George Schwandt
1997	Jim "Peaches" Gillon	Todd Knecht	Ragan Alford
1998	Nat Cazeaux	Michael Cochran	Jim "Peaches" Gillon
1999	Nat Cazeaux	Pat O'Rourke	Vic Scalise
2000	Gary Delaune (Tittie Toulouse)	Ronald Morvant	Ron Issler
2001	Gary Delaune (Tittie Toulouse)	Harry "Tip" Varnadore	Jay Cooper
2002	Brian Burke	Gary Delaune (Tittie Toulouse)	Ann Sauve
2003	Ron Issler	James Creech	Pete Eschete
2004	Ron Issler	Michael "Fish" Hickerson	Paul Van Geffen
2005	Harry "Tip" Varnadore	Rickey Callais	Randall Brown
2006	Harry "Tip" Varnadore	Ron Issler	Kenny Walker
2007	Gary Delaune (Tittie Toulouse)	Darwin Reed	George Tresch
2008	Randall Brown	Mike Moreau (Opal Masters)	Paul Davis
2009	Timm Holt	Ronnie White (Rhonda Roget)	Nick Olivares
2010	Timm Holt	Daryl Dunaway Jr.	David Aranda
2011	Barry Rutherford	Richard Hullender (Tami Tarmac)	Jerry Scavo
2012	John S. Zeringue III	Barry Rutherford	David Forth
2013	Mike Moreau (Opal Masters)	Leonard Williams (Déjà Déjà Vu)	John S. Zeringue III
2014	John S. Zeringue III	—	David Richerson
2015	John S. Zeringue III	Mike Moreau (Opal Masters)	Darwin Reed
2016	Leonard Williams (Déjà Déjà Vu)	Mina Hernandez	Chris Arthur
2017	Leonard Williams (Déjà Déjà Vu)	Regina Adams	Ronnie White
2018	Errol Rizutto	Ron Issler	Jeremy Weinberg

Krewe of Amon-Ra Royalty List

New design for the Krewe of Amon-Ra, early 1990s.
Courtesy of the Krewe of Amon-Ra.

Original pyramid design for the Krewe of Amon-Ra, 1969. Courtesy of The Historic New Orleans Collection, Williams Research Center, New Orleans, Accession No. 1980.178.167. Gift of Tracy Hendrix.

A Night in Old New Orleans 1966

Mike Moreau as the Canal Street Ferry, 1966. Courtesy of the Krewe of Amon-Ra, Mike Moreau and Darwin Reed Collection.

Invitation, 1966. Courtesy of Tulane University, Louisiana Research Collection, Howard-Tilton Memorial Library, New Orleans, Otto Stierle Collection, Manuscripts Collection 902.

James Keyes as Madame LuLu White, 1966. Courtesy of the Krewe of Amon-Ra, Mike Moreau and Darwin Reed Collection.

Everything's Coming Up Roses 1968

Invitation, 1968. Courtesy of the Louisiana State Museum, New Orleans, Accession No. 2015.026.

Jerry Gilley as Gypsy Rose Lee, 1968. Courtesy of the Krewe of Amon-Ra.

Sea Cruise 1969

Invitation, 1969. Courtesy of the Krewe of Amon-Ra.

Circus 1970

Invitation, 1970. Courtesy of The Historic New Orleans Collection, Williams Research Center, New Orleans, Accession No. 1980.178.195. Gift of Tracy Hendrix.

Inside reads: *The Krewe of Amon-Ra requests the presence of Mr. Tracy Hendrix at their Epsilon Ball. January Eighteenth in the Year of the Sphinx, one thousand nine hundred and seventy. No Admittance after 8:45 p.m. Dress Formal. Labor Union Hall. Soniat at Tchoupitoulas. B.Y.O.L.*

Carl Ricketts as the Bearded Lady with her escorts Jim Schexnayder (*left*) and Derek Maenza (*right*), 1970. Courtesy of the Krewe of Amon-Ra, Mike Moreau and Darwin Reed Collection.

Louisiana on Parade 1971

Commemorative poster, 1971. Courtesy of The Historic New Orleans Collection, Williams Research Center, New Orleans, Accession No. 1990.19.32. Gift of Tracy Hendrix.

Below: The queen's costume, representing Mardi Gras itself, and mantle were designed by Mike Moreau and executed by Suzanne Spaulding to keep the queen's identity secret from the other members, as was the tradition at the time.

Description de l'Égypte (1809–28), vol. 2, plate 52. This image, from a compendium published by scholars who accompanied Napoleon on his campaigns in Egypt, was used by the Krewe of Amon-Ra for its *Louisiana on Parade* poster and invitation. Courtesy of the J. Paul Getty Center Research Institute, Los Angeles, 83-B7948.

Mike Moreau, costume sketch for Queen Amon-Ra VI, Corky Irwin, 1971. Courtesy of the Krewe of Amon-Ra, Mike Moreau and Darwin Reed Collection.

Mike Moreau, costume mantle sketch for Queen Amon-Ra VI, Corky Irwin, 1971. Courtesy of the Krewe of Amon-Ra, Mike Moreau and Darwin Reed Collection.

Carter Church, costume sketch for captain Mike Moreau, Yambilee Sweet Potato Festival, 1971. Courtesy of the Krewe of Amon-Ra, Mike Moreau and Darwin Reed Collection.

Carter Church, costume sketch for the Crayfish Festival Queen, 1971. Courtesy of the Krewe of Amon-Ra, Mike Moreau and Darwin Reed Collection.

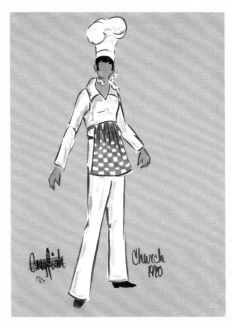

Carter Church, costume sketch for the Crayfish Festival Queen's page, 1971. Courtesy of the Krewe of Amon-Ra, Mike Moreau and Darwin Reed Collection.

Carter Church, costume sketch for the Shrimp and Petroleum Festival Queen (ball lieutenant), 1971. Courtesy of the Krewe of Amon-Ra, Mike Moreau and Darwin Reed Collection.

Carter Church, costume sketch for the Shrimp and Petroleum Festival Queen's page, 1971. Courtesy of the Krewe of Amon-Ra, Mike Moreau and Darwin Reed Collection.

Carter Church as the Crayfish Festival Queen, 1971. Courtesy of the Krewe of Amon-Ra, Mike Moreau and Darwin Reed Collection.

Captain Mike Moreau, 1971. Courtesy of the Krewe of Amon-Ra, Mike Moreau and Darwin Reed Collection.

Ball lieutenant as the Shrimp and Petroleum Festival Queen, encapsulated within an oil derrick, 1971. The captain is to the left. Courtesy of the Krewe of Amon-Ra, Mike Moreau and Darwin Reed Collection.

Alice's Adventures in Wonderland *and* Through the Looking Glass 1974

Program, 1974. Courtesy of The Historic New Orleans Collection, Williams Research Center, New Orleans, Accession No. 1980.178.331. Gift of Tracy Hendrix.

Tableau 1974

The Captain's Whistle Announces the Royal Court of 1973—King and Queen Amon-Ra VII.

Alice Enters on a Picnic and Reads When the White Rabbit Came Along and Alice Followed Him Down the Rabbit Hole.

She Comes out of the Pool of Tears with Strange Companions—The Dodo and the Beautiful Lory.

In the Woods Alice sees the Blue Caterpillar. At the House the Fish Footman Arriving with an Invitation to the Party.

The Duchess Comes to the Door Overwhelmed of Playing Croquet with the Queen.

Alice Sees the Cook with a Strange Baby and Is Told What Kind of People Live Here.

She Sees the Mad Hatter Who Is Joined by the Wild March Hare and the Dormouse, for the Celebrated Tea Party.

Also Arriving for the Affair Is the Knave of Hearts With His Strawberry Tarts Who Show Their Wares.

On Leaving for the Party of the Queen Appears a Lobster of the Quadrille.

Entering the Palace They See the Queen of Hearts Walking in the Garden Calling Her Soldiers Who Are Willing to Fill Her Demands.

Hearing Off with Their Heads, the Knave of Hearts and Alice Escape through the Looking Glass into the Garden of Live Flowers.

Where They See the Bread and Butterfly Circle about the Comical Pair of Twins Tweedle-Dee and Tweedle-Dum Who Are Accompanied by Humpty Dumpty Who Couldn't Be Put Back Together Again.

The Unicorn of Scotland Was Discovered by Alice after the Fight for the Crown and the Jousting of the Red and White Chessmen to Rescue the Damsel Alice.

And since Every Little Girl Dreams of Being a Queen, Alice as Queen Amon-Ra IX.

Selection of King Amon-Ra IX.

Inside reads: *The fascinating tale of Alice in Wonderland and Through the Looking Glass has long been acclaimed as a fantasy of joy and make-believe for the young and old alike. The simplicity of the story has caught the imagination and charm of all who fall under its magical and whimsical spell. Tonight the Krewe of Amon-Ra brings to life some of the fascinating characters that were created in this immortal and classic story by Lewis Carroll. They shall bring forth Gaiety, Excitement, Adventure and Laughter as we go along with the now generation presentation under whatever moves you on the trip with Alice to Wonderland.*

Invitation, 1974. Courtesy of Tulane University, Louisiana Research Collection, Howard-Tilton Memorial Library, New Orleans, Otto Stierle Collection, Manuscripts Collection 902.

Enchantment 1975

Commemorative poster, 1975. Design by James Schexnayder. Courtesy of Carl Ricketts.

Queen Amon-Ra X, Opal Masters (Mike Moreau), and King Amon-Ra X, Carl Ricketts, 1975. Courtesy of Carl Ricketts.

Carter Church, costume sketch for king, 1975. Courtesy of Carl Ricketts.

Royal Guards, 1975. Members of the krewe are lined up at the close of the ball, awaiting the selection of one member as the king, as was the practice at the time. Courtesy of Carl Ricketts.

A Midsummer Night's Scream 1976

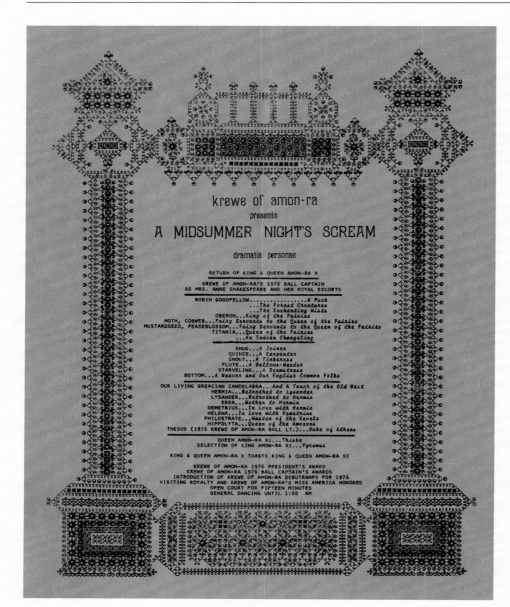

krewe of amon-ra

presents

A MIDSUMMER NIGHT'S SCREAM

dramatis personae

RETURN OF KING & QUEEN AMON-RA X

KREWE OF AMON-RA'S 1976 BALL CAPTAIN
AS MRS. ANNE SHAKESPEARE AND HER ROYAL ESCORTS

ROBIN GOODFELLOW..............A Puck
...The Forest Creatures
...The Enchanting Mists
OBERON...King of the Fairies
MOTH, COBWEB...Fairy Servants to the Queen of the Fairies
MUSTARDSEED, PEASEBLOSSOM...Fairy Servants to the Queen of the Fairies
TITANIA...Queen of the Fairies
...An Indian Changeling

SNUG...A Joiner
QUINCE...A Carpenter
SNOUT...A Tinkeress
FLUTE...A Bellows-Mender
STARVELING...A Seamstress
BOTTOM...A Weaver and Our English Common Folks

OUR LIVING GREACIAN CANDELABRA...And A Touch of the Old West
HERMIA...Betrothed to Lysander
LYSANDER...Betrothed to Hermia
EGEA...Mother to Hermia
DEMETRIUS...In Love with Hermia
HELENA...In Love with Demetrius
PHILOSTRATE...Master of the Revels
HIPPOLYTA...Queen of the Amazons
THESUS (1976 KREWE OF AMON-RA BALL LT.)...Duke of Athens

QUEEN AMON-RA XI...Thisbe
SELECTION OF KING AMON-RA XI...Pyramus

KING & QUEEN AMON-RA X TOASTS KING & QUEEN AMON-RA XI

KREWE OF AMON-RA 1976 PRESIDENT'S AWARD
KREWE OF AMON-RA 1976 BALL CAPTAIN'S AWARDS
INTRODUCTION OF KREWE OF AMON-RA DEBUTRAMPS FOR 1976
VISITING ROYALTY AND KREWE OF AMON-RA'S MISS AMERICA HONORED
OPEN COURT FOR FIFTEEN MINUTES
GENERAL DANCING UNTIL 1:00 AM

Program, 1976. Courtesy of The Historic New Orleans Collection, Williams Research Center, New Orleans, Accession No. 1976.65.48. Gift of Tracy Hendrix.

Tableau 1976
Dramatis Personae
Return of King and Queen Amon-Ra X
Captain—Mrs. Anne Shakespeare
Robin Goodfellow—A Puck
The Forest Creatures
The Enchanting Mists
Oberon—King of the Fairies
Moth, Cobweb, Mustardseed, Peaseblossom—Fairy Servants to
     the Queen
Titania—Queen of the Fairies
An Indian Changeling
Snug—A Joiner
Quince—A Carpenter
Snout—A Tinkeress
Flute—A Bellows-Mender
Starveling—A Seamstress
Bottom—A Weaver
English Common Folks
Graecian Candelabra—And a Touch of the Old West
Hermia—Betrothed to Lysander
Lysander—Betrothed to Hermia
Egea—Mother to Hermia
Demetrius—In Love with Hermia
Helena—In Love with Demetrius
Philostrate—Master of the Revels
Hippolyte—Queen of the Amazons
Lieutenant—Theseus, Duke of Athens
Queen Amon-Ra XI—Thisbe
Selection of King Amon-Ra XI—Pyramus
King and Queen Amon-Ra X Toast King and Queen Amon-Ra XI
Krewe of Amon-Ra 1976 President's Award
Krewe of Amon-Ra 1976 Ball Captain's Awards
Introduction of Krewe of Amon-Ra Debutramps for 1976
Visiting Royalty and Krewe of Amon-Ra's Miss America Honored
Open Court for Fifteen Minutes
General Dancing until 1:00 a.m.

Returning King and Queen Amon-Ra X, Carl Ricketts and Opal Masters (Mike Moreau), as the dragons, 1976. The pages carrying the mantles are Ricketts's and Moreau's partners, Henry Tebbe and Darwin Reed. Costume design by Carter Church. Courtesy of the Krewe of Amon-Ra, Mike Moreau and Darwin Reed Collection.

Carter Church, costume sketch for the Dragon King, Carl Ricketts, 1976. Courtesy of Carl Ricketts.

All That Glitters 1977

Commemorative poster, 1977. Design by Jim Schexnayder. Courtesy of The Historic New Orleans Collection, Williams Research Center, New Orleans, Accession No. 1977.307.3. Gift of Tracy Hendrix.

Inside reads: *Cunegondes Candide. And here I am, my heart broken, forced to glitter, forced to be gay. Glitter and be gay, that's the part I play. Here am I, oh sorry, forced to bend my soul to a sordid role, victimized by bitter, bitter circumstance. Alas, only had I remained, besides my lady mother. My virtue had remained, unstained until my maiden hand was gained by some grand duke or other. But was not to be harsh necessity brought me to this gilded cage. Born to higher things, here I droop my wings, singing of a sorrow nothing can assuage. And yet, of course, I rather like to read. I have no strong objection to champagne. My wardrobe is expensive as the devil, perhaps it is ignoble to complain. Enough, enough of being so tearful. I will show my noble stuff by being bright and cheerful. Pearls and ruby rings, Ah! How can such worldly things take the place of honor lost? Can they compensate for my fallen state? Purchased as they were at such an awful cost. Bracelets, lavalieres, can they dry my tears? Can they blind my eyes to shame? Can the brightest broach shield me from reproach? And the purest diamond purify my name? And yet, of course, these trinkets are endearing. I am oh so glad my sapphire is a star. I rather like twenty carat earrings. If I am not pure at least my jewels are. Enough! Enough! I will take the diamond necklace and show my noble stuff by being gay and reckless. Observe how greatly I conceal the dreadful, dreadful shame I feel.*

Superstition 1978

Commemorative poster, 1978. Design by Jim Schexnayder. *Impact Gay News* called the ball, held on Friday the Thirteenth, "most memorable" and said, "From Macbeth's witches to the Devil himself, the ball showed an incredible lusty vision of Hell." Courtesy of The Historic New Orleans Collection, Williams Research Center, New Orleans, Accession No. 1980.178.462. Gift of Tracy Hendrix.

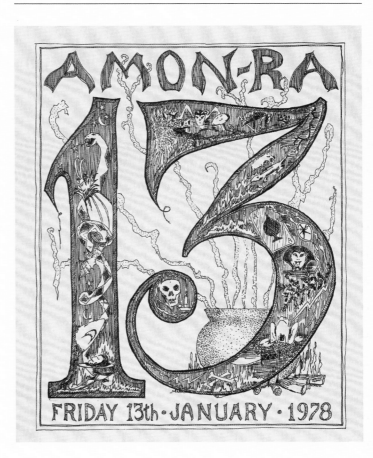

Bluebird of Happiness 1980

Invitation, 1980. Courtesy of The Historic New Orleans Collection, Williams Research Center, New Orleans, Accession No. 1980.178.522. Gift of Tracy Hendrix.

King Amon-Ra XV, Carter Church, 1980. Courtesy of Carl Ricketts.

Carter Church, costume sketch for Queen Amon-Ra XV, Carl Ricketts, 1980. Courtesy of Carl Ricketts.

Queen Amon-Ra XV, Carl Ricketts, 1980. Courtesy of Carl Ricketts.

Over the Rainbow 1981

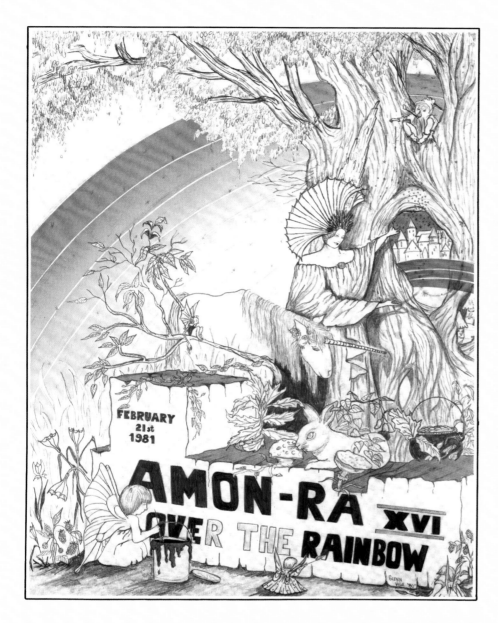

Invitation, 1981. Design by Glenn Vigé. Courtesy of Tulane University, Louisiana Research Collection, Howard-Tilton Memorial Library, New Orleans, Otto Stierle Collection, Manuscripts Collection 902.

Tableau 1981
Welcome—Amon-Ra President
King and Queen Amon-Ra XV
Ball Captain—Iris, Goddess of the Rainbow
Ball Lieutenant—The Unicorn
Maidens of the Rainbow
The Leprechauns
Pot of Gold
Gender and the Magic Lamp
Dorothy and Friends
Peter Pan and Tinkerbell
Alice and Friends
The Moon
Wind
Lightning
The Rain Drops
Queen Amon-Ra XVI
King Amon-Ra XVI

Returning King Amon-Ra XV, Carter Church, and Returning Queen Amon-Ra XV, Carl Ricketts, 1981. Courtesy of the Krewe of Amon-Ra, Mike Moreau and Darwin Reed Collection.

Carter Church, costume sketch for Returning Queen Carl Ricketts, 1981. Courtesy of the Krewe of Amon-Ra, Mike Moreau and Darwin Reed Collection.

Cocktails for Two 1982

Commemorative poster, 1982. Design by Daniel de Beau-Maltbie. Courtesy of the Louisiana State Museum, New Orleans, Accession No. 1995.010.003.

Captain Mike Moreau as the Leilani Volcano cocktail, 1982. Courtesy of the Krewe of Amon-Ra, Mike Moreau and Darwin Reed Collection.

Captain Mike Moreau, 1982. Courtesy of the Krewe of Amon-Ra, Mike Moreau and Darwin Reed Collection.

Queen Amon-Ra XVII, Robert Breaux, as the Black Russian Cocktail, 1982. Courtesy of the Krewe of Amon-Ra, Mike Moreau and Darwin Reed Collection.

That's Entertainment 1983

Invitation, 1983. Courtesy of The Historic New Orleans Collection, Williams Research Center, New Orleans, Accession No. 1983.109.2.

Inside reads: *The Captain of Amon-Ra welcomes the Russian Royalty and all of you as we prepare for the presentation of the court for 1983. We invite you to sit back, relax, and enjoy the tableau as it unfolds. Amon-Ra, as you know, has always been known for its voyages, and tonight they have spared no expense to bring you a Las Vegas Extravaganza. New Orleans like Vegas is a city without clocks, a city known for excitement, a city renowned for its entertainment. It is known for skimpy costumes, beautiful women, gorgeous men and a feather or two. As a matter of fact, if you are an avid bird watcher, the type with feathers that is, you probably haven't seen too many lately. It's certain however that you will see them all tonight: the feathers, the birds, the women and the men. But let us not linger with words. Let us bring you from Las Vegas That's Entertainment, for round and round she goes and where she stops nobody knows. Ladies and Gentlemen, live from Caesar's Palace, the Captain of Amon-Ra, Captain Capricious (Carl Ricketts), and a Bevy of Beauties.*

Tableau 1983
Russian Jewels—Returning King and Queen Amon-Ra XVII
Captain Capricious—from Caesar's Palace
Ball Lieutenant—A Fantasy with Fluorescent Dancers—From the Riviera Hotel
The Equinox and Light Variations—From the Sahara Hotel
Macho Magic—From the Frontier Hotel
Parallel Passions—From the Sands Hotel
Illuminations of Glamour—From the Stardust Hotel
Vibrant Vamps—From the Silver Slipper
Spectron—From the Flamingo Hotel
The Dancing Darlings—From the Landmark Hotel
Suggestions of Sinbad—From the Aladdin Hotel
Kaleidoscope Follies—From the Tropicana Hotel
The Ringmaster and His Ballerina Clowns—From the Circus Circus Hotel
Sensuous Syncopations—From the Four Queens Hotel
Las Vegas Dancers (Chorus Line)
King and Queen Amon-Ra XVIII

Erté, *W* from *The Alphabet*, 1976. This image inspired Chet Bush's costume for Amon-Ra's *That's Entertainment* (*Las Vegas Extravaganza*) ball, 1983. Courtesy © Sevenarts, Ltd.

Chet Bush, costume design for the Ringmaster (Don Toler), 1983. Courtesy of the Louisiana State Museum, New Orleans, Accession No. 2015.047.

Don Toler as the Ringmaster, 1983. Courtesy of Carl Ricketts.

Carter Church, costume sketch for Captain Capricious, Carl Ricketts, 1983. Courtesy of Carl Ricketts.

Carl Ricketts as Captain Capricious, 1983. Courtesy of Carl Ricketts.

Entrance on stage of Carl Ricketts as Captain Capricious and her backup dancers, 1983. Courtesy of Carl Ricketts.

Signs of the Zodiac 1984

Commemorative poster, 1984. Design by Daniel de Beau-Maltbie. Courtesy of
Howard Philips Smith.

Tableau 1984
King and Queen Amon-Ra XVIII Return
1984 Ball Captain and Ball Lieutenant—The Astrologers and Dancing Stars
The Earth Signs
    Mother Earth and Her Satyrs
    Mercury—Virgo (The Virgin)
    Saturn—Capricorn (The Goat)
The Air Signs
    The Free Spirit
    Venus—Libra (The Scales)
    Uranus—Aquarius (The Water-Bearer)
    Mercury—Gemini (The Twins)
The Water Signs
    From Poseidon's Realm
    Pluto—Scorpio (The Scorpion)
    Neptune—Pisces (The Fish)
    Moon—Cancer (The Crab)
The Fire Signs
    The Luminaries
    Jupiter—Sagittarius (The Archer)
    Mars—Aries (The Ram)
    Sun—Leo (The Lion)
Goddess of the Heavens—Queen Amon-Ra XIX
Selection and Coronation of King Amon-Ra XIX
Recognition of Special Guests
Open Court

A Picnic Fantasy 1985

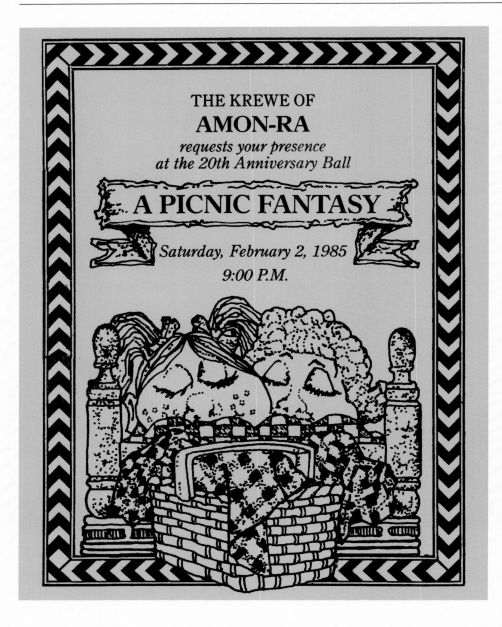

THE KREWE OF
AMON-RA
*requests your presence
at the 20th Anniversary Ball*

A PICNIC FANTASY

Saturday, February 2, 1985
9:00 P.M.

Invitation, 1985. Design by Earl Woodard. Courtesy of the Louisiana State Museum, New Orleans, Accession No. 2014.017.05.

Foam-Rubber Flowers, 1985. Courtesy of the Louisiana State Museum, New Orleans, Accession No. 2014.017.15.25.

Queen Amon-Ra XX, Buddy Rasmussen, as the Dark Moth Queen, 1985. Courtesy of the Louisiana State Museum, New Orleans, Accession No. 2014.017.15.67.

Earl Woodard and Jerry Gilley, costume sketch for Butterfly Attendant, 1985. Courtesy of the Louisiana State Museum, New Orleans, Accession No. 2014.017.13.04.

Earl Woodard and Jerry Gilley, costume sketch for Red Fire-Ants, 1985. Courtesy of the Louisiana State Museum, New Orleans, Accession No. 2014.017.13.06.

Earl Woodard and Jerry Gilley, costume sketch for Poppy Flower, 1985. Courtesy of the Louisiana State Museum, New Orleans, Accession No. 2014.017.13.05.

Earl Woodard and Jerry Gilley, costume sketch for Morning Glory, 1985. Courtesy of the Louisiana State Museum, New Orleans, Accession No. 2014.017.13.07.

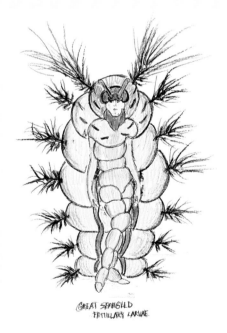

Earl Woodard and Jerry Gilley, costume sketch for Great Spangled Fritillary Larva, 1985. Courtesy of the Louisiana State Museum, New Orleans, Accession No. 2014.017.13.08.

Earl Woodard and Jerry Gilley, costume sketch for Snail, 1985. Courtesy of the Louisiana State Museum, New Orleans, Accession No. 2014.017.13.01.

The Best of Broadway 1986

Glenn Sanford, original artwork for ball invitation, 1986. Courtesy of Glenn Sanford.

Tableau 1986
Return of King and Queen Amon-Ra XX
"Gotta Dance"—Gar Williams Dance Number
"Broadway Baby"—Captain and Lieutenants
Followed by "Success" by the Weather Girls (We're Having A Ball!)
Welcome—Captain
Welcome—President Ron Ellis
Mistress and Master of Ceremonies—Becky Allen and E. J. Moran
"Shall We Dance" from *The King and I* (The King and Teacher)
"Ain't Misbehavin'"—Kenny Walker with Two Male Dancers
"Camelot"—Merlin, Arthur, Guinevere
"The Telephone Number" from *Bye Bye Birdie* (Ten Costumes)
"I Am What I Am" from *La Cage aux Folles* with Mike Edwards
"We Are What We Are" (Five Costumes)
"42nd Street"—Karen Hebert and Crescent City Movin' Company (Dance Troupe)
"I Can Do That" from *A Chorus Line*
Gar Williams Dance Number "The Ascot" from *My Fair Lady* (12 Male and 15 Female Costumes)
Queen Amon-Ra XXI as Eliza Doolittle (Enters Stage through a Large Playbill Backdrop)
Cast Presentation
King Amon-Ra XXI Selected from the Floor
Returning King and Queen Amon-Ra XX
Special Guests
Open Court

Queen Amon-Ra XXI, Richard Powell, as Eliza Doolittle, 1986. Courtesy of Glenn Sanford.

A Thousand and One Nights 1989

SOMETHING MAGICAL
IS HAPPENING

THE KREWE OF AMON-RA
INVITES YOU TO ITS
TWENTY-FOURTH BALL
JANUARY 14, 1989

ST. BERNARD
CULTURAL CENTER
DOORS OPEN 7:00 P.M.
TABLEAUX BEGINS 8:30 P.M.

STRICTLY FORMAL
NO CAMERAS

Thousand and One Nights

SOMETHING MAGICAL
IS HAPPENING

Thousand and One Nights

Invitation, 1989. Design by James Schexnayder. The invitation arrived folded down to a bottle and opened to reveal the genie inside. Courtesy of The Historic New Orleans Collection, Williams Research Center, New Orleans, Accession No. 2000.34.106.

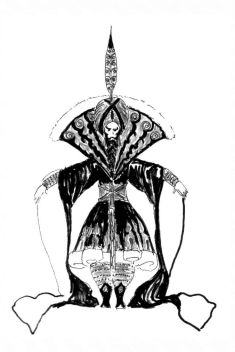

James Schexnayder, costume sketches and swatches (possibly based on Erté designs), 1989. Courtesy of the Louisiana State Museum, New Orleans, Accession No. 1993.089.

Fantasyland 1992

Jim Schexnayder as Oceanus, and two giant Seahorses, 1992. Courtesy of Krewe of Amon-Ra and Mike Moreau; courtesy of the Louisiana State Museum, New Orleans, Accession No. 1993.044.

Tableau 1992
The Garden of Eden
Captain
Ball Lieutenant
Valhalla
Oz
Disney World
Amazons
Mongo
Shangri-La
Aurora Borealis
Hades
Oceanus
Her Majesty—Queen Amon-Ra XVII
Selection of King Amon-Ra XVII
Royal Procession
Honored Guests
Open Court

Oceanus (Jim Schexnayder), his two Attendants, and two giant Seahorses (Bill McLemore and Adam Steg), 1992. Design by Alphonse "Derek" Maenza; execution by Jim Schexnayder. Courtesy of the Louisiana State Museum, New Orleans, Accession No. 1993.044.01.

KREWE OF AMON-RA

LOVE IS IN THE AIR

ALARIO CENTER
FEBRUARY 6, 2010

Invitation, 2010. Courtesy of Daryl Dunaway Jr. and David Aranda-Dunaway.

Queen Amon-Ra XLV, Daryl Dunaway Jr. (Dragonfly), and King Amon-Ra XLV, David Aranda-Dunaway (Fleur-de-Lis), 2010. Design by Mary Hyatt. Courtesy of Daryl Dunaway Jr. and David Aranda-Dunaway.

Myths and Legends 2011

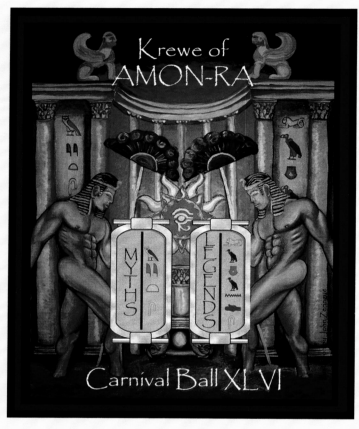

Program, 2011. Design by John S. Zeringue III. Courtesy of Wayne Phillips.

Ball lieutenant John S. Zeringue III as Mythic Rebirth (The Phoenix), 2011. Design by John S. Zeringue III. Courtesy of John S. Zeringue III.

John S. Zeringue III, costume sketches for Mythic Storyteller-Sphinx, 2011. Courtesy of John S. Zeringue III.

John S. Zeringue III, costume sketches for King and Queen Amon-Ra XLVI, Jerry Scavo and Tami Tarmac, as Legends of History: Marc Anthony and Cleopatra, 2011. Courtesy of John S. Zeringue III.

John S. Zeringue III, costume sketches for Mythic Waters, 2011. Courtesy of John S. Zeringue III.

Weighing of the Heart 2015

Firebird costume worn by Ball Lieutenant Errol Rizzuto, showing both front and back views, 2015. Design by John S. Zeringue III. Courtesy of the Krewe of Amon-Ra, Mike Moreau and Darwin Reed Collection.

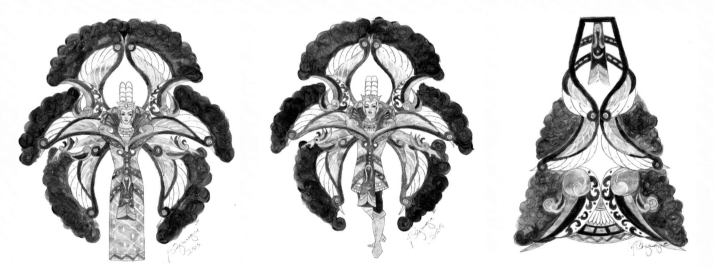

John S. Zeringue III, costume designs for Queen Amon-Ra L, Mike Moreau, and King Amon-Ra L, Darwin Reed, 2015. Courtesy of the Krewe of Amon-Ra, Mike Moreau and Darwin Reed Collection.

Queen Amon-Ra L, Mike Moreau, and King Amon-Ra L, Darwin Reed, 2015. Courtesy of John S. Zeringue III.

Captain John S. Zeringue III as Anubis, 2015. Courtesy of John S. Zeringue III.

John S. Zeringue III, costume design for captain, John S. Zeringue III, as Anubis, 2015. Courtesy of John S. Zeringue III.

Commemorative poster, 2015. Design by Livia Pirsalehy. Courtesy of Wayne Phillips.

John S. Zeringue III, costume designs for Set and Nephthys, 2015. Courtesy of John S. Zeringue III.

All That Glitters Isn't Gold 2016

John S. Zeringue III, costume design for Queen Amon-Ra LI, 2016. Courtesy of John S. Zeringue III.

Tableau 2016
Presentation of Colors
National Anthem
President's Welcome
Introduction of the Emcee
Presentation of King and Queen Amon-Ra L
The Fairy Godmother/Father
The Evil Temptress
Tiny Tim
Butterflies
Lilypad Princess and Frog Prince
Charity Number
Forest Creatures
Lady of the Dark Forest
Dragon Lady
Rainbow Unicorn
Pixie Girls (Keepers of the Forest)
Finale—Walk of King and Queen L
Announcements
Introduction of Queen and King LI

Queen Amon-Ra LI, Mina Hernandez, and King Amon-Ra LI, Chris Arthur, 2016. Courtesy of John S. Zeringue III.

A Night at the Opera . . . Ahhh . . . Opry 2017

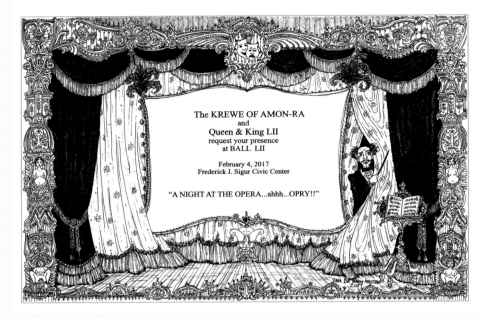

Daniel de Beau–Maltbie, original artwork for the 2017 ball invitation. Courtesy of Daniel de Beau–Maltbie.

Amon-Ra Miss America/Mr. America Summer Fund-Raiser

Commemorative program, 1980. Design by Earl Woodard. Courtesy of the Louisiana State Museum, New Orleans, Accession No. 2014.017.01.

Jerry Gillery, director, 1982. Courtesy of the Louisisana State Museum.

Miss America contestant, 1982. Courtesy of the Louisiana State Museum.

CREEPY CRAWLERS

The Ill-Fated Krewe
of Ganymede

New Orleans has always been a mutable
point in time, a collector of debris from
worn and weary Europa, gloriously
transformed by some strange alchemy
into the ever-youthful Ganymede.

—John Dodt, Krewe of Petronius

A Sign from the Gods

In Greek mythology, Zeus, king of the gods, brought the beautiful Trojan youth
Ganymede to Mount Olympus against his will to become cup bearer, consigned
to a life of immortality. Artists throughout history have depicted this abduction
and rape as the choicest moment of the myth, usually with Zeus in the form of
a giant eagle, clutching the nude boy in his talons. Rubens, Rembrandt, Correg-
gio, Ingres, Fragonard, and Michelangelo contributed to the persistent power
of this ancient tale. Traditional Carnival krewes, among them Comus, Proteus,
and Momus, recalled an ancient and heathen world with the themes for their
balls. This reverence for the classical trickled down to the gay krewes, continuing a direct line from the Carnivals of Europe through the old-line New Orleans
krewes. The myth of Ganymede's kidnapping by Zeus was an obvious target for
these gay revelers.

A Forgotten Legacy

By the time gay Carnival reached its zenith in the mid-1980s, the Krewe of Ganymede had already become a distant memory. Few community members recalled
the dazzling tableaux and troubled history of one of the earliest gay krewes. Otto
Stierle, one of those arrested in Metairie at the last Krewe of Yuga ball, was an
original signatory of the state charter granted to the Krewe of Petronius, yet he
recalled but vague fragments about the Krewe of Ganymede when compiling his

Abduction of Ganymede, from the invitation to the
Krewe of Ganymede's *Fairy Tales* ball, 1969. Courtesy
of Tulane University, Louisiana Research Collection,
Howard-Tilton Memorial Library, New Orleans, Otto
Stierle Collection, Manuscripts Collection 902.

103

master list of gay krewes many years later: "Ganymede formed in 1967 and held its first ball in 1968, disbanding soon afterwards." In reality, Ganymede had held seven balls, and they were the equal of any moment of Carnival brilliance. These balls ultimately had tremendous influence, featuring levels of daring and excesses that shaped the future of gay Carnival.

Three Capricious Captains

Vincent Indovina founded the Krewe of Ganymede in 1967 and served as captain sporadically until its demise in 1974, remaining a strong creative force throughout that time. He, Rivet Hedderel, and Jerry Koplin, chose the name to illustrate their grand ambitions. The preceding year, Indovina had been chosen king of the Krewe of Amon-Ra, but he and his partner, Scott Hoy, Amon Ra's first captain, decided to strike out on their own, creating one of the most innovative of the early gay krewes.

Many of the original members of the Krewe of Ganymede have described Indovina as completely rigid and uncompromising when considering new themes, royalty, members, and even fund-raising. More often than not, krewe meetings devolved into shouting matches. Former Tulane special collections librarian, Ken Owen, whom Koplin had urged to join the krewe, recalled Indovina and Hedderel often butting heads: when Owen tried to mediate, he incurred the wrath of both of the other men. Rivet Joseph Hedderel came from an old New Orleans family with strong ties to France. He initially became well known as the operator of a beauty salon in Old Metairie, Rivet's Coiffures Elegantes. His chic advertisements declared that he was "consultant to the most beautiful women of New Orleans," and he developed social connections to the city's most prominent families, finding seemingly effortless success in everything he touched. He became an early member of the exclusive Steamboat Club, a clandestine group of gay men known for their sophistication and social presence who had been celebrating Carnival since 1953. Hedderel's presence in the group marked him as a major force, especially during the late 1960s.

According to Vance Philip Hedderel, Rivet's nephew, Rivet Hedderel had run away to New York City to become an actor but never made it out of the chorus and returned to New Orleans and opened his eponymous beauty salon. Recalled Vance, "Uncle Rivet was always a shadowy character for me, but he was the closest thing I had to Auntie Mame: glamour incarnate. Who gives a five-year-old an elaborate wooden birdcage, sans bird, for Christmas? My Uncle Rivet!"

Rivet Hedderel become fast friends with Elmo Avet's paramour, Billy Livingston, and this connection led Hedderel to join the Krewe of Ganymede. He and Indovina served together as ball captains for the first few tableau presentations, creating magic and drama. Hedderel's greatest coup, however, was in securing Avet as a staunch and faithful benefactor.

The Gods of Mount Olympus

The first tableau ball of the newly formed Krewe of Ganymede, *The Gods of Mount Olympus*, was held in 1968 at the International Longshoreman's Association (ILA) Hall on Claiborne Avenue, one of the few venues open to the gay krewes at the time. One after another, the old gods and their pages paraded around the hall in the Grand March: Zeus and Hera, Apollo and Diana, Neptune and Saturn. And at the stroke of midnight, time stood still for a moment as Hedderel and Indovina gazed at the audience amid their great triumph, dazzling those in attendance.

Wendell Stipelcovich, who worked with Indovina on the costumes, recalled, "Indovina was a genius when it came to sets and costumes. He knew exactly what he wanted and had learned techniques from the Krewe of Amon-Ra, one of the best of the early krewes." However, Stipelcovich left the krewe after this ball to found the Krewe of Armeinius.

Fairy Tales

The 1969 ball, *Fairy Tales*, was even more sophisticated and hearkened back to the best tableaux of the nineteenth century. Owen designed and painted a giant pink backdrop with a trompe l'oeil village reminiscent of the Brothers Grimm. Hedderel, who served as captain of the ball, constantly criticized and corrected Owen's work, an approach that Owen ultimately conceded greatly improved the results. Prince Charming and Queen Cinderella (King and Queen Ganymede II) entered the stage in bejeweled white costumes astride two miniature Shetland ponies, provoking gasps from the audience. Owen was "overcome by the sheer brilliance of all the component parts, once they had come together. The ball recalled something long buried in childhood, resurrected with a sublime touch of naïveté. But the culmination, never before seen on the stages of New Orleans, surely was the two ponies with golden ribbons intertwined in their manes, groomed to perfection, and the glorious king and queen sitting upon them as they came on stage like immaculate dolls come to life. Just marvelous. With a live orchestra playing waltzes by Franz Liszt, of all things. Hedderel sure knew how to create drama."

Later in the year, George Wilson found himself in drag for the first time at a krewe fund-raiser. Such events became increasingly important for financing the ever-grander balls and costumes, and Wilson and the other young gay men flocking to New Orleans at the time sought to demonstrate that they could raise money. Looking back, Wilson remembered, "I was somehow transformed when I put on the wig, the dress, and all that makeup for the 'Dime-a-Dance' fund-raiser. I really got into the part with lots of pizazz and energy. Don't think I didn't work that room, luring in dates for dances. I raised quite a bit of money, but it took concentration."

Creepy Crawlers

For the third annual ball, captain Nick Donovan chose *Creepy Crawlers* as the theme. Donovan and his close friend, Lou Bernard, whom Donovan had recruited into the krewe, wanted to combine zany costumes with camp to produce a thoroughly entertaining show. The program followed in New Orleans's long-standing Carnival traditions, recalling Comus's *Missing Links to Darwin's Origin of Species* (1873) and Proteus's *Dumb Society* (1896), which also featured outrageous insects and animals and were part of the collective consciousness of the city. George Wilson designed the entire ball, and his incredible costumes are still considered among some of the best and most innovative of gay Carnival. During the tableau,

Peacock and Donkey costumes, Proteus's *Dumb Society* procession, 1896. Designs by Carlotta Bonnecaze. Courtesy of Tulane University, Louisiana Research Collection, Howard-Tilton Memorial Library, New Orleans.

a torchy mosquito competed with a Japanese beetle, while grasshoppers cavorted with a dragonfly, scorpion, caterpillar, snail, fruit flies, African ants, and a hilarious boll weevil who looked more like Aunt Pittypat from *Gone with the Wind* than a pesky insect. The program dubbed the boll weevil the "Queen of Camp." Donovan's Captivating Cobra was a triumph of ingenuity: in Wilson's words, "We took pieces of wire and bent then all into loops. These then were dipped into a black plastic, which would harden over time. All these were then pieced together layer upon layer until we had achieved this amazing effect of snake scales. A ton of work, but well worth the effort."

The King Crustacean, John Brumfield, wore a zigzag orange and black kimono and a gigantic orange headpiece that emulated the feathery mouth of a king crab; in his hands were his two painted claws. The Honey Covered Queen Bee and her two attendants were a brilliant gold. As Bernard reminisced, "The audience went wild over all the costumes. I loved my costume as the Sultry Spiderwoman. We called it 'saucy, *sin*tillating, and sexy.' My web was attached behind me and my dress was so tight, I found it hard to move, which only added to the camp of it all. Very melodramatic. But the snail costume worn by Fletcher Vickers—or as we called him, Miss Vicky—was the riotous showstopper. The shell, in the form of trailing appendages, was attached behind the costume made up of dry cleaning bags, and as she stepped forward a couple of steps, it would take a few beats for the shell to catch up. It was pure camp! That's what gay Carnival is all about! George had engineered an amazing ball, and the Snail costume won the best costume award at the Bourbon Street Awards that year. But it was so massive it took four of us to even get it up on the stage in the middle of Bourbon Street."

Despite the event's success, Donovan and Bernard were unhappy with Ganymede's insular board of directors controlled by Indovina and left the Krewe of Ganymede to form the Krewe of Olympus later in 1970. In addition, according to Owen, Indovina, the president of the krewe, had a lover who "hated the krewe and would throw fits at meetings. He felt that they were spending too much of their own money on the krewe, which was probably not far from the truth."

Shining Forth with Brilliance

Ganymede's last few tableau balls saw a refinement and focus that would elevate the krewe to compete with the other krewes, including Amon-Ra and Apollo. *Music Potpourri* (1971) featured lavishly choreographed musical numbers. *Queens of History* (1972), held at the Saxony on Canal Street, presented Josephine and Marie Antoinette, empresses of France; Isabella, queen of Spain; and Catherine, empress of Russia. The ball lieutenant was Mary, Queen of Scots, and the Queen of Camp appeared to lighten the mood. Queen Ganymede V reigned supreme at the close of the ball.

Tragedy Strikes

A few weeks after the 1972 ball, Miss Adolpho, the beautiful Pink Princess of the French Quarter and later a member of the Mystic Krewe of Celestial Knights, received a phone call at four o'clock in the morning. The caller told her to come quickly to La Normandie restaurant at 139 Chartres Street near the Up Stairs Lounge. It had something to do with Jerry Koplin. Miss Adolpho had helped him land a position at the seedy bar/restaurant after he had lost his other work connections. When she arrived, she learned that Koplin had been murdered, and the owner had called Miss Adolpho, Koplin's only friend, to help with the cleanup. Miss Adolpho believed that Koplin had been in the wrong place at the wrong time and had been killed in a dispute related to organized crime's control of the French Quarter's gay bars. Others, however, thought that the hit had specifically targeted the Krewe of Ganymede. According to Ken Owen, "There had been a hit by the Mafia. It was nothing extraordinary back then, but it did happen. However, I was still shocked. . . . After slashing Koplin's throat, the killer had taken a mop and made sure the blood was smeared all over the place, including the ceiling. That must have taken some time and was a clue to the nature of the crime. They wanted to make sure that this was a sensation, to strike fear rather than commit just some random crime. The krewe never recovered from it." The police accounts bear out this scenario. Koplin's roommate, John McGowan, was charged with the horrendous murder, but under the name Jack McGalen, a suspected Mafia gang member. Albert Germaine found the body when he opened the restaurant the next morning. The Krewe did hang on for another year or two, but Indovina disbanded the krewe soon thereafter, and many of the krewe members in a state of shock simply left the krewe, as fear became a factor in all meetings.

After the 1973 ball, the krewe managed one last ball with an almost melancholy theme, *Queen of Hearts* (1974). The invitation was a large-scale playing card of the red queen herself and at first glance resembled a normal card; however, *Ganymede* was printed along the sides. Indovina chose JoJo Landry as queen, despite widespread resistance among the members because Landry was always a diva and difficult to deal with. Landry had been among those arrested in the Yuga raid, but unlike the others, he had pleaded innocent to the charges. He was nevertheless convicted of the charges and had to pay a higher fine. He subsequently remained defiant, appearing at krewe meetings and in bars in full drag, seemingly taunting the police.

Rivet Hedderel, who had left the krewe after the second ball, starred in many local productions, most notably *Damn Yankees* and *Fiddler on the Roof*, at the

Krewe of Ganymede (1968)

1968

The Krewe of Ganymede was formed in 1967 by a former king of the Krewe of Amon-Ra and others who had served in the Krewe of Petronius. The first ball in 1968 was a triumph, with the *Gods of Mount Olympus* as the theme.

1969

The second ball was held at the International Longshoremen's Association Hall with *Fairy Tales* as the theme. Prince Charming and Cinderella, the reigning king and queen, rode onto the stage astride miniature Shetland ponies.

1970

Ganymede's 1970 ball, *Creepy Crawlers*, became legendary. Captain Nick Donovan as the Cobra and Lou Bernard as the Spider created a menagerie of camp creatures, including a Boll Weevil. This ball took its cue from traditional nineteenth-century balls and then, in turn, influenced other gay balls, especially Amon-Ra's *Picnic Fantasy* ball. Wendell Stipelcovich, one of the founders of the Krewe of Armeinius, also became a member of Ganymede for a couple of seasons, contributing his design and artistic genius.

1972

The *Queens of History* ball was a masterpiece of artifice and camp, showcasing elaborate period costumes and incredible staging. Unfortunately, captain Jerry Koplin was murdered by a mob assassin at La Normandie restaurant where he worked. The krewe was devastated by this attack and never quite recovered.

1974

The last ball was the *Queen of Hearts*, with JoJo Landry reigning as Queen Ganymede VII. After the murder of Jerry Koplin and the departure of Rivet Hedderel, Indovina disbanded the krewe, and it faded into relative obscurity.

Beverly Dinner Theater. He later moved to Natchez and joined the Krewe of Phoenix, a straight Carnival krewe, and was crowned their king in 1989. In Natchez, he and a partner restored the Governor Holmes House and opened it up as a bed and breakfast. Hedderel subsequently returned to New Orleans, where he, too, was murdered in 1996.

Time Regained

Ganymede was the first gay krewe to rework and expand the *bal masqué* template. Vincent Indovina, Rivet Hedderel, and Nick Donovan were visionaries who anticipated the theatrical presentations that would go well beyond the traditional Grand March and parade of costumes. The ideas they pioneered reemerged in successor krewes and particularly resonated with William Woolley in his Mystic Krewe of Celestial Knights. Wendell Stipelcovich took the expertise and creative fire he developed at Ganymede and went on to form the Krewe of Armeinius. Most notably, however, the Krewe of Olympus, formed in 1970 by former members of Ganymede, forever changed the landscape of gay Carnival with the extraordinary and groundbreaking *Camelot* ball (1971). Though the Krewe of Ganymede has long been overlooked, it remains an important facet of the history of Carnival in New Orleans.

Krewe of Ganymede Tableau Balls List	
1968	GODS OF MOUNT OLYMPUS (ALPHA BALL)
1969	FAIRY TALES
1970	CREEPY CRAWLERS
1971	MUSIC POTPOURRI (THERE'S NO BUSINESS LIKE SHOW BUSINESS)
1972	QUEENS OF HISTORY
1973	BEAUX ARTS BAL DE MASQUÉ
1974	QUEEN OF HEARTS

Gods of Mount Olympus 1968

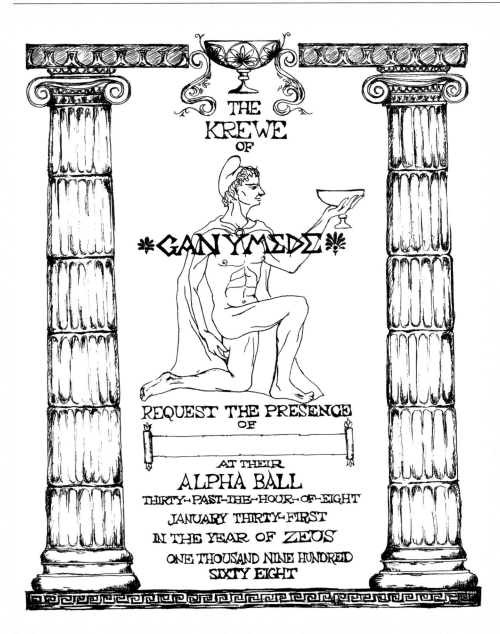

Invitation, 1968. Courtesy of the Louisiana State Museum, New Orleans, Jake and Kevin Thomas Collection, Accession No. 2015.046.04.1.

Creepy Crawlers 1970

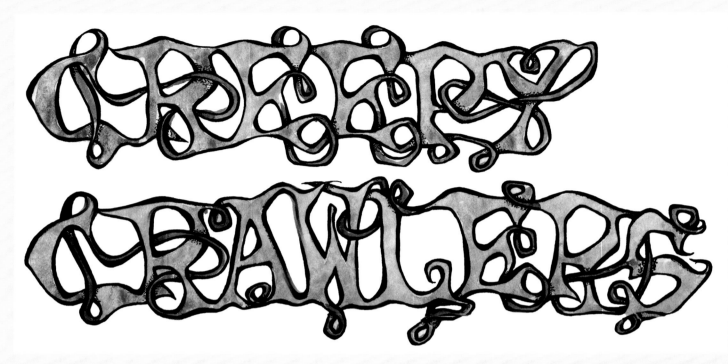

Program graphic, 1970. Courtesy of the Louisiana State Museum, New Orleans, Accession No. 1995.010.082.

Tableau 1970
Returning Royalty
Prince Charming—King Ganymede II
Her Royal Majesty—Queen Ganymede II—Cinderella and Her Attendants
    The Fruit Fly, Four Little African Ants and Their Leader, Two Grasshoppers
A Torchy Mosquito—Ball Lieutenant
A Captivating Cobra—Ball Captain
Spider—Saucy, *Sin*tillating, and Sexy
Spanish Flea—Vivacious and Vibrant
Scorpion—Slinky
Just a Bug—A Bunch of Wiggles
Japanese Beetle—Jaunty
Blue Creature—Cool and Cautious
Boll Weevil—Queen of Camp
Horny Toad—Strong and Robust
Dragonfly—Delicate
Caterpillar—Fun, Fluffy, and Very Useful
Snail—Elegant, Slow, but Definite
Call-Out Sections
His Royal Majesty—King Crustacean
Our Queen Attendants—Honey Bees
Her Majesty Queen Ganymede III—The Honey-Covered Queen Bee

Fletcher Vickers (Miss Vicky) as the Snail, 1970. The costume was made up mostly of vacuum cleaner bags. As the Snail progressed across the stage, its trappings followed at jerky intervals behind, causing riotous laughter among audience members. Courtesy of the Louisiana State Museum, New Orleans, Accession No. 2016.005.1.1.

Dragonfly costume, 1970. Courtesy of the Louisiana State Museum, New Orleans, Accession No. 1995.071.20.

Lou Bernard as the Spider, 1970. Courtesy of the Louisiana State Museum, New Orleans, Accession No. 1995.071.09.

Boll Weevil (Queen of Camp) costume, 1970. Courtesy of the Louisiana State Museum, New Orleans, Accession No. 1995.071.14.

Captain Nick Donovan as the Cobra, 1970. Courtesy of the Louisiana State Museum, New Orleans, Accession No. 1995.071.04.

King Ganymede III, John Brumfield, as King Crustacean, 1970. Courtesy of the Louisiana State Museum, New Orleans, Accession No. 1995.071.19.

Queen Ganymede II as the Honey-Covered Queen Bee, 1970. Courtesy of the Louisana State Museum, New Orleans, Accession No. 1995.071.22.

Music Potpourri 1971

Invitation, 1971. Courtesy of Tulane University, Louisiana Research Collection, Howard-Tilton Memorial Library, New Orleans, Otto Stierle Collection, Manuscripts Collection 902.

Queens of History 1972

Invitation, 1972. Courtesy of Tulane University, Louisiana Research Collection, Howard-Tilton Memorial Library, New Orleans, Otto Stierle Collection, Manuscripts Collection 902.

Queen of Hearts 1974

Invitation, 1972. Courtesy of The Historic New Orleans Collection, Williams Research Center, New Orleans, Accession No. 1980.178.349. Gift of Tracy Hendrix.

THE KREWE OF ARMEINIUS

The Boy Who
Would Be Queen

Hopefully one day a complete compilation will appear to preserve the many wonderful memories these organizations have provided. Not only Armeinius, but Petronius and Ganymede and Ishtar and Polyphemus and so on.

—Jim Willemet, Krewe of Armeinius

Great Expectations

The Krewe of Armeinius was formed in 1968 by Jerry Loner, Scott Morvant, Don Stratton, and its driving force, Wendell Stipelcovich, who guided the krewe through its first years. Tracy Hendrix, one of the members of the Krewe of Yuga arrested in 1962, also became part of the core group, along with Jimmy Hulin and Ernie Apodoca. Stipelcovich had previously been in the Krewe of Ganymede, and that bold sensibility spilled over into Armeinius, but with a more refined aesthetic. Tongue-in-cheek costumes coupled with highbrow references defined the krewe's tableaux. The origin of the krewe's name has always been up for debate. Some have claimed that Armeinius was a great Teutonic hero who challenged the might of Rome and won, while others avowed that he became Narcissus's lover after he rejected Echo. Whatever the story, the krewe takes Armeinius as its own hero and guiding force.

The First Balls

The first ball, 1969's *The Year of the Queen*, transported the great queens of history to the stage in gorgeous, glittery costumes. Jerry Loner dazzled the audience as Cleopatra, Queen Armeinius I. The following year, the krewe visited *Armeinius Gardens*, a take-off of Harmonia Gardens from *Hello Dolly!* This eponymous restaurant served up dishes as amazing costumes—Shrimp Cocktail as the captain and Cherries Jubilee as the queen, among others. The queen's costume was innovative in that it filled the stage. Stipelcovich was the captain for both of these balls, establishing

The Krewe of Armeinius's signature letter *A* transformed into *Lilies of the Field*, 1974. Design by David Peltier. Courtesy of the Louisiana State Museum, New Orleans, Accession No. 1995.010.024.

Invitation to the *Armeinius Gardens* ball, 1970. Courtesy of The Historic New Orleans Collection, Williams Research Center, New Orleans, Accession No. 1980.178.170. Gift of Tracy Hendrix.

Wendell Stipelcovich at the Krewe of Armeinius's *Among My Souvenirs* ball, 1978. Courtesy of the Louisiana State Museum, New Orleans, Jake and Kevin Thomas Collection, Accession No. 2015.046.01.

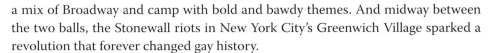

a mix of Broadway and camp with bold and bawdy themes. And midway between the two balls, the Stonewall riots in New York City's Greenwich Village sparked a revolution that forever changed gay history.

Wendell Stipelcovich

Born downriver in Buras, Louisiana, Stipelcovich grew up in Empire before moving to New Orleans. He had worked on costumes in high school and was in the Little Theater in Plaquemines Parish. He recalled, "After Ganymede, I knew we could do something better—not just balls but wonderful live shows using our own voices in live presentations. Now that's something you don't see every day. The *Year of the Queen* ball was simply electric. It was our first ball, after all, and so successful it was intoxicating. I was so taken with Carol Channing in *Hello, Dolly!* and that was the inspiration for creating our own restaurant on stage with the dishes as costumes. No one had done that before. The program itself was a large menu. Just gorgeous." He continued. "I knew everyone during the good old days, and I mean everyone—John Dodt, Jamie Greenleaf, Miss Woolley, Millie Wilson, and so on. We were competitive, for sure, but if you felt someone else had outdone you, well, you just tried harder the next time. No jealousy, just fierce competition. Nothing gets a queen going better than a chance to outshine another queen."

Dedication to Excellence

New Orleans native Albert J. Carey Jr. joined the krewe in 1970. An architect, Carey was one of the designers of the Chalmette's Saint Bernard Civic Auditorium, host of many gay balls. He served as captain for Armeinius's third ball, *Atlantis Redivivus*, set on the lost continent. The oversized invitation used Tony Robert-Fleury's painting, *Le Dernier Jour de Corinthe* (1870), renaming it *Atlantis*. Carey's tableau showed the citizenry of the lost city followed by its demise. Out of destruction arose the New Citizens of Atlantis, an amazing array of sea creatures. Tropical fish cavorted about with such oddities as the *Plecostomus punctatus* (suckermouth catfish), *Coelenterata hydrozoa* (hydras or sea serpents), *Aetobatus narinari* (spotted and colored rays), *Procanbarus clarkii* (red swamp crawfish), and *Physalia pelagica* (Portuguese man-of-wars). After this parade of natural wonders came the Dawn of a New Age and the promise fulfilled, with Queen Armeinius III.

The following year, Don Stratton became the captain of the krewe, and his ball, *A Gala Evening*, focused on the fertile realm of classic opera. This was the krewe's first grand ball, with more than a dozen splendid costumes referencing some of the greatest moments on stage from grandiose to obscure: *Carmen* and *Madama Butterfly*, *The Tales of Hoffman* and *The Magic Flute*, Wagner and Offenbach, Puccini, Strauss, Borodin, Meyerbeer, and Mussorgsky. But the most sublime moment came when Albert Carey appeared as a tornado in Giacomo Meyerbeer's *L'Africaine*. The invitation evoked the height of New Orleans society in the early nineteenth century with a drawing of the French Opera House on Bourbon Street, the city's cultural heart. Stratton was an expert in costume design, operating a costume company known for its wirework and high collars, whose clients included numerous straight krewes, among them the Venturians, Cleopatra, Choctaw, Pygmalion, Allah and most notably the Zulus. Stratton served as captain of Armeinius five more times.

Albert Carey as Tornado (from Meyerbeer's *L'Africaine*) for the Krewe of Armeinius's *A Gala Evening* ball, 1972. Courtesy of the Krewe of Armeinius and Wendell Stipelcovich.

Jon Lee Poché

Another important creative force within Armeinius, New Orleans–born Jon Lee Poché, was steeped in traditional Carnival. At one time a member of the Knights of Babylon and the Krewe of Mid-City, he served as Armeinius's captain five times beginning in 1973. That year, Poché crafted a tableau presentation around *A Midsummer Night's Dream*, focusing on the *Revelries of Titania's Court*. Poché created his own fairy world, ruling over it as the Blue Fairy. Recalled David Peltier, "Jon Lee was an extremely talented guy. He had grand ideas and he brought them to Armeinius. . . . *Revelries of Titania's Court: An Evening with the Fairies* [was] so very gay and wonderful. I designed the invitation that year—an adorable fairy with goat hooves. Each costume was a fairy, one after the other, . . . and each costume became more elaborate as they made their entrances. Of course, the queen was Titania and the king was Oberon. Such incredible costumes."

Jon Lee Poché as the German Soldier narrator for the Krewe of Armeinius's *Lilies of the Field* ball, 1974. Captain Wendel Stipelcovich as Lili Marlene stands to the left. Courtesy of the Krewe of Armeinius and Wendell Stipelcovich.

In 1979, Poché and Albert Carey joined forces as cocaptains to produce the *Do You Know What It Means to Miss New Orleans?* Featuring a walking tour of the French Quarter, this ball revealed an uncompromising love of the city itself, its history, its traditions, its foibles and idiosyncrasies, and above all its mystique. Costumes ranged from Brennan's to Buster Holmes's, a much loved soul-food restaurant, Antoine's to Messina's and the French Market. Storyville followed the St. Louis Cathedral, and the Voodoo Museum competed with the notorious Sandra Sexton 500 Club.

In 1983, Poché truly hit his creative mark, presenting one of the boldest tableau balls in the history of gay Carnival, *Great Disasters of the Western World*. Before the ball, the *New Orleans Times-Picayune* announced that the Krewe of Armeinius "has issued invitations to its ball, one of the gayest of the season. The captain, whose identity is known only to members of the krewe, in keeping with the true traditions of the prim and proper Carnival organizations, says that our maids will represent such tasteful events as a circus train wreck, a church fire, an air crash, the plague and the death of major celebrities. And just as the upper crust do, our queen will make an entrance in a gown of imported velvet encrusted with Austrian rhinestones." The ball opened with a somber funeral parlor on stage. A black-draped coffin stood in the center, topped by a huge spray of white lilies and flanked by two pillars on which hung two black wreaths. Sad Bach organ music created a grim mood. Suddenly, the lilies began to move, and the coffin popped open to reveal a hot pink throne. Jon Lee Poché took up his place as captain on the throne, wearing the lilies as his headdress. The funereal music was replaced by a peppy tune, Harry Nilsson's "I'd Rather Be Dead" (the next line: "than wet my bed"). The audience roared. The ball then depicted train wrecks; hurricanes and various fires, including the Chicago Fire; the San Francisco Earthquake; an explosion at a fireworks factory; Mount Vesuvius; a tsunami and assorted floods (including the biblical Great Flood); the Crash of the Hindenburg; and the Black Death, among other calamities. When it was time to reveal the newly crowned king and queen, the king was dead in the Blizzard of '88, and the queen was on her way to the bottom of the sea aboard the *Titanic*.

Poché encouraged Christel Robbins, who lived in the same apartment building on Orleans Avenue in the French Quarter, to accompany him to the krewe den several blocks away, and she soon became a devoted member, primarily contributing her talents as a seamstress. Echoing the straight krewes' tradition of calling out the captain's wife at the beginning of the ball, Poché would acknowledge Robbins whenever he was serving as captain. In addition, she was the onstage narrator for *The Boy Who Would Be Queen* (1985), remaining at Poché's side throughout the

Young Aristocrats of Tchoupitoulas Street (YATS) costumes for the *Evil Things* parade, Shrove Tuesday, 1982. Christel Robbins is the Red Ant with wire hangers as antennae. Photo ©Nell Campbell.

event. Robbins also became a member of the Krewe of Iris, the oldest all-female Krewe in New Orleans.

The Young Aristocrats of Tchoupitoulas Street

In 1980, several members of the Krewe of Armeinius and others—Christel Robbins, Albert Carey, David Peltier, and Jon Lee Poché—formed the Young Aristocrats of Tchoupitoulas Street (YATS), a walking club, which produced its own set of costumes and pranced about the French Quarter on Shrove Tuesday. The YATS decided that their first theme would be *Whimsical Animals*, such as the sacred cow, bird of paradise, and bears. They took the Best Group trophy in the Annual Bourbon Street Awards that year. Poché explained, "We have a couple of parties during the year. Then we get together on Mardi Gras morning and have a brunch, then we march. We do costumes that are bigger than normal for the street but not as elaborate as a ball costume."

The Artistry of David Peltier

David Peltier, King Armeinius VIII, had met Poché at the University of Southwestern Louisiana, where they pledged the same fraternity. Back in New Orleans in the early 1970s after a stint in the army, Poché urged Peltier to join the Krewe of Armeinius. Peltier subsequently designed many of the krewe's invitations. For *Great Disasters of the Western World*, he produced a line drawing of a sorrowful angel, reminiscent of a cemetery statue, holding the Armeinius letter *A* like a lamp. Perhaps Peltier's most notable work was the invitation to *The Boy Who Would Be Queen* (1985). Poché again served as ball captain and created a fairy-tale world based on the *Cinderella* story, although he substituted a little gay boy for the title character and put him at the mercy of his ugly stepsister, Oleander. The boy became queen of an imaginary kingdom where storybook creatures and characters came to life courtesy of his Fairy Dragmother. Among the other camp characters were the Good Fairy Canal, the Good Fairy Estalauda, Old Man River, Flo the Flower Fairy, a Banshee from Bucktown, and the Terrible Tiger. King Armeinius XXVII finally appeared as Sir Gregory the Gay, the Enchanted Crab; while Queen Armeinius XXVII was Prince Andrew, the Fair Mermaid Marigny. Realizing his dream, the boy had finally been transformed into a queen.

Winter Follies

Not everyone liked a dark twist to Carnival. Don Stratton, one of the founders of the krewe and a frequent captain, preferred the "showgirl" balls that showcased costumes with lots of sequins and feathers. Stratton "was not terribly fond of Jon Lee's balls. They were quirky and risqué in a way. Don't get me wrong. He was a mastermind and genius and wasn't afraid of taking huge risks, but give me a feathery ball any day." So when Stratton planned the 1989 *Winter Follies* ball, he featured a subtle pastel palette of flowing costumes and gowns. Even the invitation and program were masterworks of simplicity: a white figure clothed in large feathers holding a fan above her head while white snowflakes formed an arc against a stark blue background. As captain, Stratton began the ball with a scene from the Ice Capades, and the ball lieutenant was Fire and Ice. Subsequent scenes featured Snowflakes and Icicles caught up in blizzards, the French Alps, the Siberian Express, and Snowbirds and Unicorns that heralded the arrival of the Snow Maiden and her Winter Knight. The knight was a clever trick conceived by Wendell Stipelcovich. He appeared to be mounted on a very tall white steed, but in reality his legs were hidden inside the body of the horse on stilts, and the legs seen straddling the horse were fake.

Lee Harvey Oswald

The Krewe of Armeinius had a bizarre connection with Lee Harvey Oswald. In 1963, Oswald approached Jules Weiss (later Queen Armeinius VIII), who operated a small photography business in the French Quarter, seeking work. Weiss did not hire Oswald but did help him obtain a position with another photographer, and he apparently stayed in Weiss's extra room for several weeks, a kindness Oswald noted in his journal. A decade later, Weiss was arrested based on Oswald's journal entry and charged not only with conspiring to kill President Kennedy but also with fencing stolen goods. Though Weiss was cleared of all charges, he never recovered financially, and the long trial forced him to close shop. Weiss was much beloved in the krewe, where he was affectionately called Lovely Rita, and not only secured Le Petit Théâtre du Vieux Carré as a fund-raising venue but was active in AIDS work around the city.

The Bug Ball

In 2005, the Krewe of Armeinius returned to the insect theme with *The Bug Ball*, captained by Bill McLemore. Wrote Phyllis Denmark in *Ambush Magazine*, "Saturday night we went to the Armeinius Bug Ball. I have to say this was not your typical Armeinius Ball. The costumes were big but gone were the feathers and glitz that we have come to expect from Armeinius. Captain Bill did supply us with an array of bugs. I think it was a toss up between the Roaches and the Silverfish. Those are not my favorites around the house but they were great fun in the ball. Joel Haas came out in a stunning costume that later in the weekend won $1,000 at the Bourbon Street Awards." Haas appeared as the Firefly, while other costumes included the Gypsy Moth, the Barfly, the Love Bugs, the Bookworm, the Scarab, and the Silkworm.

Albert Carey

Albert Carey (Queen Armeinius VI and L, King Armeinius XIX and XLII) has been involved with the krewe since 1970 and has served as its historian. He was featured in Tim Wolff's documentary, *The Sons of Tennessee Williams* (2010), which shows preparations for the krewe's fortieth anniversary ball, *Let Them Eat Cake*, in 2008. The krewe became active in the gay community in the late 1980s, helping to found and maintain an AIDS hospice for Project Lazarus. Carey remains the krewe's grounding force, a constant advocate and diplomat who has guided the krewe over the years and made enormous contributions.

Krewe of Armeinius (1969)

1969

The Krewe of Armeinius was formed in 1968 by Jerry Loner, Scott Morvant, Wendell Stipelcovich, and Don Stratton. Other early members included Tracy Hendrix, Jimmy Hulin, Ernie Apodoca, and Albert Carey. Armeinius traces its lineage back to the first gay Carnival krewe, the Krewe of Yuga: Hendrix was among those arrested in the police raid. In addition, Stipelcovich came from the Krewe of Ganymede, an offshoot of the Krewe of Petronius. The first ball was *The Year of the Queen*, and Loner, as Cleopatra, became Queen Armeinius I. Stipelcovich served as captain for the krewe's first two balls. The krewe may have taken its name from a heroic German barbarian who defeated the Roman army in the Battle of the Teutoburg Forest or from the lover of Narcissus.

1970

Armeinius Gardens, like the Harmonia Gardens in *Hello Dolly!*, was a restaurant, and the costumes for the ball were the dishes on the menu, such as the Shrimp Cocktail as the captain and Cherries Jubilee as the queen. This costume was one of the first to stretch across the entire stage and at the time was a sensation.

1971

Albert Carey was the ball captain for the third Armeinius ball, in which the Queen of Armeinius proclaimed *Atlantis Redivivus*, a high-camp masterpiece set in Atlantis. The invitation was based on a nineteenth-century French painting by Tony Robert-Fleury. Carey served as cocaptain with Jon Lee Poché for *Do You Know What It Means to Miss New Orleans?* (1979).

1982

Just two weeks before the *Lido de Paris* ball, captain Danny Shuffield committed suicide, and the queen, Tom Wood, had a heart attack. However, Jon Lee Poché stepped in, and the ball was still a huge success. Several attendees came from Paris and reveled in this camp take on the City of Light.

1983

The visionary Jon Lee Poché looked death straight in the eye with his *Great Disasters of the Western World* ball, which began in a somber funeral parlor and referenced earthquakes, fires, volcanoes, floods, the Black Death, and the sinking of the Titanic, along with other tragedies. In the midst of the disasters sat Poché on a pink throne.

1985

Poché again dazzled with *The Boy Who Would Be Queen*, a gay fairy tale set in the swamps and sinkholes of New Orleans. The light-hearted transformation of Prince Andrew into the Mermaid Queen was accomplished with artistry and brilliance.

A Jolt of Creativity

J. Bruce Orgeron Jr., a native of New Orleans, joined the krewe as an accomplished costume designer, but not without controversy. He not only served as captain seven times but also served as king and queen. His ability to translate his superb designs into intricately crafted costumes served the krewe well. Among his more memorable balls were *The Blue Ball* (1999), *Armeinius Goes Looney* (2004), and the wildly popular *Makin' Groceries* (2012).

Makin' Groceries took its title from a local French phrase *faire l'épicerie*, literally translated. Often said by older women as they explained they had to do their grocery shopping, "makin' groceries" usually occurred at the Schwegmann's supermarket chain, which carried everything imaginable and was much beloved. Making the journey to a Schwegmann's was part of the city's daily routine, offering the chance to visit with neighbors and to take a break for a coffee or a poor boy at the cafeteria. Orgeron used this phrase to portray audaciously camp food-related costumes. The balcony pass was a cash register receipt from the store, and the tables for special guests featured brown grocery bags filled with provisions. Captain Orgeron was costumed as Salt. As Wayne Phillips, Carnival curator at the Louisiana State Museum, related, "I was at that ball and when [Orgeron] came out, it was a wow moment. Bruce is actually walking on stilts under that costume. I think this is one of his best costumes. The king and queen were Pepper!"

A close friend of the Lords of Leather, Orgeron also designed many of their costumes. In the second decade of the twenty-first century, divisions within the Krewe of Armeinius deepened as new members sought spots at the top, and Orgeron and several other krewe members, including Queen Armeinius LXIV, Nick Weber, refused to pay their dues and were ousted. They responded by forming the Krewe of Narcissus, which took its name from Armeinius's lover. With Orgeron as permanent captain and Weber as president, the new krewe held its first *bal masqué* in 2015.

New Blood and Renaissance

The vacuum created by the departure of Orgeron and the other veterans was filled by new, younger members. Fredrick Guess and Brent Durnin, the cocaptains for the 2015 *Architecture* ball, crafted a parade of smart and witty costumes, referencing well-known architects such as Antoni Gaudí, William F. Lamb, Jon Utzon, and Frank Gehry as well as fictional architects such as Ramases Ho-tep, Petronius Satyricon Vernaculus, Shah Abdul el Chic, Ken Mattel, Nebuchadnezzar, and Sakyapa, who supposedly built the Jocktang Temple, home of the legendary Yeti.

At the ball, Wendell Stipelcovich, Armeinius's founder and first captain, received the first Honorary Member for Life award, an honor he greatly appreciated: "I didn't realize until a year or two ago how important Armeinius has been in my life. I am very proud of our accomplishments—all the wonderful balls, shows, events, and owning our own den. Through the years we accepted many new members, some of whom make their mark and fit in like an old shoe and get along well with us older members. Such is the case right now with a recent wave of new members who will no doubt make their mark in krewe history."

Beauty and the Beast

The theme of Armeinius's 2016 ball was the age-old battle between good and evil and was interpreted in opposing pairs. According to Wayne Phillips, who attended the ball and sat at the captain's table, one pair was particularly "hilarious! Little Miss Muffet came out first, sitting on top of a giant tuffet pushed around by a couple of bare-chested boys. Then she got down from the tuffet and the creepy giant Spider came out and chased her around. Little Miss Muffet tried swatting the Spider with a giant fly swatter. At the end of their little tableau, Little Miss Muffet's wig got caught on one of the Spider's legs accidentally and was ripped off, to the cheers and roars of the audience! It was one of those hilarious unplanned moments! They both entered the Bourbon Street Awards separately, and I think Little Miss Muffet won an award in the drag category and the Spider won the Best Overall award."

Festival Fest-Evil

For the forty-ninth ball (2017), the krewe showcased an array of devilish costumes from tall skeletons to evil piñatas. Returning royalty were the Louisiana Fur and Wildlife festival. Other festivals included the American Fruit Festival, the Indian Holi Festival of Colors, Woodstock, the Cherry Blossom Festival, Cocktoberfest, Burning Man, and El Diá de los Muertos. Reigning royalty appeared as the Voodoo Festival. The ball might have been inspired in part by the 1971 *Louisiana on Parade* ball, in which the Krewe of Amon-Ra presented costumes representing various festivals around the state.

1990s

The Krewe of Armeinius continued to present balls despite the hardships, including the AIDS epidemic, that beset the New Orleans gay community, demonstrating a level of professionalism rare during this time.

2000s

The krewe experienced a resurgence in creativity during the first decade of the new millennium. Important and truly original presentations during this period were *Armeinius Goes Looney* (2004) and *Makin' Groceries* (2012), a grand departure from the more showgirl-inspired balls.

2015-17

The *Architecture* ball (2015) honored one of Armeinius's founding members, Wendell Stipelcovich, and showcased some of the krewe's new blood and energy. The *Beauty and the Beast* ball (2016) featured pairs of opposites—Miss Muffet and the Spider, Perseus and Medusa, and of course La Belle and La Bête à la Cocteau. The 2017 ball featured costumes based on festivals—with an evil edge.

Krewe of Armeinius Tableau Balls List	
1969	THE YEAR OF THE QUEEN
1970	ARMEINIUS GARDENS (A RESTAURANT)
1971	ATLANTIS REDIVIVUS
1972	A GALA EVENING
1973	REVELRIES OF TITANIA'S COURT (AN EVENING WITH THE FAIRIES)
1974	LILIES OF THE FIELD
1975	BALLS (TRIBUTE TO TRADITIONAL KREWES)
1976	GRAND ILLUSIONS
1977	GIRLS OF THE GOLDEN WEST
1978	AMONG MY SOUVENIRS
1979	DO YOU KNOW WHAT IT MEANS TO MISS NEW ORLEANS? (FRENCH QUARTER TOUR)
1980	MGM MOVIE'S GREATEST MOMENTS
1981	ALL THAT GLITTERS
1982	UN SOIR ENCHANTÉ à LE LIDO DE PARIS
1983	GREAT DISASTERS OF THE WESTERN WORLD
1984	I NEVER MET A CUNT I DIDN'T LIKE
1985	THE BOY WHO WOULD BE QUEEN
1986	THE BLACK BALL
1987	GIVE ME THAT OLE TIME RELIGION
1988	WHEN EVERYTHING OLD IS NEW AGAIN
1989	WINTER FOLLIES
1990	THE MASTER'S TOUCH
1991	I WRITE THE SONGS
1992	TAROT
1993	REFLECTIONS (TWENTY-FIFTH ANNIVERSARY)
1994	A RENAISSANCE FESTIVAL
1995	AND THE BAND PLAYED ON (THE NO BALL)
1996	OH NO! NOT HER! (THE SCARLET BALL)
1997	THE BARBARA BALL
1998	PETAL PROFUSIONS OF FLORAL FANTASIES AND FIXATIONS (THE FLOWER BALL)
1999	ARMEINIUS IN BLUE (THE BLUE BALL)
2000	THE RUSSIA BALL
2001	A DISCO ODYSSEY
2002	THE INK BALL (TATTOO BALL)
2003	REMEMBRANCES OF THINGS PAST (THIRTY-FIVE YEARS OF HELL)
2004	ARMEINIUS GOES LOONEY
2005	THE BUG BALL
2006	THE GAY BALL
2007	PIRATES, PROSTITUTES, PRISONERS, AND PIGS
2008	LET THEM EAT CAKE*
2009	THERE'S SOMETHING ABOUT MARY (THE MARY BALL)
2010	MASQUERADE
2011	HAIRBALL
2012	MAKIN' GROCERIES
2013	OH, CAPTAIN, MY CAPTAIN
2014	BAL DU BLANCHE—LES SPECTACLES DE PARIS
2015	IF YOU BUILD IT, THEY WILL COME (THE ARCHITECTURE BALL)
2016	BEAUTY AND THE BEAST
2017	FESTIVAL/FEST-EVIL
2018	LA NOUVELLE-ORLÉANS: 300 YEARS OF FABULOUS

*Featured in Tim Wolff's documentary, *Sons of Tennessee Williams*

YEAR OF TABLEAU BALL	CAPTAIN	QUEEN	KING
1969	Wendell Stipelcovich	Jerry Loner	Scott Morvant
1970	Wendell Stipelcovich	Don Stratton	Denny Dennison
1971	Albert Carey	Paul Schwartz	Henry Denoux
1972	Don Stratton	Wendell Stipelcovich	Skip Navarre
1973	Jon Lee Poché	Danny Shuffield	Larry Dodd
1974	Wendell Stipelcovich	Albert Carey	Jack Vaughn
1975	Henry Denoux	Jon Lee Poché	Tracy Hendrix
1976	Danny Shuffield	Jules Weiss	David Peltier
1977	Don Stratton	Roy Chauvin	David Daronselet
1978	Wendell Stipelcovich	Jesse Hand	Jerry Hocke
1979	Albert Carey/Jon Lee Poché	Adrian Prattini	Ronnie Bourgeois
1980	Larry Dodd	Dale Rogers	Toby Corrington
1981	Wendell Stipelcovich	Tom Wood	Jim Willemet
1982	Danny Shuffield/Jon Lee Poché	David Wagner	Wally Willemet
1983	Jon Lee Poché	John Wiggins	Ernie Apodaca
1984	Jon Lee Poché	Henry Denoux	Maurice Geisel
1985	Jon Lee Poché	John Thompson	Billy Dembrowski
1986	Jerry Hocke	Don Lemoine	Jon Lee Poché
1987	Don Downs	Earl Punch	Albert Carey
1988	Don Stratton	Jimmy Hulin	Harry Bale
1989	Don Stratton	Wally Willemet	Wally McLaughlin
1990	Don Stratton	Chip Lohner	Ed O'Halloran
1991	Don Stratton	Maurice Geisel	J. Bruce Orgeron Jr.
1992	Wally McLaughlin	Charles Rector	Scott Speak
1993	Wally McLaughlin	Don Stratton	Don Downs
1994	J. Bruce Orgeron Jr.	Charles Turberville	Larry Anderson
1995	Wally McLaughlin	Romnie Leleux	Kevin Keller
1996	Wally McLaughlin	Tracy Hendrix	Freddie Clark
1997	Wally McLaughlin	Hank Ranna	Russell Sutherland
1998	J. Bruce Orgeron Jr.	Glenn Plauché	Rusty Toups
1999	J. Bruce Orgeron Jr.	Kelly Biggs	Vinnie Pervel
2000	Charles Turberville	J. Bruce Orgeron Jr.	Bill McLemore
2001	Charles Turberville	Ricky Lenart	Nick Weber
2002	Joseph Marrione	John Cucinello	Charles Turberville
2003	Albert Carey/J. Bruce Orgeron Jr./Charles Turberville/Don Stratton (ABCD)	Rosario D'Amico	Rick Mirabelli
2004	J. Bruce Orgeron Jr.	Kevin Charpentier (Blanche Debris)	Kelly Biggs
2005	Bill McLemore	Randy Chauvin (Natasha Sinclair)	Jimmy deBlanc
2006	Charles Turberville	Joel Haas	Bill McCarthy
2007	Charles Turberville	Michael Sullivan	Adam Matthews
2008	Charles Turberville	Tommy Diestch	Charles Maddox
2009	Charles Turberville	Tim Jeansonne	Ricky Lenart
2010	J. Bruce Orgeron Jr.	Rusty Toups	Albert Carey
2011	J. Bruce Orgeron Jr.	David Scheu	Tim Goodwin
2012	J. Bruce Orgeron Jr.	Nick Weber	Kevin Charpentier (Blanche Debris)
2013	Charles Turberville	Fredrick Guess	Fred Arocho
2014	Kevin Charpentier (Blanche Debris)	Chris Leonard (Summer Rayne)	J. Bruce Orgeron Jr./Joel Haas
2015	Brent Durnin/Fredrick Guess	Chad Brickley (Dragzilla)	Tim Jeansonne
2016	Albert Carey/Fredrick Guess	John Peifer (Adrienne Andrews)	Scott Spivey
2017	Chad Brickley	Beaux DeLong-Church	Paul Meteor
2018	Barrett DeLong-Church/Fredrick Guess/Chad Brickley/Fred Arocho	Albert Carey	Wendell Stipelcovich

Krewe of Armeinius Royalty List

The Year of the Queen 1969

Captain Wendell Stipelcovich, 1969. Courtesy of the Louisiana State Museum, New Orleans, Jake and Kevin Thomas Collection, Accession No. 2015.046.01.

Queen Armeinius I, Jerry Loner, as Cleopatra, and King Armeinius I, Scott Morvant, 1969. Courtesy of the Louisiana State Museum, New Orleans, Jake and Kevin Thomas Collection, Accession No. 2015.046.01.

Armeinius Gardens 1970

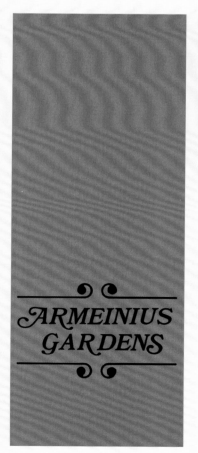

ARMEINIUS GARDENS

Don Stratton as Cherries Jubilee, 1970. Courtesy of the Louisiana State Museum, New Orleans, Jake and Kevin Thomas Collection, Accession No. SC2015.06.07.

Returning Queen Armeinius I, Jerry Loner, 1970. Courtesy of the Louisiana State Museum, New Orleans, Jake and Kevin Thomas Collection, Accession No. 2015.046.01.

Program as a menu, 1970. Courtesy of the Louisiana State Museum, New Orleans, Accession No. 1995.010.025.

Atlantis Redivivus 1971

Commemorative poster, 1971. Courtesy of The Historic New Orleans Collection, Williams Research Center, New Orleans, Accession No. 1983.109.11. Gift of Tracy Hendrix.

Tony Robert-Fleury, *Le Dernier Jour de Corinthe*, before 1870. This painting inspired the Krewe of Armeinius's *Atlantis Redivivus* poster. Courtesy of the Musée d'Orsay, Paris. Acquit de l'artiste par l'État en 1870. (INV 20123).

Coral, 1971. Courtesy of the Louisiana State Museum, New Orleans, Jake and Kevin Thomas Collection, Accession No. 2015.046.01.

Captain Albert Carey as Volcano, 1971. Courtesy of the Louisiana State Museum, New Orleans, Jake and Kevin Thomas Collection, Accession No. 2015.046.01.

A Gala Evening 1972

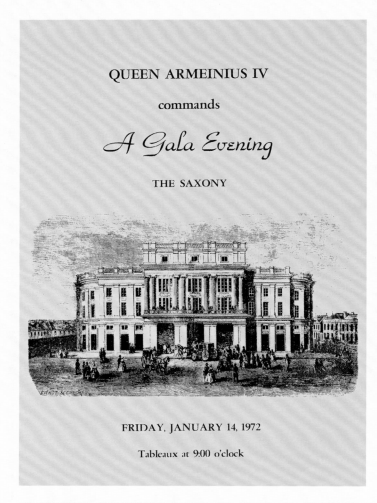

QUEEN ARMEINIUS IV

commands

A Gala Evening

THE SAXONY

FRIDAY, JANUARY 14, 1972

Tableaux at 9:00 o'clock

Program, 1972. The drawing on the cover depicts the French Opera House, or Théâtre de l'Opéra, one of the most iconic landmarks of New Orleans's past, destroyed by fire in 1919. Courtesy of the Louisiana State Museum, New Orleans, Accession No. 2014.005.15.

Inside reads: *The Krewe of Armeinius welcomes you to our fourth annual ball. Opera is music and drama wedded together. At its best, opera's grandeur can make the most incredible situations, characters, and even creatures seem perfectly real and believable to an audience. Unable to resist the challenge to recreate grandeur, we decided upon this theme for our ball. Tonight, the spectacle and the fantasy of opera become our gala evening. The Captain.*

Tableau 1972
Return of 1971 Court
    King Armeinius III
    Queen Armeinius III
Prologue
    Carmen (Bizet)—A Divertissement
    Die Frau Ohne Schatten (Strauss)—Lieutenant
    Snegourochka (Rimsky-Korsakov)—Captain
Snow Maiden on a Float
Tableaux, Act I
    L'Africaine (Meyerbeer)—Tornado
    Die Walküre (Wagner)
    Adriana Lecouvreur (Cilea)
    Die Zauberflöte (Mozart)
Entr'acte
    Madama Butterfly (Puccini)
Tableaux, Act II
    Les Contes d'Hoffmann (Offenbach)
    Parsifal (Wagner)
    Die Ägyptische Helena (Strauss)
    Prince Igor (Borodin)
Presentation of 1972 Court
    L'Étoile du Nord (Meyerbeer)—Queen Armeinius IV
    Boris Godunov (Mussorgsky)—King Armeinius IV
Grand March
    Aïda (Verdi)

Adrien Marie Persac, French Opera House, 1859–73. The etching reproduced on the program for the Krewe of Armeinius's *A Gala Evening* ball was based on Persac's drawing. Courtesy of The Historic New Orleans Collection, Williams Research Center, New Orleans, Accession No.1939.5.

Revelries of Titania's Court—An Evening with the Fairies 1973

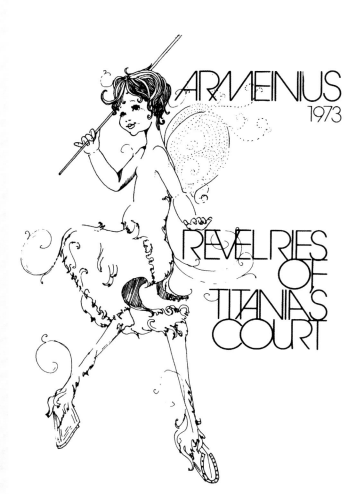

Invitation, 1973. Design by David Peltier. Courtesy of the Louisiana State Museum, New Orleans, Accession No. 2014.005.16.

Program reads: *While they waited for the arrival of the fairy queen, Titania, the fairies erected their silver dance pavilion, and assembled the fairy orchestra, who set to tuning the fairy instruments. You see, fairies are very sensible people, and when things don't seem to go just right, or they have nothing else to do, they spend their time in singing, dancing and laughing, instead of sitting down and wrinkling their brows and sighing sadly. So the fairies danced in their small pavilion hung with silver lights and illuminated inside by half a dozen or more well disposed fireflies, which sat on mushroom pedestals in the musicians' gallery.*

Tableau 1973
The Fairies
The Blue Fairy (Ball Captain)
Tinker Bell
The Fairy Truth
The Banshee
The Mermaid
The Nixie of the Mill Pond
Cinderella's Fairy Godmother
The Tooth Fairies
Glinda, the Good Witch of the North (Ball Lieutenant)
The Genie from Aladdin's Lamp
The Fairy of the Dawn
The Fairy Lagree in the Crystal Palace
The Flower Fairy
Man, Queen Mother to the Fairies
Titania, Queen of the Fairies
Oberon, King of the Fairies

Lilies of the Field 1974

Program, 1974. Design by David Peltier. Depicted in the field of lilies at the bottom of the invitation are (*left to right*) Captain Wendell Stipelcovich (*upper left*), Jon Lee Poché, Jules Weiss, Queen Albert Carey, and Don Stratton. Courtesy of the Louisiana State Museum, New Orleans, Accession No. 1995.010.024.

Tableau 1974
Lighting of the Crest—Ball Lieutenant
Lili Marlene (Captain)
Lili St. Cyr
Diamond Lil
Lili Liliuokalani
Lillian Russell
Lily Langtry
Tiger Lily
Lily Pons
Lily Dacha
Lillian Lorraine
Lillian Roth
The Gilded Lily—Queen Armeinius VI
King Armeinius VI

King Armeinius VI, Jack Vaughn, and captain, Wendell Stipelcovich, 1974. Courtesy of the Krewe of Armeinius and Wendell Stipelcovich.

Balls (Traditional Carnival Balls) 1975

Program, 1975. Courtesy of the Louisiana State Museum, New Orleans, Accession No Accession No. T0016.2001.115.

Inside reads: *Mardi Gras in New Orleans is composed of street pageants for the masses and masquerade balls for the chosen few. Tonight, you are the chosen few. Join us as we celebrate the private side of Mardi Gras, the masquerade ball. In the spirit and tradition of the Mardi Gras season, the Krewe of Armeinius honors the New Orleans Carnival captains and their krewes.*

⚜

Tableau 1975
The National Anthem
The Captain's Whistle
The Royal Court of 1974
    King and Queen Armeinius VI
Royal Crest of Armeinius
Krewe of Shangri-La
Krewe of Iris
The Royal Court of 1975
    Atlanteans
    Alhambra
    Prophets of Persia
    Jupiter
    Moslem
    Diana
    Pandora
    Helios
    Zulu
    Bacchus
    Daughters of Eve
    Bal Masqué
Her Royal Majesty, Queen Armeinius VII—Jewels of Comus
Selection of King Armeinius VII—Final Tribute to Carnival
Honored Guests Received by Their Majesties
Captain's Award
The Grand March
Call-Out Dances
Open Court
General Dancing until 1:00 a.m.

Returning Queen Armeinius VI, Albert Carey, and Returning King Armeinius VI, Jack Vaughn, 1975. Courtesy of the Louisiana State Museum, New Orleans, Jake and Kevin Thomas Collection, Accession No. 2015.046.01.

Queen Armeinius VII, Jon Lee Poché, as the Jewels of Comus, 1975. Courtesy of the Louisiana State Museum, New Orleans, Jake and Kevin Thomas Collection, Accession No. 2015.046.01.

Girls of the Golden West 1977

Invitation, 1977. Courtesy of the Louisiana State Museum, New Orleans, Accession No. T0016.2001.936.

Inside reads: *The days of the Wild West! A glorious period of man's hand-to-hand struggle with the untamable elements. The mere mention evokes visions of pitted strength—barroom brawls, cattle stampedes, shootouts and ambushes, virile struggles and honorable deaths—men everywhere! What these visions all too easily overlook is the unexciting but crucial side of life in the Wild West—the little woman by the hearth mending socks, baking bread, keeping her little house on the prairie. Tonight Armeinius pays a long-neglected tribute to these gentle ladies. The Krewe of Armeinius presents its 1977 Ball, The Girls of the Golden West.*

⚜

Tableau 1977
Prelude—The Return of King and Queen Armeinius VIII
Setting the Scene—The Captain's Dance Hall
Girls (and Boys)
The Ball Captain as Belle Starr
The Ball Lieutenant as Adah Isaacs Menken
The Golden Girls
Miss Kitty
The Dolly Sisters
Klondike Kate
Annie Oakley
Baby Doe
Dakota Lil
Lily Langtry
Lola Montez
Texas Guinan
Calamity Jane
Molly Brown
Queen Armeinius IX as La Fanciulla del West
The Golden Girl's Dream—King Armeinius IX

Among Our Souvenirs 1978

Program, 1978. Design by David Peltier. Courtesy of the Louisiana State Museum, New Orleans, Accession No. 1995.010.013.

Tableau 1978

The Return of Their Highnesses King and Queen Armeinius IX

The Captain, as That Great Star of the Hippodrome, Natasha Zinzinndorfer, Reminisces Fondly on Her Souvenirs of That Thrilling Era

First Reverie: The Scintillating Excitement of the Circus
  1. The Ball Lieutenant, Ms. Nungesser, and Her Parade of Prancing Poodles
  2. The Master of Side-Show Magicians: Houdidim the Great
  3. A Classical Clown [Italianate]: Pagliachoo

Second Reverie: Athletic Adventures of the Aquacade
  1. Fabulous Filigree of Funky Fishiness
  2. Water Sports of Bubbling Beauty
  3. A Kaleidoscope of Colorful Kinky Kelp

Third Reverie: Toe-Dancing at Its Greatest—The Ballet
  1. Our Corpse de Ballet—The Sugarplum You-Know-Whats
  2. Russia's Finest, Igor Igotscha, as the Nutcracker
  3. From Sleeping Beauty—Dame Rita Fontyn [as Her Mother]
  4. Fabulous Flaming Flurry from the Firebird

Fourth Reverie: Flirtations from the Follies
  1. Prelude—A Glittering Burst of Night and Day
  2. Robyn Gayfeather—As Sweet Simpering Spring
  3. Alice Landrieu de la Houssaye—As Serendipitous Summer
  4. Princess Fawn Yellowleaf—As Audacious Autumn
  5. Stella Stevens Snowflake—As Wondrous Winter

Queen Armeinius X—As the Follies' Queen for All Seasons

The Crowning of King Armeinius

Do You Know What It Means to Miss New Orleans? 1979

Invitation, 1979. Design by David Peltier. Courtesy of the Krewe of Armeinius and David Peltier.

Tableau 1979
St. Louis Cathedral
Storyville
Bourbon Pub
Studio Jules
Brennan's
Pharmacy Museum
Mama DiRosa's House
Halberdahl Mansion
Messina's
Buster Holmes's
French Market
Voodoo Museum
Ursuline Convent
Antoine's
809 Club
500 Club
Orleans Ballroom
Le Patio Royale

Admit card, 1979. Design by David Peltier. Courtesy of the Krewe of Armeinius.

MGM Movie's Greatest Moments 1980

Program, 1980. Courtesy of the Louisiana State Museum, New Orleans, Accession No. T0016.2001.129.

Tableau 1980
Overture—Movies Were Movies
Frankie Mann Orchestra
Introducing
    Ball Lieutenant—Cleopatra
    Ball Captain—Marc Anthony
The Wizard of Oz
    Munchkins
    The Witch
    The Wizard
Gone with the Wind
    The Burning of Atlanta
    Scarlett O'Hara
The Ten Commandments
    Moses Passing through the Red Sea
And God Created Woman
    The Epitome of Womanhood
Salute to the Magical World of Disney
    Cinderella
    Fantasia—Trip to Bald Mountain
Barbarella
    Barbarella and the Angel
The Great Ziegfeld
    The Ziegfeld Girls
Flying down to Rio
    Carnival Time in Rio
Salute to the Cult Movies
    Divine and Dr. Frank N. Furter
Mame
    Mame
My Fair Lady
Her Majesty, Queen Armeinius XII
Search for King Armeinius XII
Presentation of Captain's Award
Receiving of Royal Guests
The Grand March
Open Court

Krewe of Armeinius

1981 Bal Masque

All That Glitters

Saturday, February 28, 1981

Theatre of the Performing Arts • New Orleans, Louisiana

Program, 1981. Courtesy of the Krewe of Armeinius and Wendell Stipelcovich.

Tableau 1981
The Returns
   King Armeinius XII
   Queen Armeinius XII
The Captain—Hollywood
The Ball Lieutenant—A Rhinestone Cowboy
An Orchid Corsage
Broadway
Blackglama Mink
Vegas
Sterling Silver
Ballet
Mardi Gras
Fireworks
Crystal
Christmas
King Armeinius XIII—Solar Majesty
Queen Armeinius XIII—Lunar Majesty

Un Soir Enchanté à Le Lido de Paris 1982

Program, 1982. Courtesy of the Krewe of Armeinius and Wendell Stipelcovich.

Tableau 1982
One—Les Femmes du Lido
    The French Tarts
    The Bird of Paradise
    The Fountain of Versailles
    Pink Perfection
    The Tiger Lily
    A Special Guest—Josephine Baker
Two—Les Amis d'Armeinius
    Medusa (Ball Lieutenant)
    Pegasus
    Narcissus
    Armeinius
    Pan
    Gifts of the Gods—Nectar and Ambrosia
    The Unicorn
Three—La Forêt Enchantée
    Merlin's Enchanted Tree
    Merlin
    Morgan le Fay
    The Siren
    The Dragon
    The Lady of the Lake
    The Black Knight
King and Queen Armeinius XIV

Great Disasters of the Western World 1983

Program, 1983. Design by David Peltier. Courtesy of the Krewe of Armeinius and Howard Philips Smith.

Tableau 1983
The Hagenbeck Wallace Circus Train Wreck 1918
El Gran Circo Norte Americano 1961
The Galveston Horror 1900
The Chicago Fire 1871
The San Francisco Earthquake 1906
The Sam Jackson Fireworks Manufactory Explosion 1862
Two Thousand Ladies Burned to Death 1857
Twisters, Twisters Everywhere 1884
Vesuvius 1944
Tsunami 1960
The Johnstown Flood 1888
The Crash of the Hindenburg 1937
The Black Death 1348
Landslides in Rio 1967
Mass Asphyxiation 1944
The Deluge 2400 B.C.
The King is Dead 1985
The Blizzard of '88 1888
The Sinking of the Titanic 1912

I Never Met a Cunt I Didn't Like 1984

Program, 1984. Design by Charles Kerbs. Courtesy of The Historic New Orleans Collection, Williams Research Center, New Orleans, Accession No. 1984.46.4.

Tableau 1984
All Is Vanity
An Exercise in Poor Taste—The Captain
In the Beginning
    Mother Nature
    Eve
    Salomé
Evils of the East
    Empress Wu
    Mata Hari
    Tokyo Rose
Birds of a Feather
    The Harpies
Your Kisses Take Me to Chalmette
You Oughta Be in Pictures
    Elizabeth Taylor as Cleopatra
    Shirley Temple, Black
Let 'Em Eat Cake
    Marquise de Pompadour
    Comptesse du Barry
    Marie Antoinette
Diamonds Are Forever
    Pauline Borghese
Only Make Believe
    Queen of Hearts
    Duchess of Uganda
    Princess Thunderpussy
Hits and Misses
    Hecate
    Pope Joan
    Evita
Vanity Is Pride—Caligula
Venus Incarnate—Messalin

The Boy Who Would Be Queen 1985

Invitation, 1985. Design by David Peltier. Courtesy of Tulane University, Louisiana Research Collection, Howard-Tilton Memorial Library, New Orleans, Otto Stierle Collection, Manuscripts Collection 902.

Program reads: *Once upon a time, in the days when the fairies lived, there was a beautiful young prince who was both innocent, and gay. He lived in a fairy tale castle surrounded by lush green meadows and the bluest of lakes, and he wanted to be a Queen. This is his story. Come with us now and hear his wish. Meet the Fairy Dragmother. Follow his trek. See the many wonderful creatures along the way. And finally, witness his dream come true.*

⚜

Tableau 1985
Royal Heralds
The Great Poobah (King Armeinius XVI)
Le Grand Poop (Queen Armeinius XVI)
Oleander, the Ugly Stepsister
Andrew's Dream—The Crystal Palace
Star Dears
Fairy Dragmother
Wizard of the Weather Vane
Shrine of the Pink Virgin
Old Man River
Wicked Witch of the West Bank
Good Fairy Canal
Good Fairy Estalauda
Dragon's Graveyard
The Terrible Tiger
Geenie of the Green Weenie
The Black Elf, Cutch
Flo, the Flower Fairy
The Talisman
WASPS
Evil Emperor of the House of Lee
Banshee from Bucktown
Magic Starfish
Sir Gregory the Gay—As the Enchanted Crab

Black Ball 1986

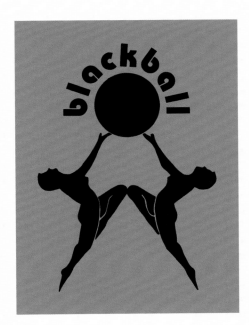

Invitation, 1986. Courtesy of The Historic New Orleans Collection, Williams Research Center, New Orleans, Accession No. 1986.156.6. Gift of Tracy Hendrix.

⚜

Tableau 1986
Blackglama
Black Russians—Queen and King Armeinius XVII
The Creature from the Black Lagoon—Captain
Black-Eyed Susans
The Black Diamond—Ball Lieutenant
The Black Sea
The Bride Wore Black
Black Pearls
Black Hawk
Black Sabbath
Black Comedy
The Black Forest
Black Mamba
The Black Queen
The Little Black Dress
Black, in Italian
Black Supremacy
Black Gold
The Black Widow
Black Sheep
Black Orpheus
The Black Madonna
The Black Hole—Queen and King Armeinius XVIII

Invitation, 1988. Design by Danny Ourso. Courtesy of The Historic New Orleans Collection, Williams Research Center, New Orleans, Accession No. 2000.34.18.

Winter Follies 1989

Poster, 1989. Design by Danny Ourso. Courtesy of the Krewe of Armeinius and Wendell Stipelcovich.

Tableau 1989
Return of King and Queen Armeinius XX
Ice Capades—Captain
Fire and Ice—Ball Lieutenant
Siberian Express
Snowflakes
Icicles
Blizzards
French Alps
Snow Bird
Unicorns
Snow Maiden
Winter Knight
Lagniappe
Poinsettias
Japanese Magnolias
Christmas Rose
White Christmas
Northern Lights
Winter Harvest
Winter Carnival
Winter Art
Winter Solstice—King and Queen Armeinius XXI

Wendell Stipelcovich as the Winter Knight, 1989. Courtesy of the Krewe of Armeinius and Wendell Stipelcovich.

Ball Lieutenant Glen Plauché as Fire and Ice, 1989. Courtesy of the Krewe of Armeinius and Wendell Stipelcovich.

Kellie Hyatt Gironda, Winter Forest sketch for Winter Harvest or Winter Art costume, 1989. Courtesy of the Louisiana State Museum, New Orleans, Accession No. 2015.054.1.

The Master's Touch 1990

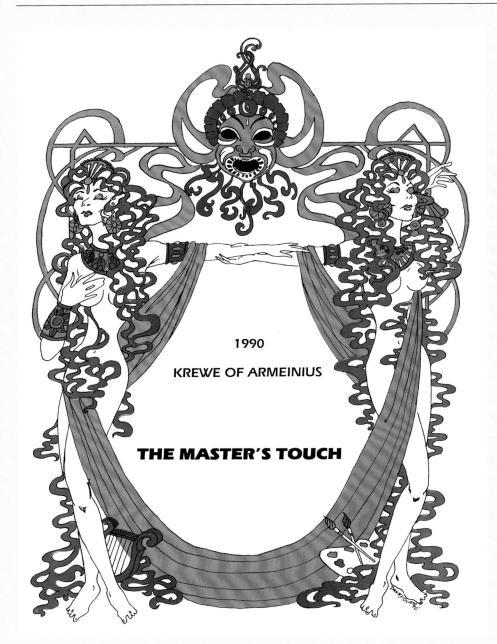

1990

KREWE OF ARMEINIUS

THE MASTER'S TOUCH

Invitation, 1990. Design by Danny Ourso. Courtesy of The Historic New Orleans Collection, Williams Research Center, New Orleans, Accession No. 2000.34.19.

Tableau 1990
Welcome
National Anthem
Returning Queen Armeinius XXI
Returning King Armeinius XXI
Choreography
    Ball Captain
    Musical Extravaganza
    Ball Lieutenant
Movies
    George Lucas
    Jerome Robbins and Robert Wise
Broadway
    Frank Loesser and Abe Burrows
    Richard Rodgers and Oscar Hammerstein
Opera
    Georges Bizet
Literature
    William Shakespeare
    Jules Verne
Art
    Michelangelo Buonarroti
Ballet
    Peter Ilyich Tchaikovsky
    Igor Stravinsky
Fashion
    Bob Mackie
    Coco Chanel
    Erté
Sculpture
    Auguste Rodin
King and Queen Armeinius XXII
Presentations

I Write the Songs 1991

Invitation, 1991. Design by Danny Ourso. Courtesy of The Historic New Orleans Collection, Williams Research Center, New Orleans, Accession No. 2000.34.21.

Tableau 1991
Welcome
National Anthem
Returning Queen Armeinius XXII
Returning King Armeinius XXII
Jules Styne—Captain
Alan Jay Lerner—Ball Lieutenant
Harry Tierney
Hugh Martin and Ralph Blane
Richard Rogers and Oscar Hammerstein
Cole Porter
Carole B. Sager
Martin Charnin
Jerry Herman
George M. Cohan
Vincent Yumans
Harry Warren
Richard Adler and Jerry Ross
Jerry Bock
Stephen Sondheim
Mark Charlap
Andrew Lloyd Webber
Irving Berlin—King and Queen Armeinius XXIII (White Christmas)
Presentations
Open Court

Danny Ourso, costume design for King Armeinius XXIII, J. Bruce Orgeron Jr., as Happy Holidays, 1991. Courtesy of the Louisiana State Museum, New Orleans, Accession No. 2015.045.1.01.

Tarot 1992

Reflections—Twenty-Fifth Anniversary Ball 1993

Commemorative poster, 1992. Design by David Peltier. Courtesy of the Krewe of Armeinius and David Peltier.

Invitation, 1993. Courtesy of the Louisiana State Museum, New Orleans, Jake and Kevin Thomas Collection, Accession No. 2015.046.01.

Danny Ourso, costume design for J. Bruce Orgeron Jr. as the Pearl, 1993. Courtesy of the Louisiana State Museum, New Orleans, Accession No. 2015.045.1.03.

A Renaissance Festival 1994

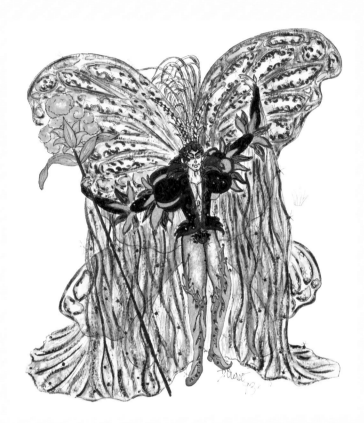

Invitation, 1994. Design by Danny Ourso. Courtesy of The Historic New Orleans Collection, Williams Research Center, New Orleans, Accession No. 1994.79.2. Gift of Tracy Hendrix.

Danny Ourso, costume design for J. Bruce Orgeron Jr. as Oberon, King of the Fairies, 1994. Courtesy of J. Bruce Orgeron Jr.

Oh, No—Not Her (The Scarlet Ball) 1996

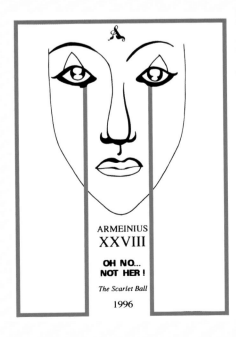

Invitation, 1996. Courtesy of The Historic New Orleans Collection, Williams Research Center, New Orleans, Accession No. 2000.34.29.

The Barbara Ball 1997

Invitation, 1997. Courtesy of The Historic New Orleans Collection, Williams Research Center, New Orleans, Accession No. 2000.34.32.

⚜

Tableau 1997
The Captain—Malibu Barbie
Barbie on TV
Jet Set Barbie
Barbie in Paradise
PMS Barbie
Barbie in a Bottle
Miss California Barbie
Desert Storm Barbie
The Ball Lieutenant—G.I. Joe
Spaced-Out Barbie
Cub Scout Ken
Barbie's Dream House
Frigid Barbie
King Armeinius XXIX
Queen Armeinius XXIX

The Flower Ball 1998

J. Bruce Orgeron Jr., costume sketch for Black-Eyed Susans or Railroad Daisies, 1998. Courtesy of the Louisiana State Museum, New Orleans, Accession No. 2015.045.1.08.

The Blue Ball 1999

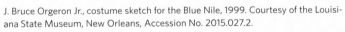

J. Bruce Orgeron Jr., costume sketch for the Blue Nile, 1999. Courtesy of the Louisiana State Museum, New Orleans, Accession No. 2015.027.2.

The Russian Ball 2000

Invitation, 2000. Courtesy of J. Bruce Orgeron Jr.

Returning King Armeinius XXXI, Vinnie Pervel, 2000. Courtesy of J. Bruce Orgeron Jr.

Queen Armeinius XXXII, J. Bruce Orgeron Jr., 2000. Courtesy of J. Bruce Orgeron Jr.

Remembrances of Things Past 2003

Armeinius Goes Looney 2004

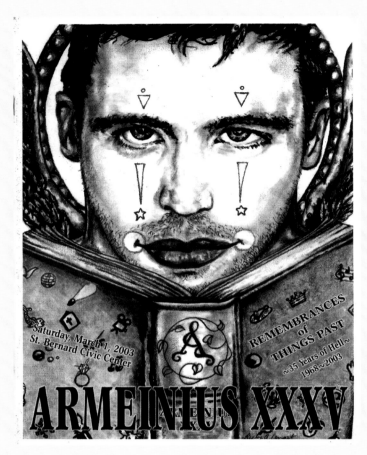

Commemorative poster, 2003. Design by Ricky Lenart. Courtesy of the Louisiana State Museum, New Orleans, Jake and Kevin Thomas Collection, Accession No. 2015.046.01.

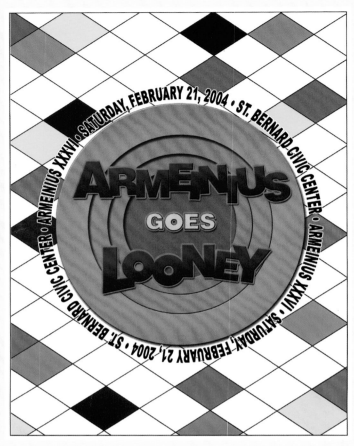

Invitation, 2004. Courtesy of J. Bruce Orgeron Jr.

Tableau 2004
National Anthem
Introduction of M.M.
Ball Dedication
Returning Royalty XXXV
Captain as That Crazy Rabbit Bugs
PU Peppy Pé Lepue
A Twisted Peppermint
That Arab and Clyde
George???
Puffs of Smoke
The Bad Boys
Purple Horney Eater
M.I.C.
The Hen House
Tweet-Tweet-Tweet
Teeny Weeney
Tooty Frooty
Queen Armeinius XXXVI
King Armeinius XXXVI
Presentations
Open Court

The Bug Ball 2005

Joel Haas, sketch for Firefly costume, 2005. This costume won Best Costume Award at the Bourbon Street Awards. Courtesy of the Louisiana State Museum, New Orleans, Accession No. 2015.056.

The Gay Ball 2006

Invitation, 2006. German Nazis forced homosexuals to wear pink triangles during the 1930s and 1940s; in the 1970s, however, the symbol was reappropriated as an emblem of gay power. Courtesy of J. Bruce Orgeron Jr.

Pirates, Prisoners, Prostitutes, and Pigs 2007

Invitation, 2007. Courtesy of the Krewe of Armeinius and Wendell Stipelcovich.

Tableau 2007
The Captain's Whistle
National Anthem
The Return of Their Royal Majesties, King and Queen Armeinius XXXVIII
Pirates!
The Bitchy Barataria Buccaneers of Bayou Segnette
The Captain as Myth
The Ball Lieutenant as Folklore
Exotic Creatures
Fabulous Fauna
Make Believe
Prisoners!
Ooh La La!
Prostitutes!
Scarlet Woman
Pigs!
Katrina!
Bianca!
Their Royal Majesties, King and Queen Armeinius XXXIX
Presentation of Special Guests to the Throne
Open Court

There's Something about Mary 2009

"MARY KAY"

Joel Haas, costume sketch for Mary Kay, 2009. Courtesy of the Louisiana State Museum, New Orleans, Accession No. 2015.045.1.30.

"MARY ANN"

Joel Haas, costume sketch for Mary Ann, 2009. Courtesy of the Louisiana State Museum, New Orleans, Accession No. 2015.045.1.35.

Makin' Groceries 2012

Captain J. Bruce Orgeron Jr. as Salt, 2012. Courtesy of the Louisiana State Museum, New Orleans, Accession No. 2015.045.5.12.

J. Bruce Orgeron Jr., costume sketch for Salt, 2012. Courtesy of the Louisiana State Museum, New Orleans, Accession No. 2015.045.1.67.

Oh Captain, My Captain 2013

Bal du Blanche 2014

Original artwork for the program and invitation, 2013. Queen of Armeinius Fredrick Guess was depicted painting himself as Scarlett O'Hara, based on Norman Rockwell's *Triple Self-Portrait*. Courtesy of Fredrick Guess.

Invitation, 2014. Courtesy of the Krewe of Armeinius and Wendell Stipelcovich.

Clarence Jackson (Ms. Ebony), 2014. Photograph by Barrett Delong-Church.

Co-king J. Bruce Orgeron Jr. with attendant, 2014. Photograph by Zachary Mason Krevitt.

Albert Carey, 2014. Photograph by Zachary Mason Krevitt.

Queen Armeinius XLVI, Chris Leonard (Summer Rayne), 2014. Photograph by Zachary Mason Krevitt.

Albert Carey, 2014. Photograph by Zachary Mason Krevitt.

The Architecture Ball 2015

Fredrick Guess, costume design for Roman Aqueduct, 2015. The architect cited in the program was Petronius Satyricon Vernaculus. Courtesy of the Louisiana State Museum, New Orleans, Jake and Kevin Thomas Collection, Accession No. 2015.046.31.

Program detail, 2015. Courtesy of Howard Philips Smith.

Bob Rooney-Leftwich as Petronius Satyricon Vernaculus and the Roman Aqueduct, 2015. Photograph by Barrett Delong-Church.

Clarence Jackson as the Tropicana Hotel in Las Vegas, 2015. Photograph by Barrett Delong-Church.

Beauty and the Beast 2016

Program, 2016. Design by Fredrick Guess from his original painting. Courtesy of the Krewe of Armeinius and Fredrick Guess.

Fredrick Guess, costume sketch for Esmeralda, 2016. Courtesy of Fredrick Guess.

Queen Armeinius XLVIII, John Peifer, and King Armeinius XLVIII, Scott Spivey, as Beauty and the Beast, 2016. Photograph by Michael Bingham.

Cocaptains Albert Carey and Fredrick Guess as the Fairy Godmothers, 2016. Photograph by Brian J. Plauché, BPNOLa Photographs.

Spider costume designed and worn by Josh Arnouville, 2016. Photograph by Brian J. Plauché, BPNOLa Photographs.

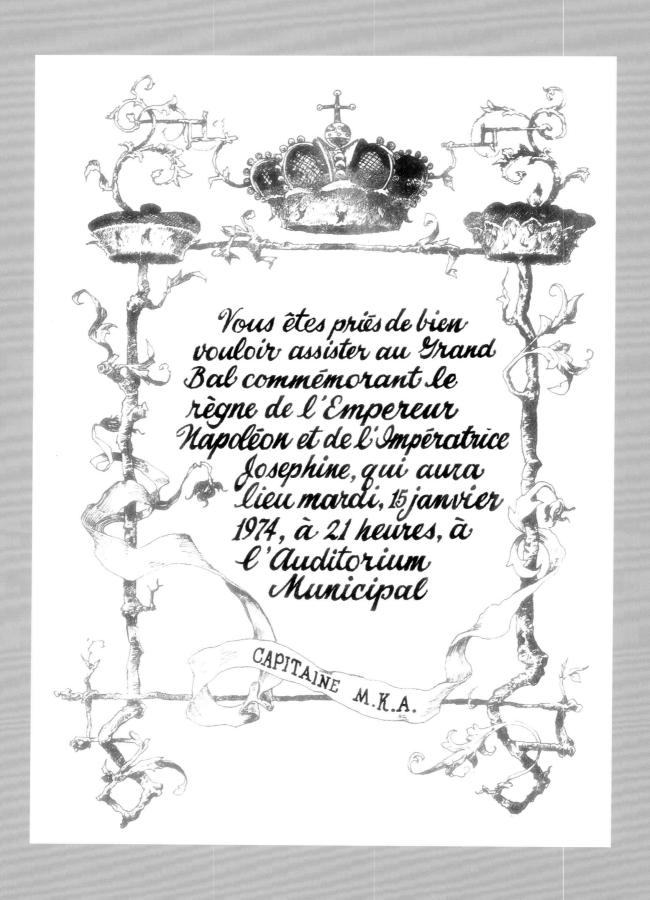

Vous êtes priés de bien
vouloir assister au Grand
Bal commémorant le
règne de l'Empereur
Napoléon et de l'Impératrice
Josephine, qui aura
lieu mardi, 15 janvier
1974, à 21 heures, à
l'Auditorium
Municipal

CAPITAINE M.K.A.

I was just a little boy, but I was there
when my dad and his friends first met to
form the Mystic Krewe of Apollo. Those
memories will live with me forever. It was
the magic of Carnival.

—D'Lon Dobson, Son of Roland Dobson

The Sun God

The ancient Roman god Apollo, known for his striking beauty and physical perfection, was a favorite among the gay krewes as well as an iconic reference in the gay male community. Recognized as the god of light and the sun, music and poetry, Apollo was often depicted by sculptors as the quintessential male physique. In addition, he was the patron god of the Muses, who gave their names to a series of street names in Uptown New Orleans. Revered in European art throughout the Renaissance, Apollo was also a special favorite of King Louis XIV of France, who portrayed the god at Versailles in many dances and tableaux by one of the early creators of French opera, Jean-Baptiste Lully, infamous even at that time as a sodomite.

The Captain as High Priest

The Mystic Krewe of Apollo was founded in 1969 by Roland Edward Dobson; his partner, Billy Langford; and their close friend, Joseph Talluto Jr. Having left his home town of Bogalusa, Dobson arrived in New Orleans in the early 1960s. He quickly ingratiated himself into the upper echelons of society and married a wealthy Uptown matron. He was seen as a Svengali figure who cured the invalid woman of her infirmities, allowing her to walk after having been confined to a wheelchair for years. He was a savvy businessman and joined the prestigious Krewe of Endymion early in the 1970s. Endymion was relatively new at that time and was one of the better-known nouveau riche straight krewes, and most of its members, like Dobson,

Invitation to the Mystic Krewe of Apollo's *Les Amours d'Apollon* ball, 1974. Courtesy of The Historic New Orleans Collection, Williams Research Center, New Orleans, Accession No. 1980.178.333. Gift of Tracy Hendrix.

Roland Dobson, founder of the Mystic Krewe of Apollo, as king of a straight krewe, early 1970s. Courtesy of D'Lon Dobson.

were businessmen. He was king of Endymion in 1973—after he had created the Mystic Krewe of Apollo—revealing how easily he moved back and forth between the straight world and the hidden gay one. In addition, he served as king of the Krewe of Noblads in 1972 and the Krewe of Shangri-La in 1976, both traditional all-female krewes. He was also a member of the Krewes of Eros and Alpheus. Many of these exquisite crowns and scepters worn by Dobson ended up in Apollo balls worn by Apollo royalty. Albert Carey of the Krewe of Armeinius recalled that as king of Endymion, when Dobson's float turned down the gay section of Rampart Street en route to the Municipal Auditorium, "he threw out tons of colorfully dyed feathers—bagful after bagful. They covered the street, and since it was raining the street became dyed as well. It took months for it to disappear. After that, according to more than one source, Dobson was booted out of Endymion for good."

Dobson's determination and acumen made him a well-known public figure, establishing New Orleans's first men's fashion house, the Salon de Roland, at 2125 St. Charles Avenue. His boutique catered to the city's elite, selling custom-designed suits at more than eight hundred dollars each. He wrote articles for local publications that not only instructed men on how to dress but elucidated the new fashion trends. He always appeared at social functions with a beautiful woman at his side, yet he was also active in the gay community and designed tableau balls for Apollo during the 1970s and 1980s.

In a 1973 *Washington Post* article, Sally Quinn summed up his vast influence: "This year Roland, at age 35, was king of four balls, turned down invitations to be king at two others, turned down countless dukedoms and is the captain of the Mystic Krewe of Apollo, the 'it' gay ball of New Orleans." The article showcased the diversity of Mardi Gras in New Orleans and frankly discussed the gay krewes: "The gay groups have been readily accepted in the community as a colorful part of the Mardi Gras but there is still some snickering among the old timers." Continued Quinn, "But if there's one thing Roland hates, it's bad taste. That's why he and a group of 'upper class' friends, mostly business and professional men, started Apollo five years ago. It's held at the Municipal Auditorium, where all the good 'straight' white balls are held, the floor is carpeted white, the format is the same, with carefully screened invitations, white tie, call-outs for the court, coronation of the king and queen and presentation of debutantes. The only difference is that they're all men."

The Municipal Auditorium and Legitimacy

One of the most creative and dramatic showmen within the gay demimonde, Dobson pounced when the Krewe of Alpheus folded, securing for Apollo Alpheus's former slot at the Municipal Auditorium on the Thursday night before Shrove Tuesday. Recalled Dan Romero, King Apollo XIII, "Roland's clever. Very clever. He bought the charter to Alpheus that was fading out. And he retained their night at the Municipal Auditorium and put Apollo in its place." Prior to Alpheus's demise, Apollo held two balls at the Monteleone Hotel in the French Quarter. Gay krewes in general had found it difficult to secure venues for their balls, but Dobson had the social standing and cachet to get his krewe in the door.

Never one to conform to norms even in the realm of gay Carnival, Dobson, as Apollo's permanent ball captain, created tableaux that hearkened back to the traditional krewes. He displayed royalty in their proper places on stage, seated on grandiose thrones in magnificent raiments of white and gold. At the height of the ball, young men paraded around the stage in drag, making their debut in high gay society, much as female debutantes did at straight balls. Dobson continued to adhere to this strict formula even as the tableaux presented by the other krewes became more and more extravagant and fantastical. Dobson was one of the last southern gentlemen, with a generally genteel and soft-spoken demeanor that coexisted with strong captain's hand and an insistence on perfection. When asked about the other gay krewes, Dobson once said, "They're just fiascoes. They get bad, dear, really bad. The ladies don't even wear long kid gloves."

Franchises

Always the innovator, Dobson franchised his krewe in other southern cities and initially served as the franchises' captain to make sure his standards were met. Thus Mystic Krewes of Apollo were formed in Baton Rouge, Birmingham, Dallas, Lafayette, Memphis, Mobile, and Shreveport, and many continue to hold elaborate Carnival balls.

Movie Madness

The first Apollo ball was held at the Monteleone Hotel's Century Ballroom on February 8, 1970, with the ornate invitation promising a "Night of High Revel." Dobson transformed the space into a glittery realm of golds and ecrus, a grand backdrop for his *Movie Madness*. Following the appearance of the Apollo crest and the captain's whistle was a short procession of costumed characters from a series of movies: *What Ever Happened to Baby Jane?*, *Midnight Cowboy*, *The Singing Nun*, and *How the West Was Won*. Dobson then appeared in his white finery as the captain of the Mystic Krewe of Apollo, followed closely by the debutantes—the lovely maids of the court from *The Birds*, *Hello Dolly!*, *20,000 Leagues under the Sea*, *Gone with the Wind*, *My Fair Lady*, *Gypsy*, *Auntie Mame*, and *What's New Pussycat?* King and Queen Apollo I appeared in white bejeweled costumes to conduct the Grand March. Glyce DiMiceli, brother of Diane DiMiceli, later founder of the lesbian Krewe of Ishtar, was the first king of the krewe. His queen was the notorious Daisy Mae (Kenneth Toncrey). After the court had their call-out dances, the guests danced until one in the morning.

King and Queen Apollo—Shreveport I, 1987. The success of this krewe in Shreveport resulted in the formation of several straight krewes, including Gemini (1989) and Centaur (1991), and contributed to the revival of Carnival there. Courtesy of the Louisiana State Museum, New Orleans, Accession No. 2015.052.3.

Descent into Hell and From Russia with Love

Devils and demons, especially on their thrones in hell, have long held a certain fascination for those with a penchant for the carnivalesque. The Mistick Krewe of Comus's first 1857 tableau featured the *Demon Actors in Milton's Paradise Lost*. A float for the Krewe of Proteus parade *The Alphabet* had for the letter *L* a gigantic horned Lucifer with a flaming red mantle and stark bat wings on the verge of throwing a pitchfork from the rising flames of hell. The Krewe of Nereus also used hell as a backdrop for its 1898 ball, *The Inferno*. In keeping with this tradition, the Mystic Krewe of Apollo's 1971 *Descent into Hell* ball elaborated on this theme, with

Orpheus descending into the netherworld before the gates of hell. The bright-red invitation and poster had demonic figures drawn with yellow-orange lines, as if burning. The finale reunited Orpheus, the son of Apollo, with Eurydice, crowning them King and Queen Apollo II. In 1972, the *From Russia with Love* ball became the first gay ball to be held at the Municipal Auditorium. Invitations were oversized Fabergé eggs with ornate depictions of the king and queen, who compelled whosoever received this royal announcement to attend. The ball re-created Imperial Russia, with Tsar Nicholas II and Tsarina Alexandra Feodorovna holding court for one last evening at the Winter Palace. As the Frankie Mann Orchestra played a jazzy tune to accompany the season's debutantes, a gigantic three-dimensional Fabergé egg slowly descended onto the stage, covered in sequins and glitter. The egg split in half, and out jumped Dobson in a white tuxedo. The egg's interior had been covered with tiny mirrors, creating a blaze of light.

B. A. Wikstrom, float design for the Krewe of Proteus Parade, 1904, The *L* is for Lucifer, a reference point for many similar ball themes. Courtesy of Tulane University, Louisiana Research Collection, Howard-Tilton Memorial Library, New Orleans.

Fifth Anniversary Ball and Beyond

For the fifth anniversary ball, *Les Amours d'Apollon* (1974), an elaborately costumed Napoleon and Josephine reigned over a beautifully sophisticated court, with Dobson introducing each costume entirely in French. With its gold emblems and crowns and its text in French, the invitation, too, recalled the lavish court of the Sun King. In 1976, the krewe went *To the Realms of Outer Space.* After the presentations of the debutantes, various costumes represented the Planets of the Bird People, Fire People, Flower People, Cobra People, Dragon People, Mermaids, Tree People, Hair People, and the Apes. The 1977 tableau presented the *Fair, Fair Ladies of Chartres Street.* Based on Christopher Stanislas Blake's short stories set in the French Quarter at Spring Fiesta time, the tableau featured Liva Hautcourt, Psyche Dearborn, and Millicent Keller, among others. A portion of the ball appeared in a segment on a *Saturday Night Live* special covering the Krewe of Bacchus parade—the first time the world was allowed to glimpse the hidden world of gay Carnival. Actress Cindy Williams (Shirley of *Laverne and Shirley*) described the queen's costume in whispers as "a floor-length gold silk gown with cathedral train and chiffon overlay encrusted and bejeweled with silver and amber on gold with a collar of pheasant feathers." The New Leviathan Oriental Fox Trot Orchestra, featuring local artist George Schmidt, performed "Rebecca Came Back from Mecca." Among those in attendance at the ball was Christine Jorgensen, "who had made international headlines with her sex change surgery in 1951." At the end of the ball, royalty from other chapters of the Mystic Krewe of Apollo were honored, as were members of the local chapter of the lesbian civil rights organization Daughters of Bilitis.

Sheet music for "Rebecca Came Back from Mecca," a popular song in the Oriental Foxtrot style written by Bert Kalmar and Harry Ruby in 1921.

The Short-Lived Golden Age

For its 1983 ball, the krewe went back to the beginning of biblical time with *Genesis Revisited.* The Gay Men's Chorus opened the ball with the krewe's anthem, *Mighty Apollo.* The returning king appeared as a pharaoh, in gold costume and headdress, while the returning queen and her four debutante attendants appeared all in white. Captain Roland Dobson appeared in his signature white tuxedo, with flourishes of pink and black, along with his attendant in a very convincing gorilla costume. After Heavy Rain and Wind, Lightning, and the Tree of Life, a dazzling Firebird appeared, covered with red and yellow feathers and with a wingspan of more than ten feet. Next came a Merman, whose scales were green jewels; lovely Grapes; and Music, a blue-sequined figure carrying a wand bearing a small beglittered piano. After the frozen Ice Castle and Three-Headed Monster, a Spiderwoman with webbed arms and dyed ostrich feathers and a Centaur with cloven hooves paraded together across the stage. Then, in rapid succession, the Marquis de Sade, Adam, Eve, and the Serpent pranced about. Finally, Dobson escorted King and Queen Apollo XIV to their silvered and sequined thrones.

Kevin Keller and a Dedication to Gay Carnival

Kevin Keller was the queen for the fifteenth annual ball in 1984, reigning in an exquisite white gown that was trimmed with white rhinestones and had a bodice and collar covered with silver sequins and edged with gemstones. Keller's king was Russell Talluto, brother of Joseph Talluto Jr., who also designed most of the invitations and posters. His deft hand had created a signature style for the club, recalling languid figures from French historical paintings. As King and Queen Apollo XV called out the costumes for the Grand March, one of the maids was Rowena, a notable female impersonator and former queen of Apollo. She appeared as a Greek nymph, with a beautiful white taffeta gown that featured a diaphanous train, and she toasted all around her with her oversized golden goblet. Rowena also served as the captain of the Krewe of Petronius, evidence of the frequent crossover between krewes. Keller, too, later joined the Krewe of Armeinius and was involved with several other krewes. He saved invitations, programs, and other ephemera and later donated them to local museums, helping to preserve the history of these events.

Queen Apollo XV, Kevin Keller, *Memories of Apollo (Fifteenth Anniversary Ball)*, 1984. Photograph by Peggy Stewart Studios. Courtesy of the Louisiana State Museum, New Orleans, Accession No. 2005.078.6.11.

The AIDS Years

Terry Thomas was chosen queen the following year, when the Mystic Krewe of Apollo hosted the *International Ball* (1985) on Valentine's Day. Guests were presented with lavish representations of love, including all red costumes. The invitation was inspired by actual Valentines given by children to each other. But the joy and revelry surrounding such a theme soon disappeared with the advent of an epidemic.

By the end of 1986, Dobson; his partner, Billy Langford; and Joseph Talluto all had died, not necessarily from the scourge of AIDS. By the 1986 Carnival season, Rowena had died as well, and the fantastic and original Mystic Krewe of Apollo was no more, though its sister krewes in other cities continue to thrive more than three decades later. Russell Talluto remained in New Orleans, riding out Hurricane Katrina with his mother in his Mid-City home, and leaving only when National Guardsmen forced them to evacuate after the city flooded. Among the few items he salvaged was the costume he wore as King Apollo in 1984, arguably the last great king of his krewe.

Roland Dobson with Governor Edwin Edwards, 1972. Courtesy of D'Lon Dobson.

Mystic Krewe of Apollo (1970)

1970

Roland Dobson, Billy Langford, and Joseph Talluto Jr. founded the Mystic Krewe of Apollo and gave their first presentation in 1970. Dobson steered Apollo to great heights, having enough clout to secure the ritzy Monteleone Hotel for the first couple of balls. Under his guidance, the group never strayed from traditional Carnival roots, imitating to the last detail the tableaux of old-line krewes. He moved easily between gay and straight New Orleans.

1972

Dobson secured the Municipal Auditorium for the krewe's third tableau ball, an almost unheard of venue for a gay krewe. As he had anointed himself permanent ball captain, Dobson was the star of *From Russia with Love*, popping out of a giant sequined Fabergé egg at the beginning of the ball.

1977

The Mystic Krewe of Apollo–Birmingham was formed, with Apollo franchise krewes following in Baton Rouge, Birmingham, Dallas, Shreveport, Lafayette, and other cities over the next few years. Dobson served as captain of the franchises for the first few years to ensure that the presentations were of the highest quality. *Saturday Night Live* was invited to film the coronation of Queen Apollo VIII at the Municipal Auditorium.

Annual fund-raising functions included a Spring Bedroom Tour of Infamous Persons, several raffles, and Apollo Weekend, where Mr. and Mrs. Apollo USA were selected. These events were wildly popular.

1986

The Mystic Krewe of Apollo held its last ball not at the Municipal Auditorium but at Sir Thomas Hall in the Faubourg Marigny and was a comparatively small affair. Dobson, Billy Langford, and Joseph Talluto Jr. all died before the end of the year.

Mystic Krewe of Apollo Tableau Balls List	
1970	MOVIE MADNESS
1971	DESCENT INTO HADES
1972	FROM RUSSIA WITH LOVE
1973	BROADWAY BABES
1974	LES AMOURS D'APOLLON (NAPOLEON AND JOSEPHINE)
1975	FOLLIES
1976	TO THE REALMS OF OUTERSPACE
1977	FAIR, FAIR LADIES OF CHARTRES STREET
1978	INFAMOUS BIBLICAL WOMEN (NAUGHTY LADIES OF THE BIBLE)
1979	CHINA (TENTH ANNIVERSARY BALL)
1980	FANTASY OF THE SEAS
1981	GARDENS OF VERSAILLES
1982	THIRTEENTH ANNUAL PRESENTATION
1983	GENESIS REVISITED
1984	MEMORIES OF APOLLO (FIFTEENTH ANNIVERSARY BALL)
1985	INTERNATIONAL BALL—VALENTINES
1986	SEVENTEENTH ANNUAL PRESENTATION

Mystic Krewe of Apollo Royalty List			
YEAR OF TABLEAU BALL	CAPTAIN	QUEEN	KING
1970	Roland Dobson	Kenneth Toncrey (Daisy Mae)	Glyce DiMiceli
1971	Roland Dobson	—	—
1972	Roland Dobson	—	—
1973	Roland Dobson	—	—
1974	Roland Dobson	Joe Black	—
1975	Roland Dobson	Billy Langford	"Teddy Bear"
1976	Roland Dobson	Roy Hermann (Rowena)	Helmut Stuhlmann
1977	Roland Dobson	Edd Smith	Dan Romero
1978	Roland Dobson	Jim "Peaches" Gillon	—
1979	Roland Dobson	—	—
1980	Roland Dobson	Anna Mae	Roland Dobson
1981	Roland Dobson	Jerry McGill (Pitti Pat)	Larry Heller
1982	Roland Dobson	Donald James/Donnie Jay	—
1983	Roland Dobson	Charles Volz	Billy Langford
1984	Jim "Peaches" Gillon	Kevin Keller	Russell Talluto
1985	Billy Langford	Terry Thomas	Eddie Orwick
1986*	Billy Langford	Joe Reine	Sterling Silva

*Held at Sir Thomas Hall on Burgundy. All three founders were ill and did not survive the year.

Movie Madness 1970

Commemorative poster, 1970. Design by Joseph Talluto Jr. Courtesy of The Historic New Orleans Collection, Williams Research Center, New Orleans, Accession No. 1980.178.197. Gift of Tracy Hendrix.

King Apollo I, Glyce DiMiceli, 1970. Costume design by San nicholas. Courtesy of Glyce DiMiceli.

Tableau 1970
Visiting Royalty
The Captain's Whistle
The Crest of Mystic Apollo
The Gay, Festive Krewe
 What Ever Happened to Baby Jane?
 Midnight Cowboy
 Singing Nun
 How the West Was Won
The Captain
The Lovely Maids of Court
 The Birds
 Hello Dolly!
 20,000 Leagues under the Sea
 Gone with the Wind
 My Fair Lady
 Gypsy
 Auntie Mame
 What's New Pussycat?
His Royal Majesty, King Apollo I
Her Royal Majesty, Queen Apollo I
Honored Guests
Big Spenders
The Krewe and Court Request Their Call-Out Dance
Grand March
General Dancing for Guests until 1:00 a.m.

Descent into Hades 1971

Commemorative poster, 1971. Design by Joseph Talluto Jr. Courtesy of Tulane University, Louisiana Research Collection, Howard-Tilton Memorial Library, New Orleans, Otto Stierle Collection, Manuscripts Collection 902.

Program reads: *Orpheus the unrivaled musician of antiquity, at whose divine music, legend tells us, trees uprooted themselves and rocks became loosened from their ledges in order to follow the wonderful sounds. For this Orpheus was the son of Apollo, god of music, and Calliope, muse of epic poetry. One day, while dancing in a field of wild flowers, a snake bit the lovely Euridice on her heel. She swooned and died in the arms of her lover. Orpheus wept day and night and all creation lamented the loss of his song. His grief was so great, darkening the sun, that Amore, the god of love, tells him he may descend to the nether world, the dark realm of Satan, there to seek the shade of Euridice. Upon his descent, the Gates of Hell are torn asunder as the legions of demons and spirits of darkness appear before him, the mortal daring to invade the land of the eternal dead. In a blaze of dazzling glory Satan himself, Lord of the Underworld, appears as his guide through the inferno. Our Orpheus is introduced to the Sins of the World. The story concludes with Orpheus personified by King Apollo II being reunited with Euridice, Queen Apollo II.*

⚜

Tableau 1971
Visiting Royalty
King Apollo I Returns
Queen Apollo I Enters
The Captain's Whistle
The Crest of Mystic Apollo
Gatekeeper of Hell Releasing the Imps
    Krewe of Apollo
The Captain of Apollo
Maids of Court—The Sins of the World
    Disobedience
    Jealousy
    Gluttony
    Laziness
    Vanity
    Drunkenness
    Hate
    Lust
    Love
His Royal Majesty, King Apollo II
Her Royal Majesty, Queen Apollo II
Royalty Entertained
Honored Guests
Call-Out Dances
Grand March
General Dancing for Guests until 11:00 p.m.
Supper Dance—Queen Anne Room 11:30 p.m.–2:00 a.m.

From Russia with Love 1972

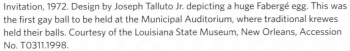

Invitation, 1972. Design by Joseph Talluto Jr. depicting a huge Fabergé egg. This was the first gay ball to be held at the Municipal Auditorium, where traditional krewes held their balls. Courtesy of the Louisiana State Museum, New Orleans, Accession No. T0311.1998.

Program reads: *The Mystic Krewe of Apollo by command of Nicholas II, the Imperial Tsar of Russia and Tsaritsa Alexandra Feodorovna, compel that you be present at their ball Monday, January seventeenth, Nineteen hundred and seventy-two at nine of the clock. The Auditorium. Saint Peter Street entrance. Strictly Personal. Formal. Please present this admit card for entrance. The committee reserves the right of admission. Imperial Russia during the days of the Tsars was filled with exciting and dazzling balls. The last reigning Tsar of Russia was Nicholas II and his wife Tsarina Alexandra Feodorovna. They reigned during the last decade of the 19th century and the first decade of the 20th century, entertaining with breathtaking, elaborate and splendrous balls in the Winter Palace, the Hermitage in Leningrad. Tonight you are invited to revisit one of those great balls.*

Broadway Babes 1973

Invitation, 1973. Design by Joseph Talluto Jr. Courtesy of Howard Philips Smith and Wendell Stipelcovich.

Tableau 1973
The Captain's Whistle
Lighting of the Crest
Debutantes of the 1973 Season
The Mood Is Set for an Evening with Broadway Babes
His Majesty, The King of 1972 (*Camelot*)
Her Majesty, The Queen of 1972
The Ball Lieutenant (Follies)
The Captain
The Dukes
Our Lovely Broadway Babes
    Coco Chanel (*Coco*)
    Magnolia (*Showboat*)
    Laura Lee (*Gentlemen Prefer Blondes*)
    Fanny Brice (*Funny Girl*)
    Sally Bowles (*Cabaret*)
    Dolly Levi (*Hello, Dolly!*)
His Majesty, MKA IV
Her Majesty, MKA IV
Royalty and Guests Entertained (*No, No, Nanette*)
Court Receives General Guests
Grand March
General Dancing in Scheuering Room
    10:30 p.m. to 12:30 a.m.—Tickets at Door

Les Amours d'Apollon 1974

Invitation, 1974. Design by Joseph Talluto Jr. Courtesy
of The Historic New Orleans Collection, Williams
Research Center, New Orleans, Accession No.
1980.178.333.

Tableau 1974
Le Coup d'Envoi Sera Donné par le Capitaine
L'Hymne Nationale Américaine
Illumination des Armoires
Acceuil des Invités
Présentation des Débutantes 1974
Le Thème du Bal 1974—Les Amours d'Apollon
Le Capitaine
La Cour de Napoléon
   Les Ducs
   Les Reines des Années Précédentes de MKA
Sa Majesté—La Reine du Quatrième Bal
Sa Majesté—La Reine du Troisième Bal
Sa Majesté—La Reine du Deuzième Bal
Sa Majesté—La Reine du Premier Bal
Sa Majesté—L'Impératrice Josephine—La Reine du
Cinquième Bal de MKA
Son Majesté—L'Empereur Napoléon—Le Roi du
Cinquième Bal de MKA
Présentations à Leurs Majestés
Les Divertissements
Promenade de la Cour
La Cour Reçoit
Et Réjouissance Générales jusqu'à 23:30 h.

Follies 1975

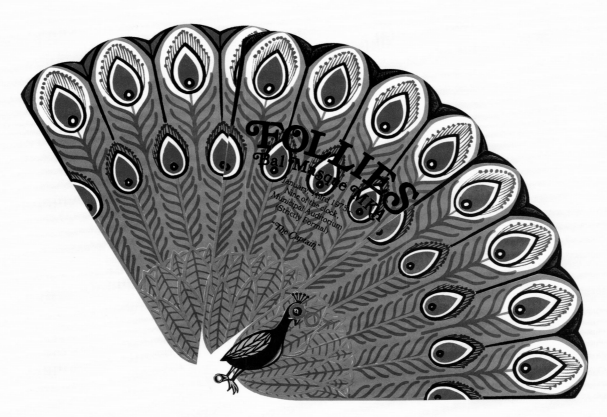

Invitation, 1975. Courtesy of Howard Philips Smith and Wendell Stipelcovich.

Program reads: *The house-lights dim. The curtain rises. The stage is set. The ambers spotlight the figure at the top of the stairs. As the orchestra begins to play softly "A Pretty Girl is Like a Melody," the figure descends the stairs. She is clad—or unclad—in beads and feathers, this exquisite Show Girl. Not a bead or feather of her costume is displaced as she walks rhythmically to the music. She is joined by other beauties. Yes, this is the Follies as created by Florenz Ziegfeld. But there are other Follies—perhaps the Folies-Bergères, or French Follies. Or personal follies. Oh, you haven't experienced any? You've missed a lot! MKA Follies—as exemplified by James Bond and his exciting cohorts.*

Tableau 1975
Captain's Whistle
National Anthem
Crest of MKA
Debutantes of the 1975 Season
Her Majesty, the Queen of 1974
The Captain
Ball Lieutenant
Royal Dukes of MKA
007's Exciting Girls
    Goldfinger
    Live and Let Die
    Thunderball
    From Russia with Love
    You Only Live Twice
His Majesty, MKA VI
Her Majesty, MKA VI
Royalty and Guests Entertained
Court Receives Royalty of Visiting Clubs
Grand March
Court Receives General Guests
General Dancing to 11:30 p.m.

Program, 1980. Courtesy of Howard Philips Smith and Wendell Stipelcovich.

Inside reads: *There has always been a mystery about the excitements and fantasies of the sea. Out of its depths evolve mysterious stories of excitement, love, and outrage. In its compass holds the beauties of world, alluring sea creatures, precious jewels, delicate marine life, and breathing coral formations. Tonight we delve into its mysteries and reveal to you the excitement of the Water World.*

Tableau 1980
Captain's Whistle
Crest of MKA
King MKA X
Queen MKA X
Entrance of the Captain
Ball Lieutenant
Dukes of MKA—Sea Captains
World Wind
Maids of the Sea
    Flying Fish
    Sea Weed
    Sponge
    Tropical Sea Bird
    Sea Shell
    Sea Devil
Creature from the Depths of the Sea
Queen MKA XI
King MKA XI
Honored Guests Received
Grand March
Open Court—General Dancing

Gardens of Versailles 1981

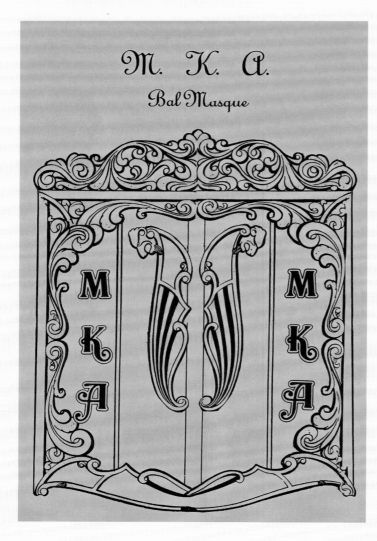

Program, 1981. Courtesy of Howard Philips Smith and Wendell Stipelcovich.

Inside reads: Only at Versailles did Louis XIV admit his humble subjects and allow them to approach him. Tonight, from the Bassin d'Apollo in the Marble Courtyards, we await our opportunity to approach the Royal Throne in the Apollo Room. Imagine if you will, a portrait of our Louis XIV by Rigaud, savonnerie rug and tapestries representing royal audiences.

We await our audience with a stroll in the gardens and palace. The color and magnificence of the Latona flowerbeds with decorations inspired from the Legend of Apollo brings us to the botanical gardens where we find sweet smelling flowerbeds, the colours and scent combinations of which are changed every day. Here a glimpse of Marie Antoinette by the Petit Trianon built by Gabriel. Within the palace we come upon Ladies of the Court. With orchestra of the Royal Opera moving us, the beauty of the Pajou sculptures, the colours of velvets and silks transport us to the Royal Court.

We greet our King and his lovely Queen in the Room of the Nobles. Above on the ceiling, we see Mercury in the Company of Poetry and Science in the coverings, celebrated women of antiquity are evoked, Sappho, Penelope, Aspasia, and Cesisene. Our audience is over and we return to our own lives, while remembering theirs. No, they are us—we are they, both of us and some of us—colorful, flamboyant, and gay. February 26, 1981. New Orleans Municipal Auditorium.

⚜

Tableau 1981
Captain's Whistle
National Anthem
Introduction of Visiting Royalty
Crest of MKA
Welcome
Our Captain Marie Antoinette
King and Queen MKA XI
Ball Lieutenant
Ladies of the French Court
    Madame Pompadour
    Countess Jeanne du Barry
In the Gardens of Versailles
    The Rose
    The Peacock
    French Lily
    Swan
    Mystical Tree
    The Tulip
    The Butterfly
    The Black Orchid
The Morning Glory
King MKA XII
Queen MKA XII
Honored Guests
The Grand March

Queen Apollo XII, Jerry McGill (Pitti Pat), 1981. Courtesy of Jerry McGill.

King Apollo XII, Larry Heller, and Queen Apollo XII, Jerry McGill, with their court, 1981. Courtesy of Jerry McGill.

Genesis Revisited 1983

King Apollo XIV, Billy Langford, 1983. Photograph by G. Andrew Boyd.
Courtesy of Wayne Phillips.

Spiderwoman, 1983. Photograph Courtesy of G. Andrew Boyd. Courtesy of Wayne
Phillips.

The Firebird, 1983. Photograph by G. Andrew Boyd. Courtesy of Wayne
Phillips.

Tableau 1983
President of Apollo
Master of Ceremonies—Roberts Batson
Captain of Apollo
Crest of Apollo
Ball Captain of Apollo
Debutantes of the Season
Apollo Presents *Genesis Revisited*
    Heavy Rain and Wind
    Lightning
    The Tree of Life
    A Firebird
    Merman
    Grapes
    Music
    Ice Castle
    Three-Headed Monster
    Spiderwoman
    The Marquis de Sade
    Centaur
    Adam
    Eve
    The Serpent
King Apollo XIV
Queen Apollo XIV
Court Receives Royal Guests
Open Court and Dancing

Memories of Apollo 1984

International Ball (Valentines) 1985

Program, 1984. Courtesy of The Historic New Orleans Collection, Williams Research Center, New Orleans, Accession No. 2000.34.102.

Invitation, 1985. Courtesy of The Historic New Orleans Collection, Williams Research Center, New Orleans, Louisiana, Accession No. 1985.107.3, Gift of Mr. Tracy Hendrix.

Tableau 1984
Crest of MKA
MKA Welcomes Guests to the Bal Masqué
King Apollo XIV
Queen Apollo XIV
Captain's Entrance
The Ball Lieutenant
Memories of Mardi Gras
King and Queen Apollo XIII
King and Queen Apollo XII—The Gardens of Versailles
King and Queen Apollo X
King and Queen Apollo IX
King and Queen Apollo VII—Naughty Ladies of the Bible
King and Queen Apollo VI—From Beneath the Sea
King and Queen Apollo V
King and Queen Apollo III—The Birds
King and Queen Apollo I—The Movies
His Majesty—King Apollo XV
Her Majesty—King Apollo XV
The Grand March
Presentations to the Court
Open Court

THE KREWE
OF OLYMPUS

From Camelot to Houston

My time as Queen Olympus V was magical. At the height of the ball, I was revealed as the reigning queen on my birthday. When my partner, Nick Donovan, came up on stage to pay homage to me as the reigning monarch, he presented me with a glorious diamond ring. What more could a queen ask for?

—Lou Bernard, Krewe of Olympus

Camelot

The mere mention of the word *Camelot* within the secretive realm of gay Carnival still evokes a sense of wonder, magic, awe, and ultimately envy. No tableau ball has excited more passion or praise. The first ball of the Krewe of Olympus in 1971 was a touchstone in gay Carnival annals: few other balls have come close to surpassing such artistry. Formed in 1970 by Lou Bernard, George Wilson, and Nick Donovan, Olympus was intended to embody a new type of "high-quality krewe with great theatricality and professionalism." Donovan, who had been captain of the Krewe of Ganymede for the *Creepy Crawlers* ball earlier that year, Bernard, and Wilson had all become disillusioned with the krewe, and they began to talk of forming a new group, half in jest but with a note of excitement. They met with a few others at Tony Moran's restaurant above the Old Absinthe House on Bourbon Street to flesh out the deal, selecting Pat Hamberg as president, Gene Cheatham as secretary, and George Wilson as lieutenant. In keeping with their goal of maintaining artistry, Wilson thought of Jamie Greenleaf to serve as captain

Invitation to the Krewe of Olympus's *Camelot* ball, 1971. Design by Jamie Greenleaf. In a nod to the rituals of traditional Carnival, this large poster was hand-delivered as the invitation. Courtesy of Kenneth Owen and James McAllister.

of the first ball, recalling, "Jamie himself was secretly disenchanted with Petronius after the *Glorification* ball. Miss Woolley and Jamie would often clash over almost everything, so for him to join a new krewe was very tempting. He and I got along just fine, and he came on board almost immediately. Now that left a bitter taste in Petronius, but what are you going to do?"

The Creative Force

Lewis S. "Jamie" Greenleaf III had already made his mark as an accomplished set and costume designer with the Krewe of Petronius. He and his partner, Harvey Benson Hysell, had met in college in Texas, where Hysell was studying dance. They subsequently moved to Manhattan, where Hysell became a soloist with the New York City Ballet and later the company's principal costume designer. In 1966 he and Greenleaf moved to New Orleans, where Hysell had grown up, and formed Greenleaf-Hysell Associates, a costume design firm specializing in work for Mardi Gras krewes and local theater groups. They soon became quite popular and were hired to create the costumes and sets for the 1967 production of *Gypsy* at the Gallery Circle Theatre.

Greenleaf joined the Krewe of Petronius around this time and by 1969 had become captain, producing the spectacular *Glorification of the American Girl*, which showcased an array of exotic costumes—sassy pink-feathered showgirls, enigmatic creatures made out of flowers, and gold-disc-encrusted bodysuits with layers of sequined ruffles. Even the program, shaped like a fan and covered in pink feathers, was a marvel of ingenuity. Greenleaf and Hysell continued to work together and by 1970 were designing costumes for the straight krewe Rex, a major coup for any designer. Charged with fabricating more than 265 individual costumes for Rex's one hundredth anniversary parade in 1971, the studio worked for months to complete the assignment. Between 1967 and 1970, Greenleaf and Hysell also did design work for the straight Krewe of Anubis, a nonparading krewe formed by and primarily for men who worked in the pharmaceutical industry. The design for the 1970 queen's costume had the typical crook and flail of Egyptian royalty, and she appeared in the standard arms-crossed pose. But when her hands went down, her breasts appeared to be exposed. Greenleaf was summarily fired, but the costume lived on in the Miss America pageant fund-raiser for the Krewe of Amon-Ra.

The perpetual bickering among the members of the Krewe of Petronius drove Greenleaf away, and he joined Olympus soon after its inception. Named after the fabled mountain in Greek mythology, the krewe also brought back memories of the fictitious Olympus Carnival krewe featured in the 1938 Bette Davis movie *Jezebel*. In the film, Davis's character wore a red dress to the annual Olympus ball, shocking her beau and the rigid social set and setting in motion her downfall.

Wilson was especially excited when Greenleaf joined: "At the time, there were about twenty members on board for Olympus. As ball lieutenant, I had saved the space for Jamie as

"Aztecs on Iberville? Hard to believe, but true enough, Harvey Hysell and visiting New Yorker Lewis Greenleaf are hiding behind those masks." *Dixie-Roto Magazine* (Sunday supplement to *New Orleans Times-Picayune*), February 5, 1967. Courtesy of the Louisiana State Museum, New Orleans, Carnival Reference Collection.

captain, but the board had to vote. I told them to trust me since I could not reveal his name. They voted for the mysterious Madame X, which was really Jamie, and so he was in. He was already known, however, for saying that if something was worth being done, it was worth being overdone. I knew we were in for a wonderful experience."

The Saint Bernard Civic Center

Like other gay krewes at the time, Olympus had difficulty finding a suitable venue for its first ball, particularly because Greenleaf's vision of a storybook castle and a fairytale wonderland with King Arthur and Lady Guinevere required a larger space. According to Lou Bernard, although Chalmette was not known as the most gay-friendly parish, "the auditorium in St. Bernard Parish was discussed since the manager was secretly gay. We approached him with the idea of a gay ball, and he thought about it but decided that we should meet with the Chalmette sheriff and the head judge to get their approval. George and I met with them and presented Jamie's sketches of the costumes and his drawings of the proposed set. They were duly impressed and immediately asked for invitations to our ball." Wilson remembered that "Jamie wanted the auditorium at all costs. We didn't hide the fact that we were a gay krewe, but we guaranteed that there would be no drag queens in the audience and only costumes on stage. The staff were apprehensive at first, but when they saw how serious we were, they pitched in and helped get things rolling." It is, however, likely that parish leaders agreed to allow the ball to be held in St. Bernard not merely out of benevolence or because it was a source of revenue (though that consideration became increasingly important) but also because, in the words of Arthur Hardy "more than likely a secret had been discovered and exploited to great benefit." That is, the krewe had knowledge that would have embarrassed the parish government. At least one other krewe member has confirmed the existence of secret deal. Whatever the reasons, once the first Olympus ball took place there, other gay krewes relocated their balls to Chalmette, and a tentative détente emerged and ultimately benefited both sides. St. Bernard Parish police always protected the balls and directed traffic. The St. Bernard Civic Center became synonymous with gay Carnival balls until 2005, when Hurricane Katrina forced its temporary closure.

A Calculated Debut

The theme for the first Olympus ball, *Camelot*, reflected a story that had also attracted traditional krewes, whatever the historical veracity of the story of King Arthur and the Knights of the Round Table. As George Wilson explained, Greenleaf had seen a Broadway production of the Lerner and Loewe musical *Camelot* "and wanted this as the theme of our first ball. He came from a very rich family in Greenwich, Connecticut. At the age of twelve, Jamie boldly stated that he wanted to become a costume designer. Later on, his mother sent him to Paris to study with the legendary Erté. Many people thought this story an exaggeration, but Jamie swore that he became very close to Monsieur Erté—so close,

Invitation to the Krewe of Proteus's *Romance of Wales* ball, 1909. Gay Carnival krewes often took inspiration from traditional Carnival themes, as in this example that may have influenced Olympus's *Camelot*. Courtesy of The Historic New Orleans Collection, Williams Research Center, New Orleans, Accession No. 1961.69.13.

in fact, that Erté gave him almost thirty prints of his work. This is how he learned to make exquisite costumes—from the master himself."

The Creation of a Masterpiece

When guests arrived at the Saint Bernard Civic Auditorium on February 6, 1971, they were greeted by a fairy tale forest built out from the stage. Greenleaf stood hidden within the towering set, costumed as Merlin the Magician wearing a dark blue robe lined with sequined stars and with a mechanical owl, Archimedes, perched on his shoulder. His white hair looked like silver flames shooting up, an illusion created by piecing together translucent Lucite. Two silver branches framed his face. Across his shoulders, a long purple-pink cape featured intricately sequined flames. When the ball began, the bird squawked and sputtered, Merlin shot fire from his magic wand, and the forest split in half, revealing a storybook castle that stretched across the stage and into the background. The knights sported plumed golden helmets with large crested shields and swords. Other crusaders wore short red tunics covered in large white crosses with long plush red capes trimmed in golden fringe. Pages and valets wore shining metallic armor and helmets, sparkling white capes, and long white boas. A black raven menaced those onstage. Morgan le Fay (Hysell), a dewy, red-haired maiden, demurely held a cluster of pink flowers to match her diaphanous pink gown. Bearded King Arthur (Nick Donovan) wore a gold crown and robes of gold-lined mail trimmed in Russian fox fur ending in a train that flowed around him like a purple and gold river. With the fabled sword Excalibur in hand, he bestowed his beneficence upon the audience, as his pages turned his train lined in velvet and sequins. Queen Guinevere (Gene Cheatham) wore gold robes that clung to her body as well as an even more intricate train. Her closely fitted gold crown shone like sparkling fire.

According to Wilson, "Sequins come in blankets, with each containing several thousand individual sequins. The king's costume alone was made with over a hundred blankets. But the queen's costume was even more difficult and literally took months to complete. We used glass jewels to make the bodice and the sleeves. Each sleeve was a separate piece with a zipper. Same thing with the bodice. We had Gene come into the studio and we glued the jewels on him as he lay on a table. I think the whole thing ended up weighing over eighty pounds, but it was stunning!"

Hysell choreographed a dance interlude to accompany his appearance as Morgan le Fay. Lou Bernard appeared as one of the four forest creatures accompanying the enchantress, but narrowly avoided disaster: "As I walked from backstage, the peacock feathers in my headdress touched the candles in my staff, and I caught fire. Harvey just picked up his cape and knocked out the fire. Everyone wondered why one of the forest creatures had smoke coming out of his headdress. I was terrified, but Harvey told me to just start dancing to the beat of the music all over again."

George Wilson was Sir Lancelot and appeared on stage in a real suit of armor. "I was surprised when Jamie told me that we suddenly had to go to New York," Wilson recalled. "We arrived at the family house in Connecticut to pick up the suit of armor. It was an authentic piece. The white boa we picked up in Manhattan. It was twisted with strands of Mylar, which was reflective. Jamie wanted something to bedazzle when I came out. I spent months polishing the armor, and it all blazed like a shooting star."

The audience included members of the Krewes of Ganymede, Amon-Ra, Armeinius, and Petronius, as well as William Woolley (who later formed the Mystic

Krewe of Celestial Knights), and the production challenged all of them to create their own dazzling spectacles. Another of those in attendance, Michael Hickerson, described the night as "sheer magic. . . . It was one of those splendid moments that literally took your breath away."

According to Lou Bernard, the costumes were displayed on a balcony in the French Quarter on Fat Tuesday: "Jamie Greenleaf had an apartment on Royal Street with a balcony that curved around the corner. That was when parades still came into the Quarter on Royal Street and then up Orleans to the Municipal Auditorium for the balls. The beautiful costumes of King and Queen Olympus I were displayed on that balcony all day, and when Comus came rolling down Bourbon Street at twilight, well, he stopped the parade and toasted us on that balcony with his golden goblet. Now it didn't get any better than that. The trains were draped over the balcony as well, reaching almost to the ground. Before we knew it, someone had taken the king's train. We were devastated."

The Second Ball

Olympus's 1972 ball, *Red, White, and Blue*, lasted a scant thirty minutes but nevertheless left the audience spellbound. The set was stark: a blindingly white staircase that led from the stage to the floor. One by one, a dozen showgirls dressed in identical red headpieces and tight red gowns made their way to the top of the stairs and then descended to the floor

Intersection of Royal and St. Peter Streets, French Quarter, 1938. Costumes and mantles for King and Queen Olympus I were displayed on this balcony on Shrove Tuesday in 1971. Comus himself raised a toast as he paraded past. Photograph by Frances Benjamin Johnston. Courtesy of the Louisiana State Museum, New Orleans, Accession No. 1981.132.128.

of the auditorium, where they paired up and bowed in a choreographed sequence. Next came men in white tuxedos and top hats, dancing down the steps, followed by showgirls in pink gowns and white headpieces with boas. Those ten couples danced on the steps to "Tea for Two." Then came Greenleaf, the captain, dressed in a skimpy showgirl costume with boas cascading down from his arms and around his head. Four tuxedoed men accompanied him around the stage and then placed him atop a pedestal to the strains of "What A Peach of a Girl." The dancers gathered round, the house lights dimmed, and Greenleaf lit up like a torch. Revealed George Wilson, "Jamie had everyday lightbulbs inside his boas and headpiece, and all we had to do was plug him in to a socket hidden in the pedestal. To this day, I can't believe how thrilling this simple device was at the time. The audience was beyond disbelief as they clapped and cheered."

Next, as "Lovely to Look At" played, three gentlemen in dark blue tuxedoes descended the stairway, each with two matching showgirls on his arms. Then as they twirled around the floor, the music segued into "The Most Beautiful Girl in the World." All of the performers came together, creating the title palette, and the music changed to "Strike Up the Band" as showgirls arrived on stage with huge red, white, and blue striped headdresses and bustles.

Wilson, the reigning queen, came out wrapped in a red, white, and blue fur cape with the American Flag over his head and began tap-dancing to "Yankee Doodle Dandy." He threw off his cape to reveal a snug, flesh-colored bodysuit with thousands of sequins: it appeared that he was dancing in the nude. The stunt shocked not only those in attendance but also those who subsequently heard about it. Green-leaf left for Atlanta soon thereafter. According to Wilson, Greenleaf and Hysell had ended their romantic relationship, and Greenleaf wanted his new boyfriend, Larry Kelley, to serve as captain. Wilson believed that Kelley "was not capable of running a ball. He couldn't even pay his dues. So I proposed that we would serve as cocaptains. Well, Jamie would have none of it and left the krewe. He soon afterwards left New Orleans, so that put an end to that." Hysell remained in New Orleans and formed the Ballet Hysell, which became synonymous with theatricality and polish. Hysell later brought Greenleaf back to serve as technical director for a production of *Coppélia* at the New Orleans Theater for the Performing Arts.

The Third Ball

George Wilson captained the Krewe of Olympus for its 1973 an *Evening of Enchantment* ball, a peek into the hidden realms of twilight, with a mysterious invitation designed by Dal Kimberling. According to Wilson, "Everything in the ball was depicted in the invitation: there was no color, only shades of black, white, or gray, until the king and queen entered, representing the rising sun. I was captain and returning queen, representing the Evening Star. There were dewdrop costumes, starry sky costumes, night creatures, peacocks, wind, and of course a storm—a fantastic night storm the likes of which were never again seen on the stages of Chalmette."

Rodney Dugas served as Queen Olympus III in 1973 but left New Orleans soon thereafter. Wilson chose his friend for the role not because of their close ties but, as Wilson remembered, because Dugas was an extremely talented artist and "an invaluable member of the Krewe. He was the best and only choice for my queen." A native New Orleanian with his family home in the Carrollton area, Dugas had frequently appeared on the stages of Le Petit Théâtre du Vieux Carré and Gallery Circle theaters. Most notably, he had starring roles in *Everybody Loves Opal*, written by John Patrick, and in the *Fatted Calf Revue*, directed by George Patterson. Dugas moved to New York by the mid-1970s "to try his hand on Broadway" and never returned to New Orleans. He appeared in many East Coast productions and eventually settled in Connecticut.

The Talented Mr. Woodard

In 1974, the krewe took advantage of the graphic design talents of Earl Woodard, a new recruit who designed not only the invitations but also the costumes, staging, and poster for *Gay Bars of America*. Woodard served as lieutenant for the 1975 ball, *The Court of Louis XIV*, and again created intricately crafted and stylized costumes, sets, and choreography that brilliantly evoked the period. He made his entrance on a silver sedan chair carried by two bare-breasted ladies of the court in outrageous pink costumes. The opulent white and silver set enhanced all the costumes in subtle shades of blue and lavender, pink and orange, yellow and gold.

George Wilson recalled the occasion as "one of those perfect balls. Everything came together flawlessly. *Camelot* was indeed a sensation, but behind the scenes, we were all scrambling. For the French ball, all aspects from choreography to the lighting and especially the detailed costumes were executed without a snag. It was a visual delight, taking everyone to another realm, one of opulence and luxury. The costumes were just works of art, all designed by Earl, who was so into his period character. There was no narration and the ball was barely over forty minutes, but what a perfection! We even had to learn the minuet!"

The queen, Lou Bernard, learned of the honor when he was "invited to celebrate my birthday by the ball captain and lieutenant. At the end of the dinner, Gene Cheatham, the captain, handed me a wrapped box. Inside was a silver bracelet with QOV [Queen Olympus V] engraved on the underside. At first I was stunned. I didn't feel ready yet to be queen, but they insisted, and they were right. It was the most spectacular Carnival season ever. The costumes were simply brilliant and were of such quality and class—just works of art. Earl was a magician, and then some. After the ball, when I'd go into a bar in the Quarter, everyone would announce that I was Olympus royalty, and the whole bar would bow. That was the way it was back then. Everything centered on Mardi Gras. Nothing else mattered. Even D. H. Holmes displayed our costumes right out in the middle of the store for the entire city to see, thanks to Miss Woolley. She fell in love with our costumes."

The Later 1970s

For 1976's *Baubles, Bangles, and Boobs*, Woodard's invitation featured a showgirl holding an invitation for the krewe's sixth presentation. The showgirl was replicated on the set itself, with her hands and fingers extended on either side of the stage. The ball opened with showgirls descending a set of stairs onto the palms of the hands and then another set of stairs to the stage. At the *Illuminations* ball the following year, Woodard was King Olympus VII, while Ben Jones was Queen Olympus VII. *Olympus Reads the Comics* (1978) constituted a departure from the trend toward glamorous costuming, with comic strip characters coming to life on stage and Snuffy Smith (the petite Dale Triché) and his wife, Loweezy (Jay Verona, almost six feet, six inches tall), as the king and queen. At this ball, captain Bryan Tatum did a wonderful albeit unsteady curtsy in a ten-foot hoopskirt made of newspapers, and a bevy of Little Orphan Annies tap-danced the night away. For Olympus's tenth anniversary, Woodard again designed sets, costumes, and invitations, and the ball was staged not only in New Orleans but also in Houston. During the year, the krewe's fund-raisers included the Folies-Bergère and a Las Vegas Night.

Houston Beckons

Ben Jones moved from Houston to New Orleans in 1972 and joined the krewe in 1974. He and Bill Walters met in 1978, and Bill moved from Mississippi to join the krewe and live with Ben. They moved to Houston in 1980, keeping an apartment in New Orleans for several years. By 1991, the program for the *Olympus Goes West* ball signaled that something new was in store: "Twenty years ago a group of people had a dream called Olympus. That dream has gone on, evolving and changing, and we are still dreaming. Tonight we bring back those dreams, not as they were, for dreams are always changing, but as we dream today." The krewe was struggling, largely as a consequence of the AIDS crisis, and Jones and Walters decided that the solution was to move Olympus to Houston, where they continue to thrive.

Krewe of Olympus (1971)

1970

The Krewe of Olympus was formed by Lou Bernard, Nick Donovan, and George Wilson in 1970. As the first captain, they recruited Jamie Greenleaf, who had brought the Krewe of Petronius to such grand heights with the *Glorification of the American Girl* ball in 1969. The krewe was the first to hold a ball at Chalmette's Saint Bernard Civic Auditorium, which could accommodate the growing number of attendees. Other krewes quickly followed suit.

1971

The first Olympus ball, *Camelot*, was an artistic tour-de-force that provided other gay krewes with a wake-up call. Greenleaf broke new ground with costumes, sets, music, and theme. King Olympus I was Nick Donovan and Queen Olympus I was Gene Cheatham.

1972

The patriotic *Red, White, and Blue* ball was a crowd-pleaser. Queen George Wilson tap-danced in a sheer body suit that made her appear nude, a daring and risqué stunt.

1973–74

Despite Greenleaf's departure, the Krewe of Olympus continued to prosper with Lou Bernard and George Wilson at the helm and the arrival of such newcomers as Earl Woodard, who went on to design invitations and costumes for many balls, and Ben Jones.

1975

The *Court of Louis XIV* ball featured costumes that replicated a lavish historical era. The costumes worn by Lou Bernard as queen and Earl Woodard as ball lieutenant were placed on public display in the foyer of the D. H. Holmes Department Store on Canal Street.

1976

Baubles, Bangles, and Boobs reached new heights with flamboyant showgirl costumes designed by Earl Woodard.

1980s

Though the Krewe of Olympus celebrated its fifteenth anniversary in 1985 with the *Space Ball*, an elaborate voyage to outer space, and put on a fantastic *Folies-Bergère* ball the following year, its membership was being decimated by AIDS, leading to a crisis.

1991

The krewe held its last ball in New Orleans, with Ben Jones serving as captain and Bill Walters as lieutenant. The entire operation moved to Houston, where it prospered and continues to hold presentations.

Krewe of Olympus Tableau Balls List	
1971	CAMELOT
1972	RED, WHITE, AND BLUE
1973	AN EVENING OF ENCHANTMENT
1974	GAY BARS OF AMERICA
1975	THE FIFTH SEASON—THE COURT OF LOUIS XIV
1976	BAUBLES, BANGLES, AND BOOBS (SHOWGIRLS)
1977	ILLUMINATIONS
1978	XANADU
1979	OLYMPUS READS THE COMICS
1980	OLYMPUS X
1981	A CHILDHOOD FANTASY
1982	STORYVILLE
1983	MAGIC
1984	UNDER THE BIG TOP
1985	OLYMPUS XV—SPACE BALL
1986	WORLD WAR II
1987	DESERT SONG
1988	JUST DESSERTS
1989	LAWN ORNAMENTS
1990	OLYMPUS XX—A JOURNEY OF DREAMS
1991	OLYMPUS GOES WEST

Krewe of Olympus Royalty List

YEAR OF TABLEAU BALL	CAPTAIN	LIEUTENANT	QUEEN	KING
1971	Lewis "Jamie" Greenleaf III	George Wilson	Gene Cheatham	Nick Donovan
1972	Lewis "Jamie" Greenleaf III	—	George Wilson	—
1973	George Wilson	—	Rodney Dugas	Doug Massey
1974	Lou Bernard Jr.	Dal Kimberling	Richard West	Frank Wright
1975	Gene Cheatham	Earl Woodard Jr.	Lou Bernard Jr.	Frank Balthazar
1976	Ben Jones	George Wilson	Danny McNamara	Paul Veret
1977	Danny McNamara	Earl Woodard Jr.	Ben Jones	Earl Woodard Jr.
1978	Garland Humphries	—	Skip Kibodeaux	Fred Lutz
1979	Bryan Tatum	David Tringali	Jay Verona	Dale Triché
1980	Lou Bernard Jr./ Earl Woodard Jr.	—	Bryan Tatum	Mister Glenn
1981	David Tringali	Michael Lambert	Garland Humphries	Dariel Miller
1982	Jim Shively	Robert Richards	William Walters	Gene Haus
1983	Bryan Tatum	David Tringali	David Tringali	Carl Benoit
1984	Johnny Wescott	Michael Lambert	Michael Genovese	Austin Roundtree
1985	Carl Benoit	Larry Holbron	Pat McCormick	Brian Hoffmann
1986	William Walters	Jim Willemet	Will Hughes	Skip Kibodeaux
1987	Garland Humphries	Michael Eldred	Larry Moranz	Courtney Craighead
1988	Irv Schluntz	Will Hughes	Garland Humphries	Vic Walter
1989	Ben Jones	Lloyd Reid	Glenn Plauché	Irv Schluntz
1990	Ben Jones/Lou Bernard Jr.	—	Lloyd Reid	Ben Jones
1991	Ben Jones	William Walters	Luckie Itow	JJ Kenworthey

Camelot 1971

Queen and King Olympus I, Gene Cheatham and Nick Donovan, as Queen Guinevere and King Arthur, 1971. Photograph by Peggy Stewart Studios. Courtesy of Kenneth Owen and James McAllister.

Lou Bernard as Morgan le Fay's fairy attendant in a dance sequence choreographed by Greenleaf's partner, Harvey Hysell (Morgan le Fay), 1971. Photograph by Peggy Stewart Studios. Courtesy of the Louisiana State Museum, New Orleans, Accession No. 2016.005.2.

Rodney Dugas as the May Girl, 1971. Photograph by Peggy Stewart Studios. Courtesy of George Wilson.

George Wilson as Sir Lancelot, 1971. Photograph by Peggy Stewart Studios. Courtesy of George Wilson.

Captain Jamie Greenleaf as Merlin the Magician, 1971. Photograph by Peggy Stewart Studios. Courtesy of the Louisiana State Museum, New Orleans, Accession No. 2016.017.

An Evening of Enchantment 1973

Poster, 1973. Design by Dal Kimberling. Courtesy of the John C. Kelly and Michael J. Rosa Collection, Earl K. Long Library, University of New Orleans.

Queen Olympus III, Rodney Dugas, 1973. Photograph by Peggy Stewart Studios. Courtesy of George Wilson.

Gay Bars of America 1974

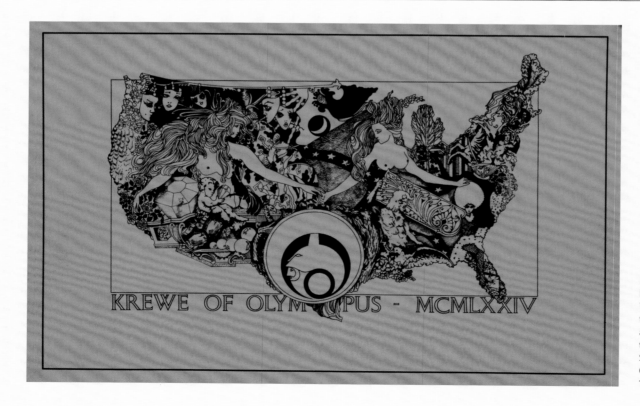

Poster, 1974. Design by Earl Woodard. Woodard also created the costumes, staging, and invitations. Courtesy of the Louisiana State Museum, New Orleans, Accession No. 1995.010.095.

The Court of Louis XIV (The Fifth Season) 1975

Program, 1975. Design by Earl Woodard. Courtesy of The Historic New Orleans Collection, Williams Research Center, New Orleans, Accession No. 1980.178.387. Gift of Tracy Hendrix.

Captain Gene Cheatham, 1975. Courtesy of George Wilson.

King Frank Balthazar and Queen Lou Bernard, 1975. Courtesy of the Louisiana State Museum, New Orleans, Accession No. 2012.014.06.

Lieutenant Earl Woodard, 1975. Courtesy of the Louisiana State Museum, New Orleans, Accession No. 2012.016.02.

Costume sketch for ball lieutenant Earl Woodard, 1975. Design by Earl Woodard. Courtesy of the Louisiana State Museum, New Orleans, Accession No. 2016.025.21.

Baubles, Bangles, and Boobs 1976

Invitation, 1976. Design by Earl Woodard. Courtesy of The Historic New Orleans Collection, Williams Research Center, New Orleans, Accession No. 1980.178.417. Gift of Tracy Hendrix.

Set design, 1976. Design by Earl Woodard. Courtesy of the Louisiana State Museum, New Orleans, Accession No. 2012.016.12.

Earl Woodard, sketches for showgirl costumes, 1976. Courtesy of the Louisiana State Museum, New Orleans, Accession Nos. SC2012.01.4, SC2012.01.8.

Xanadu 1978

Invitation, 1978. Design by Earl Woodard. Courtesy of Howard Philips Smith and Wendell Stipelcovich.

Olympus Reads the Comics 1979

Invitation, 1979. Original artwork by Earl Woodard. Courtesy of the Louisiana State Museum, New Orleans, Accession No. 2012.016.28.

Olympus X 1980

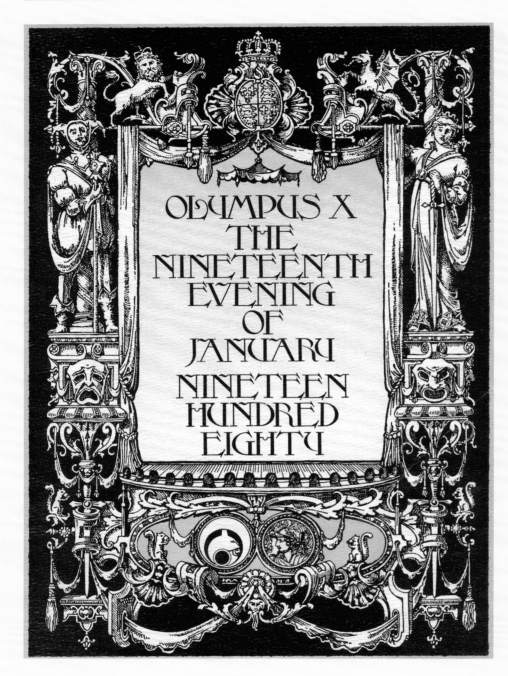

Invitation, 1980. Design by Earl Woodard. Courtesy of Tulane University, Louisiana Research Collection, Howard-Tilton Memorial Library, New Orleans, Otto Stierle Collection, Manuscripts Collection 902.

Program reads: *So saying, Minerva, the goddess azure-eyed, rose to Olympus, the reputed seat eternal of the gods, which never storms disturb, rains drench, or snow invades, but calm the expanse and cloudless shines with purest day. There the inhabitants divine rejoice for ever. Oh, Homer. Please!*

Tonight we celebrate our tenth anniversary. In the past we have taken you from Camelot to the Comics. From unknown creatures of the night to the never-known Land of Make Believe. From the gayest bars in America to the Mystic East. From Flo Ziegfeld's women to our own women of Burlesque, and the opulence of the French Court. Our presentation this evening is our retrospect of the members of the Krewe of Olympus. We thank you for joining us in the past, we welcome you tonight, and we fondly look forward to seeing you many times in the future. With pleasure, we give you Olympus X.
—*The Captains*

Tableau 1980
Olympus X—The Captains
Olympus IX
The Sunday Comics—King and Queen Olympus IX
Olympus VIII
Xanadu: An Eastern Adventure—King and Queen
    Olympus VIII
Olympus VII
The Land of Make Believe—King and Queen Olympus
    VII
Olympus VI
Baubles, Bangles, and Boobs—King and Queen
    Olympus VI
Olympus V
An Evening in the Court of France—Queen Olympus V
Olympus IV
A Tour of Our Favorite Bars—King Olympus IV
Olympus III
A Journey from Dusk to Dawn—King Olympus III
Olympus II
A Visit with Florenz Ziegfeld
Olympus I
Camelot—King Olympus I
A Royal Dance
Olympus—The First Decade
King and Queen Olympus X
Presentation of Distinguished Guests
Grand March
Call-Out Dances
Open Court

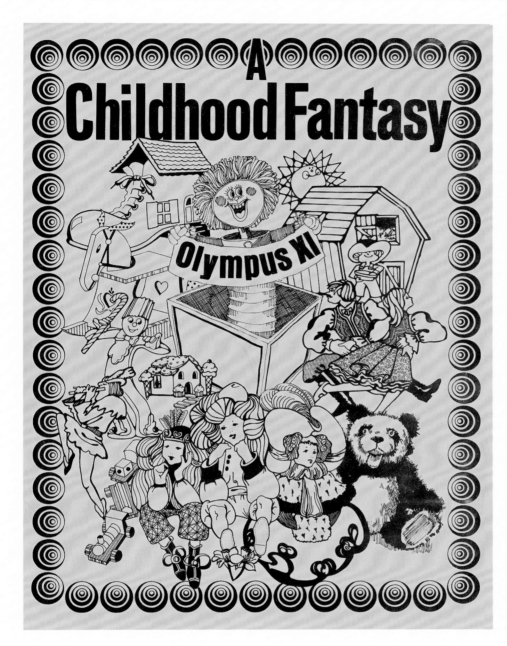

Invitation, 1981. Courtesy of The Historic New Orleans Collection, Williams Research Center, New Orleans, Accession No. 2000.34.91.

Program reads:

As night descends our toymaker works, while deep in the shadows the Sandman lurks,
Ready to sprinkle the grains of sleep, the joys of dreamland he hopes to reap.
But now the Fairy of Night sweeps on and our toyland lives until the dawn.
Toys and trinkets, castles with dolls, all come to life, even the walls.
And then a storm, a sudden change. Why is our toyland now so strange?
It's now a forest of fairy-tale size from which some magical creatures rise.
A spot of light, eternal youth, the search for beauty, an icy truth.
An evil spirit invades the night, seeking to fill our souls with fright.
But never fear, for from above dawn's rays pierce the dark with love.
And mother's songs come back to mind, leaving all bad dreams far behind.
As morning comes our dreams must end, but please remember this, my friend,
The dreams of a child who's loved shall be ideals of Happiness and Serenity.
—Captain

⚜

Tableau 1981
Part I
A Visit to Mystical Toyland Starting with Reality
     The Old Toymaker
     The Sandman
     The Fairy of the Night (Ball Lieutenant)
And Entering into the Surreal
     Olympus' Building Blocks
     Magical Movements
     Jack-in-the-Box (Ball Captain)
     Raggedy Andy and Friend
     The Tears of A Clown
Part II
The Magic Castle of Dolls and Dreams
Dolls from in, around, and out of This World
     Guardians of the Castle (Her Majesty's Toy Soldiers)
     The Doll of the Future (Queen Olympus X)
     From Russia with Love (Siberian Dolls)
     An Arena in Madrid (Matador Doll and Opponent)
     The Hills of Athens Georgia (An Antebellum Doll)
     Saint Peter's Basilica in Rome (Bride Doll)
     Outside No. 10 Downing Street (English Bobby Doll)
Part III
Entering an Enchanted Forest, Children's Stories, Rhymes, and Fairy Tales
     The Light of Eternal Youth (Peter Pan and Tinker Bell)
     The Missing Slipper (Cinderella and Prince Charming)
     The Magic Lamp (Aladdin)
     A Fright of a Different Color (A Composite Witch)
     Cavalier Cat (Puss-in-Boots)
     Ice Maiden (The Snow Queen)
     The Great Fall (Humpty Dumpty)
     A Needle in a Haystack (Old MacDonald's Farm)
Part IV
The Dawn of a Grand New Day
The Serenity and Happiness of Childhood—King and Queen Olympus XI

Invitation, 1984. Courtesy of Tulane University, Louisiana Research
Collection, Howard-Tilton Memorial Library, New Orleans, Otto
Stierle Collection, Manuscripts Collection 902.

Lawn Ornaments 1989

Olympus XIX

Lawn Ornaments

Program, 1989. Courtesy of the Louisiana State Museum, New Orleans, Accession No. 2015.044.24c.

⚜

Tableau 1989
Gazing Balls
King Olympus XVIII
Ball Captain—White Trash
Ball Lieutenant—Blue Mary
We Never Promised a Rose Garden
Autumn Leaves
Grape Arbor
Rose Trellis
Banana Tree
Please Don't Feed the Animals
Dog House
Bird Feeder
Curb Your Dog
Stoned Statues
Buddha
Lions
Breaking Wind
Whirligigs
Chimes
Wishing Well
Make a Wish and Support Buzzy's Boys
Water, Water, Everywhere!
Goldfish
Lily Pond
Sprinkler
Umbrella Table
Flamingos
Wrought Iron
Their Royal Majesties King and Queen Olympus XIX
A Chalmetian Christmas
    Krewe of Olympus—Lawn Ornaments 1989

A Journey of Dreams 1990

OLYMPUS XX

Invitation, 1990. Courtesy of The Historic New Orleans Collection, Williams Research Center, New Orleans, Accession No. 2000.34.93a.

⚜

Tableau 1990
The National Anthem—Star Spangled Banner
Overture
Master of Ceremonies—Sugar Plum Fairy (Honorary Ball Lieutenant)
King and Queen Olympus XVII—Spearmint
Bon Bons
    Captain Olympus XVIII—Rio Kisses
    Orange Slices
Bubble Gum
Cakes
    Red Velvet
    Birthday
    Angel Food
    Devil's Food (Captain's Award)
    Wedding Cake (Honorary Ball Lieutenant)
Peppermints
Candy Apple
M&Ms
Banana Split
Godiva Chocolate
Fruit Tart
Grand March
King and Queen Olympus XVIII—Compulsion and Satisfaction
Introduction of Special Guests
Open Court

THE KNIGHTS
ARE COMING!

The Mystic Krewe of
Celestial Knights

We're going to do it again next year. And it will be
bigger and better, because we love your applause
and we love you. You are beautiful!

—William Woolley, Mystic Krewe of Celestial Knights

The Birth of a Legend

Once heralded as the gay krewe par excellence, the Mystic Krewe of Celestial
Knights achieved splendor and a certain notoriety with its first ten balls. Some
revered this krewe, claiming that no other krewe had ever come close to such
artistry, while others reviled it. All of these strong reactions were provoked by its
captain, the vainglorious William M. Woolley, five-time captain of the Krewe of
Petronius and once its queen. Woolley had left Petronius in a huff, forming the
Mystic Krewe of Celestial Knights with a few other disgruntled members. He was
determined that the new krewe would maintain high standards, and indeed, the
quality of Woolley's costumes and tableaux has rarely been matched.

Miss Woolley

The role of captain of a krewe is important, with responsibility for choosing the
theme of the ball, the costumes, and, most important, the queen—the most powerful and glamorous royal in the gay world. The king was usually chosen at the end of
the ball, although some krewes integrated the kingship into the selection of all royalty at the beginning of the year's planning. Though Woolley (and many others, both
before and since) insisted on occupying the captain's seat, he never operated as a
dictator, instead working democratically with the others in his krewe. He expanded
the number of costumes, creating smaller roles that required less money to include
most members. Pages, dancers, attendants, and footmen elevated the presentations

Program for the Mystic Krewe of Celestial Knights's
Command Performance—Tenth Anniversary ball, 1986.
Design by Charles Kerbs. Courtesy of Howard Philips
Smith.

187

to a new level of pageantry. During Woolley's tenure in the krewe, he wielded his real power by controlling the quality of the presentations. His creative depth and knowledge of the stage, coupled with what he had learned from Elmo Avet, allowed him to reach new heights, and his designs for costumes and staging became reference points for the future of gay Carnival.

Power Struggle

In the wake of the Krewe of Petronius's 1976 *Memories* ball, two accomplished members sought the position of captain: longtime member Millard Wilson (Aunt Millie, who had already served twice as captain and once as queen) and newcomer Daniel Jones. After Jones won the election, Wilson charged that the vote had been rigged, resulting in a seemingly endless catfight. Woolley, who had had enough of this kind of incessant bickering, and several others followed Jones out the door and headed for the Golden Lantern.

After a few drinks, this group of men—William Crotty, Danny Jones, Francis Jones, Hank Ranna, James Keyes, and James Weaver—began planning a new krewe, which they named the Mystic Krewe of Celestial Knights. Woolley already had in mind the krewe's crest, a crescent moon and a single star, paying homage, whether directly or inadvertently, to the mysticism of the Orient or the Order of Freemasonry or perhaps getting the idea from city manhole covers with a similar graphic: said JoJo Landry, "It really takes a lot to find inspiration from the gutter. Now that's a real queen!" The krewe decided to apply for an official state charter, thus ensuring its longevity and legitimacy. Keyes designed the crest as well as the artwork for the first ball invitation, poster, and doubloon. As a later program explained, "In June of 1976, the captain, with an initial membership of twenty, decided upon a new concept for a Carnival krewe, one conceived with a permanent captain and largely permanent board. Initial members were recruited for their talents and artistic abilities. God knows not for their looks, but good buns helped!" That winter, krewe members plastered the French Quarter with announcements warning, *The Knights Are Coming! The Knights Are Coming!* Recalled William Crotty, who became King Celeste I, "That is all that was said so everyone was in semidarkness until the invitations arrived around town. It was an exciting time, full of promise and mystery. This is the essence of Carnival, in my experience."

Local newspapers announced the Krewe's incorporation under the name Margot-Eve, Inc., a nod to the movie *All about Eve*, in which Bette Davis played aging actress Margot Channing and her nemesis was the ingénue Eve Harrington. Woolley had always taken an exaggerated Davis persona as his default alter ego.

Heavenly Bodies

The first Celestial Knights ball, *Heavenly Bodies* (1977) was much anticipated within the gay community. With membership still small, several people affiliated with Petronius lent a hand with what Woolley called his "extravaganza." He promised an over-the-top presentation with as much glitz and glitter as possible. Many believe to this day that the elaborate props and lighting came directly from the storage vaults of the Canal Street department stores, where Woolley and many other Celestial

Knights worked. Thousands of spectators came to the Saint Bernard Civic Center for the initial ball, which not only referenced the solar system but displayed fantastically clad (and unclad) heavenly bodies in brightly colored costumes.

Recalled Crotty, "Bill Woolley designed each and every costume, and I sewed them all myself. Talk about numb fingers. The decorations and trimmings were done by the other members of the club, a total of only eight people. Needless to say, we had to expand the membership by having 'guest' roles for that first year. Jones and Woolley supplied the sets, as they both headed display departments in major department stores. We intended to make it one of the grandest entrances of any club thus far, and Bill outdid himself. He designed a large half-moon with tiny white lights inserted into the design for stars. This became our coat of arms and was hoisted way above the curtains on a wooden porch swing as the prelude music began. Bill was scared—really scared. Everything depended on this ball. Much of the feathers used that first year actually came from Philadelphia, where we found the company that supplied Las Vegas showgirls. On that same trip, Danny and I selected our fabric for our entrances as King and Queen Celeste I. We chose orange chiffon with sequins over a yellow watermarked moiré. The chiffon was from a Christian Dior collection, but we asked them to alter the placement of sequins to our specifications. They agreed, but for a price. This was 1976, and we spent almost five thousand dollars on each costume as royalty." The krewe soon attracted dancers, choreographers, window dressers, and costume and set designers, who combined their talents to produce surprisingly professional stage productions.

Woolley grew up in Memphis and visited New Orleans as a small child with his parents. He found the city both exciting and otherworldly, and after a stint in the army during World War II, he settled there, quickly becoming part of the French Quarter coterie of gay men who gathered at the Bourbon House or the Coffee Pot. Woolley started off working at Canal Street's prestigious Gus Mayer department store, the high-fashion destination at the time. Stewart Gahn, the art director at D. H. Holmes, soon lured Woolley over. Part of the gay clique centered at Miss Dixie's bar, Woolley attended several Krewe of Yuga balls and escaped the police dragnet at the last one. Unbowed, Woolley and his cohorts boldly continued on in the Krewe of Petronius, now a legitimate Carnival club, with Woolley serving as its first real Queen when he reigned at the fourth annual ball, *The Wicked Bitches of History*. He earned a reputation as difficult and exacting, prompting both high praise and rancor. Woolley quickly learned the complex lessons of gay camp sensibility and took them directly to the stage, where he transformed them into a new mode of gay expression.

Perfumes

Designed by Michael Murphy, the poster for the Knights' second ball, *Perfumes* (1978), depicted the set as an opulent boudoir with a gigantic mirror and dresser in the middle. But in a departure from previous practice, the dominant color was red, which invigorated the stage and costumes. Performers dressed in costumes that referenced exotic and expensive fragrances—Chanel No. 5, Patchouli, Jungle Gardenia, YSL Opium, and L'Air du Temps—popped out of the mirror and paraded around the audience while enveloped in a cloud of perfume.

James Keyes, costume design for the Mystic Krewe of Celestial Knights's *Carnival in Rio* ball, 1979. Courtesy of Howard Philips Smith.

Gay Carnival for the Public

With *Carnival in Rio* (1979) Woolley and company explored more fully their staging with colors and feathers. Bold reds, oranges, yellows, greens, and blues came together in unexpected combinations. Further, Brazilian Carnival was sexy and hedonistic, and the Celestial Knights brought this same energy and aesthetic to the stage, with notably revealing costumes. *New Orleans Magazine* ran a piece on the ball, which was subsequently restaged for the public at the New Orleans Theater for the Performing Arts. James Keyes's playful poster encouraged revelers to *Go Bananas and Come to Carnival in Rio with the Krewe of Celestial Knights.* "Our past two balls have been stylized and chic. This year we plan to be gaudy," explained Woolley. The highlight of the ball came with the appearance of a wildly colorful butterfly with nine-foot-high rhinestone-studded wings that spread out to more than ten feet.

Les Plumages d'Hiver (Winter Feathers)

For the Knights' fourth ball, *Les Plumages d'Hiver* (1980), an all-white stage showcased an array of soft pastel costumes. An elaborate set of carved silver doors led to a snowy garden dotted with statues of Venus. Woolley and his cocaptain, Jim Weaver, wearing subtle pink gowns and plumes, rode onstage in a sled and introduced the frolicking Snowflakettes, who were scantily clad and wore pearls draped over their arms and headpieces of white and silver feathers. Each carried a snowflake, which was a hoop draped with white spangles, waved to and fro as a fan. After four toy soldiers marched up and down this winter wonderland to the Nutcracker's *Dance of the Flowers*, the Sugar Plum Fairies danced around a fountain with shining blue streamers dangling from silver tiers. Next came the Winds, who sported bluish-pink chiffon costumes with capes and pink and white glittery feather headpieces, followed by the Huntsmen, who chased and shot a white feathery-furry Lion, who pulled out two red streamers to symbolize blood. The Bell wore a silver lamé jumpsuit with a knee-length cape edged in purple fur and a four-foot-high headpiece adorned with giant silver bells and white feathers. The finale was a masquerade given by the reigning king and queen in their winter palace. King André Picou, in his white tunic trimmed with hundreds of rhinestones, reigned over his court, whose members wore pastel wigs that matched their costumes. Queen Gene Davis, in a gold lamé gown and crown, blazed against the white set, waving her magic wand. James Keyes's poster and invitation for the ball showed a rather mysterious figure in a snowy landscape, with bare trees and icicles and snowflakes in subtle shades of white and blue. Keyes used the wintry scene from Erté's series *The Seasons* but did so with a minimalist sensibility. Gone were the subtle ochres and greens and the deep blues of the sky, replaced with the icy white of a dazzling frozen world.

This ball, too, was repeated for the public in a showing at the New Orleans Theater for the Performing Arts with the participation of a local favorite, the New Leviathan Oriental Fox-Trot Orchestra. The newspaper advertisement portrayed the ball as a "lighthearted, tongue-in-cheek approach to the theme with spectacular sets, all glitter and icicles and snow, and the costuming defies description." George Dureau, a well-known local gay artist, was asked to create a second poster specifically for the public performance, and he reimagined the tableau as a bacchanal scene right out of the *Satyricon*. His bold lines and flesh-colored tints were simple yet suggested another world, decadent and flirtatious. The poster was sold as a limited edition fine art print. It also announced the event as the second annual presentation, keeping secret the presentation's origins as a gay Carnival ball.

A Golden Age

For *An Oriental Fantasy* ball in 1981, the Celestial Knights dazzled their audience with the mysteries of the Far East. This was not the first time Carnival had tapped into these exotic realms. In 1885, the Krewe of Proteus's *Myths and Worships of the Chine*se had featured floats recalling the Birth of Confucius and Paradise. The narrator at the beginning of the Celestial Knights' ball quoted lines from Gilbert and Sullivan's *Mikado*, mixing them up a bit for dramatic effect: "If you want to know who we are, we are gentlemen of Japan—on many a vase and jar, on many a screen and fan, we figure in lively paint. Our attitude's queer and quaint—and if you think we ain't, you're wrong! If you think we are worked by strings, like a Japanese marionette, you don't understand these things. It is simply court etiquette. Perhaps you suppose this throng can't keep it up all day long? If that's your idea, you're wrong!" The presentation featured boldly colored costumes on a black lacquered set, with performers descending a series of steep stairs from the stage to the audience. Woolley, dressed as a dark Fu Manchu figure, opened the ball before being joined by a red dragon manned by at least a dozen men with a huge papier-mâché head. The rather avant-garde soundtrack for the ball came from a popular album by Yellow Magic Orchestra, a Japanese electronic group that played on recognizable oriental motifs.

Burlesque Revival

The 1982 ball, *An Evening of Burlesque*, charted new territory, as the krewe set out to re-create great moments from the vaudeville stage and to recall such famous strippers as Gypsy Rose Lee. As captain and master of ceremonies, Woolley appeared in a flamboyant blue-sequined costume. The performance included dance numbers and costumed characters, all announced by Woolley with acid wit and camp. When intermission was announced (another innovation), Woolley stepped behind a screen onstage and began to change his costume, again evoking the vaudeville strippers. As more than a thousand spectators watched, he explained what would happen next: "In order not to get raided by the police after the war, burlesque houses staged this big finale. How big? 42D and I won't tell you what the D is for either! They had to do a salute to America. It was very patriotic. Needless to say, we need more of it today!" He later reappeared on stage for another musical number in yet another lavish and fantastic costume. One of the great numbers in this ball was a re-creation of the pregnant bride skit from *Funny Girl*.

The finale, "Stars and Stripes Forever," included performers in red, white, and blue costumes cavorting around the stage in front of a backdrop of flags and eagles. Woolley came out as a majorette with her attendants all carrying huge American flags. The king and queen arrived wearing red garments with red sequins and rhinestones, red-feathered collars, and tall, glittering crowns and scepters.

Artist George Dureau in his French Quarter studio, 1977. Photograph by Sarah Benham.

Rivalries, Rivalries, and More Rivalries

The Mystic Krewe of Celestial Knights and the Krewe of Memphis became particular rivals, and by chance, both groups chose blues-related themes for their 1983 balls—not terribly surprising given that the blues and jazz form such an integral part of New Orleans culture. The Krewe of Memphis's ball, *Memphis Blows the Blues*, took place before the Celestial Knights' presentation, *Symphony in Blue*, and Woolley threw down the gauntlet early in the evening, just after the opening musical number, "Blue Skies": "Now that we've blown blue skies away, let's see if we can blow Memphis away. Not the krewe, darlings, the city. Shame on you for thinking naughty thoughts, just because they didn't invite me. I heard they needed applause. See I took a nasty pill today, so watch it, you bitches." He continued on with one of the major inspirations for the ball: "In the 1920s in Memphis there was this marvelous black man who wrote music that typified the times. We would like to pay tribute to this wonderful man, W. C. Handy, who wrote so many of the blues numbers we'll be doing for you tonight."

After intermission, Woolley reappeared in an even more elaborate blue and silver costume with blue feathers and long shining blue train. Woolley reenacted "Hello Bluebird," a Judy Garland song from the film *I Could Go On Singing*. In addition to Garland, the movie starred Dirk Bogarde, another gay icon, and the film was released not long after Garland's Carnegie Hall concert, where she had reached an apotheosis within the gay community. While introducing another lively number, Woolley touched on inspiration itself, the threat of failure always lurking behind the next tableau ball and the level of scrutiny that greeted every number: "The next number I wanted to do, they wouldn't let me. They told me I couldn't dance well enough. I don't know what the hell I'm doing up here besides making a fool out of myself. There are a few here tonight who would love to see me do that, wouldn't you? That's all right, bitches. I haven't fallen in seven years. I mean, if you want me to, I could just fall right now and we could get it over with.

I Could Go on Singing movie poster, 1963.

Judy at Carnegie Hall, 1961.

But I got another number to do. I better not break these heels. Now back to seriousness. It's a gorgeous number, and it's simply called "Shaking the Blues Away"!" The rest of the ball featured different interpretations of George Gershwin's *Rhapsody in Blue*.

This ball was also noteworthy because an African American man, Allen Lombard, was selected as queen. According to Woolley, "Others in the krewe did not like the fact that we were having an African American queen, so they shortened the queen's royal costume by several inches. I threw a fit. I wasn't about to send my queen to the stage with an imperfect garment. I just couldn't figure out such mean-spiritedness. And besides, Allen deserved to be queen. He had worked harder than anyone else in the krewe, and I took it upon myself to fix the situation. There wasn't any more of the fabric, so I went to Metairie Fabrics and bought a contrasting strip to lengthen the gown. I also bought teardrop pearls to attach around the hem. The fix, if you can believe it, cost as much as the whole gown. It was a spectacular triumph. Allen's gown tinkled like little bells as he walked, giving him that certain something that only a queen could pull off."

The Celestial Knights also had a rivalry with Jon Lee Poché and the Krewe of Armeinius, with the two men battling on the streets of the French Quarter, on the stage in Chalmette, and in the local newspapers. Poché had started the feud by publishing prank photos that supposedly showed members of the Celestial Knights dressed in tacky drag with bitchy captions. Woolley parried by publishing photos of his krewe members in even tackier drag with captions indicated that members of Armeinius were envious.

In 1985, both Woolley and Poché came up with imaginative and unique ball themes as they sought to best each other onstage. Woolley again channeled Elmo Avet and his love of Hollywood. Through its various incarnations—a play by Edward Knoblock, a silent movie, a Vitascope extravaganza, a 1944 movie starring Marlene Dietrich (a particular favorite of Avet's) and Ronald Coleman, a Broadway musical, and a 1955 Vincente Minnelli film of the musical—*Kismet* had become a touchstone for the gay community. The camp musical version particularly resonated for Woolley and the Celestial Knights, and it inspired their *1001 Arabian Nights*. Using subtle shades of green, blue, purple, brown, orange, and yellow, Woolley created a palace backdrop for all the musical's central characters, with the Sultan and Sultana of Baghdad becoming King and Queen Celeste IX. The production emphasized the parallels between the musical's depiction of the wonderfully liberated life in Baghdad and New Orleans, where gay men and women could pursue their lives "with the zeal we feel here," as the lyrics to "Not since Nineveh" put it. In attendance was Poché, who then fought back as captain of Armeinius with an elaborate fairy tale wherein a boy dreamed of becoming the queen of a storybook kingdom and then realized his dream.

Midstream Changes

With their tenth anniversary ball, *Command Performance* (1986), the Celestial Knights looked back and contemplated what they had achieved. At the top of their game, they showcased the themes of past Celestial Knights balls. Wayne Phillips, costume curator at the Louisiana State Museum, described *Command Performance* as "a historicist masterpiece of Age of Enlightenment design. Calling on his many years of work in eye-popping visual merchandising for department stores, Woolley as captain imbued the whole ball with an eighteenth-century style and grace but with a definite gay spin. The color palette consisted of nearly universal pastel shades, his own opening costume being a sweet pistachio green with matching wig. Drag costumes incorporated panniers under the wide froufrou satin skirts, and the faces of the men were as powdered and populated with as many beauty spots as those of the 'women.' Such attention to detail sets Woolley apart as a true devotee of the unashamedly gay tableau tradition."

But by the mid-1980s, AIDS had begun to slash its way through the New Orleans gay community, and the annual ball programs were dedicated to deceased members. By the end of 1986, Woolley had left his beloved New Orleans, with some observers claiming that he had been ousted from the krewe and others contending that he had departed to take care of his sister, who was ill. In reality, many of the Canal Street department stores were closing, and Woolley took a job in Mobile as vice president of visual merchandising for Gayfer's Department Store.

Despite Woolley's departure and its shrinking membership, the krewe forged ahead. Danny Jones, Queen Celeste I, became captain, and Celestial Knights continued

Mystic Krewe of Celestial Knights (1977)

1976–77

The Mystic Krewe of Celestial Knights was formed by disgruntled members of the Krewe of Petronius in 1976. Leading the Celestial Knights as permanent captain was the strong-willed William Woolley, one of the creative forces behind Petronius. Conceived as presenting "extravaganzas" rather than ordinary tableau balls, the new krewe would accept few compromises. The first ball, *Heavenly Bodies* (1977), took place at the Saint Bernard Civic Auditorium.

1978

The Celestial Knights' second ball featured costumes that depicted famous perfumes. The performers appeared onstage by popping out of a huge mirror atop a red dresser.

1979

The Celestial Knights' next ball, *Carnival in Rio*, was a bawdy trip to Brazil with skimpy costumes and lots of attitude. Woolley and krewe remounted the entire ball for the public at the New Orleans Theater for the Performing Arts.

1980

With *Les Plumages d'Hiver*, Woolley took his krewe to a winter wonderland, snow-covered and pristine. After the ball, the production was again presented to the public at the New Orleans Theater for the Performing Arts.

1982

Woolley charted new territory with *An Evening of Burlesque*, which revisited the risqué world of Vaudeville. The krewe presented a tightly focused romp with choreographed song-and-dance numbers and a sensational intermission during which the captain changed clothes onstage behind a screen.

1985

1001 Arabian Nights found both the krewe and gay Carnival at the top of their games. Reworking Minnelli's *Kismet* musical, Woolley presented a pastel journey through the palaces of Baghdad.

1986

The krewe's tenth anniversary ball was the last for which Woolley served as captain, though he helped his successor, Danny Jones, with the next ball.

1992

The Mystic Krewe of Celestial Knights held its final ball, *In the Land of the Pharaohs*. Though the production was less spectacular than its predecessors, the krewe retained its standards. Members then decided to disband on a high note.

to hold balls. According to Gabe Nassar, who joined the krewe around this time, "We were going strong in 1987 despite the void created by Miss Woolley's absence. We had well over three thousand attendees at the *Celebración de Fiestas* ball. And the next year we moved to the Municipal Auditorium. Can you imagine that? Our little ol' krewe among the finest balls in New Orleans. So when it came time for me to be king, well, I couldn't rely on the krewe itself, which always, always paid for the costumes for royalty. I had to make it even bigger, with all the feathers I could find in New York. Yes, that was when all the lights were at their most brilliant, but it couldn't last forever."

In the 1990s, the krewe replaced the tableau balls with smaller gatherings held at a dinner club at which costumes were revealed. Woolley seldom traveled back to New Orleans and become nearly a complete recluse, holing up in Mobile with his sister and permitting only the closest of friends to remain part of his life. In 2008, however, he consented to be interviewed by Tim Wolff for his groundbreaking documentary, *The Sons of Tennessee Williams*, looking forward to a future in which gay men and women would demand nothing less than full equality.

The Legacy of the Celestial Knights

Otto Stierle, an early member of the Celestial Knights who had also been a member of the Krewes of Yuga and Petronius, reflected, "Celestial Knights gave sixteen years of lavish extravaganza balls. Eleven of the balls were at the Saint Bernard Civic Center, followed by four at the Municipal Auditorium, and the final presentation in 1992 at the Clarion Hotel Grand Ballroom in a totally new format. Although ending in a financially sound status, the board of directors decided to dissolve, because of the ever-shrinking base of interested working members and the general economic conditions of the local area. The AIDS crisis had put an ever-increasing financial burden on the gay community, and Carnival organizations were fighting for the same dollar support of the community. It was thought best to dissolve with success and dignity intact. This organization was well-known for its choreographed production numbers, large and lavish costumes, and spectacular presentations. Many of its costumes could be seen decorating store windows on Canal Street each year following its ball during the weeks preceding Mardi Gras." Many decades later, the Celestial Knights still cast a long shadow.

Mystic Krewe of Celestial Knights Tableau Balls List	
1977	HEAVENLY BODIES
1978	PERFUMES
1979	CARNIVAL IN RIO
1980	LES PLUMAGES D'HIVER
1981	AN ORIENTAL FANTASY
1982	AN EVENING OF BURLESQUE
1983	SYMPHONY IN BLUE
1984	FASHION
1985	1001 ARABIAN NIGHTS
1986	COMMAND PERFORMANCE—10TH ANNIVERSARY
1987	CELEBRACIÓN DE FIESTAS
1988	SALUTE TO LAS VEGAS
1989	BIRDS OF A FEATHER
1990	AN AMERICAN VIEW OF PARIS
1991	ROMANCING THE STONE
1992	IN THE LAND OF THE PHARAOHS

Ronald DeLise, stained-glass crest of the Mystic Krewe of Celestial Knights, based on design by James Keyes, 1977. DeLise also designed the stained glass crest for the Knights d'Orléans motorcycle club. Courtesy of Wayne Phillips.

Mystic Krewe of Celestial Knights Royalty List			
YEAR OF TABLEAU BALL	**CAPTAIN**	**QUEEN**	**KING**
1977	William Woolley	Daniel Lee Jones	William Mullen Crotty
1978	William Woolley	James Weaver	John Nelson
1979	William Woolley	Francis Jones	Hank Ranna
1980	William Woolley/James Weaver	André Picou	Gene Davis
1981	William Woolley	Donnie Lloyd	Leo Cappell
1982	William Woolley	Weldon Brackett	(unknown—not a krewe member)
1983	William Woolley	Allen Lombard	Vic Rodi
1984	William Woolley	Joey Bennett	Charles Barr
1985	William Woolley	George Roth	Frank Marquez
1986	William Woolley	Carlos Rodriguez	André Boudreaux
1987	Daniel Lee Jones	Joey Bennett	Gabe Nassar
1988	Daniel Lee Jones	Dale Rogers	Otto Stierle Jr.
1989	Allen Lombard	—	—
1990	Allen Lombard	Brandi Rodi (female)	David Learned
1991	Wayne Bell/Allen Lombard	Jerry McGill (Pitti Pat)	Jim Keaton
1992	Wayne Bell/Allen Lombard	—	—

Heavenly Bodies 1977

Poster, 1977. Design by James Keyes. Courtesy of The Historic New Orleans Collection, Williams Research Center, New Orleans, Accession No. 1997.307.13.

Captain William Woolley, 1977. Courtesy of the Louisiana State Museum, New Orleans, Accession No. 2016.026.11.1.

King Celeste I, William Crotty, and Queen Celeste I, Danny Jones, 1977. Courtesy of the Louisiana State Museum, New Orleans, Accession No. 2016.011.03.03.

Perfumes 1978

Poster, 1978. Design by Michael Murphy. Courtesy of the Louisiana State Museum, New Orleans, Accession No. 1995.010.053.

John C. Scheffler, costume sketch for *Perfumes*, Krewe of Helios, 1966. This design may have inspired the Mystic Krewe of Celestial Knights's *Perfumes* ball. Courtesy of the Louisiana State Museum, New Orleans, Accession No. 2014.032.008.04.

Captain William Woolley and entourage, 1978. Courtesy of the Louisiana State Museum, New Orleans, Accession No. 2016.011.04.01.

Carnival in Rio 1979

Poster, 1979. Design by James Keyes. *Carnival in Rio* was the first gay ball to be restaged for the general public at the New Orleans Theater for the Performing Arts. Courtesy of the Louisiana State Museum, New Orleans, Accession No. 1995.010.035.

Captain William Woolley, 1979. Courtesy of the Louisiana State Museum, New Orleans, Accession No. 2016.011.05.38.

Queen and King Celeste III, Francis Jones and Hank Ranna, 1979. Courtesy of the Louisiana State Museum, New Orleans, Accession No. 2011.026.05.09.

Les Plumages d'Hiver (Winter Feathers) 1980

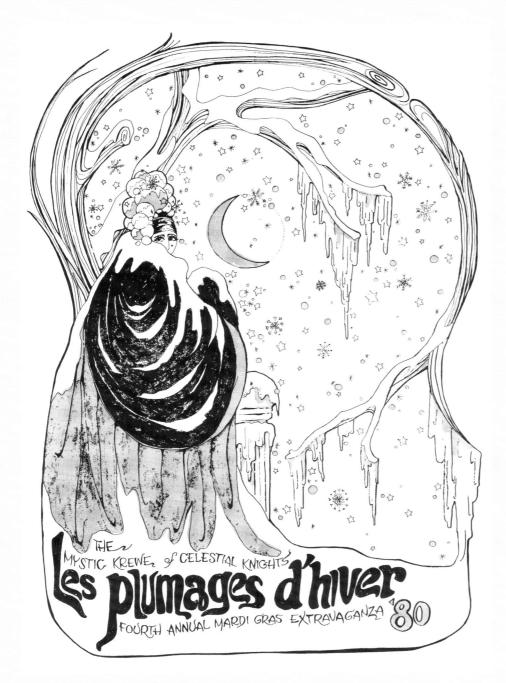

Poster, 1980. Design by James Keyes. Courtesy of the Louisiana State Museum, New Orleans, Accession No. 1995.010.038.

Erté, *Hiver* (Winter), from *Seasons*, which inspired the *Plumages d'Hiver* invitation. Courtesy © Sevenarts, Ltd.

Poster for the restaging of the *Plumages d'Hiver* ball, 1980. Design by George Dureau. Courtesy of the Louisiana State Museum, New Orleans, Accession No. 1995.010.039.

An Oriental Fantasy 1981

Program, 1981. Design by James Keyes. Keyes was inspired by Utagawa Hiroshige's ukiyo-e prints and his *36 Views of Mount Fuji*. Courtesy of the Louisiana State Museum, New Orleans, Accession No. 1995.010.041.

An Evening of Burlesque 1982

Poster, 1982. Design by Susan Stutts. Courtesy of the Louisiana State Museum, New Orleans, Accession No. 1995.010.042.

Burlesque showgirls, 1982. Courtesy of the Louisiana State Museum, New Orleans, Accession No. 2016.011.09.02.

Captain William Woolley and attendants, 1982. Courtesy of the Louisiana State Museum, New Orleans, Accession No. 2016.026.14.01.

Symphony in Blue 1983

Program, 1983. Design by Susan Stutts. Courtesy of the Louisiana State Museum, New Orleans, Accession No. 1995.010.051.

Fashion 1984

Program, 1984. Courtesy of The Historic New Orleans Collection, Williams Research Center, New Orleans, Accession No. 2000.34.55.

Tableau 1984
Act I
Overture—Fashion Moods
The Gift Wrap Stomp—The Boyettes
Big Bucks—The Captain
Midnight Lace—Returning King and Queen
Millinery—A Shopper's Delight
Buttons and Bows, English Style
For Ladies Only
Beautiful Face Needs Beautiful Clothes
Imagination—The Designer's Tools
Beautiful Thoughts

Act II
Think Pink—Captain and Dressmakers
Bathing Suits—A Look at Tomorrow
Sportswear in Space
Jazzercise—New Wave Style
Lipsticks
Jewels
After Five—The Captain
Bride and Groom of the Future—King and Queen Celeste VIII
A Final Bow—King and Queen Celeste VII
Honored Guests
Open Court

Captain William Woolley and fashionistas, 1984. Courtesy of the Louisiana State Museum, New Orleans, Accession No. 2016.026.15.03.

1001 Arabian Nights 1985

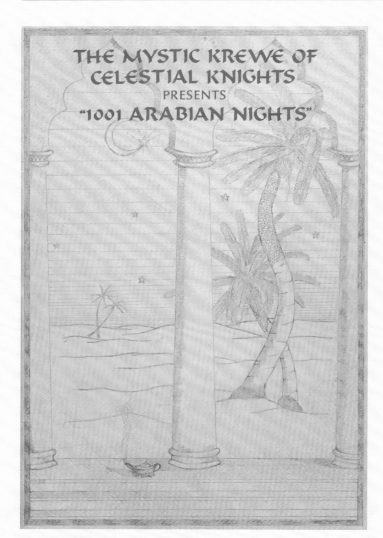

Program, 1985. Design by James Keyes. Courtesy of Howard Philips Smith.

Program reads: *Congratulations and Best Wishes to King and Queen Celeste IX. Love, Norma Desmond. To King and Queen Celeste IX, Congratulations, but never forget, we're still Number One! Bill and Dan, King and Queen Celeste I.*

Tableau 1985
Overture
Lighting of the Crest
Presentation of Officers
Welcome to Baghdad—Captain
The Bride and Groom Return from the Garden of Allah—Returning King and Queen
Palace Guards
The Wazir
Rahadlakum—A Love Potion
Arabi Traffic Jam—Flying Carpets
Zubbediya
Snake Charmers and Cobra Woman
At the Marketplace
    Beads and Jewels
    Perfume
    Silk Merchant
    Shalimar
Passions of the Oasis
    Palms and Exotic Fruit
    Desert Flowers
    Desert Bird
Concubines and Nubians of the Caliph
The Sultan and Sultana—King and Queen Celeste IX
Caravan—Finale

Captain William Woolley, 1985. Courtesy of the Louisiana State Museum, New Orleans, Accession No. 2016.026.10.

Queen Celeste IX, George Roth, 1985. Courtesy of the Louisiana State Museum, New Orleans, Accession No. 2016.026.16.2.

King Celeste IX, Frank Marquez, 1985. Courtesy of the Louisiana State Museum, New Orleans, Accession No. 2016.026.16.3.

Celebración de Fiestas 1987

Salute to Las Vegas 1988

Program, 1987. Courtesy of the Louisiana State Museum, New Orleans, Accession No. 1995.010.055.

Program, 1988. Design by Otto Stierle. Courtesy of the Louisiana State Museum, New Orleans, Accession No. 1995.010.063.

Showgirl, 1988. Courtesy of the Louisiana State Museum, New Orleans, 2016.011.11.20.

An American View of Paris 1990

Program, 1990. Courtesy of The Historic New Orleans Collection, Williams Research Center, New Orleans, Accession No. 2000.34.64.

Tableau 1990
Paris by Night
Folies-Bergère (Captain)
Crystal—Returning King and Queen Celeste XIII
Champagne
Pastries
Perfumes
Left Bank
Haute Couture
Museums
The Classics
Landmarks
Music
Fleur-de-Lis
King and Queen Celeste XIV

THE KREWE OF ISHTAR

I Am Woman

Ishtar was the first gay women's Carnival club in the city and was embraced by the whole gay community. We were so proud of our krewe. I attended all the balls. . . . I even had the honor of meeting Miss Dixie through my close friend Alice Brady, another legendary lesbian.

—Diane DiMiceli, King Ishtar I

The Lesbian Community

During the Golden Age of Gay Carnival in the early 1980s, bars had already become an important part of the lesbian community as meeting places, clearinghouses of information, and havens from intolerance. The bar scene had grown steadily from the 1950s through the 1970s, until lesbian bars were sprinkled not only throughout the French Quarter proper but also through the Faubourg Marigny and even Jefferson Parish. These early years, especially with frequent police raids, were difficult. Several lesbian bars sprung up on the waterfront near Tchoupitoulas Street during the 1950s but soon were forced to close. At the Goldenrod Inn on Frenchmen Street, a straight bar in front and a lesbian bar in the back, almost fifty lesbians were arrested in a 1953 police raid. By the early 1960s, women had been frequenting many of the gay male bars in the French Quarter, including Dixie's Bar of Music and the Galley House, but women wanted their own places. Unlike Hattiesburg, Mississippi, for example, a town with no gay bars where lesbians had weekly get-togethers to read poetry, listen to music, and bake bread, New Orleans was too spread out and needed a more focused section of town for interaction. The only lesbian social group, the Gourmet Club, did not last very long. By the mid-1980s, the center of the New Orleans lesbian universe was Charlene's Bar on Elysian Fields Avenue in the heart of the Faubourg Marigny. Proprietor Charlene Schneider was a community activist who created "a safe place for lesbians

The goddess Ishtar on her chariot with her seven lions. Design by Gunter. This graphic became identified with the krewe and was seen on many of its invitations and posters. Courtesy of the Louisiana State Museum, New Orleans, Accession No. 1980.177.1.

207

Jenny Wilde, float designs for the Mistick Krewe of Comus's Izdubar parade, 1904. Float No. 8, *At the Shrine of Ishtar*, a possible influence on gay Carnival. Courtesy of the Louisiana State Museum, New Orleans, Accession No. 1971.036.41.

when attitudes toward them were less tolerant." By this time, other lesbian bars included Brady's, Diane's, Pino's, Vicki's, the Quarter Horse, Pinstripes and Lace, Les Pierres, the Blue Odyssey, Kathryn's, and Club 621.

According to *Last Call: New Orleans Dyke Bar History Project*, "Dyke bars were once a common fixture in New Orleans. In the 1970s and 1980s, there were more than a dozen such spaces in New Orleans—Charlene's, Pino's and Brady's to name a few. Bars have historically functioned as community centers for queer and trans people who were often shunned by their families. New Orleans has an especially rich history as a haven for LGBTQ people from all over the South for generations." From these bars sprang New Orleans's first (and to date only) lesbian krewe, which took its name from the Babylonian goddess of war, power, love, sex, and fertility.

The Birth of the Goddess

Alice Brady's bar on Rampart Street served both men and women but soon became more known for its lesbian clientele, and Diane DiMiceli took over Brady's in the late 1970s. Kitty Blackwell opened Miss Kitty's bar on Burgundy Street and also welcomed a mixed crowd. Not until Rosemary Pino and Charlene Schneider opened their bars on Elysian Fields did the lesbian community have its own bars. Strengthened by this success, Pino, DiMiceli, and Sue Martino formed the Krewe of Ishtar in 1980 and held their first ball the next year. DiMiceli served as krewe president, Martino became the captain, and Pino held the post of secretary-treasurer. Jan Moran, who served as vice president for a time, was also president of the board of the Academy of the Golden Goddess Inc. (AGGI) Awards. The krewe's namesake female goddess had previously appeared in more traditional Carnival parades, such as the 1904, the Mistick Krewe of Comus parade. According to the legend, as Ishtar descended into the netherworld, she was forced to remove one garment for each of the gates she entered, and after the seventh gate, she was naked. While she remained in hell, all sexual activity ceased on earth. As she ascended back to earth, her garments were restored. The krewe's ball invitations depicted the goddess driving a chariot led by seven lions and carrying a bow and arrow at the ready to defeat her foes.

Alice Brady

A pioneer in the New Orleans gay community, Alice Brady started out working in the Galley House, a gay male bar on Chartres Street, in the 1950s and quickly became a strong voice within the community. She opened up the Mascarade Bar on St. Louis Street in 1952 and then Brady's on Rampart several years later. According to Diane DiMiceli, "She was tough as nails, and she had seen it all. Back then, you had to be either butch or femme. That's just the way it was. There was a tough woman's bar on Decatur Street named Vicky's. Alice would tell me stories of going there and always getting into a tangle with some butch. But by the 1980s, things had started to change. These stereotypes were slow to disappear, but that seems like another world now. The openness and support she provided, however, helped strengthen the lesbian community, and I don't think we could have pulled off a real Carnival krewe without her."

The First Balls

For its first ball in 1981, the two dozen members of the Krewe of Ishtar presented *The Modern Gods and Goddesses of Babylon* on the stage of the St. Bernard Civic Center in Chalmette. This was the krewe's Alpha Ball and Sue Martino as ball captain produced a masterful tableau, featuring the queen as the Lioness. For the 1982 Beta Ball, *I Am Woman*, the krewe channeled famous women in history, most notably Amelia Earhart, who descended onto the stage in an airplane in full pilot regalia at the close of the tableau. *Music, Music, Music* (1983) heralded a more light-hearted approach, with costumes representing Broadway shows glittering beneath the spotlights as spectators heard—what else?—music.

Somewhere in Time and *Tarot Cards*

The krewe's Delta Ball, *Somewhere in Time* (1984), offered "a salute to those abstract feelings in life that bring us joy and pleasure," and the captain hoped that it would "continue to delight and surprise you." The costuming reached a high level of artistry, with the Butterfly, Valentine, Rainbow, Mermaid, and Peacock strutting around Queen and King Ishtar IV. The *Tarot Card* ball (1985) represented a huge leap in not only ambition but aesthetics and composition. The krewe brought divining the future alive with a Gypsy Fortune Teller as the captain and her lieutenant as the Fool, one of the most enigmatic cards. The returning king and queen were the High Priestess and the Empress. Then came forth the Lovers, followed by Justice, Death, Temperance, the Sun, and the Angel of Judgment. King and Queen Ishtar V were the King of Cups and the World, represented by a nude woman surrounded by a wreath and mysterious heads at each corner. As the program explained, "No other subject conjures up more secrecy, superstition, and mystery than the exciting Tarot Cards. Sometimes ominous, often forewarning but always entertaining, these colorful pieces of cardboard never fail to hold our fascination." Wally Sherwood reported in *Ambush Magazine* that "the wonderful women in the gay community came up not only with one of the season's most illustrious themes, but perhaps the most attractive program of all, a full-sized deluxe edition in black, red and mustard uncluttered by an excess of commercialism. Each presentation was matched by a reproduction of the card in the program, and as part of the table centerpiece. The Crescent City Movin' Company, a popular dance troupe, lifted the Carnival spirit of everyone in the St. Bernard audience and The Lovers card especially touched a cord. The fun continued with post-ball partying at Pino's Club 621."

Love

The invitation to the Krewe of Ishtar's 1986 ball, *Love*, featured a dove. Although gay men could not join Ishtar, they had been involved in all of the krewe's balls as designers, choreographers, and consultants, and the AIDS epidemic had taken many of the krewe members' friends; nonetheless, the ball retained a sense of celebration of life, a cornerstone of the lesbian community's philosophy.

Arson Attacks

With the increased visibility of New Orleans's gay community in the 1970s and 1980s, a backlash was perhaps inevitable, and a number of establishments catering to homosexuals suffered arson attacks. The Club My-O-My, which featured female impersonators, operated first in the French Quarter and then on the Lakefront from the 1930s until 1972, when it was destroyed by fire. After briefly returning to the French Quarter, the club closed for good. A 1973 fire at the Up Stairs Lounge resulted in the deaths of thirty-two patrons. And over Easter weekend in 1985, a fire started in a storage area at the back of Pino's Bar and "almost the entire roof of the bar was destroyed." The fire was considered suspicious, especially because the bar had recently prevailed against an excessive-noise complaint brought by a nearby hotel and other neighbors.

Charlene Schneider

Charlene Schneider became a gay activist after she was arrested in a raid on a gay bar and lost her job at NASA during the mid-1960s. In 1991, her efforts led the New Orleans City Council to pass an antidiscrimination ordinance, earning her the Human Rights Campaign Equality Award and the Forum for Equality Community Service Award. Her bar especially functioned as a clearinghouse for news and a safe haven for women. And its focus was unapologetically lesbian: declared a sign on the door, "If You Ain't Gay, You Can't Stay." However, gay men occasionally frequented Charlene's bar. Ed "Blanche" Norton, a bartender at the Golden Lantern and lead diva for the Demented Women drag troupe, often relaxed at Schneider's bar, eventually becoming so close to her that she gave him a key to the back door, a symbol of supreme trust. "She was like a mother hen," recalled Norton. "If someone needed money, Charlene was always there to lend a hand, and believe me, I needed it from time to time. No questions asked. And for the dykes in this town, she represented respect and love above all else. She made sure that her girls were taken care of."

Diane DiMiceli

Diane DiMiceli was born and raised in New Orleans's Gentilly neighborhood. She came out by encountering other lesbians in the French Quarter and soon began frequenting gay-friendly establishments. In 1978 she bought Alice Brady's bar on Rampart and continued to welcome both men and women, though she renamed the bar Diane's. When she opened another Diane's in Metairie, she brought the first woman's bar to Jefferson Parish. DiMiceli's devotion to gay Carnival was evident in her commitment to the Krewe of Ishtar. She hosted fund-raisers at her bars and participated in all aspects of the gay community, with a special focus on lesbians. "It would be hard to separate out friendships and lovers from the group that kept Ishtar together. I had been romantically involved with several bar owners myself, and these relationships and breakups contributed to and at times hindered our efforts, but we viewed ourselves as one big family, a community of brothers and sisters who happened to enjoy going out to the bars and going to all the gay balls." DiMiceli, Marsha Robert, and other women from Ishtar were also at one time members of the Krewe of Venus, a traditional women's parading krewe.

Flyer for Krewe of Ishtar rummage sale, July 27, 1980. Courtesy of the Louisiana State Museum, New Orleans, Accession No. 1980.177.1

Rosemary Pino

Rosemary Pino was another pioneer in New Orleans's gay and lesbian community in the city and in Ishtar, helping to fuel the city's growing lesbian presence with her Club 621 Bar on Elysian Fields. Pino worked closely with the Krewes of Polyphemus and Armeinius, helping with fund-raising and events and serving on the board of the Academy of the Golden Goddess Inc. (AGGI) Awards. Tragically, Pino died in 2005 in the flooding caused by Hurricane Katrina when water inundated the nursing home where she was convalescing in St. Bernard Parish.

An Enduring Legacy

The creation of a lesbian-only krewe unquestionably represented a milestone. Just as noteworthy, however, was the relationship between New Orleans's lesbians and the gay male krewes. Members of both communities came together to celebrate Carnival and to toast each other's successes. This commitment to a shared community served members of both groups when the AIDS epidemic hit.

Women in Other Krewes

Women had appeared in the gay krewes early on, although most of these women were straight, at least at first. In 1976, Amon-Ra chose Carmen Huffer as its king. The short-lived Krewe of Vesta, founded in 1983, proclaimed itself "a newly formed carnival krewe consisting of gay men and women and duly chartered by the State of Louisiana. We are proud to now be a part of the Gay Community of New Orleans and offer you our support in the years ahead." The Mystic Krewe of Satyricon, founded by Mickey Gil in 2002, like the Krewes of Eros and Mwindo, included both men and women. And in 2015, Petronius chose an African American lesbian couple to serve as king and queen.

Krewe of Ishtar (1981)

1980

The Krewe of Ishtar was formed late in 1980 and was built on the foundation established by New Orleans's lesbian bars, including Charlene's, Miss Kitty's, Pino's, and Diane's. The krewe represented not only a collaboration among prominent lesbian leaders but also a much-needed celebration of women.

1981

Ishtar's Alpha Ball, *The Modern Gods and Goddesses of Babylon*, featured many women in tuxedoes, à la Marlene Dietrich in *Morocco*. The ball introduced the magnificent lioness goddess Ishtar in her golden chariot. Royalty for the following year was chosen at the close of the ball. This new tradition continued for several years.

1982

The Beta Ball, *I Am Woman*, celebrated women's accomplishments. The captain played the role of Amelia Earhart, descending onto the stage in an airplane.

1983

Ishtar's Gamma Ball, *Music, Music, Music*, offered a salute to "food for the soul." The captain bid everyone welcome and hoped "to delight the ears with fanciful melodies and dazzle the eyes with all the glitter and glamour of the ball season."

1986

Ishtar held its final ball, *Love*.

Krewe of Ishtar Tableau Balls List	
1981	THE MODERN GODS AND GODDESSES OF BABYLON
1982	I AM WOMAN
1983	MUSIC, MUSIC, MUSIC
1984	SOMEWHERE IN TIME
1985	TAROT CARDS
1986	LOVE

Krewe of Ishtar Royalty List				
YEAR OF TABLEAU BALL	CAPTAIN	LIEUTENANT	QUEEN	KING
1981	Sue Martino	Judy Thompson	Rosemary Pino	Diane DiMiceli
1982	Sue Martino	Judy Thompson	Diana Brisolara	Jackie Ducros
1983	Sue Martino	Jan Moran	Jay Bowman	Marsha Robert
1984	Sue Martino	Diana Brisolara	Brenda Laura	Jan Moran
1985	Sue Martino	Saundra Boudreaux	Nesha Benoit	Judy Thompson
1986	Diana Brisolara	Carrie Connell	Bonnie LeBlanc	Barbara Price

The Modern Gods and Goddesses of Babylon 1981

King Ishtar I, Diane DiMiceli, and Queen Ishtar I, Rosemary Pino, 1981. Courtesy of Greta Reckner.

Music, Music, Music 1983

Program, 1983. Courtesy of Tulane University, Louisiana Research Collection, Howard-Tilton Memorial Library, New Orleans, Otto Stierle Collection, Manuscripts Collection 902.

Tableau 1983
Mistress of Ceremonies
President of Ishtar
The Return of King Ishtar II
The Return of Queen Ishtar II
Captain of Ishtar
Ball Lieutenant
Solid Gold
Jezebel
Copacabana
That Ol' Black Magic
Ishtar Clowns
Baby Face
Hooked on Classics
Hooray for Hollywood
Stormy Weather
Crescent City Movin' Co. (Special Guest Appearance)
Magnificent Seven
Lee Austin (Special Guest Appearance)
New York, New York
Vicki Sanders (Special Guest Appearance)
A Chorus Line—Ishtar Girls
Queen Ishtar III

King Ishtar III, Marsha Robert, and Queen Ishtar III, Jay Bowman, 1983. Courtesy of Greta Reckner.

214

Somewhere in Time 1984

Friday
February 10
1984
St. Bernard Civic Auditorium

Invitation, 1984. Courtesy of The Historic New Orleans Collection, Williams Research Center, New Orleans, Accession No. 1984.170.17. Gift of Tracy Hendrix.

Program reads: *In 1981 the Krewe of Ishtar proudly presented its Alpha Ball Modern Gods and Goddesses of Babylon, thus introducing the magnificent lionesses, captain and the krewe to New Orleans. In 1982, the Krewe of Ishtar presented I Am Woman followed in 1983 with its dazzling Music, Music, Music. For 1984 Ishtar now presents their Delta Ball with a salute to those abstract feelings in life that bring us joy and pleasure. The captain bids you welcome with the hope to continue to delight and surprise you. Somewhere in Time is meant to recall those wonderful feelings that we have and hopefully will continue to experience.*
—The Captain

⚜

Tableau 1984
Lighting of Crest and National Anthem
Ishtar's Mistresses of Ceremonies
President of the Krewe of Ishtar
Returning King Ishtar III
Returning Queen Ishtar III
Somewhere in Time
Captain of the Krewe of Ishtar
Ball Lieutenant
Butterfly
Valentine
Rainbow
Mermaid
Crescent City Movin' Company
Peacock
Leather
Lee Austin
Snowflake
Crescent City Movin' Company
Queen Ishtar IV
King Ishtar IV

Diane DiMiceli and Necha Benoit, 1984. Courtesy of Marsha Roberts.

Tarot 1985

THE KREWE OF ISHTAR
presents

TAROT

WHEEL of FORTUNE.

CARDS

Program, 1985. Courtesy of The Historic New Orleans Collection, Williams Research Center, New Orleans, Accession No. 1985.107.14. Gift of Tracy Hendrix.

Inside reads: *No other subject conjures up more secrecy, superstition and mystery than the exciting Tarot Cards. Sometimes ominous, often forewarning but always entertaining, these colorful pieces of cardboard never fail to hold our fascination. Tonight the Captain and Krewe of Ishtar are pleased to present to you their Fifth Anniversary Ball Tarot Cards and hope that you too will be delighted and surprised by this revealing experience. Sue Martino, Captain. Saundra Boudreaux, Ball Lieutenant. Costumes and headpieces: Derek Maenza.*

❧

Tableau 1985
Lighting of the Crest
Mistress of Ceremonies
The Return of King Ishtar IV
The Return of Queen Ishtar IV
The Gypsy Fortune Teller—Captain
The Fool—Ball Lieutenant
The High Priestess
The Emperor
The Empress
The Lovers—Crescent City Movin' Company
Venus Personified
The Conquering Warrior
Justice
Death
Ishtar Dancers
Temperance
The Sun
The Angel of Judgement
The World—Queen Ishtar V
King of Cups—King Ishtar V

Captain Sue Martino, 1985. Courtesy of Necha Benoit.

King Ishtar V, Judy Thompson, and Queen Ishtar V, Necha Benoit, 1985. Courtesy of Necha Benoit.

Rosemary Pino as the High Priestess, 1985. Courtesy of Necha Benoit.

Love 1986

Program, 1986. Costume and set designs by Neil Bordelon. Courtesy of The Historic New Orleans Collection, Williams Research Center, New Orleans, Accession No. 1986.156.18. Gift of Tracy Hendrix.

♣

Tableau 1986
Lighting the Crest
National Anthem
Mistress of Ceremonies
President's Message
Eternal Love—Captain
Young Love—Ball Lieutenant
Love around the World
Rhapsody of Love
Jealous Love
Love's Sweet Song—Crescent City Movin' Company
Bittersweet Love
Twisted Love—Rage
Gifts of Love
Love Birds—Crescent City Movin' Company
Love's Passion—Ecstasy
Erotic Love—Seduction
Love Aflame—Desire
The Sentiments of Love—King and Queen Ishtar VI

Returning Queen Ishtar V, Necha Benoit, and attendants, 1986. Courtesy of Necha Benoit.

We were all young and extremely close. We went out to bars and social events together and even lived in one large apartment complex. We were more than just a Carnival krewe.

—Gary Martin, Krewe of Polyphemus

The Eye of Polyphemus, symbol and crest of the Krewe of Polyphemus. Courtesy of Gary Martin.

The Eye of Polyphemus

Polyphemus, the cyclops and the son of Poseidon, is one of the most interesting figures in Homer's *Odyssey*. When Polyphemus captures Odysseus and his men, they must blind the one-eyed giant to escape. This mythological creature attracted attention among New Orleans's Carnival community as early as 1884, when the Krewe of Proteus chose to represent the moment when Polyphemus saw Odysseus and his men arrive on the island.

In 1982, just under a century later, Michael Hickerson, Gary Martin, Eugene Fenasci, and David Smith revisited the creature as inspiration for their new Krewe of Polyphemus. It was among the very few gay krewes that allowed blacks to become members, and it attracted many of the best people, who quickly became a close-knit group. According to Martin, who served as the krewe's first captain, "We were drunk one night and pulled the name out of a hat. It was so weird no one could pronounce it at first. We became very close and we went everywhere together as a group. We were young and carefree but with a fierce pride in our krewe. Our balls were serious affairs and we wanted to be on top."

Polyphemus, Float 7, Krewe of Proteus's *Aeneid* parade, 1884. Design by Benjamin Briton. Mythology inspired both the traditional krewes and the gay krewes. Courtesy of Tulane University, Louisiana Research Collection, Howard-Tilton Memorial Library, New Orleans.

Gems

The krewe's first ball, 1983's *Gems*, revealed not only a polished presentation but also a fully formed group of creative individuals who would go on to deliver a mix of sophistication and glamour. Michael Hickerson reigned as Queen Polyphemus I, while David Smith was King Polyphemus I. Hickerson, known affectionately as "Fish," was one of the first African American members of any krewe, and he received the Krewe of Amon-Ra's President's Award in 1985 for his work. His Cherries Jubilee costume was a tremendous camp hit, and Hickerson had found his calling. He was also among the founders of the short-lived all-black Krewe of Somnus and later on the more successful Krewe of Mwindo.

I Do! I Do!

Based on the brides of the world, Polyphemus's third ball was a spectacular succession of fabulous costumes. *I Do! I Do!* showed incredible attention to detail: each of the tables for special guests had a two-tiered white wedding cake topped with two male grooms, one a redhead, the other a blond, representing the king and queen. The returning king and queen appeared as the Unicorn and Maiden, with more than five hundred live orchids on the returning Queen Polyphemus II's beaded collar. The captain was a bride from New York, and his lieutenant was from Spain. Paris, Russia, and the silken brides of China and Japan followed an unbelievable Bride of the Arctic. A duo draped in chiffon and sequins came from India, and immense headdresses from Africa competed with mountains of plumes from Rio. As Britain's Princess Diana, Philip Hull wore a tightly fitted white dress embellished with glittering rhinestones and a tiara. Wrote Rip Naquin and Marsha Delain in *Ambush Magazine*, "It was hard to believe anything could top the festivities thus far, but believe us the new royalty did just that. King (Kevin Bergeron) and Queen Polyphemus III (Gregory Pichon) dazzled the audience with their thousands of plumes and stones, the most breathtaking costumes we have ever seen. The captain of Polyphemus is certainly to be congratulated on the superb costuming, choreography, and showmanship of this exquisite production." In just its third ball, Polyphemus served notice that it had already become a force, taking the AGGI Awards for Returning Queen, Reigning King, and Solo Performance and taking first runner-up in two additional categories as well as four honorable mentions.

The Focus on AIDS Charities

By 1985, the krewe began actively supporting AIDS organizations, including the AIDS Hot Line, NO/AIDS Task Force, and Tau House, and Hickerson later founded a support group, In This Together. Many if not all gay krewes echoed this approach during the late 1980s and early 1990s, shifting their focus to fund-raising for AIDS organizations. Already organized and networked, gay krewes had a head start when the dimensions of the AIDS crisis began to become apparent, and New Orleans was one of the first cities where the gay community began to fight the disease. Nevertheless, HIV/AIDS decimated the population, and Hickerson reflected many years later that "some of the artistry and craftsmanship of Carnival died when so many men died of AIDS, and it also shifted priorities away from spending money on costumes to saving and spending so much money on their medical treatment."

Deco and Design

For the 1986 *Deco and Design* ball, the Krewe of Polyphemus channeled the artistry of the art deco movement, taking as inspiration not only the clean lines and allure of the 1920s period but also the designs of Erté. The returning King and Queen Polyphemus III appeared at the beginning of the ball as the Futuristic Bride and Groom, a nod to the previous ball, before a parade of exquisitely tailored and embellished costumes representing the Charleston, Chandeliers, Indochina and the Red Sea, the Portrait, the Vamps, the Golden Calf, R, and the Six and Nine graced the stage of the Saint Bernard Cultural Center. Next came a stunning interpretation of the Folies-Bergère of Paris: Taps, the Snob, the Mistress, Diva, and Guys and Dolls. Finally, King and Queen Polyphemus IV were presented to their subjects under the aegis of Deco.

The program's notes provide some indication of the camaraderie that existed among various krewes: "Best wishes and continued success to a fantastic krewe. Looking forward to working with you again in 1986. The Mystic Krewe of Celestial Knights and Congratulations to My Boys! Your Mother, Pino." Rosemary Pino, owner of several lesbian bars that hosted krewe events, including Hallelujah Holidays at Christmastime, was a member of the Krewe of Ishtar and an honorary member of the Krewe of Polyphemus. Polyphemus and the Celestial Knights considered themselves sister krewes; Gary Martin was dating a member of the Celestial Knights, and the two groups conducted some joint fund-raisers. One of the more successful events was a double feature of John Waters films, *Female Trouble* and *Pink Flamingos.*

Another Polyphemus fund-raiser, Prom Night, became a wildly popular summer event, with attendees encouraged to don prom dresses and dance the night away.

The Broadway Ball

For the fifth anniversary ball, *The Envelope Please* (better known as the *Broadway Ball*, 1987), Daniel Ourso was called on to design all the costumes. Ourso had helped various krewes over the years prepare music for their balls and was an expert, primarily in classical music and opera, who worked at Smith's Record Shop on St. Charles Avenue. He also sang arias. While working on incidental music for a Polyphemus ball, Gary Martin saw some of Ourso's costume sketches and asked him to design the next ball. The krewe was so taken with his work that they immediately made him a member, with the owner of the shop, Miss Annette, paying his dues. As Ourso set to work on the costumes, he "knew that for the ball to stand out I'd have to design in Technicolor. And that's just what they got, a ball of bold and fantastic colors. No shrinking violets here."

Several months before the ball, the finished sketches were stolen from Martin's car while he was at Metairie Fabrics selecting material for the costumes. Ourso quickly resketched the entire ball so that the krewe could finish up the costumes. Ourso wore his own *My Fair Lady* costume, created in shades of lavender, for the Ascot Races scene. Ourso's mother loved lavender and attended the ball, her first gay ball. The krewe never used sequins but nevertheless sought to "set the mark for high quality," in Gary Martin's words, meaning that Ourso was limited to silver, gold, and clear rhinestones. In addition, featherwork was prominent on every costume, courtesy of Arnie Claudet, a florist who integrated feathers into costumes using the same layering techniques he used in floral arrangements. His costume from *Kismet* was red and gold with magic lamps on the shoulders and a headpiece that featured a ziggurat covered in pheasant feathers that accentuated his every move. Norman Millis, who also designed invitations and costumes for the krewe, was an expert in wirework, enabling the construction of light, wearable costumes.

Bomb Scare in Chalmette

The Queen of the Night costume was one of three very important and extremely ornate costumes on which the entire ball tableau hinged. However, the krewe member tasked with constructing the costume had fallen so far behind schedule that the krewe became worried. A couple of days before the ball, that member was thrown out of the krewe, and other members began what Ourso called a "crash" session—a nonstop marathon of several days during which they worked round the clock to finish the costume. Kevin Keller, a prominent member of the Mystic Krewe of Apollo who had subsequently joined Polyphemus, agreed to perform in the costume at the last minute. But when he came onstage, an announcement was made that the auditorium had to be cleared out immediately. Someone had called the police and reported that the queen's clutch contained a bomb. Ourso blamed the member who was originally supposed to wear the costume: "She was so incensed that she called the police and dreamt up this bomb nonsense. Now that's hateful. We sat in the parking lot on top of cars, sipping champagne. Most people didn't leave, and we did finish our ball. It was a night to remember." Almost two hours later, the police allowed the crowd and the performers to return to the auditorium, and Keller picked up where he had left off.

From the Sea and *Let Me Take You Dancin'*

Danny Ourso also designed the costumes for Polyphemus's 1988 ball, *From the Sea*, working captain Gary Martin's theme into an underwater ballet sequence that spotlighted the returning king and queen. Martin appeared as the Sea itself, followed by a brilliant lineup of jellyfish, Siamese fighting fish, dolphins, lion- and angelfish, mermaids, a whelk and clam, and a stingray and a lobster. The new king and queen appeared as Poseidon, God of the Sea, and his wife, Amphitrite, Goddess of the Sea. Ourso also designed all the costumes for the next year, when the theme was *Let Me Take You Dancin'* (1989). But in the voting for the captain, Pat McKinny recorded an upset victory over Gary Martin. Not surprisingly, according to Ourso, "Gary was devastated. I accompanied him back to his apartment after the election. He was silent and pensive, but not angry. I didn't want him to be alone, but to his credit, he helped the krewe all that year and attended the ball as a sign of good faith. Of course he was back on top the next year. Gary was a force of nature and came back not with bitterness but with renewed vigor and creativity."

Fiery Destruction on New Year's Eve

But the 1990 ball never took place. A New Year's Eve arson fire gutted the krewe den at 1424 Frenchmen Street, destroying all the costumes.

The 1997 Lords of Leather ball, *Before the Fire*, referenced Polyphemus's catastrophe. As Wayne Phillips of the Louisiana State Museum remembered, "All the costumes related to historic fires. One of the costumes was inspired by the 1990 fire that took place in the Krewe of Polyphemus den, destroying all the costumes. Even seven years after the fact, it was still a Carnival legend."

Long Live the Queen

As Polyphemus prepared to hold its tenth anniversary ball, krewe members knew that it would be their last: the group was preparing to fold. Having returned to the captaincy, Gary Martin chose to fulfill a longtime dream by also serving as Queen Polyphemus X. The ball, *Holidays*, served up camp versions of well-known holidays. Polyphemus's demise, signaled the end of the Golden Age of Gay Carnival.

Krewe of Polyphemus Tableau Balls List	
1983	GEMS
1984	THE GARDEN BALL
1985	I DO! I DO!
1986	DECO AND DESIGN
1987	THE ENVELOPE PLEASE (FIFTH ANNIVERSARY BALL)
1988	FROM THE SEA
1989	LET ME TAKE YOU DANCIN'
1990	—
1991	A NIGHT AT THE OPERA
1992	HOLIDAYS (TENTH ANNIVERSARY BALL)

Krewe of Polyphemus Royalty List			
YEAR OF TABLEAU BALL	CAPTAIN	QUEEN	KING
1983	Gary Martin	Michael "Fish" Hickerson	David Smith
1984	Gary Martin	Eugene Fenasci	Dave Moynan
1985	Gary Martin	Gregory Pichon	Kevin Bergeron
1986	Gary Martin	Chris Rhodes	Pat McKinny
1987	Gary Martin	Thomas Pecora	Rory Centanni
1988	Gary Martin	George Howard	Steve Rojas
1989	Pat McKinny	Tito Toledo	Wayne Cassard
1990	—	—	—
1991	Gary Martin	Philip Hull	Joseph McLaughlin
1992	Gary Martin	Gary Martin	David Tringali

Krewe of Polyphemus (1983)

1983

Founded by Gary Martin in 1982, the Krewe of Polyphemus gave its first ball, *Gems*, the following year. This krewe was composed mainly of young, energetic gay men with a strong interest in performing on stage and outshining the older krewes, and they sparked a reinvigoration of gay Carnival. The first queen of Polyphemus was Michael "Fish" Hickerson, a cofounder of the krewe who subsequently made his mark in the Krewe of Amon-Ra. He later joined Mwindo and became known in the city for his work with AIDS organizations, founding In This Together, a support group for those with HIV/AIDS.

1985

I Do! I Do! featured brides from around the world. The tables closest to the stage had two-tiered wedding cakes topped by two grooms representing both the king and queen. The returning king made his entrance as a unicorn, while the returning queen portrayed a maiden, wearing a pink gown with a high collar covered with more than four hundred live orchids. The reigning king and queen wore all-white costumes covered in silver rhinestones and billowy white feathers, the perfect bride and groom.

1986

During the summer, the krewe inaugurated its Prom Night fundraiser. Held at the Bakers Union Hall in the Marigny, the event was wildly successful, particularly because many members of the gay community had not been able to attend their high school proms with their dates of choice.

1990s

A New Year's Eve fire gutted the krewe's den and resulted in the cancellation of the 1990 ball. The krewe again hosted balls in 1991 and 1992 but then folded after being decimated by the AIDS epidemic.

Gems 1983

Queen Polyphemus I, Michael Hickerson, and King Polyphemus I, David Smith, 1983. Courtesy of Gary Martin.

The Garden Ball 1984

Program, 1984. Design by Norman McDole Millis. Courtesy of Tulane University, Louisiana Research Collection, Howard-Tilton Memorial Library, New Orleans, Otto Stierle Collection, Manuscripts Collection 902.

Queen Polyphemus II, Eugene Fenasci, 1984. Courtesy of Gary Martin.

King Polyphemus II, Davy Moynan, 1984. Courtesy of Gary Martin.

I Do! I Do! 1985

Program, 1985. Costumes designed by Norman Mc-Dole Millis. Courtesy of Gary Martin.

Tableau 1985
National Anthem
Mistress of Ceremonies
King and Queen Polyphemus II—The Unicorn and the
    Maiden
Captain—New York
Ball Lieutenant—Spain
Can-Can—High Kickers
Paris
England
Russian
Arctic
China
Japan
International Ballet—High Kickers
India
Africa
Rio
Hawai'i
Hollywood
Chalmette—Wash and Wear Bride
King Polyphemus III
Queen Polyphemus III
Open Court

Deco and Design 1986

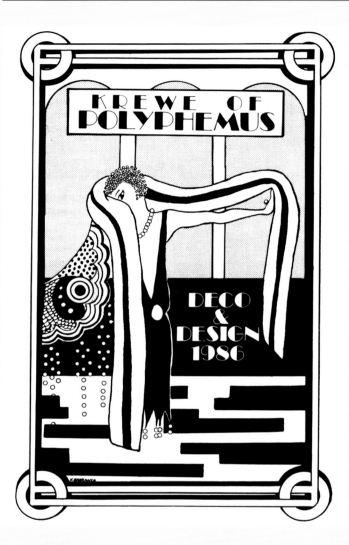

Program, 1986. Design by K. Barranco. Courtesy of Gary Martin.

❧

Tableau 1986
National Anthem
Mistress of Ceremonies
King and Queen Polyphemus III—The Futuristic Bride and Groom
Design
The Bird Cage—Captain
The Charleston
Chandeliers
Indochina and the Red Sea
The Portrait
The Vamps
The Golden Calf
R
The Six and Nine
Folies-Bergère
Taps
The Snob
The Mistress
Diva
Guys and Dolls—Ball Lieutenant
Deco
The Reigning Royalty—King and Queen Polyphemus IV
Open Court

Guys and Dolls scene, 1986. Courtesy of Gary Martin.

From the Sea 1988

Program, 1988. Design by Robert G. Lee. Costumes designed by Danny Ourso. Courtesy of The Historic New Orleans Collection, Williams Research Center, New Orleans, Accession No. 2000.34.258.

Tableau 1988
National Anthem
Mistress of Ceremonies
King and Queen Polyphemus V—Underwater Ballet
The Sea—1988 Ball Captain
Jellyfish
Siamese Fighting Fish
Dolphin
Lion Fish
Angel Fish
The Mermaids
Welk
Clam
Sting Rays
The Lobster and Condiments
King Polyphemus VI—Poseidon
Queen Polyphemus VI—Amphitrite

Let Me Take You Dancin' 1989

Let Me Take You Dancin

Program, 1989, and costume designs by Danny Ourso. Courtesy of The Historic New Orleans Collection, Williams Research Center, New Orleans, Accession No. 2000.34.260.

Tableau 1989
The Leading Citizens From Atlantis
    King and Queen Polyphemus VI
Latin
    The Latin Rhythms
    Cha Cha
    Mambo
    Conga
    Tango
    Samba—1989 Ball Captain
Ethnic
    Africa
    American Indian
    Apache
    Kabuki
Theatrical
    Spring Waters
    Broadway Gypsies
    Ballet Slippers
Las Vegas
    Showgirls and 1989 Ball Lieutenant
American Pop
    Fifties—At the Hop
    Sixties—John Pela
    Seventies—Discothèque
Futuristic Trippin' on the Moon
Waltz (Hapsburgs)
Their Royal Highnesses
    King Polyphemus VII
    Queen Polyphemus VII
Presentations
Open Court

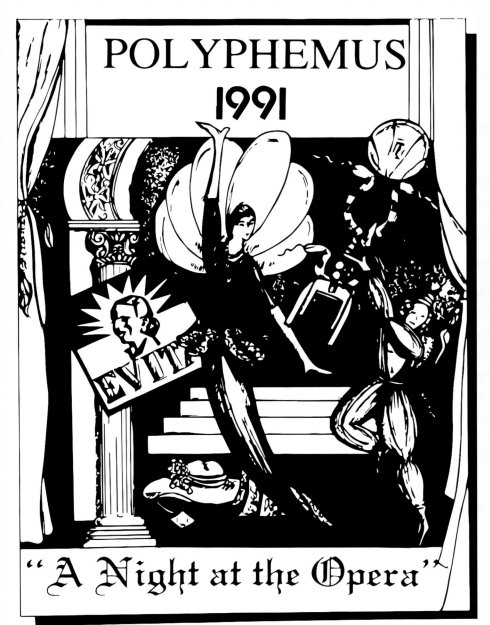

Program, 1991. Courtesy of The Historic New Orleans Collection, Williams Research Center, New Orleans, Accession No. 2000.34.264.

Tableau 1991
Le Ballet Russe—King Polyphemus VII
Soap Opera
    Falcon Crest—1991 Ball Captain
    The Bold and the Beautiful—1991 Ball Lieutenant
    Another World
    General Hospital
    Generations
    Dark Shadows
Grand Ol' Opry
    Texas Star
    Minnie Pearl
    Cotton-Eyed Joe
Rock Opera
    Jesus Christ Superstar
    Joseph and the Amazing Technicolor Dreamcoat
    Hair
    Starlight Express
Classical Opera
    A Thousand and One Arabian Nights
    Carmen
    Madama Butterfly
Lohengrin—King Polyphemus IX
Lucia di Lammermoor—Queen Polyphemus IX

Holidays (Tenth Anniversary Ball) 1992

Program, 1992. Courtesy of The Historic New Orleans Collection, Williams Research Center, New Orleans, Accession No. 1993.110.25. Gift of Tracy Hendrix.

Tableau 1992
National Anthem
Master of Ceremonies
Grand Opera—King and Queen Polyphemus IX
Overture
The 1992 Polyphemus Calendar
February 4th—Chinese New Year—1992 Ball Captain
December 31st—New Year's Eve in Times Square—1992 Ball Lieutenant
February 14th—Saint Valentine's Day
March 19th—Saint Joseph's Day
November 1st—All Saints' Day
Mardi Gras
Carnival in Rio de Janeiro, Brazil
Carnival in Cape Town, South Africa
Carnival in Venice, Italy
40 Days Later—Easter Parade
May 5th—Cinco de Mayo
2nd Sunday in May—Mother's Day
July 4th—Independence Day
Last Thursday in November—Thanksgiving
December 25th—Christmas
A Special Polyphemus Holiday
February 2nd, 1992—The Anniversary
King Polyphemus X
Queen Polyphemus X

Queen Polyphemus X, Gary Martin, 1992. Courtesy of Gary Martin.

Prom Night Summer Fund-Raiser

Prom Night Summer Fund-Raiser, 1986. Courtesy of The Historic New Orleans Collection, Williams Research Center, New Orleans, Accession No. 1986.156.30. Gift of Tracy Hendrix.

Kevin Bergeron, 1986. Courtesy of Gary Martin.

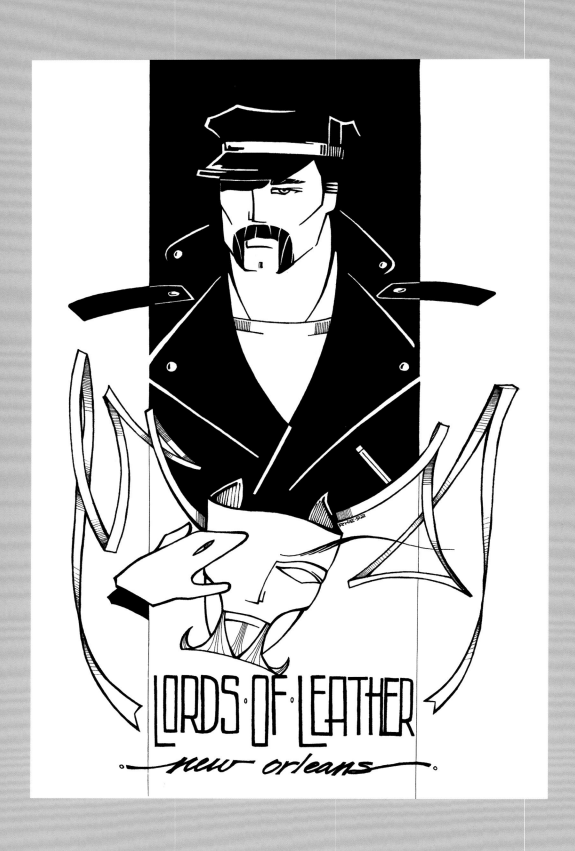

New Orleans, for me, was not just a city.
It was a temple.

—Wally Sherwood, Lords of Leather

Leather, Love, Laughter

In the early 1980s, New Orleans's gay community was thriving, with numerous new Carnival krewes joining in the city's Mardi Gras celebrations. In addition to the Krewes of Ishtar and Polyphemus, the Krewes of Vesta, Perseus, and David joined the party, generally following the gay Carnival template.

But the Crescent City's gay scene also featured different sorts of groups. Gay motorcycle clubs, such as the Cavaliers and the Lancers MC, and well-established leather groups, including deSade & Men and the Knights d'Orléans, had been popular for years. In 1983, members of the leather community decided to create a Carnival club that fit their sensibilities and lifestyle, and the result was the Lords of Leather. Like the other krewes, the Lords would hold an annual ball, but the court and presentations would take on a more masculine tone, eschewing drag and camp for a more dramatic and serious tableau, and the krewe would be run by two governing bodies, the House of Lords (the officers) and the House of Commons (the rest of the board). A lord king would reign alongside his lord consort rather than a queen. The ball initially was held on Shrove Monday Eve, with both coronations taking place at the stroke of midnight, making the event the final gay ball of the Carnival season.

The Eagle

During the July 1983 deSade & Men's Bastille I Run, a weekend event where this leather club welcomed out-of-town organizations, several attendees discussed the

Original artwork for a Lords of Leather commemorative poster, 1992. Design by Harry Sherman (Rhie). Courtesy of the Louisiana State Museum, New Orleans, Accession No. 2009.089.72.

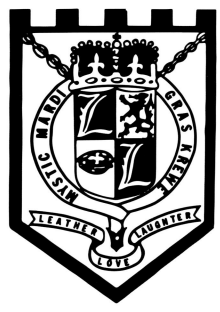

Official crest of the Lords of Leather. Courtesy of the Louisiana State Museum, New Orleans, Accession No. 2009.089.06.

formation of a new gay Carnival krewe, and within a month, plans were proceeding. Longtime friends Don "Eagle" Bury and Wally Sherwood met with Daniel Hallock, Robert Ravoira, David Robertson, and Jerry Zachary at the St. Luis Crepe Shoppe and sketched out the idea for "a Mardi Gras krewe composed of leather men as an alternative to the usual style of dress and behavior found in other krewes." The founders were very cautious about letting the krewe grow too quickly and enjoined members "to work together, stay close, and be dedicated to the fun and party of the club." The official colors of the newly minted krewe would be the traditional Carnival colors (green, purple, and gold) plus black. In a departure from the standard practice among gay krewes, members would choose the king by secret ballot rather than appointed by the captain. Sherwood, a writer and well-known leather-man, would be the first captain. A dwarf who was frequently photographed by local artist George Dureau, Sherwood enjoyed a type of celebrity in the demimonde of the French Quarter.

At a second meeting, the krewe further clarified its purpose: "We will be the fifteenth Mardi Gras krewe. We are not competing with any other cycle clubs, leather groups, or krewes, as our primary purpose is for one function on Mardi Gras Eve. The ball should be invitational and require either tuxedo formal, full leather, or club uniform. Not levi and not drag." Women were not allowed to join the krewe and initially were not to be permitted to attend the ball, though this rule changed before the first event took place. The krewe also chose *Leather, Love, Laughter* as its motto.

The Leather Lifestyle

The leather tradition dates back to just after World War II, when the so-called Old Guard among gay communities mentored new members in groups such as the Black and Tans in Los Angeles and the Crescent City's Knights d'Orléans. By the early 1970s, New Orleans had a strong leather community, and some members of gay krewes were also members of these leather groups and motorcycle clubs. For example, Otto Stierle of the Mystic Krewe of Celestial Knights was also a member of the Knights d'Orléans. The Old Guard rules were rigid and unquestioned. Most large cities had several exclusively leather bars, though the first such establishment did not open in New Orleans until 1981, when the Phoenix Bar began doing business on Elysian Fields Avenue. Prior to that time, Jewel's Tavern, TT's, and the Golden Lantern had hosted occasional leather events. As the leather community's visibility increased, the Lords of Leather came into being. By 1988 the krewe was hosting the Mr. New Orleans Leather contest: Paul Vicknair took home the first title and the accompanying leather sash. This contest served as the precursor to the more organized Mr. Louisiana Leather contests that began in 1993. The Ms. Louisiana Leatherette title (always a camp drag queen) came along later, as did the Mr. Marigny Leather and the Mr. Big Easy Leather, sponsored by the Knights d'Orléans. Winners of these local contests, especially Mr. Louisiana Leather, went on to compete in the International Mr. Leather contest in Chicago. Several motorcycle clubs also rose to prominence during this time, among them the Crescent City Outlaws, the Cavaliers, and the Lancers Motorcycle Club, which held motorcycle christenings at the Golden Lantern from time to time. And for about a decade starting in the late 1990s, New Orleans hosted a national event, the Pantheon of Leather.

Mr. Louisiana Leather

The annual Mr. Louisiana Leather contest, which drew leather-men not only from around the state but also from surrounding states, served as a very successful fund-raiser for the Lords of Leather, enabling them to increase the size and complexity of their tableau balls. The krewe is one of the few gay groups that survived the AIDS epidemic, and it has bolstered its numbers by creating various levels of membership, among them Lord (full membership) and Baron (limited responsibilities and lower annual dues), with Viscount and Viceroy in between.

The First Ball

On Shrove Monday 1984, the Lords of Leather held their first ball at the Bakers Union Hall in the Marigny. According to *Around the Clock* magazine's "Mardi Gras Wrap-Up," at the stroke of midnight, Lord Chancellor Bob Brown proclaimed that "the leather community had been a part of Mardi Gras for many years and now had its first krewe." The Lord of Misrule, Don Bury, who had replaced Wally Sherwood as captain, introduced the House of Lords, and, after pages proceeded onto the stage, the lord king, Jerry Radtke, and his royal consort, Bob Keesee, knelt at Brown's feet and received their leather crowns. Several local leather groups paid homage to their majesties, including deSade & Men, Knights d'Orléans, and Lancers MC.

Though Bury's involvement with the Lords of Leather ended after the first ball, he was extremely important to the krewe, since he and Sherwood had redefined the notion of a gay Carnival krewe. Bury had moved from Chicago to New Orleans in 1973 and quickly joined the Lancers Motorcycle Club and deSade & Men. Swept up in the Carnival scene, he also became a member of the Krewe of Petronius and the Krewe of Armeinius. But he and Sherwood ultimately rejected the drag sensibilities of the other krewes in favor of a more male-centered organization. Bury almost singlehandedly paid for and organized the first ball and created the guidelines that the Lords of Leather continued to follow long after his departure.

Partners Bar advertisement, 1980s. Partners Bar on Rampart Street was owned by Bob Keesee and Jerry Radtke (depicted in advertisement), the first lord king and lord consort of the Lords of Leather. Courtesy of the Louisiana State Museum, New Orleans, Accession No. 2014.005.25.

Gargoyles

For the Lords of Leather's second tableau ball, the theme was *Gargoyles*, in keeping with the krewe's emphasis on darker motifs. The tableau featured the Lord Herald (Hyperborean Warrior), the Captain (Lord Overseer and Living Gargoyle), the Contemporary Leatherman, and the Middle Ages Leatherman (Marquis de Sade). During the royal coronation ceremony at midnight, the Lord of Misrule, Jerry Radtke, crowned the new lord king, Jim Williams, and his consort, Tom Greenwood. Wrote

Wally Sherwood, "Following the two-hour leather ball, the Mardi Gras krewe ushered in Fat Tuesday festivities with a midnight coronation before Parliament. The presentation was rendered with much masculine finery and finesse, accompanied by plenty of appropriate fanfare. A Contemporary Leatherman complemented the appearance of a Living Gargoyle, a Hyperborian Warrior, and the Marquis de Sade himself. The stage setting was simple, but eloquent, and the entire affair was marked with pomp and circumstance, truly a joy to behold."

Over the next few years, the krewe's ball themes included *Spell of the Sultans*, *Before Sin*, *Warriors of the World*, *Crown Royal*, and *Games People Play*, continuing the tradition of darker and more sinister tableau costumes and decor. However, as the leather community itself changed from the strict lines of the Old Guard, the spirit of the Lords of Leather changed as well. Commented Lord of Misrule Gary Vandeventer, "The Lords of Leather ball provides an entertaining alternative to the high drag pageantry of the other remaining gay Carnival krewes. The other krewes focus on glamour, beautiful and elaborate costumes, and a drag aesthetic in an often serious manner. The Lords of Leather krewe celebrates the sexual aspect of our leather psyche, often tongue in cheek, with sometimes risqué costumes, still elaborate and colorful presentations but in a more light-hearted spirit."

Emphasis on Extravagance

This shift was evident in the 1994 *Magic* ball. The krewe presented a tableau filled with warlocks and magic potions, with costumes representing the Wing of a Bat, the Eye of a Newt, and the Wart of a Frog as well as the Crystal Ball, the Pentagram, the Scarab, Tarot Cards, and Out of the Hat. Two years later, the visionary *Where No Man Has Gone Before* recast the *Star Trek* television show as a tableau while remaining true to the Carnival traditions of extravagant costuming and bold presentation. Designed by Bruce Orgeron, a member of the Krewe of Armeinius, the costumes included Captain James T. Kirk, Mr. Spock, Red Alert, Klingon Empire, Romulus, Stratos, Scalos, Omicron Delta Amusement Planet, and Janus VI.

For the 2008 *Superheroes* ball, the krewe used strong primary colors to re-create comic book heroes—Aquaman, Superman, Ghost Rider, Conan the Barbarian, Spiderman, and the X-Men. However, Orgeron's costumes expanded on the original iconic designs by adding three-dimensional flourishes. Lord king and royal consort were Batman and Robin, and the Lord of Misrule crowned them both on Shrove Sunday night, a shift from the traditional Monday night ball.

Orgeron again designed the costumes for *That's Entertainment!* (2015), which explored different types of show business—Find Me a Primitive Man, When in Rome, Welcome to Burlesque, TV Land, Jocks, Join the Circus, and Hooray for Hollywood. The most impressive costumes were reserved for lord king Troy Powell and his consort, Tommy Stubblefield, and represented "What Happens in Vegas": geometric shapes in grays and silvers and lined with jewels. When the performers moved, the costumes swirled. Orgeron had taken his inspiration from Siegfried and Roy, and the costumes' colors evoked the duo's white tigers.

Into the Future

Troy Powell represents the new spirit of the krewe. He became interested in the leather lifestyle after attending the 1988 Los Angeles Gay Pride festival, and he believes that the Lords of Leather "have a unique perspective to convey. It's a fine line to walk between masculine and feminine aspects of gay Carnival. To be bejeweled and in leather at the same time is something that we do and do well. The dichotomy of it all is what I like. I can still be a very masculine man in leathers and have a Swarovski crystal–studded costume on, and no one thinks that the two should not go together." Powell won the Phoenix Bar's Mr. Phoenix Leather title in 2010 and was named Mr. Louisiana Leather the following year. In his view, "The krewes not only put on a ball but build friendships that last a lifetime. The Lords are one small part of that rich history. We will continue to promote our core values as they are expressed in our motto, *Leather, Love, and Laughter*."

Lords of Leather Tableau Balls List	
1984	FIRST ANNUAL BALL
1985	GARGOYLES
1986	MEN OF MYTH
1987	SALUTE TO MARDI GRAS
1988	ONE TO GO
1989	BEFORE SIN
1990	WARRIORS OF THE WORLD
1991	CROWN ROYAL
1992	GAMES PEOPLE PLAY
1993	KANSAS . . . NOT!
1994	MAGIC
1995	CAT SCRATCH FEVER
1996	WHERE NO MAN HAS GONE BEFORE
1997	BEFORE THE FIRE
1998	KING OF KINGS
1999	LEATHER, LOVE, AND LAUGHTER
2000	LIGHTS, CAMERA, ACTION
2001	LORDS OF TIME, MYTHS AND LEGENDS
2002	IN THE LORD'S FOREST
2003	A DIFFERENT DRUMMER
2004	A WILD, VERY WILD WEST SHOW
2005	GREAT EXPECTATIONS
2006–7	THE GREAT WHITE WAY
2008	SUPERHEROES
2009	A LORDLY CELESTIAL EVENING
2010	LOST NEW ORLEANS: IT AIN'T HERE NO MORE
2011	CIRCUIT
2012	THE SCI-FI BALL
2013	CAN'T STOP THE MUSIC
2014	TALES AND ADVENTURES
2015	THAT'S ENTERTAINMENT!
2016	THERE'S NO CURE LIKE TRAVEL
2017	MAGIC TO DO

Lords of Leather (1984)

1984

The first ball was held on the night before Shrove Tuesday at the Bakers Union Hall in the Marigny. The first king was Jerry Radtke, and his consort was Bob Keesee; their coronations began at midnight. Wally Sherwood, a columnist for *Ambush Magazine*, served as the krewe's first captain but withdrew before the ball took place and was replaced by Don Bury.

1985

Under captain Jerry Radtke, the second annual ball took *Gargoyles* as its theme. The king was Jim Williams, and his consort was Tom Greenwood. The krewe had been formed to showcase the leather lifestyle, and the costumes for this ball particularly fulfilled this requirement. The lord herald was a Hyperborian Warrior, while the captain was a Living Gargoyle. A Contemporary Leatherman was followed by the Marquis de Sade. The krewe was governed by the House of Lords (the officers) and the House of Commons (the rest of the board).

1990s

By the early 1990s, the Lords of Leather's balls had expanded to include thematic presentations with more elaborate costumes. For *Magic* (1994), many of the costumes referenced the casting of spells—the Wing of a Bat, the Eye of a Newt, the Wart of a Frog, and finally the Magic Potion. Other costumes included the Pentagram, Scarab, and Tarot Cards, culminating in a Broken Heart and Mistletoe. This tableau, with its precise story arc, marked a new creativity while maintaining the krewe's link to pagan themes. In addition, the ball moved from the Monday to Sunday before Mardi Gras, and the coronation took place much earlier than midnight.

2000s

The krewe widened its focus to explore myths, Wild West shows, and even a leather publication *Drummer Magazine*. In the wake of Hurricane Katrina, the krewe turned to Broadway, superheroes, and the changing face of the city (*Lost New Orleans*, 2010).

2015

For *That's Entertainment!*, Bruce Orgeron designed colorful yet restrained costumes that were powerful and whimsical. The lord king and his consort appeared in full regalia for the opening night of a Presbytère exhibition, *From the Big Apple to the Big Easy: Two Carnival Artists in New York*, that featured traditional Carnival drawings curated by Wayne Phillips from the Louisiana State Museum. Sketches by Bruce Orgeron were also on display.

2016–17

For the 2016 ball, captain Gary Vandeventer chose *There's No Cure Like Travel* as the theme. The poster for the event referenced vintage travel advertisements featuring luxurious ocean liners and trains. In 2017, Bruce Orgeron reigned as lord king over the *Magic to Do* ball.

Lords of Leather Royalty List			
YEAR OF TABLEAU BALL	**CAPTAIN**	**LORD KING**	**LORD CONSORT**
1984	Don "Eagle" Bury	Jerry Radtke	Bob Keesee
1985	Jerry Radtke	Jim Williams	Tom Greenwood
1986	Jim Williams	Bob Keesee	Roy Bell
1987	—	George Simons	Joe D'Antoni
1988	Dannie Brunson	Bill Floyd	John Peters
1989	Dannie Brunson	Guy Flanary	Paul Shifflet
1990	George Simons	Neil Gordon	Jared Campo
1991	David Stranger	Michael Edwards	George Hester
1992	David Stranger	David Eisenlord	Ron Polar
1993	David Stranger	David Stranger	Brian Eschette
1994	Kevin Mauldin	Jay Pennington	Jamie Temple
1995	Kevin Mauldin	Jared Campo	Roy Dugas
1996	Jared Campo	George Hester	Lee Sills
1997	David Stranger	Ernie O'Steen	Neil Gordon
1998	Danny Alford	Jamie Temple	Christian Kean-Johnson
1999	Danny Alford	Gregory Cain	Mickey Hebert
2000	Danny Alford	Damon Veach	Sam Favaro
2001	Mickey Hebert	Timm Holt	Matt Scott
2002	Mickey Hebert	Todd Cole	Wayne Monroe
2003	Timm Holt	Tommy Darensbourg	Elmer Godeny
2004	Timm Holt	Jack Pruitt	Gerard Beaudoin
2005	Timm Holt	Alan MacLachlan	Keith Istre
2006	—	—	—
2007	George Hester	Danny Alford	Danny Starnes
2008	David Boyd	Michael Ducote	Doug Minich
2009	David Boyd	Gary Vandeventer	J. Bruce Orgeron Jr.
2010	David Boyd/Ben Bourgeois	Alan Kelley	Tim Lott
2011	Gary Vandeventer	Ben Bourgeois	Pat Johnson
2012	Gary Vandeventer	Ed Azemas	Jason Ashford
2013	Gary Vandeventer	Pat Johnson	Joey Landry
2014	Gary Vandeventer	Terry Conerly	Don Bordelon
2015	Gary Vandeventer	Troy Powell	Tommy Stubblefield
2016	Gary Vandeventer	J. Kelley Terry	Kyle Robin
2017	Gary Vandeventer	J. Bruce Orgeron Jr.	Brock Andersen

Lords of Leather
A MYSTIC MARDI GRAS KREWE
SECOND ANNUAL
CORONATION BEFORE PARLIAMENT
* * *

Ten O'Clock P.M. to Twelve O'Clock Midnight
PRE-CORONATION LEATHER BALL
* * *

Twelve O'Clock Midnight
FANFARE
NATIONAL ANTHEM
LIGHTING OF COAT OF ARMS
ENTRANCE OF THE LORD HERALD
– Hyperborian Warrior
ROYAL PROCLAMATION
LORD OVERSEER
– Living Gargoyle (Acting Captain)
REIGNING ROYALTY
– Returning Lord King I
– Returning Lord Consort I
SYMBOLIC LORD OF LEATHER
– Contemporary Leatherman
MIDDLE AGES LEATHERMAN
– Marquis deSade
THE TRANSITION OF POWER
ROYAL CORONATION
– Lord Consort II Elect and Entourage
– Coronation and Investiture of Lord Consort II
– Lord King II Elect and Entourage
– Coronation and Investiture of Lord King II
ROYALTY AND NOBILITY OF OTHER KINGDOMS
OPEN COURT

* * * * * * * * * *

HOUSE OF LORDS
Lord Jerry R. – Lord Chancellor(President)
              Lord of Misrule(Captain)
Lord Shawn S. – Lord Mayor(Vice President)
Lord Roy B. – Lord Exchequer(Treasurer)
Lord Bob K. – Lord Privy(Secretary)
Lord George S.– Lord Temporal(Lieutenant)
      HOUSE OF COMMONS
          Lord Joe D.
          Lord Tom G.
          Lord Jim W.

Program, 1985. Courtesy of the Lords of Leather.

✢

Tableau 1985
10 o'clock to Midnight
Pre-Coronation Leather Ball
Midnight
Fanfare
National Anthem
Lighting of Coat of Arms
Entrance of the Lord Herald—Hyperborean Warrior
Royal Proclamation
Lord Overseer—Living Gargoyle (Acting Captain)
Reigning Royalty—Returning Lord King I
Returning Lord Consort I
Symbolic Lord of Leather—Contemporary Leatherman
Middle Ages Leatherman—Marquis de Sade
The Transition of Power
Royal Coronation
Lord Consort II Elect and Entourage
Coronation and Investiture of Lord Consort II
Lord King II Elect and Entourage
Coronation and Investiture of Lord King II
Royalty and Nobility of Other Kingdoms
Open Court
House of Lords
House of Commons

Games People Play 1992

Commemorative poster, 1992. Design by Ron
Aschenbach. Courtesy of the Louisiana State Museum, New Orleans, Accession No. 2009.089.71.

Ron Aschenbach, costume sketch for Monopoly,
1992. Courtesy of the Louisiana State Museum, New
Orleans, Accession No. 2009.089.34.

The Lords of Leather bring you MAGIC 1994

Program, 1994. Courtesy of the Louisiana State Museum, New Orleans, Accession No. 2009.089.09.

✣

Tableau 1994
Presentation of the Coat of Arms
National Anthem
Returning Royalty—Lord King I
The Ball Tableau
The Zodiac—1994 Ball Captain
The Warlocks
The Wing of a Bat
The Eye of a Newt
The Wart of a Frog
A Magic Potion
The Crystal Ball—Ball Lieutenant
The Pentagram
The Scarab
The Witch Doctor
Blue Magic
Tarot Cards
Out of the Hat
A Broken Heart
Puff
Mistletoe
Presentation of 1994 Royalty
Call-Outs
Open Court

Where No Man Has Gone Before 1996

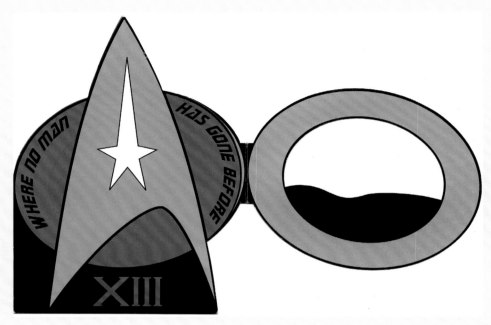

Invitation detail, 1996. Courtesy of the Louisiana State Museum, New Orleans, Accession No. 2009.089.11.

J. Bruce Orgeron Jr., costume design for McCoy, Lords of Leather's *Where No Man Has Gone Before* ball, 1996. Courtesy of the Louisiana State Museum, New Orleans, Accession No. 2009.089.35.

Great Expectations 2005

Joel Haas, costume sketches for Fighting the Wall Flowers (Matador, worn by Mr. Louisiana Leather 2005, Alan Bowers) and Florida Sunshine, 2005. The emcee explained that one of the milestones of a young person's life is a first school dance, but so many people spend that dance as wallflowers: it takes the courage of a matador to get up and dance. The Florida Sunshine costume was a reference to Anita Bryant, former Miss Oklahoma and longtime spokesperson for the Florida Citrus Commission, who became an outspoken enemy of gay rights in the 1970s, resulting in an LGBT boycott of Florida orange products and ultimately in the commission ending its relationship with her. Courtesy of the Louisiana State Museum, New Orleans, Accession Nos. 2009.089.52, 2009.089.58.

Joel Haas, costume sketches for Lord King and Lord Consort, 2005. Lord King Alan MacLachlan and Lord Consort Keith Istre initially appeared with their backs to the audience, recalling a Roman fountain motif, and then turned around to reveal their costumes. Courtesy of the Louisiana State Museum, New Orleans, Accession Nos. 2009.089.54, 2009.089.55.

Superheroes 2008

J. Bruce Orgeron Jr., costume designs for Lord King Batman and Lord Consort Robin, 2008. Courtesy of the Louisiana State Museum, New Orleans, Accession Nos. 2009.089.55, 2009.089.56

⚜

Tableau 2008
Opening Ceremonies
The Return of Their Majesties Lord King XXIV and Lord Consort XXIV
The Lords of Leather Dancers
The Year 2525
Aquaman
Superman
Ghost Rider
Conan the Barbarian
Spiderman
X-Men (Archangel)
Lone Ranger and the Cowpoke Dancers
Musical Interlude
Robin Hood
Catwoman
Spawn
Batman and Robin—Lord King XXV and Lord Consort XXV
Grand March
Closing Ceremonies
Open Court

That's Entertainment 2015

Lord King, Troy Powell, and Lord Consort, Tommy Stubblefield, 2015. Photograph by Barrett De-long-Church.

There's No Cure Like Travel 2016

Program, 2016, and two of the vintage travel posters from the 1920s and 1930s, that inspired it: Adolphe Mouron Cassandre's *Nord Express* (1927) and *Normandie* (1935). Courtesy of Wayne Phillips.

Ball captain (Lord of Misrule) Gary Vandeventer, 2016. Photograph by Barrett Delong-Church.

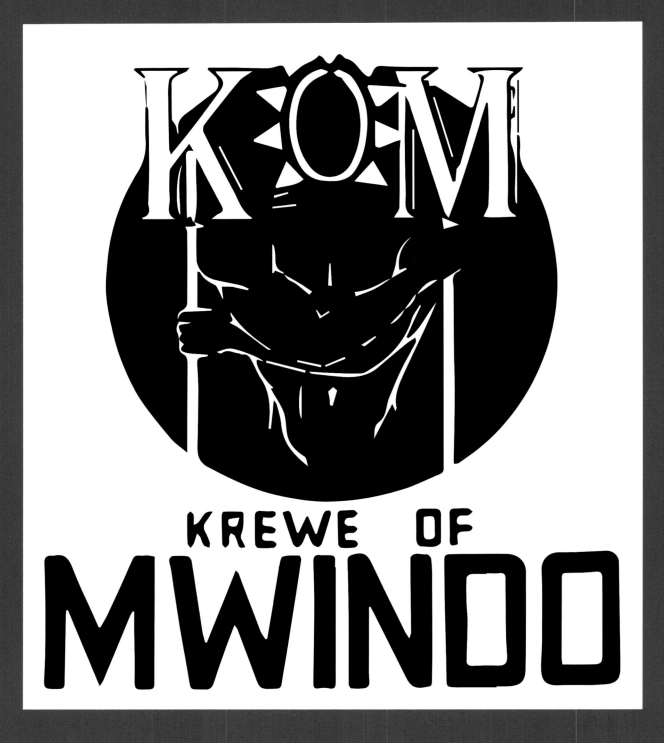

THE KREWE OF MWINDO

A Strong Black Voice

We stole the fire from the heavens
and lived to tell the tale.

—Michael Hickerson, Krewe of Mwindo

A Firm Foundation

The Krewe of Mwindo was formed in 1998 by Evans Alexander, Carlos Butler, Michael Forest, Thomas Franklin, Michael Hickerson, Byron Hogans, and Jacob Simmons. Mwindo was the first all-black gay Carnival krewe with membership open to both men and women. Following in the footsteps of the Zulu Social Aid and Pleasure Club, a straight black krewe founded in 1909, the krewe took its name from the African continent. The Mwindo epic comes from the Nyanga people of the Congo and tells the tale of Mwindo, a powerful chief with supernatural powers. Mwindo's quests included a visit to the underworld, where he had to perform tasks for its ruler, Muisa. After serving his punishment for killing a sacred dragon, Mwindo returned to his people and ruled in peace as a majestic lord. The Nyanga people continue the storytelling tradition today, with a bard dressed in a colorful costume adorned with bells and gourds recounting the tribe's long oral tradition while adding his own personal experiences.

Exclusion

Excluded from the traditional white krewes of the nineteenth century, blacks had always participated in New Orleans's Carnival parades as flambeau carriers and were seen at Congo Square, where the African bamboula dances were held. The city had many free men of color who settled in the Faubourg Marigny, the former plantation of Bernard de Marigny, and their traditions were woven into the first

Krewe of Mwindo crest. Courtesy of the Krewe of Mwindo.

black club organizations, such as the Original Illinois Club and later the Zulus. Blacks also developed the Mardi Gras Indian tradition, in which men and women appear on the street on Fat Tuesday wearing elaborate handmade "suits" with many feathers and beads, as a way to celebrate the bond between slaves and the Native Americans who helped them "escape the tyranny of slavery."

The Black Gay Experience

Black gay men in New Orleans faced many difficulties, especially segregation and prejudice, along with the laws forbidding homosexuality. Gay bars in and around the French Quarter generally attracted a loyal clientele that was segregated by race and gender. In the 1960s and 1970s, many French Quarter gay bars sought to restrict the admission of African Americans by requiring them to produce two or three forms of identification, though this practice began to die away by the early 1980s. Only Gigi's, the Safari House, and Café Lafitte in Exile welcomed men of color. One of the reasons the Southern Decadence party began at a home in Tremé was that African Americans felt they did not belong in the streets. According to Frederick Wright, the first grand marshal of Decadence, "In the early seventies there were places where blacks wouldn't have been welcomed in the Quarter."

Separate black gay bars had flourished, especially the Golden Feather on St. Bernard Avenue and the Dream Castle on Frenchmen Street. Drag bars, which had long encouraged black performers, eventually bridged this gap in the gay community. Travis's Bar on Rampart Street showcased such drag queens as Alotta Mulatta and Gilbertine Liveaudais. Performers came from Atlanta, Houston, Memphis, and especially Pensacola, where the legendary Red Garter promoted drag shows every weekend. On the Mississippi Gulf Coast, the Casablanca Club welcomed not only white gay men and lesbians but also those of color, providing an oasis when segregation reigned throughout the South.

Predominantly White Gay Krewes and African Americans

One of the few venues that welcomed the earliest gay balls was the International Longshoremen's Association, a black dockworkers' union, which hosted events by Petronius, Amon-Ra, and Ganymede during the 1960s. The Krewes of Amon-Ra and Polyphemus were among the first gay krewes to allow African Americans to join. The first king and queen of Polyphemus were not only black but a couple. Allen Lombard, an African American dancer and member of the Mystic Krewe of Celestial Knights, choreographed all the musical numbers for the krewe's balls. The Lords of Leather also had black members early on and by the mid-1990s began to designate black members as royalty. One out-of-town krewe, the Mystic Krewe of Apollo de Lafayette, identifies itself as a "racially inclusive gay men's krewe that has run an annual Mardi Gras masqué ball in Lafayette since 1976." Nevertheless, as Michael Hickerson, one of the first African Americans to join a gay krewe and to attend gay balls, including the 1971 *Camelot* ball put on by the Krewe of Olympus, remembered, "Most black gay men didn't even attend the balls, much less belong to a krewe. Black gays were a rather underground community for a long time. We were doubly excluded from mainstream society."

Michael "Fish" Hickerson

Hickerson was one of the most important forces behind the creation of the Krewe of Mwindo. In the early 1980s, Hickerson became well known in the French Quarter, working various jobs in gay bars, most notably the Phoenix Bar and Café Lafitte in Exile. He served as the director of Gay Pride and along with Gary Martin formed the Krewe of Polyphemus, a successful biracial gay krewe whose original members also included Gregory Pichon, who was selected as Queen Polyphemus III in 1985. Hickerson and his partner at the time, David Smith, became King and Queen Polyphemus I. However, Hickerson soon left the krewe because, he believed, "too much power came into the organization too quickly, and it split up."

Hickerson and several other former members of Polyphemus then found a home in the Krewe of Amon-Ra, an established krewe with a good reputation. He received Amon-Ra's President's Award in 1985, and his Cherry Tart costume became a sensation at that year's *Picnic Fantasy* ball, which included not only terrorizing insects but tempting dishes for the picnic. He made the enormous costume from an inverted plastic child's pool covered in foam rubber and fake cherries, cutting a hole in the middle for his body. Hickerson also served as the grand marshal of Southern Decadence in 1985.

In 1981, Hickerson formed the Krewe of Somnus (named for the god of sleep) "so more African Americans could be in a ball," but the krewe folded without presenting a staged tableau. Nevertheless, Somnus constituted an important effort to increase the black community's visibility and involvement in Carnival.

Hickerson played the role of Bubblin' Brown Sugar in Amon-Ra's 1987 *Kaleidoscope* ball and served as captain for the 1988 *Outer Worlds* ball. All of the costumes represented objects from outer space, and all of the chairs on the floor had seat belts. The queen, Arthur Wallace, was a girl who was abducted by aliens and then rescued, while Hickerson descended onto the stage from the ceiling. Hickerson became queen in 2004 and left the krewe after his return as queen the following year.

Queen Amon-Ra XXXIX, Michael Hickerson, *Fiction* ball, 2004. Courtesy of the Krewe of Amon-Ra.

The Dream of Mwindo

But even while he was becoming royalty in Amon-Ra, Hickerson and several friends were working to create an all-black gay Carnival krewe. The Krewe of Mwindo was formed in 1998 and presented its first ball the following year. Mwindo also maintained ties to other African American organizations, including sporadic collaborations with People of Substance, a gay black pride organization founded by Darrell Keith Sims. Beginning in 2000, People of Substance sponsored its own black krewe, the Krewe of Anubis, which included both men and women and held its first ball in 2001. Mwindo, however, thrived.

Once the Krewe of Mwindo was up and running, Hickerson moved on, preferring to devote himself to organizing and fund-raising for HIV/AIDS charities. He served on the board of directors of Belle Rêve, a hospice, and eventually became the volunteer coordinator. In addition, in 2004 he and his partner, David Munroe, created In This Together, a social services agency that provides direct support for HIV medications and services, mostly to members of the black gay community.

The First Ball

Mwindo Dreams in Colors (1999) included the Dream Maker as the master of ceremonies, accompanied by the Performing Purple, a dance troupe, as well as Recovering Red, the Black Hole, Gaily Gold, and drag superstar Teryl-Lynn Foxx as the Rainbow Personified. Other fantasy colors followed—Fierce Fuchsia, Gentle Green, Tan and Tasty, Yonder Yellow, Boisterous Blue, and Winter White Wonderland. King and Queen Mwindo I proudly conducted the Grand March of costumes at the close of the ball.

Attendant, *Mwindo Goes Sight-Seeing Downtown* ball, 2015. Courtesy of the Krewe of Mwindo.

Indulge in Madness

Nearly two decades later, the Krewe of Mwindo is still going strong. One of its more noteworthy balls was *Indulge in Madness* (2011), held at the St. Bernard Civic Center in Chalmette. As Tony Leggio wrote in *Ambush Magazine*,

> The members satisfied all our indulgences that night. President Joseph McCrory welcomed us that evening and then there was the presentation of colors by the New Orleans Bear and Trapper Social Club. The National Anthem was belted out by Tahtianah Kresha, whose melodious voice reverberated throughout the building. This young lady is talented. The Master of Ceremonies that evening was Thomas Franklin III who was One Mad Hat and he truly lived up to his title. I have to give it to Thomas, he had a good time on that stage as did the rest of the krewe. After a brief award presentation from NOLA Masquerade (Black Gay Pride) to the krewe from President Ryan Rochon, the tableau began. The ball was separated in five sections. The first was Smoke with Ball Captain XII Joe Blow the caterpillar coming out in a Technicolor outfit that would make Lewis Carroll proud. He was followed up by the royal return, the King of Hearts. Throughout the night the Rising Stars dance group performed some wonderful interludes for the audience's enjoyment. Then we went Walking in the Park with Alice in all her sassy glory, then we got to see the ball captain transformed into the Butterfly. The Cheshire Cat came next before we entered the Path of Transformation. This segment included All the King's Horses and Men, the Knave of Hearts and the Bird from McDonoghville. Ms. Zhane Kennedy, the newly crowned Miss Louisiana America 2010–2011 performed a tribute remembering those who are no longer with us. The ensuing portion was called Tea Time with Hennessey and had some great costumes such as March Hare, Mad Hattress Transformed, Mr. and Mrs. 100-Proof Old Grand Dad and Chocolate Rabbit. The finale was Reality Redux and King and Queen Mwindo XIII came out as the King and Queen of Chess. Their costumes were beautiful and very elegant. Congratulations to Queen Mwindo XIII Dennis E. Walton II. You were gorgeous and to your King Reuben Collins Filmore may your reign be a very special one.

King Mwindo, *Mwindo Goes Sight-Seeing Downtown* ball, 2015. Courtesy of the Krewe of Mwindo.

2015–Present

For its 2015 ball, Mwindo took a lighthearted approach with *Mwindo Goes Sight-Seeing Downtown.* The locations visited included Canal Street, formerly a shopping destination. Mwindo's semiofficial home is the Page Bar on Rampart Street (formerly the Society Page). Krewe meetings and various fund-raisers are held here, and the bar has become a center of the gay black community on the periphery of the French Quarter. For its 2016 ball, the Krewe of Mwindo had another success with *Candy Shop*, and 2017 took Mwindo to Broadway.

Krewe of Mwindo Tableau Balls List	
1999	MWINDO DREAMS IN COLORS
2000	AIR MWINDO, FLIGHT 2000
2001	ALL BETS ARE OFF
2002	MWINDONOPOLY
2003	DAWN OF CREATION
2004	VERSES, RHYMES, AND FAIRY TALES
2005	FEATHERS AND WINGS
2006	—
2007	GAMES PEOPLE PLAY
2008	JUICY FRUITS
2009	FOLLOW THE YELLOW BRICK ROAD
2010	DO YOU?
2011	INDULGE IN MADNESS
2012	MWINDO'S CALENDAR
2013	FIFTEENTH ANNUAL BALL
2014	SIXTEENTH ANNUAL BALL
2015	MWINDO GOES SIGHT-SEEING DOWNTOWN
2016	MWINDO CANDY SHOP
2017	MWINDO ON BROADWAY

Krewe of Mwindo Royalty List			
YEAR OF TABLEAU BALL	CAPTAIN	QUEEN	KING
1999	Byron Hogans	Thomas Franklin III	Byron Hogans
2000	Byron Hogans	James Swire	Evans Alexander
2001	Byron Hogans	Connie Marcel	Norman Zardes III
2002	Thomas Franklin III	René Bryant	J. Kelley Terry
2003	Evans Alexander	Willie Hyams	Paul Matthews
2004	Evans Alexander	Katie Rivers	Larry Jones
2005	Thomas Franklin III	Herbert Holmes	Duane Jenkins
2006	—	—	—
2007	Chad Dominick/J. Kelley Terry	Saline Victoria	Joseph McCrory
2008	J. Kelley Terry	Chad Dominick	Laurin Lawless
2009	Byron Hogans/J. Kelley Terry	Corey Mickel	Kenneth Moses
2010	Joseph McCrory	Queen Lemon	Bobby Wagstaff III
2011	Kenneth Moses	Dennis Walton II	Reuben Filmore III
2012	Bobby Wagstaff III	Liza Cooper	Grace Benjamin
2013	Bobby Wagstaff III	Dennis Walton	Bobby Wagstaff III
2014	Bobby Wagstaff III	Mercedes L'Oréal	Hillary Hardy
2015	Bobby Wagstaff III	Shantell Thomas	Willie Mackie
2016	Bobby Wagstaff III	Barbara Mathers	Glenn Johnson
2017	Bobby Wagstaff III	Darren Gilmore	Willie Glaze

Krewe of Mwindo (1999)

1999

The Krewe of Mwindo was organized in 1998 by Evans Alexander, Carlos Butler, Michael Forest, Thomas Franklin III, Michael Hickerson, Byron Hogans, and Jacob Simmons. The founders took the name from a legendary African hero who used his strength and tenacity to conquer obstacles. On January 18, 1999, the krewe held its first ball *Mwindo Dreams in Colors,* at the St. Bernard Civic Auditorium.

2000s

The Krewe of Mwindo continued to present exciting balls and expanded its fund-raising efforts to support black organizations such as Black Pride New Orleans and to partner with the NO/AIDS Task Force and the Community Awareness Network.

2003

Mwindo dazzled its audience with the *Dawning of Creation,* in which, as Wally Sherwood wrote, "subtle starlight faded into the glare of spotlights."

2015–17

Held at the newly refurbished Carver Theater in Tremé, *Mwindo Goes Sight-Seeing Downtown* (2015) was a huge success. *Mwindo Candy Shop* (2016) and *Mwindo on Broadway* (2017) continued the string of first-class presentations, with royalty parties following at the Page bar.

Dawn of Creation 2003

Program, 2003. Courtesy of the Louisiana State Museum, New Orleans, Jake and Kevin Thomas Collection, Accession No. 2015.046.07.4.

Games People Play 2007

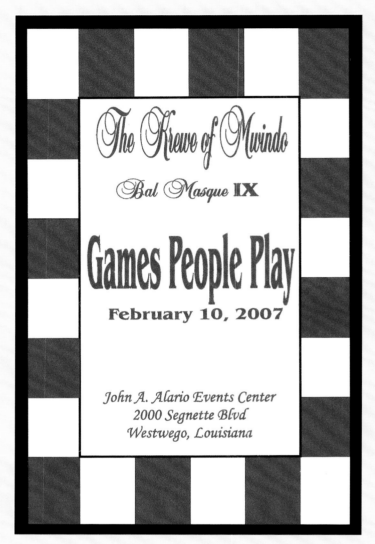

Program, 2007. Courtesy of the Louisiana State Museum, New Orleans, Jake and Kevin Thomas Collection, Accession No. 2015.046.07.5.

The Krewe of Mwindo

Ball Masque X

JUICY FRUITS

Saturday, January 26, 2008
Laborer's Union Hall
400 Soniat Street
New Orleans, Louisiana

Program, 2008. Courtesy of the Louisiana State Museum, New Orleans, Jake and Kevin Thomas Collection, Accession No. 2015.046.07.6.

Tableau 2008
Music Prelude
National Anthem—Davell Crawford
Master of Ceremonies—Gregory Dawson
President's Welcome
Byron Hogans
Parade of Past Royalty
    King Mwindo I, IV, V, VI, VII, IX
    Queen Mwindo I, II, III, IV, VI, IX
A Salute to King Mwindo II—Evans Alexander
Co-Master of Ceremonies—Carmen Miranda
The Return—King and Queen Mwindo IX—African
    Royalty
Tropical Itch—The Captain as Dragonfruit
Chiquita Banana—Ball Lieutenant
Succulent Edibles
Bacchus Rising—Ball Lieutenant
Georgia Peach
Norman Michael Bardes Community Fund Presents
Ms. Opal Vanderhurst—Ms. Bold and Beautiful
    2006–2007
Sweet Beginnings—The Mwindo Debutantes
    Fire and Ice
    The Mango Goddess
    Cherries Jubilee
    Real Fruit—Good Golly Miss Molly
Welcome Fruit—Pineapples—King and Queen
Mwindo X
Special Awards
Captain's Guests
Royal Guest
Krewe Guest
Open Court

Follow the Yellow Brick Road 2009

Indulge in Madness 2011

Program, 2009. Courtesy of the Louisiana State Museum, New Orleans, Jake and Kevin Thomas Collection, Accession No. 2015.046.07.7.

Queen Mwindo XIII, Dennis Walton II, as Reality Redux: The Queen of Chess, 2011. Courtesy of the Krewe of Mwindo.

Do you all believe in fairies?
Well, I sure do!

—Mickey Gil, Mystic Krewe of Satyricon

Genesis Revisited

After the Krewe of Petronius held its 2002 *Fly with Us* ball, the voting for krewe
captain began almost immediately. For thirteen of the preceding fourteen years,
Mickey Gil had won the post, but now Wally McLaughlin, previously a member of
the Krewe of Armeinius, defeated Gil and became Petronius's captain. Gil was devastated. Recalled local diva Becky Allen, "Mickey found his niche when he found
Mardi Gras. He loved glamour. He loved beauty. He loved people. Being the captain
of the ball satisfied his soul." In the words of George Patterson, who was Gil's longtime
companion and who had worked behind the scenes with him in Petronius, "he walked
out of the krewe, followed by sixteen others, and formed a new organization, the
Mystic Krewe of Satyricon." Named for Petronius Arbiter's decadent Roman epic, the
Satyricon, it became the darling of gay Carnival, reshaping the notion of a gay krewe.

Gil and Patterson found themselves well positioned to bring together a more
diverse group. Patterson and Allen were close—he had chosen her for her first
big role, the lead in *Gypsy* at Le Petit Théâtre du Vieux Carré—so it seemed only
natural that she and others linked to the theater would help shape the new krewe's
identity. Female impersonators Bianca del Rio and Varla Jean Merman brought a
strong mastery of the stage and artifice, while Patterson brought expertise in stage
design, lighting, costume wizardry, and thematic magic. Other members including Ted Jeansonne, David Boyd, Carl Mack, Joe Brooks, Wedon Brown, Richard
Read, and Stephen Rizzo added a creative energy that contributed to a series of
balls that would define the new millennium for gay krewes.

Official crest of the Mystic Krewe of Satyricon,
designed by Mickey Gil. Courtesy of Howard Philips
Smith.

Captain Mickey Gil. Courtesy of the Mystic Krewe of Satyricon and George Patterson.

The First Presentation

His sense of purpose renewed, Gil sought to present not only a great tableau but something the audience had never before seen or experienced. He chose *Some Like It Hot* as the theme, spotlighting what was hot and what was not. The new krewe membership, which included both men and women, gay and straight, rose to the occasion. Becky Allen reigned as the first queen.

Satyricon in Bloom

For *Satyricon in Bloom* (2004), Gil called on nature itself to fill the St. Bernard Civic Center. With Gil as the Flower Goddess, petunias, hydrangeas, lilies, poppies, foxgloves, snapdragons, nasturtiums, cherry blossoms, irises, magnolias, Queen Anne's lace, tulips, forget-me-nots, and a shy wall flower burst forth on stage. Drag favorite Varla Jean Merman served as the master of ceremonies; king and queen Danny Boyd and Bianca del Rio appeared as Monet's Water Lilies.

Carnival in Rio

Choosing Carnival itself and especially the Grand Carnival in Rio as a theme was a risk. Only the Mystic Krewe of Celestial Knights under the leadership of Bill Woolley had ever done this topic any kind of justice. But for Satyricon, former Celestial Knight Jimmy Keyes created lavish and beautiful costumes for such characters as Brazilian Coffee, Girls from Ipanema, the Social Butterfly, Flying Down to Rio, and the much-anticipated Carmen Miranda, and Gil's idea resulted in another masterpiece. Varla Jean Merman again served as master of ceremonies. In addition to the newly crowned King and Queen of Twelfth Night, appearing onstage were the New Orleans Gay Men's Chorus; the winner of Satyricon's Star Search, Miss Tiffany; the

Casa Samba dance troupe; and the Southern Decadence Grand Marshals Lisa Beaumann and Regina Adams (with a Parrot King and some Brazilian Bananas).

The Mickey Ball

At the beginning of March 2010, just after the end of the Carnival season, Gil died of complications from gallbladder surgery. The following year, Satyricon paid tribute to its former leader with the *Mickey Ball*, opening with a jazz funeral segment, an appropriate send-off for someone who so loved New Orleans. With Gil no longer in charge, the krewe decided to have a committee plan the ball each year rather than selecting a ball captain, a seismic shift for the New Orleans Carnival community.

Satyricon Makes Scents: Le Bal des Parfums

In the program for the 2015 ball, *Satyricon Makes Scents: Le Bal des Parfums*, krewe president Wedon Brown explained, "Whether you douse yourself in designer perfume or draw the line at hand soap, fragrance is a great equalizer. Like taste, scent affects all of us, conjuring up memories in ways that startle and delight: a high school friend, a former lover, your grandmother's kitchen. The power of fragrance is universal and undeniable." The tableau presentation featured Bond No. 9, Axe Body Spray, Shalimar, Chanel No. 5, Le Male, Polo, Joy, the Avon Lady, and White Diamonds.

George Patterson and Mickey Gil as Marlene Dietrich. Courtesy of the Mystic Krewe of Satyricon and George Patterson.

Le Bal des Beaux-Arts/A Night at the Museum

In 2016, Carl Mack reigned as the queen of Satyricon, with Darric Cavalier as king. Mack's gown, an Erté-inspired masterpiece, bore silver sequins from top to bottom, as did her attached greyhound mascot. Mack, a longtime member of the New Orleans gay community, founded a chapter of the Radical Faeries in the early 1990s.

In addition to carrying on Mickey Gil's legacy of creating fantastic tableaux, the krewe has established the Mickey Gil Scholarship to benefit musical theater students at the New Orleans Center for the Creative Arts. The primary fundraiser is the Twelfth Night Ball, which takes place as close to Epiphany as possible. At the ball, the krewe introduces the king and queen of Satyricon, announces the theme of the upcoming ball, and crowns the king and queen of Twelfth Night.

Mystic Krewe of Satyricon's Twelfth Night Ball, 2015. Courtesy of the Mystic Krewe of Satyricon.

The Mystic Krewe of Satyricon (2003)

2003

Mickey Gil and his partner, George Patterson, broke away from the Krewe of Petronius and formed Satyricon, which soon became the toast of the town. New Orleans diva Becky Allen reigned as Queen Satyricon I.

2004

Many different types of flowers were the inspiration for the second ball, and Bianca del Rio (Roy Haylock), winner of *RuPaul's Drag Race*, reigned as the queen, who, along with the king, was dressed as Monet's Water Lilies.

2005

Satyricon's ball, *Carnival in Rio*, returned to a familiar theme, but James Keyes's designs for the invitation and costumes made it unusual and flamboyant.

2015

The krewe took on the perfume theme with *Satyricon Makes Scents/ Le Bal des Parfums*. In addition, by this time, Satyricon had done away with the office of elected captain; rather, a core group of members planned and executed the balls by vote. Satyricon remains unique in this approach.

2016

The *Bal des Beaux-Arts* (A Night at the Museum) in 2016 exhibited the stage talents of krewe members who regularly performed in plays and musicals around town.

Mystic Krewe of Satyricon Tableau Balls List	
2003	SOME LIKE IT HOT
2004	SATYRICON IN BLOOM
2005	CARNIVAL IN RIO
2006	ALONG THE SILK ROAD
2007	SATYRICON PLAYS WITH TOYS
2008	FANTASTIC DREAMS
2009	COCKTAILS AT 7
2010	ALL THAT JAZZ
2011	THE MICKEY BALL
2012	THE ARMAGEDDON BALL
2013	SATYRICON GOES GREEN
2014	BAL D'AMOUR
2015	SATYRICON MAKES SCENTS—BAL DES PARFUMS
2016	LE BAL DES BEAUX ARTS—A NIGHT AT THE MUSEUM
2017	—

Mystic Krewe of Satyricon Royalty List			
YEAR OF TABLEAU BALL	CAPTAIN	QUEEN	KING
2003	Mickey Gil	Becky Allen	Ted Jeansonne
2004	Mickey Gil	Roy Haylock (Bianca del Rio)	David Boyd
2005	Mickey Gil	Stephen Rizzo	Don Westerman
2006	Mickey Gil	Joe Brooks	Todd Blauvelt
2007	Mickey Gil	Hoyle Byrd	Tony Leggio
2008	Mickey Gil	Carl Mack	Scott Lloyd
2009	Mickey Gil	Wedon Brown	Richard Read
2010	Mickey Gil	Ty Johnson	Paul Metoyer
2011	—	Brian Peterson	Kent Roby
2012	—	Stephen Rizzo	Brick Bishop
2013	—	Todd Blauvelt	Todd Shaffer
2014	—	Brick Bishop	Christopher Santilli
2015	—	Becky Allen	Marshall Harris
2016	—	Carl Mack	Darric Cavalier
2017			

Notes: Beginning in 2011, the ball was planned by committee rather than a single captain. In 2014, the krewe chose a mystic consort rather than a queen. The krewe did not present a tableau ball in 2017.

Some Like It Hot 2003

Commemorative poster, 2003. Design by Clint Delapasse. Courtesy of the Louisiana State Museum, New Orleans, Accession No. 2004.061.1.

Queen Satyricon I, Becky Allen, and King Satyricon I, Ted Jeansonne, 2003. Photograph by Mitchel L. Osborne. Courtesy of LGBT+ Archives Project of Louisiana Grant.

Purple Iris, 2003. Photograph by Mitchel L. Osborne. Courtesy of LGBT+ Archives Project of Louisiana Grant.

Satyricon in Bloom 2004

Commemorative poster, 2004. Design by Clint Delapasse. Courtesy of the Louisiana State Museum, New Orleans, Accession No. 2004.061.2.

Tableau 2004
God Bless America—Varla Jean Merman
Hot Love—Returning King and Queen Satyricon I
The Flower Goddess—Captain MG
Dazzle Dazzle—Tommy Elias
Twelfth Night Royalty Presentation
A Thorny Flower
Purple Rose of Cairo—Ball Lieutenant
Flowers of Evil
Dance of the Flowers—Lyle Guidroz and Co.
Petunias
Hydrangea
Allium
Star Gaze Lily
Toxic Poppy—Coca and Co.
Wall Flower
Fox Glove
Snap Dragon
Habanera—Varla Jean Merman
Sexy Nasturtium
Audrey II
Cherry Blossom
Iris
Tiptoe through the Tulips—Lyle Guidroz and Co.
Steel Magnolia
Queen Anne's Lace
Forget-Me-Not—Rusty LaRoux
Awards and Honors
Water Lilies—King and Queen Satyricon II
Special Guests
Sister Krewes
Open Court

Queen Satyricon II, Roy Haylock (Bianca del Rio), and King Satyricon II, David Boyd, as Monet's Water Lilies, 2004. Photograph by Mitchel L. Osborne. Courtesy of LGBT+ Archives Project of Louisiana Grant.

Snap Dragon, 2004. Photograph by Mitchel L. Osborne. Courtesy of LGBT+ Archives Project of Louisiana Grant.

Carnival in Rio 2005

Commemorative poster, 2005. Design by James Keyes. Courtesy of the Louisiana State Museum, New Orleans, Accession No. 2005.081.

Tableau 2005
National Anthem—New Orleans Gay Men's Chorus
Returning Royalty—King and Queen Satyricon II
Brazil—Captain MG
Case Samba (dance troupe)
King and Queen of Twelfth Night
Varla Jean Merman—Co-Emcee
Special Honors
Brazilian Coffee
Social Butterfly
At the Carnival—New Orleans Gay Men's Chorus
Flying Down to Rio
Casa Samba (dance troupe)
Tiffany—Winner of Satyricon's Star Search
Carnival Revelers
Football in Brazil
Girl from Ipanema
Water Sprite
The Evening's Beneficiaries
New Orleans Gay Men's Chorus
Varla Jean Merman
Copa Star with the Copa Girls
Southern Decadence Grand Marshals
Parrot King
Brazilian Bananas
Carmen Miranda
King and Queen Satyricon III
Casa Samba (dance troupe)
Special Guests
Sister Krewes
Open Court

James Keyes, costume design for Brazilian Coffee, 2005. Courtesy of the Louisiana State Museum, New Orleans, Accession No. 2015.027.6.

James Keyes, costume design for Girl from Ipanema, 2005. Courtesy of the Louisiana State Museum, New Orleans, Accession No. 2015.027.4.

Satyricon Makes Scents—Bal de Parfums 2015

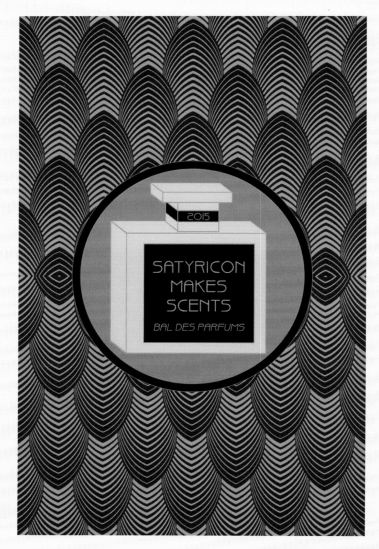

Program, 2015. Courtesy of Wayne Phillips.

Queen Satyricon XIII, Becky Allen, and King Satyricon
XIII, Marshal Harris, 2015. Photograph by Barret
Delong-Church.

Le Bal des Beaux-Arts 2016

Queen Satyricon XIV, Carl Mack, and King Satyricon, XIV Darric Cavalier, 2016. Photograph by Frank Stansbury.

Tableau 2016
Women of Algiers (Pablo Picasso)
Mona Lisa (Leonardo da Vinci)
Balloon Dog (Jeff Koons)
A Portrait of Bobby Jindal
Napoleon Crossing the Alps (Jacques-Louis David)
Elvis on Velvet—Varla Jean Merman
Learn to Paint with Bob Ross
The Persistence of Memory (Salvador Dali)
Marilyn Monroe (Andy Warhol)
An Homage to George Dureau
Summer Days (Georgia O'Keeffe)
Canna-Bloom (Georgia O'Keeffe)

Napoleon Crossing the Alps, 2016. Photograph by Frank Stansbury.

The Yuga Regina was one of the most spectacular sights I've ever seen in my life. When the lights reflected off her royal raiments, the room was filled with explosions and bursts of light like fireworks. Who would have guessed that her children would take up the mantle of Carnival and run with it like they were possessed?

—John Henry Bogie, Krewe of Yuga and Steamboat Club

The history of gay Carnival and its decades of hiding behind locked doors in union halls and small venues has been only partially reclaimed. Many short-lived gay krewes and groups that only celebrated Carnival in the French Quarter bars or with Fat Tuesday parades left little evidence of their existence. In some cases, such as that of the Krewe of Jason, all that is known is the krewe's name. The Krewe of Memphis presented at least eight balls at the St. Bernard Civic Center, but only a handful of invitations have survived, and no former members have been identified. For its first ball in 1976, the theme was *That's for the Birds*. The 1977 ball was *An Evening in Paris*, and in 1978 it was *When the Stars Go Marching In*. The 1979 ball featured the *Daughters of Evil: A Bunch of No-Goods*. Early ball invitations featured a Star of David, an indicator that this krewe may have had a predominantly Jewish membership. The krewe also hosted an annual Miss Vieux Carré contest. Only a single ball program testifies to the existence of The Queen's Men (TQM), who presented a tableau that featured the Pharaohs of the Upper and Lower Kingdoms of Egypt as well as Queen Tequemen, the Sacrifice, also known as the Queen of Camp, demonstrating that the group was most definitely a gay krewe. They presented at least two tableau balls. The Mystic Krewe of Phoenix presented a ball in 1975. No other references have been found to date.

The Satin and Sequins krewe encouraged its guests to wear drag, but more traditional gay krewes required formal wear. Founded by habitués of the Post Office Lounge, the Frollicking Krewe of PO usually celebrated Carnival in the bar in costume. The invitations to Snow White's costume balls at St. Mark's Community Center on Rampart Street were handmade silver snowflakes. The queen was always Snow

Krewe of Yuga ball at the Rambler Room dance studio, Metairie, 1961. Attendees included Bob Phillips, Joey Bausch, and George Roth. The scenery and props suggested a Wild West theme. Courtesy of Louisiana State Museum.

White, while guests wore only white. Miss Blanche (Ed Norton) of the Golden Lantern bar formed the Krewe of Kancellation when a 1979 police strike resulted in the cancellation of Carnival. The following year, police shut down the group's walking parade because organizers had failed to obtain a permit.

La Krewe Mystique de Désimé was formed by Daisy Mae (Kenneth Toncrey), a drag queen from Biloxi, Mississippi, where he frequented KoKo's Café, a gay piano bar. According to legend, after having an affair with the son of a prominent businessman, he was forced to leave Biloxi and headed for New Orleans, where he had contacts. Once there, he set up shop in an apartment in the French Quarter and housed all his friends from the Gulf Coast when they were in town. The 1968 novel *Queens of the Quarter*, which mixed in real historical events and real queens and drag queens, depicted Daisy Mae as a "big blonde stud with a penal record who always wore drag." Toncrey worked for a time as a bouncer at Café Lafitte's before opening Daisy Mae's Gift Shop at 830 North Rampart in the late 1960s. La Krewe Mystique de Désimé presented large tableau balls at Chalmette's St. Bernard Civic Center in 1975 and 1976 and at the Superdome in 1977. "Anything you've heard about me, I did it, says the French Quarter's most candid character, Daisy Mae," wrote Bob Mann in *Contact Magazine*. "Ex–hair burner, bartender, bouncer, entrepreneur, Daisy Mae has been into everything. His shop is overflowing with Indian headdresses, oil paintings, chastity belts, bicycle parts, frames, and last year's Mardi Gras drag."

Among Daisy Mae's friends and fellow krewe members were Crispy Critter, Tinker Bell, Numa, Miss Ella, and Foxie, a car mechanic who imitated Barbara Streisand and wore fox furs. In the late 1960s, Miss Daisy Mae held court at the Finale Bar at 1041 Royal Street. A patron of the bar at the time recalled that this was where "police raids were still a threat at the time but we always had our cadre of fag hags for cover. Touching between men was frowned upon by the bar owner. Someone was always posted at the door to alert the patrons if they suspected a possible raid. If I remember correctly, a change in the lighting on the dance floor was the signal. Most everyone knew each other and if a stranger wandered in, Daisy Mae and her court quickly sized them up. Their gaydar was usually spot-on. I pitied the poor souls who didn't pass muster as they were dished mercilessly by the royalty. No one could read beads like Miss Daisy Mae." According to George Wilson, who managed the Finale with his partner, Nick Donovan, Daisy Mae "was the muscle at Lafitte's, and despite his bleached and permanented hair, he was a very tough guy. Once when a straight thug stood at the entrance making derogatory remarks and challenging Daisy to a fight, he got what he wanted. After Daisy thoroughly whipped his ass, he looked down at the thug now prostrate on the sidewalk, and said, 'Now go home and tell your momma a faggot whipped your ass!'"

Dorothy "Dirtie Dottie" Pelletier ran the DeGeorge Cleaners and Laundry at 826 North Rampart. According to *Contact Magazine*, she earned her nickname "by spicing her language, regularly, with words not meant for tender ears. She dearly loves the gay kids, goes to all the Carnival balls, and makes spectacular Mardi Gras costumes. If you can take her riverfront vocabulary, you'll love Rampart Street's Dirty Dottie." A Canadian, she was reputed to have been a stripper on Bourbon Street and was a seamstress who repaired the flags for the *Natchez* steamboat. Some of her krewe's costumed presentations took place in Chalmette, but their quality was uneven. According to Pat O'Rourke, the first three-time royal in the Krewe of Amon-Ra, "The Krewe of Dirtie Dottie was populated by people who couldn't get into other krewes, such as hustlers and street people." Pelletier also served as secretary-treasurer for the Krewe of Dionysus, which presented at least one ball, *Gone with the Wind*, presided over by Queen Roz.

On a list of gay krewes compiled in the early 1990s, Otto Stierle mentioned that the remnants of the Krewe of Memphis joined the Krewe of David; when that group folded, they went on to help found the Krewe of Eros. Its membership included both men and women, and A. J. Fayard served as the first captain. The Krewe of Trash was a bar crawl in which participants wore black or multicolored trash bags as costumes. Pickup trucks chauffeured the king and queen from one bar to another, and a buffet was held in their honor at the Mississippi River Bottom bar. Cerci was among the groups slated to hold tableau balls in 1985 but did not and soon disappeared. Though the Krewe of Vesta was short-lived, Ed Cox's artwork for its 1983 *Flight of Fancy* ball was impressive.

Evidence of the Mystic Krewe of Tragoidia appears in several legal documents. Linked to the Clinic, a French Quarter gay bar, the krewe was formed in 1983 by Scott Bloom, Donald Moore, John Kahl, and Mercedes Canedo and took its name from the Greek word for tragedy. The name evoked the Greek pagan world. Tragoidia's first major fund-raiser, Speakeasy Night, was supposed to be held on a steamboat, but the New Orleans Steamboat Company refused to comply with an agreement with the krewe even after it had paid a three-hundred-dollar deposit. According to one document, "An employee of the company had phoned a representative of the krewe to inform the group that, on a prior charter by a different group, homosexuals became uncontrollable when they drank alcohol. A company officer explained that on a previous charter on a different boat in New York the homosexuals chased the deckhands around the ship." After the krewe filed suit, the company eventually agreed to host the fund-raiser on the steamboat free of charge, but the krewe disbanded without presenting a tableau ball. Bloom reused *Tragoidia* as the name of his documentary film company after moving to Los Angeles and produced several groundbreaking films associated with gay culture.

More recent groups include the Krewe of Queenateenas, which since 1987 has basically been a Carnival costume party held at the Bourbon Street home of Rip Naquin and Marsha Delain, publishers of *Ambush Magazine*, complete with a bead toss from the balcony. The Mardi Gras Merrymen began an annual Riverboat Cruise in 1992. The Krewe of La Cage aux Folles (2000–2003) sought to become the first gay krewe to parade down St. Charles Avenue onto Canal Street, as the traditional krewes do. Captain Anthony Chad Williams led the group, with Timm Holt (Lord King XVIII of the Lords of Leather) and Amber Nicole Welch (the reigning Miss Crescent City America). The New Orleans City Council refused to issue the required permit on the grounds that only a limited number could be granted, but many observers accused the city of discrimination. Formed in 2000, Anubis held its first ball the following year. The core of the group was the People of Substance, a gay Black Pride organization founded by Darrell Keith Sims, and both men and women were members. In 2003 the krewe presented the *Birds of a Feather* ball at the Saint Bernard Cultural Center. A black lesbian social group, the Krewe of Kemet (LIPS), presents a supper ball a month or so after Carnival season. In 2014, local historian Frank Perez as the Lord of Misrule inaugurated the Mistik Krewe du Rue Royale Revelers, a Twelfth Night party at the corner of Royal and St. Ann attended by more than three hundred revelers. The court of the Krewe of Queenateenas, including the King Cake Queen, came to pay honor to the Mistik Krewe at the beginning of the Carnival season, mirroring the meeting of Rex and Comus at the end. In 2015

Jeffrey Palmquist was crowned as the first Grand Reveler, followed by William Antil (2016) and Rip Naquin (2017). In 2015, the Krewe of Narcissus, made up of former members of the Krewe of Armeinius, held its first ball, *Reflections*, at the Healing Center on St. Claude Avenue in the up-and-coming Bywater neighborhood, with Bruce Orgeron as captain. In the old style of gay Carnival, all the tickets were bestowed, not sold. Costumes reflected the theme of Narcissus gazing at his own image—mirrors, eyes, and shields. Queen Narcissus I (Rick Mirabelli) was presented to her subjects along with her page, a young Narcissus (Jason Doyle), though in another throwback to early gay Carnival balls, no king was chosen. Unable to secure a venue in 2016, the krewe did not present its second ball until 2017, when it presented a tableau and named Rusty Toups as Queen Narcissus II. Founded in 2016 by former members of the Mystic Krewe of Satyricon, the Krewe of Stars seeks "to encourage, nurture, and promote the talents of the New Orleans performance art community." Led by captain Carl Mack, the krewe held its first ball, *Show Ball*, in 2017. Local legend Angela Hill was queen, with Dennis Assaf as king. Local favorite Becky Allen was chosen as the grand duchess.

THE KREWE OF THE QUEEN'S MEN (1973)

Invitation, 1973. Courtesy of Tulane University, Louisiana Research Collection, Howard-Tilton Memorial Library, New Orleans, Otto Stierle Collection, Manuscripts Collection 902.

Tableau 1973
Prelude
Welcome by C. Ed Hammett, President
Herald
Presentation of Pharaoh of Lower Kingdom I
Presentation of Pharaoh of Upper Kingdom I
Presentation of Queen Tequemen II
Overture
Entrance of Ball Captain
Royal Guards
Ambassador of the Incas
Ambassador of the Mayas
High Priest
Sacrifice (Queen of Camp)
Sun God
Presentation of Pharaoh of Lower Kingdom II
Presentation of Pharaoh of Upper Kingdom II
Grand March and Elevation of New Court
Presentation of Awards
Presentation of Court and Krewes of New Orleans
Open Court

THE MYSTIC KREWE OF PHOENIX (1975)

Invitation to the *Gift of the Nile* ball, 1975. Courtesy of the Louisiana State Museum, New Orleans, Accession No. T0016.2001.741.

Reverse reads: *The Story. Once in the shadow of a thousand years, from the ashes of its flaming body, rises the magnificent phoenix bird. Since not the days of Egypt's glory, when the Pharaohs ruled the world, has this event been witnessed. Now, you are invited. January 3, 1975.*

LA KREWE MYSTIQUE DE DÉSIMÉ (1975)

The Captain
of
La Krewe Mystique De Desimé
requests
the honor of your presence
at its
first annual ball
"How Gay Can You Be"
to be held at the
St. Bernard Civic Auditorium
on the
sixth day of February
in the year of
nineteen hundred and seventy-five
to commence promptly
at the
stroke of nine of the clock

1975

Invitation to the *How Gay Can You Be* ball, 1975. Courtesy of the Louisiana State Museum, New Orleans, Accession No. T0016.2001.261.

Daisy Mae, captain of La Krewe Mystique de Désimé. Photograph by Bruce Gilden/MAGNUM Photos.

Cover of the paperback *Queens of the Quarter* by William B. Tressner Jr. (1968). This early gay pulp fiction masterpiece portrayed many of the real denizens of the French Quarter, including Daisy Mae, as a backdrop to a gay romance.

Adrian St. Clair and others getting ready for the *How Gay Can You Be* ball at the Superdome, 1975. Photograph by John McMillan. Courtesy of the Don Lee Keith Collection, Earl K. Long Library, University of New Orleans.

THE KREWE OF MEMPHIS (1976)

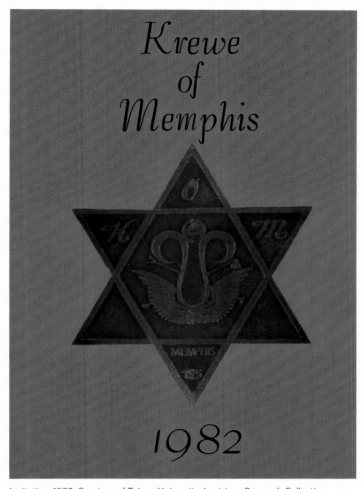

Poster for the *Memphis Blows the Blues* ball, 1983. Courtesy of The Historic New Orleans Collection, Williams Research Center, New Orleans, Accession No. 1983.109.35. Gift of Tracy Hendrix.

Invitation, 1982. Courtesy of Tulane University, Louisiana Research Collection, Howard-Tilton Memorial Library, New Orleans, Otto Stierle Collection, Manuscripts Collection 902.

Tableau 1979
Evil of Evils—The Devil (Captain)
Daughter of the Bride of Frankenstein (Ball Lieutenant)
Entertainment
The Debutantes
King and Queen Memphis III
Entertainment
The 1979 Court of the Krewe of Memphis
King and Queen Memphis IV
Entertainment
Reigning Royalty of Other Krewes
Special Guests of the Queen
Special Guests of the King
Special Guests—Title Holders
The Captain of the Krewe of Memphis
The Ball Lieutenant of the Krewe of Memphis
The Captain's Award
Grand March
Open Court
General Dancing till Midnight

FROLLICKING KREWE OF PO (1977)

THE KREWE OF DIRTIE DOTTIE (1977)

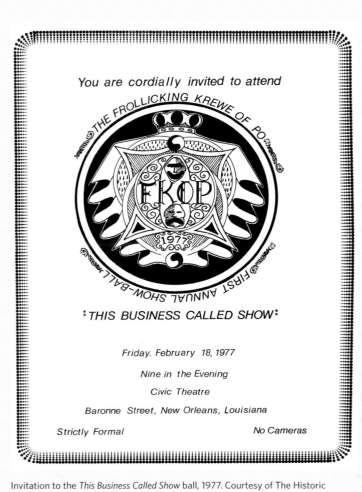

Invitation to the *This Business Called Show* ball, 1977. Courtesy of The Historic New Orleans Collection, Williams Research Center, New Orleans, Accession No. 1977.307.37a. Gift of Tracy Hendrix.

Invitation to the *Leather* ball, 1982. Courtesy of the Louisiana State Museum, New Orleans, Accession No. 1995.010.079.

Dirtie Dottie and friend, 1982. Courtesy of the Louisiana State Museum, New Orleans, Accession No. 1995.010.080.

THE KREWE OF SNOW WHITE (1978)

1981 SNOWBALL

THE MANY AND ASSORTED
DWARFS HAPPILY INVITE YOU TO FROLIC
WITH THEM AS THEY HONOR

SNOW WHITE
1981

AT HER FIRST ANNUAL SNOW BALL, TO BE
HELD AT JACKSON'S PLACE, 1212
ROYAL STREET, ON MONDAY EVENING,
MARCH 2, 1981, BEGINING AT 9 00PM

FORMAL ATTIRE OR ALL WHITE DRESS
IS APPROPRIATE FOR THIS FESTIVE
CELEBRATION
(A TOUCH OF COLOR IS PERMITTED)

RSVP BY TELEPHONE AT (504) 522 4468
FOR FURTHER DETAILS AND THE REQUIRED
SNOW FLAKE NEEDED FOR YOUR ENTRY
TO THE LAND OF SNOW

ALL OF THE DWARFS HOPE YOU WILL
ATTEND!

Invitation, 1981. Courtesy of the Louisiana State Museum, New Orleans, Accession No. 1981.043.08a.

Dwarf ensemble, 1981. Courtesy of the Louisiana State Museum, New Orleans, Accession No. T0070.1998.1.

THE KREWE OF DIONYSUS (1979)

Krewe of Dionysus crest. Courtesy of the Louisiana State Museum, New Orleans, Accession No. T0016.2001.277.

THE KREWE OF VESTA (1983)

THE KREWE OF TRASH (1984)

Invitation to the *Flight of Fancy* ball, 1983. Design by Ed Cox. Courtesy of Ed Cox.

Krewe of Trash logo. Design by Ed Cox. Courtesy of Ed Cox.

THE KREWE OF DAVID (1984)

Program for the *Fables and Fairytales* ball, 1986. Courtesy of Howard Philips Smith and Wendell Stipelcovich.

Inside reads: *It has been a rough year but the strong survive. I look forward being able to give you a night of fulfillment to relax and enjoy. On behalf of myself and my Ball Lieutenant and our Krewe, we thank you for being our honored guests. I look forward to now and seeing you next year.*

King Tony Rizzuto, 1986. The 1986 queen was Larry Federico; the captain was Perry Stamm. Courtesy of Glyce DiMiceli.

THE KREWE OF PERSEUS (1984)

Invitation, 1985. The April 6, 1988, issue of the *Rooster* reported, "The Krewe of Perseus, no longer functioning as a Carnival organization, has liquidated its treasury and donated $1,000 to Buzzy's Boys at Charity Hospital. Buzzy says that the money will be used to buy appliances to make the boys more comfortable. Thanks to Perseus for their generosity!" Founded by Buzzy Fanning, Buzzy's Boys (later Buzzy's Boys and Girls) was an HIV/AIDS charity. Courtesy of The Historic New Orleans Collection, Williams Research Center, New Orleans, Accession No. 2000.34.125.

Inside reads: *It is dark. You have followed the concrete path from the city and entered the hall of brick and glass. Now seated in the great room filled with others, allow yourself to be alone. Glance around quickly. Were you noticed by the others? Were they aware that you noticed them? Now it all begins. So many crown heads in one room. The elite of the elite and somewhere in the shadows, the Captains! My men carry me in to you and I shall carry you away in my mad dream. Let yourself be alone. Come with me on A Winter's Night Fantasy. Daniel Romero, The Captain.*

⚜

Tableau 1985
Overture
Master of Ceremonies
Presentation of the Crest
Miss Gay World of Louisiana 1984–85
Presentation of Honored Royalty
King and Queen Perseus I
Captain
Ball Lieutenant—Opium
Snowflake
Winter Star
The Moon
Horns of Plenty
White Rose of Winter
Iceberg
Creature from the Sea
King and Queen Perseus II
The Grand March
Perseus Recognizes
Open Court

The Krewe of Queenateenas (1987)

1987

On Fat Tuesday, more than four hundred guests joined Rip Naquin and Marsha Delain, publishers of *Ambush Magazine*, at their Bourbon Street home, which features one of the largest balconies in the French Quarter.

1988

Jay Loomis officially named the krewe, and the balcony became known as the Queenateenas Balcony Float No. 69.

1994

For the first time, a King Cake Queen was chosen to celebrate the day. The tradition has continued, with official titles and colors added and the balcony decorated to reflect the official theme.

1995

The new queen was introduced to society three weeks before Carnival at the KCQ Coronation Bash, where she was joined by other members of the King Cake Queen Royalty Club. The queen leads the Official Gay Mardi Gras Bead Toss on Fat Tuesday.

2008

King Cake Queen XV, Marsha Delain, selected *The Fleur-de-Lis Queen* as her theme, channeling French royalty from the days of Louis XIV. Opal Masters designed and built the intricate royal raiments.

2010

King Cake Queen XVII Opal Masters led the festivities, which took the theme *Passport to Versailles, No Guillotines, Please*. Reigning as the Parisian Queen as well as designing and executing her gown, Opal was presented to Carnival Society for the seventeenth annual King Cake Queen Coronation on January 23, kicking off Gay Mardi Gras.

2015–17

In 2015, King Cake Queen XXII Aubrey Synclaire headlined the twenty-eighth Official Gay Mardi Gras Bead Toss, in which thousands of beads were thrown from the balcony. On May 2, 2015, the Krewe of Queenateenas participated in the Gay Krewe of Krewes parade, which traveled down Bourbon Street in the French Quarter. Queen Synclaire continued her reign the following year. In 2017, Monica Synclaire-Kennedy was designated as King Cake Queen XXIV.

YEAR	QUEEN	THEME
1994	—	—
1995	Jay A. Loomis	*Jewel of the Nile*
1996	Smurf Murphy	*The Rainbow Queen*
1997	Reba Douglas	*Pearl of the Sea*
1998	Elizabeth Simms	*The She Devil*
1999	Christine Cheridon	*The Czarina*
2000	Stephanie Williams	*Sex Goddess*
2001	Phyllis Denmark	*The Peacock Queen*
2002	Lisa Beaumann	*The Freedom Queen*
2003	Teryl-Lynn Foxx	*The Voodoo Queen*
2004	—	—
2005	Savanna DeLorean	*The Amazon Queen*
2006	Raven Kennedy	*The Diamond Queen*
2007	Princesse Stephaney	*The Fantasy Queen*
2008	Marsha Delain	*The Fleur-de-Lis Queen*
2009	Tami Tarmac	*The Grandee Queen*
2010	Opal Masters	*The Parisian Queen*
2011	Rona Conners	*The Chrysanthemum Queen*
2012	Nicole DuBois	*The Samba Queen*
2013	Dusty Debris	*The Platinum Queen*
2014	Barbara Ella	*The Borghese Queen*
2015	Aubrey Synclaire	*Queen of the Opera—Part I*
2016	Aubrey Synclaire	*Queen of the Opera—Part II*
2017	Monica Synclaire-Kennedy	*Pridelicious: Rainbows, Stars and Stilettos!*

Krewe of Queenateenas—King Cake Queen List

Official crest of the Krewe of Queenateenas. Courtesy of Rip Naquin and Marsha Delain.

King Cake Queen XXII/XXIII, Aubrey Synclaire, 2015–16. Photograph by Larry Graham. Courtesy of Rip Naquin and Marsha Delain.

King Cake Queen XV, Marsha Delain, 2008. Photograph by Larry Graham. Courtesy of Rip Naquin and Marsha Delain.

THE KREWE OF EROS (1987)

THE KREWE OF LA CAGE AUX FOLLES (2000)

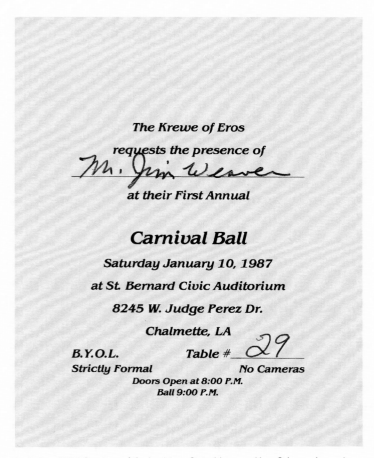

Invitation, 1987. Courtesy of the Louisiana State Museum, New Orleans, Accession No. 1995.010.081.

Publicity poster, 2002. The krewe sought to stage a 165-unit procession, *Legends of Screen and Stage*, including 20 floats saluting such divas as Lucille Ball, Madonna, and Barbra Streisand and popular shows such as *A Chorus Line*, *Little Shop of Horrors*, and the *Rocky Horror Picture Show*. In addition to the standard marching and parade units, the krewe proposed the novel inclusion of 20 choirs from across the country. Captain Anthony Chad Williams led the efforts from his home in Algiers Point. The krewe disbanded after the city refused to grant a parade permit. The graphic of the Eiffel Tower and the Can-Can Dancer became synonymous with the krewe. Courtesy of Tulane University, Louisiana Research Collection, Howard-Tilton Memorial Library, New Orleans.

THE KREWE OF ANUBIS (2003)

Program for the *Birds of a Feather* ball, 2003. Courtesy of the Louisiana State Museum, New Orleans, Jake and Kevin Thomas Collection, Accession No. 2015.046.27.

THE KREWE OF NARCISSUS (2015)

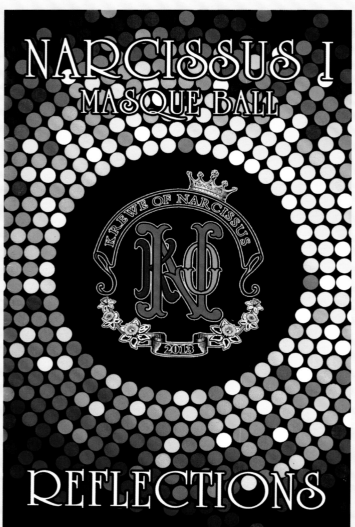

Program for the *Reflections* ball, 2015. Courtesy of J. Bruce Orgeron Jr.

J. Bruce Orgeron Jr., costume sketch for Mirror, Mirror, 2015. Courtesy of the Louisiana State Museum, New Orleans, Accession No. 2015.045.3.3.

ACADEMY OF THE GOLDEN GODDESS, INC. (1978–1991)

A.G.G.J.

Academy of the Golden Goddess, Inc. Annual Awards—1985
An Example of a Typical Awards Year
March 30, 1985, St. Bernard Cultural Center

AWARD	NOMINEES	WINNER
BEST BALL THEME	Amon-Ra, Armeinius, Polyphemus	Amon-Ra
BEST MUSIC	Amon-Ra, Armeinius, Olympus	Armeinius
BEST SET DESIGN	Amon-Ra, Armeinius, Polyphemus	Amon-Ra
BEST COSTUME DESIGN	Amon-Ra, Armeinius, Polyphemus	Amon-Ra
BEST RETURNING KING	Amon-Ra, Armeinius, David	David
BEST RETURNING QUEEN	Amon-Ra, Polyphemus, Ishtar	Polyphemus
BEST SOLO PERFORMANCE	Armeinius, Olympus, Polyphemus	Polyphemus
BEST GROUP PERFORMANCE	Amon-Ra, Ishtar, Polyphemus	Ishtar
BEST REIGNING KING	Armeinius, Olympus, Polyphemus	Polyphemus
BEST REIGNING QUEEN	Amon-Ra, Armeinius, Polyphemus	Amon-Ra
BEST BALL LIEUTENANT	Amon-Ra, Armeinius, Perseus	Armeinius
BEST BALL CAPTAIN	Armeinius, Olympus, Polyphemus	Armeinius
BEST KREWE COSTUME	Amon-Ra, Olympus, Petronius	Petronius

AGGI Statuette, from the 1984 AGGI Awards program. Courtesy of the Louisiana State Museum, New Orleans, Accession No. 1995.010.133.

Beginning in 1978, the Academy of the Golden Goddess, Inc. (AGGI) Award was the gay Carnival award for excellence. Among the categories were Set Design, Costume Design, Best Theme and Music, Returning King and Queen, Solo Performance, Group Performance, Costume, Ball Lieutenant, Reigning King and Queen, and Ball Captain. However, the most prestigious award was always Reigning Queen. Although the Mystic Krewe of Celestial Knights was nominated every year, its members refused to attend the award ceremony. Jan Moran, a member of the Krewe of Ishtar, served as the Academy's longtime president, while Garrett Stearns was a devoted fund-raiser for the group.

By 1985, the award ceremony, usually held a month after Ash Wednesday, took place at the Saint Bernard Cultural Center in Chalmette. The show featured entertainment by local dance troupes such as the AGGI Dancers or the Crescent City Movin' Co. In addition, some of the nominated costumes and dances were presented again during the awards ceremony. The Academy folded after presenting the 1991 AGGIs.

THE ARTISTS
OF GAY CARNIVAL

A Hidden World Revealed

I have always been in awe of gay Carnival. I sat in the audience at many balls simply mesmerized by the beauty and magic of it all. What an honor to have contributed to it all!

—Daniel de Beau-Maltbie, Artist

Remnants of the Golden Age

The year 2017 marked the sixtieth anniversary of gay Carnival in New Orleans. During that long and glorious span of time, many different artists contributed to the visual representations associated with the gay krewes. The Golden Age of Gay Carnival is now long past, but it survives in the invitations, posters, doubloons, and programs that some participants saved as mementos of their revelry. The artists who created these ephemeral items often lacked training, but that did not stop them from crafting original and inventive items, many of which referenced historical artworks. Nevertheless, most were reluctant to sign their names to their work because of laws against homosexuality and masking in public, and more often than not these important artists remained relatively unknown to the outside world.

Early Artworks

From the beginning, gay krewes took advantage of members' artistic abilities and imposed few restrictions on their creativity, though budget and time constraints meant that early invitations frequently lacked professional polish, with hand-stenciling and large press-on letters. Many invitations for fund-raisers and parties featured clever illustrations taken from the history of art, such as special invitations inspired by Aubrey Beardsley, who illustrated the works of Oscar Wilde. The invitations for the Krewe of Amon-Ra's 1971 ball used a dramatic illustration from

Invitation to the Krewe of Petronius's holiday party at the home of John Dodt, 1973. The invitation features Aubrey Beardsley's frontispiece for *The Mirror of Love* (1895). Courtesy of Tulane University, Louisiana Research Collection, Howard-Tilton Memorial Library, New Orleans, Otto Stierle Collection, Manuscripts Collection 902.

Inside reads: *Saturday, December 15, 1973. 920 Saint Louis Street. 9:00 p.m. to 1:00 a.m. Dress—Endimanche.*

Napoleon's campaign as well as hieroglyphs printed in embossed gold relief. The Krewe of Armeinius used an obscure painting by nineteenth-century Frenchman Tony Robert-Fleury for the 1971 *Atlantis Redivivus* ball.

Elmo Delacroix Avet

Elmo Delacroix Avet (1896–1969) was an early leader of New Orleans's gay community and an original member of the Krewe of Yuga. Avet created a simple yet stunning program for the Krewe of Petronius's 1967 ball, *Around the World with Auntie Mame—It's Sheer Camp*. The ball invoked *Mame*, a musical version of a book by Patrick Dennis that opened on Broadway in 1966 with Angela Lansbury in the title role. Avet was friends with Dennis. All costumes and headpieces for the ball were designed by ball captain JoJo Landry, while William Woolley and Aunt Millie (Millard Wilson) designed the sets. Otto Stierle, another founding member of the krewe, was crowned Queen Auntie Mame.

Chester G. (Chet) Bush

For almost fifteen years, Chester G. Bush (1921–1996), another native of New Orleans, worked closely with Mike Moreau in his costume business. According to Moreau, "Chet was a wonderful friend and a great artist. He had never done sequin appliqué work before he started with me, but he succeeded in making his work look like paintings. He was the best at what he did." Bush was a self-taught artist as well as a hair stylist who co-owned a hair salon and worked for a long time on Canal Street in window display. He was a member of the Krewes of Ganymede (serving as king) and Amon-Ra.

Stewart K. Gahn Jr.

A member of the Krewe of Yuga, Stewart K. Gahn Jr. (1928–2009) was among those arrested in the 1962 police raid. He attended the New Orleans Academy of Arts and Tulane University and designed costumes for the Krewe of Bacchus for many years. He also worked as art director for D. H. Holmes department store on Canal Street and was a staunch supporter of the revitalization of the French Quarter as an active member of the Vieux Carré Property Owners Association. An early gay presence in the city, Gahn lived openly with his partner, Robert Abramson. Gahn's invitation for the 1962 Yuga ball, though simple on the surface, contained references to the hidden world of gay Carnival.

George Valentine Dureau

Born in New Orleans, George Valentine Dureau (1930–2014) was famous for his paintings and photographs but also contributed his talents to the gay community and was no stranger to the underground society that permeated the Faubourg Marigny and the French Quarter. Dureau's drawing for the Krewe of Petronius's tenth anniversary ball (1971) featured revelers with the number *10* and the letter *P*

Program for the Krewe of Petronius's *It's Sheer Camp— Around the World with Auntie Mame* ball, 1967. Design by Elmo Avet, featuring Angela Lansbury as Auntie Mame. Courtesy of Tulane University, Louisiana Research Collection, Howard-Tilton Memorial Library, New Orleans, Otto Stierle Collection, Manuscripts Collection 902.

Stewart K. Gahn Jr., costume for the king of the Krewe of Bacchus, 1999. Courtesy of the Louisiana State Museum, New Orleans, Accession No. 2011.026.13.01.

almost consumed in fleshly celebration. The figures incorporate the presence of this underground society, with a proud nude standing in front of castaways and hedonists attending yet another bacchanal, oblivious to the outside world. Dureau's 1970 painting, *Black Tie to Petronius*, offers a nod to the veneer of formality required to attend a gay ball and the rigid exclusivity. The following year, Dureau designed the cover of the original menu for Marti's Restaurant on Rampart Street, one of the centers of gay café society. He also designed the poster for the Mystic

Artist George Dureau in his studio, early 1970s. Photograph by Sarah Benham.

George Dureau, *Black Tie to Petronius*, 1977. This painting illustrates the formal rituals of gay Carnival. From *Selected Works, 1960–1977*, exhibition, New Orleans Contemporary Arts Center, 1977. Courtesy of the ONE National Gay and Lesbian Archives, University of Southern California Libraries, Los Angeles.

Krewe of Celestial Knights's public restaging of the 1980 *Les Plumages d'Hiver* ball at the New Orleans Theater for the Performing Arts, revealing a hidden world of bold exaggerations and camp gestures, rivalries, and gossips. Dureau's commemorative poster for Petronius's thirtieth anniversary in 1991 featured a striking drawing of white figures on a black background.

James Keyes

James Keyes (1932–2010) became involved with gay Carnival early on, attending many of New Orleans's first gay balls. After Keyes served as Queen Petronius XV in 1976, he and his close friend William Woolley moved on to the Mystic Krewe of Celestial Knights. Keyes helped design the krewe's signature crest—a crescent moon with a single star—and produced some of the most spectacular posters and doubloons for its first balls. The *Heavenly Bodies* poster was a finely executed line drawing showcasing the moon and a river of stars flowing through the Milky Way. *Carnival in Rio*, *Les Plumages d'Hiver*, *An Oriental Fantasy*, and *An Evening of Burlesque* were also fine examples of color and composition.

James Keyes, costume design for Grasshopper, *Thoth's All Mixed Up* ball, 2010. The ball's theme was cocktails. The Krewe of Thoth is an all-male parading krewe that produced its first parade and ball in 1947. With a current membership of more than seventeen hundred, Thoth is one of the five largest krewes in New Orleans. Courtesy of the Krewe of Thoth.

James Keyes, costume design for Coral Sea, *Thoth's Aquatic Adventures* ball, 2009. Courtesy of the Krewe of Thoth.

For many years, Keyes designed costumes and sets for the krewe. In addition, he was involved with straight krewes, designing the court costumes for the Krewe of Thoth's *The Wonderful World of Color* (2003), among others, as well as the all-female Krewe of Shangri-La, for which he created costumes. His Hercules costume for the Lords of Leather's *A Salute to the Krewes of New Orleans* used only leather, chains, and studs. And he designed many costumes for Mickey Gil's balls with the Krewe of Petronius as well as the Mystic Krewe of Satyricon.

James H. Schexnayder

James H. Schexnayder (1932–92) was another member of the Krewe of Yuga who was arrested in 1962, and he went on to help found the Krewe of Amon-Ra in 1965. He grew up in Morgan City, Louisiana, but spent most of his life in New Orleans, where he attended Tulane University, and graduated from the Parsons School of Design in New York City. Schexnayder designed costumes for the krewe, but his early invitations, mostly based on the art nouveau style, are particularly noteworthy. Depicting various Egyptian figures, he deftly wove Amon-Ra's identity into his artwork. In 1985's *Picnic Fantasy*, he was one of the garden snails, which had their large shells on wheels to move them about the stage. Schexnayder also served as King Amon-Ra III, as Queen Amon-Ra XVI, and as captain for the *Superstition* (*Friday the 13th*) ball (1978) and the *Thousand and One Nights* ball (1989), for which he designed the costumes and sets.

William Woolley, 2015 re-creation of sketch for Woolley's captain costume, Krewe of Celestial Knights' *Symphony in Blue* ball, 1983. Courtesy of the Louisiana State Museum, New Orleans, Accession No. 2016.003.5.

William Woolley, 2015 re-creation of sketch for Sagittarius costume, Krewe of Petronius's *Signs of the Zodiac* ball, 1973. Courtesy of the Louisiana State Museum, New Orleans, Accession No. 2016.003.1.

William Woolley

Born in Memphis, Tennessee, William M. Woolley (1933–) moved to New Orleans after a stint in the U.S. Navy. Woolley made an early mark in the Krewe of Petronius but went further and crafted amazing and original extravaganzas after he founded the Mystic Krewe of Celestial Knights in 1976. He worked creating window displays for many of the stores on Canal Street, the epicenter of the city, where he gained the experience that enabled him to design and execute exquisite costumes for numerous balls. His costume design and tailoring stand among the best of Carnival in New Orleans.

Lewis S. (Jamie) Greenleaf III

Originally from Connecticut, Lewis S. Greenleaf III (1935–2002) designed many balls for Petronius (most notably in 1969, when he served as captain) and Olympus, which he joined in 1970, although few of his creations survive. He and his partner, Harvey Hysell, met while in college in Texas and subsequently lived in New York before returning to New Orleans, Hysell's hometown. They designed all the float costumes for Rex's one hundredth anniversary (1971). Greenleaf also was responsible for the striking large-format poster for the first Krewe of Olympus ball, *Camelot.* He left New Orleans in the early 1970s and continued to design sets and costumes in Anchorage, Alaska, for the International Imperial Court.

Jamie Greenleaf, costume design for Marco Polo, Rex Parade, 1971. Courtesy of the Louisiana State Museum, New Orleans, Accession No. 2008.067.01.14.

Joseph Nicholas Talluto Jr.

Along with Roland Dobson, Joseph Nicholas Talluto Jr. (1939–86) was one of the founding members of the Mystic Krewe of Apollo in 1969. Talluto showed a penchant for art at an early age and painted portraits of friends and family for years until he settled on iconic religious imagery as an expression of his Italian Catholic heritage. The krewe's invitations and posters frequently called on Talluto's artistic talent. His signature style featured elongated figures with a painterly flare and colorful backgrounds, recalling the oeuvre of the School of Fontainebleau. His depiction of the god Apollo for the first ball is a masterpiece of subtle innuendo and classic gay male beauty.

Charles Kerbs (aka Matt)

Charles Kerbs (1940–2002) was a native of New Orleans who grew up in the world of Carnival, with its pageantry and artifice. Known primarily as an erotic artist in the leather community, he started out working for the Athletic Model Guild but soon was illustrating novels and stories under the pen name *Matt.* Doug McClemont, editor of *Honcho Magazine,* not only published Matt's work but also became his close friend. Kerbs had his first exhibition in the Galley House bar on Chartres Street and a later exhibition at the Leslie-Lohman Art Gallery in New York. His varied talents led him into acting and writing plays and a brief stint in the New York theater. He returned to New Orleans and began creating window displays for the department stores on Canal Street, which his longtime partner, Jeffrey

Charles Kerbs (aka Matt), poster for *Dior Merchant of Happiness: The Private Collection of Mrs. Robert J. Newman, 1947–57,* exhibition, Louisiana State Museum, 1988. Courtesy of the Louisiana State Museum, New Orleans, Carnival Reference Collection.

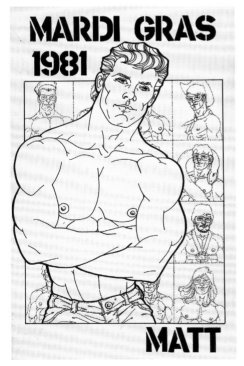

Charles Kerbs (aka Matt), Mardi Gras poster, 1981. Courtesy of the Louisiana State Museum, New Orleans, Accession No. 2009.089.68.

Johnson, described as "a perfect apprenticeship for . . . Mardi Gras krewe work," since both media "needed to be flashy, attention-getting, and witty." Gay krewes sought out Kerbs for invitations, costumes, and sets. For the Krewe of Petronius's *Space Ball* (1978), Kerbs created a comic strip poster depicting the queen's perilous journey to Chalmette. For the twentieth-anniversary ball, *Clowns*, Kerbs depicted lines of dancing Pierrots.

Michael Murphy, poster for the First Annual Gay Festival, 1979. Courtesy of the Louisiana State Museum, New Orleans, Accession No. 2015.007.13.

Mardi Gras 1979, *Impact Magazine*. Design by Michael Murphy. Courtesy of the Louisiana State Museum, New Orleans, Accession No. 2016.018.02b.

Michael Murphy

Michael Murphy (1941–86) was a fine artist who was quite popular in New Orleans during the 1970s and 1980s. He primarily created woodblock prints and showed his work at his studio at 511 Dumaine Street and at the Elizabeth Alexander Gallery and Stone and Press Gallery as well as at New York's Alan Brown Gallery. Murphy's work has been described as modernist and has been sold at the New Orleans Auction Galleries. A native New Orleanian, his single poster for the Mystic Krewe of Celestial Knights stands out as a beautiful example of a master artist. He also designed one of the first posters for New Orleans's 1979 Gay Festival, a forerunner of the Gay Pride celebration.

Carter Church

Carter Church (1943–) was born in Jackson, Mississippi, but his family moved to New Orleans before his first birthday to join his grandfather. A long-standing member of Rex, Church's grandfather fueled the boy's passion for Carnival, which guided him for the rest of his life. Local designer John C. Scheffler, who created costumes for the Krewes of Venus, Alla, Cleopatra, and Aphrodite while living in Manhattan, gave Church a start in the costume business, and after a brief stint at New York's Traphagen School of Design, he began designing costumes for the Krewe of Iris. He later designed costumes for the Krewe of Sparta and the Krewe de la Noblesse, both in Lake Charles, Louisiana, and the Krewe of Nereids in Bay St.

Carter Church, costume for maid, Knights of Sparta, 1995. Courtesy of the Louisiana State Museum, New Orleans, Accession No. 2008.066.06.

Carter Church, costume for king, Knights of Sparta, 2005. Courtesy of the Louisiana State Museum, New Orleans, Accession No. 2008.066.22.

Carter Church, costume sketch for Water, Krewe of Amon-Ra's *In the Beginning* ball, 1979. Courtesy of Carl Ricketts.

Louis, Mississippi, where he eventually moved. He and Mike Moreau cofounded the Krewe of Troy in 1983, and Church designed its costumes for almost a decade. He also helped found the Krewe of Amon-Ra and designed costumes for many of its balls, including *Circus* (1970), *Enchantment* (1975), and *Bluebird of Happiness* (1980). As Carl Ricketts recalled, "Carter was a master and his sketches prove it. They are exquisite renderings of what proved to be beautiful and completely wearable designs. I was queen and king and captain several times, and Carter designed them all. I couldn't have done it without his genius. He never designed the same costume twice. That's what makes him so unique. He also knew the legendary Erté when he lived in New Orleans."

Mike Moreau (Opal Masters)

Born in Opelousas, Louisiana, Mike Moreau (1943–) moved to New Orleans in 1963 and became a regular at Miss Dixie's Bar of Music on Bourbon Street. Soon after the Krewe of Amon-Ra was founded, Moreau was asked to join by his close friend and fellow designer, Carter Church. The two men worked together closely for years, and Moreau established himself as a sought-after costume designer not only for Amon-Ra but also for a number of traditional krewes, including Diana, Gemini, and the Slidellians. A devotee of all things Carnival, Moreau has maintained his dedication to the Krewe of Amon-Ra for more than half a century.

David Peltier

David Peltier (1950–) was born on Banks Street and grew up in Old Metairie. After serving in the U.S. Army, he ran into an old college friend, Jon Lee Poché, at Café Lafitte in Exile on Bourbon Street. They soon joined the Krewe of Armeinius, and Peltier, who had always been interested in art and excelled as a

Poster for Daughters of Eve's *Gotta Sing, Gotta Dance* ball, 1974. Design by David Peltier. Courtesy of the Louisiana State Museum, New Orleans, Accession No. 1995.010.188.

David Peltier, Mardi Gras poster, 1979. The poster depicts Edd Smith (*in hard hat*), the master of ceremonies for the Bourbon Street Awards in the 1980s; David Peltier (*middle, almost hidden*); and Queen Armeinius XVII, John Thompson (*large face below fairies*). Courtesy of the Louisiana State Museum, New Orleans, Jake and Kevin Thomas Collection, Accession No. 2015.058.15.

commercial artist, used his talents to produce some of the krewe's most memorable invitations, often basing them on illustrations from his extensive collection of children's books from the early 1900s. For *Revelries of Titania's Court* (1980), he created a fairy that incorporated a child's head and horse's hooves. Peltier's graphic for *The Boy Who Would Be Queen* (1985) came from a series of cartoon figures he had been doing at the time. He also provided one of the most memorable images in gay Carnival history for *The Great Disasters of the Western World* (1983). Peltier and now lives in Bywater with his partner of more than thirty years, Steve Biel.

Earl Woodard

Earl Woodard (1950–) worked as a graphic designer with David Peltier, but Woodard joined the Krewe of Olympus rather than joining his friend in Armeinius. He remained a member for less than a decade, but during that time he created excellent invitations that featured bold graphics. Woodard and his partner, Spencer Lindsay, went on to work with other krewes, most notably designing the poster and costumes for the Krewe of Amon-Ra's *Picnic Fantasy* (1985). According to Jerry Gilley, "Earl was a very serious artist and came through with everything on time and with such creative flair. It was a pleasure to work with him. He was a quiet guy, and very few people knew the breadth and depth of his work in the gay community. He did the famous Carnival parade mural at the Parade Disco upstairs at the Bourbon Pub that everyone remembers. He also did the marvelous Calla Lily mural which ran all the way up the stairs at the old Menefee's bar. Just wonderful. He designed the logos for both the Bourbon Pub and Menefee's, among so many other things. . . . I still recall that Earl and Spencer were always called up together to greet the reigning king and queen at the close of all the balls."

J. Bruce Orgeron Jr., costume design for Ghost Rider, Lords of Leather's *Superheroes* ball, 2008. Courtesy of the Louisiana State Museum, New Orleans, Accession No. 2009.089.63.

Joseph Bruce Orgeron Jr.

Another native New Orleanian, Bruce Orgeron (1952–) was originally a member of Armeinius and not only served as captain seven times but designed many of their balls. He also designed balls for the Lords of Leather, which awarded him a lifetime membership, and continued to do so even after founding the Krewe of Narcissus with Nick Weber in 2013. He also designed for the Knights of King Arthur and the Grand Marshals of Southern Decadence.

Recent developments beyond the showgirl drag aesthetic in gay Carnival costume design can be traced back to Orgeron's tenure in the Krewe of Armeinius. Though the straight krewes had long featured elaborate royal costumes with rhinestones, sequins, and jewels, the gay krewes always exaggerated these drag sensibilities. Orgeron's contribution was to add three-dimensional attachments that protruded out from the body for a literal and physical interpretation of the ball theme, drawing attention to the individual costume. Examples typical of this design trend were Orgeron's 1998 Black-Eyed Susan costume for the Krewe of Armeinius and his Ghost Rider costume, with its spaceship attachment that seemed to explode outward, for the 2008 Lords of Leather ball. Some observers described these designs as wearable floats.

Glenn Sanford

Born in Hattiesburg, Mississippi, Glenn Sanford (1952–) studied fine art at the University of Southern Mississippi and Jackson State University. Sanford and his partner, Bill Jones, routinely traveled from their Jackson home to visit friends in New Orleans and to make costumes and sets, although they never became krewe members. Sanford used his signature pointillist style to create one of the most unusual artworks for a gay ball. At a cocktail party thrown by Carl Ricketts of the Krewe of Amon-Ra, Richard Powell, slated to be Queen Amon-Ra XXI as Liza Doolittle, asked Sanford to design an art piece for the 1986 *Best of Broadway* ball. Inspired by *Playbill* magazines, Sanford incorporated a rose, pearls, top hats, and a *Playbill* into his composition. The following year, he produced another work solely for the queen's return, incorporating visual references to the previous year's poster. Sanford's artwork has been exhibited widely and in 2000 was the subject of a retrospective at the Meridian Museum of Art.

Glenn Sanford, *Old Mirrors, Reflections, and Reality*, 1987. This print references the other side of gay Carnival, the devastation of the AIDS epidemic, as seen by the slow deterioration reflected in the mirror. Courtesy of Glenn Sanford.

Fredrick Guess

Cocaptain Fredrick Guess (1953–) designed costumes for the Krewe of Armeinius's 2015 *Architecture Ball*. Born in Florida, he moved to New Orleans in 1997 and opened a fine art studio in the French Quarter. A longtime member of Armeinius, he also was crowned Queen Petronius XLVIII in 2009. Guess believes that "life is a wonderful thing. The colors, movements, sounds and shapes that surround us all still inspire me. It doesn't matter whether I am looking at French Quarter architecture or a pelican flying over the bayou or a pile of hot, boiled crawfish—they all move me." Both Armeinius and Petronius commissioned Guess to produce paintings to commemorate their 2016 royalty.

Fredrick Guess, costume design for Daphne, Krewe of Armeinius's *Beauty and the Beast* ball, 2016. Courtesy of Fredrick Guess.

Daniel de Beau-Maltbie

Daniel de Beau-Maltbie (1955–) was born in Merced, California, and raised on a farm. After graduating from high school, he entered the seminary to become a priest, which brought him to New Orleans. His plans changed, and he found a job working in window display at D. H. Holmes department store. He met several members of Amon-Ra, including Robert Breaux, Queen Amon-Ra XXVI, and eventually joined the krewe. De Beau-Maltbie's passion for Victorian architecture influenced his creation of one of the masterworks of gay Carnival, the poster and invitation for Amon-Ra's *Cocktails for Two* (1982), in which naughty flourishes are cleverly

Dan de Beau-Maltbie, drawing of Victorian house, 1981. Courtesy of Daniel de Beau-Maltbie.

hidden within the architectural details. It echoes the work of Aubrey Beardsley, who created the artwork for Oscar Wilde's *Salomé* in a similar vein. For the *Signs of the Zodiac* (1984), de Beau-Maltbie created a masterful tribute to the celestial signs. Now living in Florida with his husband, de Beau-Maltbie created Amon-Ra's 2017 invitation as well.

Edward Cox, poster for the Krewe of Olympus's Folies-Bergère fund-raiser, 1986. Courtesy of the Louisiana State Museum, New Orleans, Accession No. 1995.010.098.

Edward Cox, logo design for Second Skin Leather, 1984. Courtesy of Ed Cox.

Edward R. Cox

Edward R. Cox (1956–) is a native of New Orleans who has appeared in numerous movies, commercials, and stage productions. In addition, his talents extend into production design, sets, costumes, photography, and graphic design. He has worked for several gay krewes, including Vesta and Olympus, and maintains a high profile in the New Orleans gay community. According to *StageClick*, he "has built an impressive career over the past four decades in the fields of theatre, Carnival design, animation and graphic art. His lively designs and brilliant artistic interpretations have graced the stages of thousands of theatrical stages across the country as well as hundreds of Carnival krewes' parades and ball-masques, ballets, operas and many more presentations throughout Louisiana and the Gulf Coast, and decorating the walls of collectors around the world."

Daniel Ourso

Born into a Carnival family in New Orleans, Daniel Ourso (1959–) learned to design costumes from his mother, and at age fifteen, he designed costumes for a straight women's krewe. Ourso joined the Krewe of Polyphemus and designed many of their costumes, beginning with *The Envelope Please* (1988). He has also designed for

Armeinius, the Lords of Leather, and Apollo–Baton Rouge as well as for a handful of straight krewes, including Diana, Mid-City, Carrollton, and Centurions, and for the Ballet Hysell. A member of the group of gay men who worked in window display for the New Orleans's major department stores, Ourso creates designs that reveal an immense knowledge of opera, theater, and ancient history.

Kellie Hyatt Gironda and Mary McCleland Hyatt

One of the few straight women artists who design for Carnival, Kellie Hyatt Gironda (1959–) has over the past three decades produced some of the most interesting and dramatic costumes for both gay and straight krewes, though she has worked primarily with the Krewe of Armeinius, creating the exquisite regalia for the king and queen at the *Winter Follies* ball (1989). Her work for the Krewe of Olympus was so highly respected that it garnered her an honorary membership in the krewe. At a young age, Gironda began creating Mardi Gras costumes with her designer mother, Mary Hyatt (1933–2013), a costumer for numerous Mardi Gras organizations in and around New Orleans and along the Gulf Coast. Mary began her career by working for Larry Villemure, the owner of Metairie Fabrics, assisting Mardi Gras designers and krewe captains with their costumes for Carnival balls and parades. After she developed a rapport with numerous Carnival organizations, she formed Designs Unlimited, specializing in creating costumes that featured lights and movement. Mary and Kellie worked for the Krewes of Pegasus and Saturn as well as for Adonis, a krewe in Morgan City. Kellie went on to graduate from the prestigious New Orleans Center for Creative Arts and the John McCrady Fine Arts School in the French Quarter. In 1982, *New Orleans Magazine* recognized both Kellie and Mary Hyatt as "People to Watch." Seeking an education in the fashion field, Kellie moved to Dallas to attend Wade College, where she earned an associate's degree in design and won the school's 1984 Designer of the Year award. Gironda eventually returned to New Orleans and resumed her partnership with her mother . The Louisiana Jazz and Heritage Festival commissioned the two women to represent the Louisiana Exhibit in 1997, and Gironda's artwork became part of the Louisiana State Museum's archives in 2000.

Joel M. Haas

Joel M. Haas (pronounced *Hayes*; 1961–) grew up on the West Bank in a Carnival family. His father served as king of the Krewe of Poseidon and chose Joel as one of his pages. The boy thus had the opportunity to see the inner workings of Carnival and learned how sketches and designs were turned into costumes: recalled Haas, "As children, my brother and I had the good fortune of being able to go with my father, to meet with Mr. [Jules] Greenburg at his shop. He would allow us to go to the second floor of his

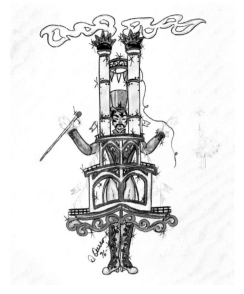

Daniel Ourso, costume design for Steamboat, ball unknown, 1996. Courtesy of the Louisiana State Museum, New Orleans, Accession No. 2009.089.37.

Kellie Hyatt Gironda, sketch for captain Cindy Quartana Dana of the Krewe of Octavia, a straight West Bank krewe, 1984. Courtesy of the Louisiana State Museum, New Orleans, Jake and Kevin Thomas Collection, Accession No. 2015.058.14.01.

Joel Haas, costume sketch for Queen Mary, Krewe of Armeinius's *There's Something about Mary* ball, 2009. Courtesy of the Louisiana State Museum, New Orleans, Accession No. 2015.045.1.33.

store, where the seamstresses were working on king and queen costumes and float rider costumes. I had the opportunity to become friends with most of the seamstresses, and over the years they allowed me to look through the bolts of fabric they were working with. I would pay close attention to the discussions of the design and construction of the costumes, and that was part of the motivation that pushed me in that direction." Haas tried his hand at design when he became a member of the Krewe of Armeinius, eventually winning first place and Best in Show at the Bourbon Street Awards several years in a row.

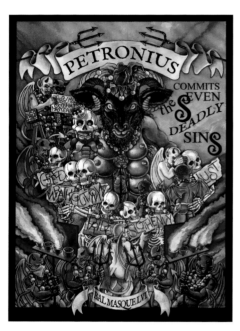

Michael Meads, poster for the Krewe of Petronius's *Seven Deadly Sins* ball, 2017. Courtesy of Michael Meads.

Michael Meads, *The Intercession*, 2010. Courtesy of Michael Meads.

Michael Wayne Meads

After earning a master of fine arts degree from the State University of New York at Albany, Michael Wayne Meads (1966–) briefly returned to his hometown, Anniston, Alabama. In 1998, he and his partner moved to New Orleans, where he finetuned his over-the-top style of combining historical and contemporary figures. According to Bradley Sumrall of the Ogden Museum of Southern Art, Meads creates "a magical world where Valkyries and Roman gods mingle with frat boys and firemen. Plague doctors and Pulcinella roam the streets of the Vieux Carré, and winged putti struggle to support the crumbling edifices of historic architecture. With a masterful hand, Meads creates a graphite opera where each work is a complex visual libretto." Meads sees New Orleans as possessing "a certain degree of insanity that goes beyond any desire for conformity, and a wonderful disregard for fashion and trends. I think it ties into the larger culture—what everyone that has lived and died here had to go through to be here. Those shared experiences create a somewhat insulating effect from outside influences." His 2017 poster for the Krewe of Petronius illustrates the *Seven Deadly Sins*, a theme dear to the denizens of New Orleans.

John S. Zeringue III

John S. Zeringue III (1973–) was born in New Orleans but raised in Plaquemines Parish. He became a fine artist whose paintings were exhibited in various New Orleans galleries and at the city's Contemporary Arts Center. He and Mike Moreau worked together for the Krewe of Troy in Slidell before Zeringue began producing sketches and wirework for the Krewe of Amon-Ra. He later joined the krewe, serving as ball lieutenant, king, and captain. His costume took first place at the 2015 Bourbon Street Awards. He has also worked for other krewes, among them Alla, the Knights of King Arthur, Apollo–Baton Rouge, and Queenateenas. His designs are known for their complexity and visual delight, emphasizing the use of feathers for larger-than-life headdresses, collars, and mantels. Hearkening back to the Ziegfeld Follies and Broadway, Zeringue's masterful touch has become synonymous with the New Renaissance of gay Carnival. He served as captain for the Krewe of Petronius's 2017 ball, the *Seven Deadly Sins.*

John S. Zeringue III, original artwork for poster and program for *A Year through the Eye of Amon-Ra* ball, 2014. Courtesy of John S. Zeringue III.

Clint Delapasse

Born near Baton Rouge, Clint Delapasse (1979–) left his mark on gay Carnival even though he only lived in New Orleans between 2000 and 2005. He worked on costumes for the Krewes of Petronius, Satyricon, and Armeinius, and Mickey Gil commissioned him to produce posters for the Mystic Krewe of Satyricon's *Some Like It Hot* (2003) and *Satyricon in Bloom* (2004) balls. Delapasse's posters are explosions of color and graphics, recalling the psychedelic 1960s. He also worked on the costumes for Queens Becky Allen and Bianca Del Rio. His program for Armeinius's *Looney Tunes* ball (2004) featured a paper doll cut out in the image of Blanche Debris.

Clint Delapasse, advertisement for Blanche Debris's Can-Can Cabaret, 2004. Courtesy of the Louisiana State Museum, New Orleans, Jake and Kevin Thomas Collection, Accession No. 2015.046.01.

Other Artists

Claire Evangelista, Joseph Marrione, Norman McDole Millis, Dal Kimberling, Ricky Lenart, Don Stratton, Ron Aschenbach, Brandon Schau, James Lenormand, Chad Brickley, John Burton Harter, San nicholas, James G. Jay, Susan Stutts, and Harry Sherman (Rhie) are among the other artists who have made notable artistic contributions to gay Carnival. Evangelista designed numerous invitations for the Krewe of Petronius, most notably for 1967's *It's Sheer Camp* ball. Her use of color and camp language recalls the Antonio Sotomayor's exaggerated illustrations of the *Satyricon.* An accomplished artist who exhibited her

Joseph Marrione, costume for the reigning king as Jesus Christ, Krewe of Petronius's *Decadence and Decay* ball, 2005. Courtesy of the Louisiana State Museum, New Orleans, Accession No. 2013.014.4.

Don Stratton, costume design for Cleopatra, Krewe of Pygmalion, 2011. Courtesy of the Louisiana State Museum, New Orleans, Jake and Kevin Thomas Collection, Accession No. 2015.058.13.04.

Norman McDole Millis, Mardi Gras poster, 1981. Courtesy of the Louisiana State Museum, New Orleans, Accession No. 2016.004.05.

J. Burton Harter, Carnival poster, 1980s. Courtesy of the Louisiana State Museum, New Orleans, Accession No. I.1993.0027a.

work locally and across the South, Evangelista later taught fine art at the University of Southern Alabama, where her work became primarily sculptural.

Raised in Chalmette, Joseph Marrione joined the Krewe of Polyphemus during the early 1980s; when it folded, he joined the Krewe of Armeinius. As captain for the *Ink Ball* (2002), he designed costumes inspired by the art of tattooing. He then became a member of Petronius and served as captain until 2005, when he settled in Atlanta in the wake of Hurricane Katrina.

Norman McDole Millis designed invitations for the Krewes of Petronius and Polyphemus in the early to mid-1980s. He also designed costumes for Polyphemus and was known for his mastery of wirework.

Both Dal Kimberling and his lover, Jim York, were members of the Krewe of Olympus. Kimberling had studied at Parsons School of Design in New York City.

Ricky Lenart served as Queen Armeinius in 2001 and King Armeinius in 2009 and designed several program covers for the krewe. He is known locally as an accomplished artist and collects teddy bears.

Don Stratton, captain of the Krewe of Armeinius, had a huge influence on the group, designing many of their costumes. He has also designed costumes for the straight Krewe of Pygmalion and for the Daughters of Eve.

Ron Aschenbach was active in the Lords of Leather and not only designed costumes for the *Games People Play* (1992) but also created a commemorative poster for the krewe. He also worked with the Krewe of Armeinius.

Brandon Schau redesigned the Krewe of Petronius's crest and designed several of costumes for its 2016 ball, including the captain's costume, which evoked Elton John as the Queen of England.

James Lenormand designed for the Krewe of Amon-Ra and for traditional krewes.

William McCarthy and Chad Brickley have twice served as cocaptains of the Krewe of Petronius. Brickley, who is also a member of the Krewe of Armeinius, has designed and fabricated costumes for the Mystic Krewe of Satyricon as well.

A former curator at the Louisiana State Museum, Burt Harter was an accomplished fine artist whose primary medium was painting, and he produced various posters for Mardi Gras. His unapologetic depictions of gay men were at once sensual and masterful. Reputed to have been a member of the Steamboat Club, Harter may also have briefly joined the Krewe of Petronius.

San nicholas, who deliberately did not capitalize his last name to give it distinction, designed for the straight Krewe of Endymion and for the Mystic Krewe of Apollo.

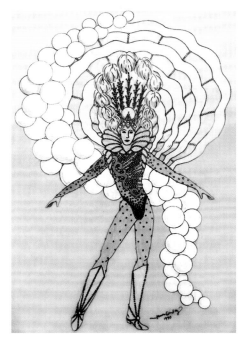

James G. Jay designed costumes for the Krewe of Petronius, especially for the thirtieth anniversary ball, *Petronius Salutes Royalty*, in 1991. His costume for captain Mickey Gil was a masterpiece with a sequined bodysuit and large pearls cascading from high atop a shell shoulder-piece all the way down to the floor in a twisting swoop behind him. The head-piece spotlighted a coral couronne with a dazzling centered pearl.

Susan Stutts trained as a graphic designer at the University of Southern Mississippi in Hattiesburg, Mississippi, and was a successful fashion illustrator and art director for Waldoff's and McQuillan and Breckenridge Advertising as well as a cartographic technician at Lockheed/NASA in Bay St. Louis, Mississippi. She worked with King Celeste IX Frank Marquez at Wiener Associates in New Orleans, and he commissioned her to design the two posters for the Mystic Krewe of Celestial Knights.

In 1992, Harry Sherman designed a bold black and white commemorative poster for the Lords of Leather. He also served as Southern Decadence Grand Marshal in the same year. He was mostly known by his drag name, Rhie.

Little is known beyond the names of other artists who contributed to gay Carnival, including R. Mullins, Glenn Vigé, Lumpkin, Gunter, Smith, Calvert, Allen, W. T. Bell, K. Barranco, Robert G. Lee, and Ronald DeLise. However, the works they created form part of the rich history of New Orleans's celebrations.

James G. Jay, costume design for captain Mickey Gil as "Pearls," *Petronius Salutes Royalty* ball, 1991. Courtesy of the Mickey Gil papers, Louisiana Research Collection, Tulane University.

IT'S SHEER CAMP!

The Legacy of
Elmo Delacroix Avet

The last time I saw Elmo he was dressed as a
mermaid and had a splendidly muscled young man
carrying him about, which was part of the costume,
don't you know. He could barely walk even without
a fish tail at that point.

—Tommy Griffin, New Orleans Writer

The Yuga Regina

It was Saturday, February 24, 1962. The returning queen of the fourth annual Krewe
of Yuga ball appeared, a ghostlike figure in shades of gray and dusty blue, at the
appointed hour. Her Royal Majesty, Yuga Regina IV, waved her scepter, and her attendants removed her cloak to reveal a sparkling golden goddess. "Let the festivities
begin," she cried. And all the costumed characters, her loyal servants, bowed low and
shouted, "Long live the Yuga Regina!" Captain John Henry Bogie came forward and
escorted her around the perimeter of the Rambler Room, a dance studio in Metairie.
As the clock struck ten, the maids and debutantes came forward. The returning king
came forth, music played, and guests drank and danced under the soft lights. In the
wings, Elmo Avet awaited the stroke of midnight, when he would appear as the newly
crowned Queen of Yuga. He had seen Hollywood and Broadway, but nothing had
prepared him for this night. It was to be an apotheosis, his ascension to something
extraordinary. And he wondered how history would remember this night.

Avet sat as still as a statue while his attendants lined up for their grand entrance.
As hands of the clock moved closer and closer to the 12, the anticipation was inter-
rupted by a shout and a scream, and suddenly all was mayhem. Avet fled through
a side door, shedding his glittering silver and bronze costume and heading to the
nearby woods, which would offer him shelter from what he instinctively realized
was a police raid. As searchlights flashed, a policeman grabbed him. But when Avet
stood up, he saw the face of a family friend. Fate had smiled on him. The friend led
Avet to a trail, and he escaped the dragnet. Later that morning, he returned to the

Elmo Delacroix Avet as the Marquis de Vaudreuil,
in front of his Flea Market Antique Shoppe on
Royal Street on Fat Tuesday, 1954. JoJo Landry lies
in the gutter. Courtesy of The Historic New Orleans
Collection, Williams Research Center, New Orleans,
Accession No.1982.147.2. Gift of Clay Watson.

French Quarter, where others who had escaped alerted the community, though Avet remained tight-lipped. The first gay krewe was no more.

The arrests initially brought gay Carnival to a halt. Many denizens of this discrete demimonde never again attended a gay ball. The Krewe of Petronius, which had held its first ball at the same location just a week earlier, struggled along until 1966. However, the krewe obtained an official state charter that charged Petronius with celebrating Carnival for ninety-nine years, paving the way for gay krewes to become full participants in the great celebration that is Carnival in New Orleans. Elmo Avet was central to this process.

The Scarlet Empress movie poster, 1934.

From Plaquemine to Hollywood

Elmo Delacroix Avet Gianelloni was born in the small town of Plaquemine in 1896 to Portuguese immigrant parents. After serving in the U.S. Navy during World War I, Avet settled in Los Angeles, where he began working in Hollywood. He not only learned the art of movie production but also discovered an overtly gay culture that permeated the studios. He moved within this realm with ease and was involved in such noteworthy films as *Glorifying the American Girl* (1929), *Shanghai Express* (1932) and *Scarlet Empress* (1934), the latter two starring Marlene Dietrich. Avet eventually landed at MGM Studios, working under art director, Cedric Gibbons, who took over from Erté when he got tired of working with Louis B. Mayer. Avet regularly joined many others who worked in the studio's costume and art departments at gay cocktail parties at the home of George Cukor, rubbing shoulders with such members of the gay Hollywood elite as Vincente Minnelli, Orry-Kelly, and Adrian. Avet left Hollywood during World War II: his final picture was *The Wizard of Oz* (1939), for which he helped create the sets for the Yellow Brick Road and the Emerald City.

Patrick Dennis, *Little Me: The Intimate Memoirs of that Great Star of Stage, Screen, and Television, Belle Poitrine,* 1961.

Manhattan

During the 1940s, Avet then became a dealer in antiques and objets d'art, which he sold at a series of Flea Market Antique Shoppes in Manhattan. In New York, Avet became close friends with Patrick Dennis (creator of *Little Me* and *Auntie Mame*) and his troupe of actors, providing them with costume designs for parties or plays. In 1949, Avet created the decor, props, and costumes for a truck float in the annual Mummers Parade in Philadelphia, which almost ended in disaster.

New Orleans Beckons

By the early 1950s, Avet had settled permanently in New Orleans, having bought a house on Bourbon Street, where he lived an openly gay lifestyle with his paramour, Billy Livingstone, in the safe haven of the Vieux Carré. Avet's eclectic and eccentric home was featured in Henry Lionel Williams and Ottalie K. Williams's *America's Small Houses: The Personal Homes of Designers and Collectors* (1964), an impressive large-format book that showcased "some of the country's most attractive and original homes owned by people of taste and distinction." After taking readers through the living room and bedroom, with their huge and ornate ceiling medallions and intricate chandeliers, the authors warned that "the third room of this suite . . .

Postcard from Elmo D. Avet Antiques, 819 Bourbon Street, early 1950s. Courtesy of Henri Schindler.

Reverse says: *Visit The Most Fabulous Antique Shop In New Orleans. See Our Furniture, Decorations and Garden Accessories in Actual Twenty-Two Room Settings. When in New York Stop at Elmo's Flea Market, 1003 Second Avenue at 53rd St.*

The den of Elmo Avet's Bourbon Street home as depicted in *America's Small Houses: The Personal Homes of Designers and Collectors* by Henry Williams and Ottalie Williams, 1964.

presents the ultimate in bohemian unconventionality": a period painting of Mary, Queen of Scots, and her son; a mahogany sleigh bed used as a daybed; a life-sized bull's head with a glass top for a side table that had once been the sign for a French butcher's shop; a large nineteenth-century Dutch desk; a sofa made of buffalo horns upholstered in antelope skin that had once belonged to Kurt Weill; a zebra-skin rug; tribal weapons; porcelain bowls; the metal breastplate from a suit of armor used as a wall sconce; and a death mask of Napoleon Bonaparte.

Avet later established his last Flea Market Antique Shoppe at 540 Royal Street, where he sold odd curios and unique items such as vintage Christmas cards from Germany (with pop-up angels and Santa Clauses) and Mae West's golden swan bed from the Broadway comedy *Catherine Was Great*. In addition, patrons could find an array of bronze statues, Chinese urns, and a set of Marie Antoinette's china specially

Poster for Mae West's stage show, *Catherine Was Great*, 1944.

Elmo Avet in his Royal Street antique shop, 1950s. Courtesy of Tulane University, Louisiana Research Collection, Howard-Tilton Memorial Library, New Orleans.

Jewel Box Revue promotional flyer, 1950s. Courtesy of Howard Philips Smith.

ordered by the empress from the Sèvres porcelain factory. Avet kept other items hidden in storage vaults throughout the city. A crusty businessman with a wicked sense of humor and a volatile temper, he frequently threw people out of his shop.

Alvin Payne and Ray Cronk, both former Krewe of Petronius royalty, bought many pieces from him for their house on Dumaine Street, including a stained glass window panel. According to Payne, "He had exquisite taste, and nothing was ever too precious to sell. Once we were invited to his house on Bourbon Street for drinks, and everything, including the furniture and glassware, had a price tag." Remembered Cronk, "We briefly lived next door to Elmo on Bourbon Street in a small apartment across his courtyard. At night the bullfrogs were so loud, it was deafening—just deafening. We didn't sleep for a month, and then we had to move. I always wondered how Elmo could sleep through it all, not to mention all those Hollywood types running in and out."

"Those Hollywood Types"

While in Los Angeles working on films, Avet had made the acquaintance of Rae Bourbon, who had appeared in the early films of Mae West, mostly in drag. His Jewel Box Revue stopped in New Orleans periodically to play at Dixie's Bar of Music. Another close friend was the legendary Barbette, who became a huge star in Paris during the 1920s as a female impersonator aerialist. Born Vander Clyde in Texas, Barbette appeared at the Folies-Bergère, Casino de Paris, and the Moulin Rouge and was not only photographed by Man Ray but had starring roles in many of his avant-garde films. After an accident on the high wire forced Barbette into semiretirement, he continued as a consultant on numerous Hollywood films. He also frequently stayed with Avet when traveling across the country.

Avet also counted Kaye Ballard and Mae West among his friends and was especially close to Helen Hayes, who enjoyed the local cuisine, especially spicy boiled shrimp piled up on newspapers. She and her pet poodle, Chiquita, felt right at home at 819 Bourbon Street, and Avet took her sightseeing and out to dinner every night.

True Royalty

In his later years, Avet became completely focused on Carnival. At the 1969 *Glorification of the American Girl* ball, his Tribute to the Flower Children costume featured hundreds of live flowers, and he refused to let his frequent bouts of emphysema prevent him from performing. In attendance was his close friend and confidant, Henri Schindler. He remained a key player in the Krewe of Petronius, occasionally foul-mouthed and spiteful but revered by other krewe members, who referred to him as "that old queen." Avet was slated to become the queen of Petronius at its 1970 *Space Oddity* ball, but once again, fate intervened to prevent him from wearing the crown: he died in December 1969. Schindler was in New York when Avet died and returned to find Livingstone distraught over the loss of his longtime companion, whom he called "Madame": "I just don't know what I'm going to do. Madame had so wanted to be queen of Petronius, and to think she didn't get to wear her rightful crown. And to top it all, boxes and boxes of rhinestones just keep arriving. What am I going to do with all those rhinestones, for God's sake?"

Though Avet never did wear the crown, there is no question that he belongs in the pantheon of gay Carnival royalty. He formed the first gay krewe and was instrumental in the development of the Krewe of Petronius, helping to create the template that all the other gay krewes followed. He exemplified the ultimate queen, the epitome of gay culture at the time, both masculine and feminine, and served as a role model for an emerging gay sensibility—quick-witted, bitchy, and creative, drawing on a vast knowledge of literature and film, antiques, history and culture, and especially aesthetics. He stands as a New Orleans cultural phenomenon.

Barbette (Vander Clyde), photographed by Man Ray, 1926. Jean Cocteau likened Clyde's transformation into Barbette both to Dr. Jekyll and Mr. Hyde and to the human metamorphosis into flora prevalent in Greek and Roman mythology. Courtesy of the J. Paul Getty Museum, Los Angeles, ©Man Ray Trust ARS-ADAGP.

Elmo Avet as Mary, Queen of Scots, and Billy Livingstone as his page, in the courtyard of Miss Dixie's Bar, early 1950s. Photograph by Jack Robinson. Courtesy of the Jack Robinson Archive, Memphis.

Elmo Avet as the Marquis de Vaudreuil, Shrove Tuesday, 1954. Courtesy of The Historic New Orleans Collection, Williams Research Center, New Orleans, Accession No. 1982.147.1. Gift of Clay Watson.

Elmo Avet helped his friend Patrick Dennis with his book *Little Me* (1961) and was rewarded with an appearance in a photo collage as Mary, Queen of Scots (Avet appears far right). Collage by Chris Alexander.

RUE DE L'AMOUR

Gay Café Society and the Once Brilliant Lights of Rampart Street

New Orleans is a strange place.

—Truman Capote, *Local Color*

The early 1980s constituted the Golden Age of Gay Carnival in New Orleans. The krewes were at their best, and restaurants and bars brimmed with colorful characters, love, and drama. One of the high points of the era occurred on November 27, 1982, when Erté's ninetieth birthday party took place at the Restaurant Jonathan in the heart of what had become the French Quarter's gay café society. By this time, Gay Carnival not only filled the stages during the Mardi Gras season but spilled over into the rest of the year, creating a vibrant social scene that included fund-raising events, meetings, and celebrations. Krewe members and friends attended cocktail parties, honored community milestones, and exchanged gossip and news. Erté was a key figure in the gay community, with his designs providing inspiration for numerous balls. The following re-creation of his birthday celebration offers a peek into this world, revealing the dynamic scope of this unique society.

The Erté Salon at Restaurant Jonathan was abuzz with anticipation regarding the arrival of Monsieur Erté. Chef Tom Cowman and sous chef John Estrada were preparing a sumptuous banquet, while the din in the second-floor dining room reverberated through the etched glass panel that hung at the far end. This frosted marvel depicted a woman gazing into the distance with flowers cascading down from her head into the Night and Day Lounge, where Erté had stopped to have a quick Absinthe Sazerac with the owners Jack Cosner and Jay Schwab. The legendary artist was radiant in a pink shirt, a pink blazer, pink trousers, and a pink bow tie.

"His eyes sparkled like Cartier's. After all, it was his ninetieth birthday celebration at the most beautiful art deco palace in the heart of New Orleans," recalled Gilbertine Liveaudais, a café society regular during the early 1980s. Erté was indeed a

Night and Day cocktail lounge, Restaurant Jonathan, with a view of Dennis Abbé's two-story frosted glass panel, *Paradise*. Photograph by Jaime Ardiles-Arce. Courtesy of Tulane University, Louisiana Research Collection, Howard-Tilton Memorial Library, New Orleans.

popular figure in New Orleans and especially in the Vieux Carré, where he appeared from time to time to oversee the sale of his bronze figurines and colorful prints at the prestigious Dyansen Gallery. And here he was on Rampart Street at Restaurant Jonathan, on the fringes not only of conventional society but also of the original city—literally the ramparts. When the city was founded in 1718, it was known as the Rue de l'Amour.

Moving upstairs and taking his honored place at the head of the table, Erté surveyed his kingdom, with its high-deco splendor dominated by silver-gray and blue. The owners had bought a suite of original Erté prints and had the best displayed in the bespoke dining room. Everyone's favorite was the rapturous and fecund siren of Spring from the series *The Seasons*, an assessment with which Erté heartily agreed, raising his glass of Veuve Clicquot to toast the owners for creating such a space and himself for having lasted so long. At the end of the dining room, the frosted glass panel depicted Paradise, with its exotic birds and flowers and with two horizontal figures floating above, strangely joined at the hip and gazing up toward the stars while below them flowers floated all around the siren. Dennis Abbé, whom Erté once called "my spirit and my long-lost brother," had created the breathtaking glass masterpiece. Even more impressive was the colorful entryway mural, which depicted mermaids and sea horses riding gigantic waves and a stark white egret surveying the scene from a vantage point high above the Gulf of Mexico.

Gilbertine Liveaudais had somehow leveraged herself an invitation to the birthday bash, just as she managed to attend all the galas, balls, and soirées. She had already proclaimed herself heiress to the title *Scarlet Empress*, once held by another rather well-known figure in gay café society, Elmo Avet. Gilbertine was a beautiful drag queen who moved effortlessly throughout gay society at a time when Rampart Street was a glittering yellow brick road and Bourbon Street's bars and discothèques were packed every night of the week. A self-described and unapologetic "quadroon" with coffee-colored skin, Gilbertine had begun life in the Magnolia Housing Development.

"It's a clever girl who can carve out a career from just two letters!" Gilbertine often would say. And it was true. To escape scandal with his prestigious Russian family, Romain de Tirtoff dropped everything but his initials and elided them together to form the name *Erté* and became a famous gay Parisian fashion designer who almost single-handedly helped turn the art deco movement into an international sensation. "That's *R* and *T* in French," explained Gilbertine. "Just two letters! Imagine that!" After Paris, Erté's reputation landed him a brief sojourn in Hollywood at MGM Studios to art direct films. Louis B. Mayer spoiled and cajoled Erté, but they clashed almost immediately, and their collaboration lasted for only a few films.

Downstairs in the Night and Day Lounge, the oxblood-lacquered piano tinkled over the muffled conversations of elegantly bedecked couples on their way to the Municipal Auditorium across the street. Earl Woodard and Spencer Lindsay sat sipping champagne cocktails before heading off to catch one of the last gay balls of the 1982 Carnival season. The Mystic Krewe of Apollo's annual tableau ball was held on the same evening as the Knights of Momus, and this year's theme was a closely guarded secret. Woodard and Lindsay were members of the Krewe of Olympus and thus assured of the best seats up front. The two immaculately groomed men in black wool tuxedos provided the perfect accent to the chrome and frosted glass that shone throughout the bar and restaurant proper.

"Remember that stormy New Year's Eve last year?" asked Woodard, a king of Olympus. "Good thing we were old friends with the host. He let us borrow the limousine that was waiting for some drama queen to reappear from dining in the posh Leontyne Price Room on the third floor! They even have the diva's tiara from a performance of Tosca at the Met in a glass case."

William Woolley and his partner, André Boudreaux, formally dressed to the nines, were also waiting to cross over to Armstrong Park. As permanent captain of the Mystic Krewe of Celestial Knights, Woolley was another honored guest. His krewe's den was only a few blocks down the street, and this year's ball had been held in Chalmette at the St. Bernard Civic Auditorium, where most gay balls were now held. "Jean Harlow would have loved this art deco palace of a restaurant," said Woolley. His date, also a member of the Celestial Knights and maître d' at Menefee's, nodded in agreement. After all, the owners of Restaurant Jonathan had framed Harlow's wedding announcement and placed it in the restroom, along with other treasures from the age of deco wonder. Harlow had also appeared on the poster for the krewe's ball.

By the early 1980s, Rampart Street had become the epicenter of a sparkling gay café society, with Ginger Rogers, John Travolta, Liza Minnelli, and other stars landing at Restaurant Jonathan when in town. It also became the restaurant of choice for members of the gay krewes on the nights when they were not working on costumes for the next tableau ball. The restaurant was now filled to the brim and was thoroughly infused with the spirit of celebration.

Further along the street lay other centers of gay café society: Marti's Restaurant, Menefee's Restaurant and Bar, Miss Kitty's, Alice Brady's, and Travis's Bar. In 1971, Martin Shambra had opened Marti's restaurant with chef Henry Robinson from Mississippi. Hungry night owls and socialites soon thronged the Old Gentilich Building to sample the crab bisque, the andouille sausage, and Madame Begue's legendary *boeuf bouilli*. Crisp white linen tablecloths contrasted sharply with the red walls and cork ceiling. Combined with the mirrors lining the far wall, the delicately sheer curtains hanging halfway down the large windows recalled a French bistro. Off to the side, an intimate bar was decorated with a colorful mural of City Park rescued from the old DeSoto Hotel that depicted swans and boats floating in the placid lake along with smartly dressed figures waiting on the steps down to the water's edge. A closer look revealed that the among the mural's characters were two men together holding hands. Marti especially loved the fringes here on Rampart Street and was one of the first pioneers to conquer the wilds of the outskirts, which some people thought too dangerous even for cars. Never one to shy away from the spotlight, Marti had caused a seismic scandal at a Krewe of Armeinius ball by wearing a Nazi armband over his Rubenstein Brothers tuxedo. He was quickly thrown out of the auditorium and was said never to have attended another gay ball.

The morose figure at the end of the bar at Marti's, in his usual corner sipping a bourbon cocktail, was Thomas Lanier Williams III, lost within the whirl of the ceiling fans rotating above his head. By 1982, Williams had become a fixture in the city he loved the best, writing in his *Notebooks* that it "will always seem kind of home-like to me." He lived in a house right across the street from the restaurant entrance on Dumaine Street.

Ray Cronk and Alvin Payne, former queens of the Krewe of Petronius, had sold their successful Uptown beauty salon and opened the New Orleans Guest House on Ursulines Avenue, contributing to the revival of Rampart Street. The most vital piece of this resurrection, however, was located across from Marti's on Rampart Street, where Jerry Menefee had opened an eponymous sprawling complex that included a huge bar and disco, a chic restaurant upstairs, and a lavish health club, complete with a swimming pool in the back. Menefee had been ensconced in New Orleans for years, starting out as a bartender, along with his partner, Tex Knight, at Café Lafitte in Exile on Bourbon Street. Knight and Menefee had earned enough money to renovate the Caverns, a sleazy hustler bar at the corner of St. Ann and Bourbon that had concrete stalactites hanging from the ceiling. The Caverns was a curious nod to the Cave, a once-famous restaurant in the basement of the old Grunewald Hotel on University Place (now a laundry room in the Roosevelt Hotel) that had plaster and cement stalactites and stalagmites hiding the pipes and conduits, with stucco nymphs in all their disrobed beauty watching over the goings-on.

When Tex and Jerry took over the Caverns, they booted out the drugs and thugs and converted the building into another center of gay café society. The Bourbon Pub downstairs served as a proper cocktail bar, while the upstairs was transformed into the fantastic Parade Discothèque, where patrons could dance the night away to a playlist that was a fixture on *Billboard Magazine*'s Top 10 listings. The Parade started the trend of giving away a custom-designed doubloon with the entry fee, which meant a free drink at the bar. The Parade was accented by a colorful mural of costumed revelers holding balloons as they stood expectantly before large floats, anticipating the trinkets that soon would shower down from heaven. The celebrants also gazed at the traditional Fatted Calf or *boeuf gras*, with garlands of multihued flowers around its pale neck. Earl Woodard had created this iconic graphic in the mid-1970s, so it was no surprise that Jerry Menefee again called on Woodard to complete Menefee's, the monster palace on Rampart Street. "Even the sconces along the walls were works of art," Woodard recalled. "They were a series of arms holding stylized red neon flames like torches. Simply gorgeous!" Menefee was a fearless and confident gay presence in the French Quarter. His mother was a relative of a former governor, and his family had previously been quite prominent in Louisiana. "He had loads of charisma," Knight recalled. "No one could resist him once he got going. And he was a flamboyant man. He wore tons of jewelry, gold necklaces, silver rings on every finger, earrings, and enormous hats. You couldn't miss him in a room. No sir!"

But another Rampart Street club also drew in crowds every weekend: Travis's Bar, where "All the Beautiful Girls Were Boys," was New Orleans's only serious drag venue since the closing of the Club My-O-My on the Lakefront. Travis's Bar was a smallish affair, with barely enough room for an audience. Owned by Travis Hickman and his partner, Clifford Rednour, along with Ron Smith, the club featured performers who became famous within this demimonde: Rowena, Mister Boobie (David Parker), Alotta Mulatta, Ginger Snap, Sable Starr, Tarrah, and Donnie Jay. Mister Boobie's rendition of the flamboyant Rae Bourbon earned him the title Miss Gay Vieux Carré. Adrian St. Clair and Gilbertine Liveaudais came close to winning the Miss Drag Universe Pageant, but the title always went to Adrian, who had survived the 1973 Up Stairs Lounge fire.

The revival of and focus on Rampart Street could not have been possible without the presence of gay bars in the French Quarter. Dixie's Bar of Music at 701 Bourbon Street opened in 1949 and not only welcomed gay men but also established a sense of community over the next decade. Dixie had previously helped her sister at the bar's former location on St. Charles Avenue near Canal Street, and she took care of "her boys" when needed. Café Lafitte was another place where gay men felt a home. After it settled into its present location during the 1950s, Café Lafitte in Exile attracted gay men from around the world, who stepped through the corner doors into a world filled with regulars who knew each other and were more than likely members of the gay Carnival krewes. Though the café had lost the lease to its original location (currently home to the Lafitte Blacksmith Shop Bar), it had not surrendered its will to remain visible and open to a community with a growing sense of history, worth, and excitement. Gay liberation was in full swing, and by the end of the 1970s, New Orleans had become a destination for those wanting to escape the rest of the repressive South and its intolerance.

Pete Fountain's became a popular dance bar in the mid-1970s, around the same time that the Parade Disco opened. The Bourbon Street Awards had long celebrated this section of the thoroughfare on Mardi Gras. First conceived by Arthur Jacobs in 1963 to promote his Clover Grill diner, the contest had turned into a gay extravaganza by the 1980s. The awards had originally been held on platforms constructed in the middle of Bourbon Street in front of the Clover Grill, which was also in front of Café Lafitte in Exile. Edd Smith had provided the energetic spirit that held the event together until he became an early victim of AIDS. The awards took place after the midday Rex Parade, with revelers packing themselves into Bourbon Street like sardines to view the incredible costumes, many of which came directly from the gay balls.

Further down toward the river on Royal Street, the Golden Lantern offered many members of the gay community a quiet haven from the restless energy of Bourbon Street and became the starting point for another uniquely gay experience, the Grand March of Southern Decadence. Miss Blanche, a bartender at the Golden Lantern and agent provocateur, hosted motorcycle christenings along with owner Danny Wilson, a member of deSade & Men leather club, and terror drag shows with her infamous troupe, the Demented Women. "Oh, the drugs. Don't forget the drugs!" cautioned Blanche. Yes, there were drugs. Quaaludes, Ativan, Seconal, cocaine. It was the drug decade, and French Quarter establishments served as a pharmacy.

In 1978, two former bartenders from the Golden Lantern, David Jolly and Jack White, reopened Jewel's Tavern, transforming the former sailor dive at the wrong end of Decatur Street into an even raunchier bar with a back room. The bar's notorious Full Moon parties attracted standing-room-only crowds throughout the night, with the DJ booth in the back playing some of the best experimental music in the city, such as Klaus Nomi's "Total Eclipse" or the latest hit by Gang of Four. Offering an alternative to drugs, however, the krewes stepped in with renewed focus, grounding the gay community with a sense of purpose, camaraderie, and pride.

Miss Gilbertine could occasionally be found at Jewel's Tavern, but to be seen around town, she usually ended up at Flamingos on St. Charles Avenue or the Fatted Calf on St. Peter Street. The Fatted Calf attracted mostly the gay set, especially for lunch, and was convenient for the long evening bar crawl. The old Bourbon House had closed, so everyone moved on to the Fatted Calf or the Coffee Pot around the corner. But most locals preferred the Apple Barrel, originally located on Dauphine Street in the Faubourg Marigny, away from the French Quarter and all its tourists. The Apple Barrel's popularity reflected the growing settlement of the Marigny by gays relocating into the city, a group who also frequented the Phoenix Bar and Charlene's. Charlene's, a prominent lesbian bar, was located on Elysian Fields Avenue and hosted fund-raising events for the Krewe of Ishtar, the first lesbian krewe. "I used to go to the Barrel for breakfast a lot," said Miss Gilbertine. "Everybody ended up there. After a night out, there's no other place to recover with tons of coffee and attitude. But give me Restaurant Jonathan any day. Especially during the Carnival season!"

And, indeed, Miss Gilbertine returned to Jonathan the next weekend. Jack and Jay were sitting at the bar, and the laughter from the Paradise Dining Room echoed

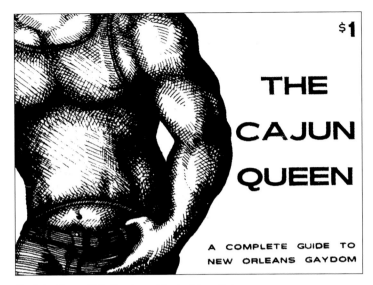

The Cajun Queen, 1974. Courtesy of the Louisiana State Museum, New Orleans, Accession No. 2016.018.01.

along with the music. The glow from the etched glass along the back of the bar silhouetted them against the mirrors and chrome. Tuxedoed couples happily sang along with the piano player in the lounge as the bright lights shone over the old Rue de l'Amour. Miss Liveaudais and her date celebrated the Carnival season with yet another champagne cocktail, but all talk centered on Woolley's extravaganza, *An Evening of Burlesque*, one of those nights when all the stars had for an instant aligned perfectly. And when the ball began, somewhere among the celestial orbs, perhaps Jean Harlow had been watching from her chrome-plated deco heaven.

But the dazzling brightness soon gave way to a lingering darkness. New Orleans's first AIDS casualties were also the city's most recognizable. Five men who owned gay businesses on Rampart Street died almost at the same time. Jack Cosner and Jay Schwab had eventually sold their portion of Restaurant Jonathan to Michael Morris, settling down in San Francisco for only a few months before they died. Jerry Menefee soon followed, taking along his dreams of the resurrection of Rampart Street. Marti Shambra, too, was gone by 1987.

Among the explanations for the restaurant's enigmatic namesake, one recalled Seth Jonathan, who had come to New Orleans from the pine forests of Hattiesburg, Mississippi, via New York City, and had ingratiated himself with this selective group as a companion, confidant, paramour, and eventually charlatan. His outlandish claims included the ability to channel the Archangel Gabriel, who not only served as Jonathan's spiritual guide but gave him esoteric knowledge of the future. But Seth Jonathan left town as suddenly as he had appeared, without a word to anyone. With him went thousands of dollars, jewelry, and even an Alfa-Romeo convertible. He was rumored to have landed in Los Angeles, where he spent a decade of his life and was last seen living in the decadent luxury of Palm Springs. With him, seemingly, went the life force of the old Rue de l'Amour.

Postcard for the Club My-O-My on the Lakefront, 1950s. Courtesy of Howard Philips Smith.

Club My-O-My (Lake Pontchartrain Lakefront)

Female impersonation had commonly been associated with the New Orleans gay community, especially within the French Quarter. In 1936, after much police harassment, Emile Morlet relocated his operation, the Wonder Bar, from Decatur Street near Canal to the Lakefront and renamed it the Wonder Club. Like Mama Lou's and many other Lakefront camps, the bar itself rested on pilings in Lake Pontchartrain or close to the shore. In the 1940s Pat Waters took over the business, and Club My-O-My was born. The club's reputation soon drew busloads of tourists, who packed the tables each weekend. The performers not only looked like real women but also sang, and Jimmy Callaway landed a recording contract with Planet Records. Though the club reopened after a 1948 fire, a devastating January 5, 1972, blaze closed the venue permanently. Arson was suspected in both cases but was never proven.

Travis's Bar (834 North Rampart Street—early 1970s)

At around this time, Travis Hickman and Clifford Rednour opened Travis's Bar at 834 North Rampart Street, a seedy location in the French Quarter, continuing the tradition of female impersonation but adding a real drag sensibility that included both raunch and refinement. For more than a decade, Travis's Bar was the city's only legitimate venue for drag, and during that time, Rampart Street gained new life as a center of gay café society with the emergence of Restaurant Jonathan, Marti's Restaurant, and Menefee's, among others. Many of the stars who performed at Travis's—Rowena, Mr. Boobie, Donnie Jay, Alotta Mulatta, Gilbertine Liveaudais, and Adrian St. Claire—became well known. By the mid-1980s, Andy Boudreaux bought the bar and renamed it Wolfendale's.

Dixie's Bar of Music (701 Bourbon Street—1949)

Opened in 1939 by Yvonne "Miss Dixie" Fasnacht and her sister, Irma, Dixie's Bar of Music originally stood at 204 St. Charles Avenue. In 1949 the bar moved to 701 Bourbon Street, where Miss Dixie played saxophone with her jazz group, much to the delight of her gay boys. Recalled Alvin Payne, who arrived in New Orleans from Beaumont, Texas, in the early 1960s, "Miss Dixie ruled her bar with an iron fist, but with respect. Miss Irma, Dixie's sister, ran the cash register. She didn't trust anyone else. . . . The place was small, with that huge mural looming across an entire wall. The bar itself was round, in the center of the room, and she only employed black bartenders, all dressed up like waiters. She had very strict rules. No boys could touch in her bar, and if you happened to get on her outs list, well, heaven help you. Miss JoJo Landry pissed her off once, and it was over a year before she was let back in. There was always the threat of a raid, especially on weekends. But that only added to the excitement. It still takes my breath away, just remembering it all, the way it used to be."

Bruce of LA's physique catalog, 1960. Physique photographer Bruce of LA journeyed to Carnival in 1960 to find and photograph muscular men. Volume 16 of his *Male Figure* catalog, a Mardi Gras special edition, featured Dixie's Bar of Music and some of the costumes he found on Bourbon Street. Courtesy of Howard Philips Smith.

Xavier Gonzalez, *Jazz Mural*, 1940s. Dixie's Bar of Music opened in a very narrow building at 204 St. Charles Avenue on October 19, 1939. The mural was painted by artist Xavier Gonzalez in the late 1940s. The owners were sisters Yvonne (Dixie) and Irma Fasnacht. Dixie played clarinet, a lady named Sloopy played piano, Johnny Senac played bass and Judy Erle played trumpet. It became a hang-out for entertainers and, in a short time, for World War II servicemen. In late 1949, the operation was moved to 701 Bourbon Street along with the mural. Courtesy of the Louisiana State Museum, New Orleans, Accession No. 1978.061.

Café Lafitte in Exile (901 Bourbon Street—1954, or earlier)

The Café Lafitte was originally located in the space that is now home to Lafitte's Blacksmith Shop Bar. In 1954, when the bar lost its lease, it moved down the block to its current location and became known as Café Lafitte in Exile. It is one of the oldest gay bars in the country. Originally owned by a

Café Lafitte in Exile advertisement, 1980s. Courtesy of Howard Philips Smith.

Post Office Lounge advertisement, 1980s. Courtesy of Howard Philips Smith.

Flamingos poster, 1980s. Courtesy of Howard Philips Smith.

straight man, the bar was a destination within the French Quarter for those who called it their neighborhood bar and for those who journeyed from around the South to find others like themselves. Inside was a welcoming space with a special sculpture and its "eternal" flame. Tom Wood eventually bought the bar and assured its place in history by hosting the annual Bourbon Street Awards just outside. "You can blow out the candles, but you can never blow out the flame!"

The Post Office Lounge (940 St. Louis Street—1970s)

The Post Office had a drag queen dancing troupe, the Male Bags, who appeared every Saturday night. The owner launched a short-lived krewe, the Frollicking Krewe of PO, which held a ball in 1977.

Flamingos Café and Bar (1625 St. Charles Avenue—1980s)

Flamingos Café and Bar, opened by Paul Doll and Tom Struve in 1977, was a big hit during the early 1980s with not only the gay crowd but also Uptowners. The interior was filled with hundreds of hot pink lawn flamingos, and the accent colors of green and lavender only focused attention on the feathers and balloons. The menu featured quiches, salads, and omelets, but most people were attracted by the promise of an excursion out of the French Quarter and for the cheap cocktails and ambience, with the waiters joining in the fun with everything from a bitch fight to a serenade.

Bourbon Street Awards (1963)

Young Aristocrats of Tchoupitoulas Street (YATS), Krewe of Armeinius, winners of the Group Costume Award at the 1980 Bourbon Street Awards: Ed Lepoma (*Oriental costume*), Christel Robbins (*Queen Bee*), Albert Carey (*Red Bird*), Jon Lee Poché (*Sacred Cow*), and Henry Denoux (*Bird of Paradise*). Photograph by Mitchel L. Osborne. Courtesy of LGBT+ Archives Project of Louisiana Grant.

Bourbon Street Awards poster, 1966. Courtesy of the Louisiana State Museum, New Orleans, Accession No. 2000.100.1.

George Wilson as A Melodic Mimsy of Musical Motion, Bourbon Street Awards, 1969. He won second place. Courtesy of the Louisiana State Museum, New Orleans, Accession No. 2016.025.07.

Bourbon Street Awards, 1975. Courtesy of the Louisiana State Museum, New Orleans, Accession No. 2015.043.01.

Bourbon Street Awards and grand prize winners, 1960s. Courtesy of the Louisiana State Museum, New Orleans, Accession No. 1995.071.35.

Little Orphan Annies from the Krewe of Olympus, Bourbon Street Awards, 1979. The founder of the awards, Arthur Jacobs, is seated on the upper right. Photograph by Mitchel L. Osborne. Courtesy of LGBT+ Archives Project of Louisiana Grant.

Live the Life You Love

Before World War II, merchants near certain city markets held costume competitions that attracted large crowds. "Such a contest is held each year in the Vieux Carré; it attracts all types of contestants, many with bizarre costumes," wrote Leonard Huber in his 1977 Mardi Gras history. The Bourbon Street Awards first took place on Shrove Tuesday 1963, when the owner of the Clover Grill, Arthur Jacobs, sought to promote his diner by hosting the ceremony in the late afternoon in the middle of Bourbon Street, between the Clover Grill and Café Lafitte in Exile. Over the ensuing years, the streets surrounding the event became so crowded with people that moving was nearly impossible. But the costumes were

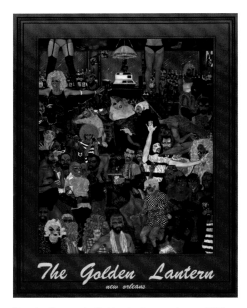

Douglas Bourgeois, Golden Lantern poster, ca. 1982. Courtesy of the Louisiana State Museum, New Orleans, Accession No. 2009.089.70.

Earl Woodard, Golden Lantern advertisement, ca. 1985. Courtesy of Howard Philips Smith.

Earl Woodard, Bourbon Pub and Parade Disco advertisement, 1970s. Courtesy of Howard Philips Smith.

always the star attraction, and many of them came from the tableaux of the gay krewes. In the mid-1980s, the Play It Again Sam bar began hosting the awards, which shifted to Burgundy Street at St. Ann; when the Bourbon Pub took over the sponsorship, the ceremony moved yet again, this time to Bourbon Street at St. Ann. In 1984 *Around the Clock Magazine* reported that "the Best Male honors went to Dan Boudreaux for his costume which literally hung from his shoulders representing the Gardens of Versailles on one side and the Hall of Mirrors on the other." As for the costumes from the gay krewes, "Polyphemus was judged as the Best Krewe with their Captain being dressed as a rose and their King as an orchid."

The Golden Lantern (1239 Royal Street—1966)

Though Danny Wilson owned the Golden Lantern, Miss Blanche ruled it, especially when it came to the annual Southern Decadence street celebrations held on the Sunday before Labor Day. She reinvented this exercise in bad taste by having drag queens tour all of the French Quarter's straight bars. The Demented Women, as she dubbed her group, wreaked havoc on the streets throughout the day and well into the night, much to tourists' horror and amusement.

The Golden Lantern was a popular hangout for playing pool and scoring drugs. After Wilson served as grand marshal of Southern Decadence in 1983, his bar became the center not only for Southern Decadence but also for all things Carnival. Even the Lancers MC christened their motorcycles there late at night as the music blared and libations flowed. And next door was a laundromat, so a cocktail was always welcome for the spin cycle.

The bar's name supposedly came from the tales of the Arabian Nights, but no one really bought into the idea of the place as full of genies—in fact, patrons insisted on calling it the Golden Latrine, or the Latrine for short. Whether a magic lamp or piss bucket, the Golden Lantern became a sort of porthole into the lives of those who lived and loved within its sphere of influence.

The Bourbon Pub and Parade Discothèque (801 Bourbon Street—1975)

According to the *Cajun Queen*, "a complete guide to New Orleans gaydom" and the only local guide for incoming queens, Cajun or otherwise, the Bourbon Pub was *the* place to be on a Sunday afternoon for Tea Dance. Tex Knight and Jerry Menefee transformed the rundown hole-in-the-wall known as the Caverns into the dazzling Bourbon Pub and Parade Disco. Queens came from miles around to drink and dance the night away within the swirling lights of the disco ball haze. Located on the second floor, the Parade Disco was so popular that it appeared every week on *Billboard Magazine*'s Top 10 playlist. For years, the owners advertised on the back cover of *Blueboy* magazine, one of the early gay cultural bibles, along with *After Dark* and *Christopher Street*. The advertisements were designed by Earl Woodard, at the time a member of the Krewe of Olympus.

The mural at the Parade Disco stretched from wall to wall and depicted colorfully costumed Carnival revelers holding balloons and watching a stream of parade floats, including the traditional boeuf gras. One panel showed Jerry Menefee himself, peering out at the throng from behind his Carnival mask.

Restaurant Jonathan (714 North Rampart Street—1976)

On the edge of the French Quarter, on historic North Rampart Street, was a door with a silver nameplate that read *Jonathan, A Restaurant*. On the other side of the door, patrons found a magnificent art deco interior (featuring such relics of famous stars as Jean Harlow's wedding announcement, which reposed in an upstairs bathroom, and a tiara worn by Jessye Norman during a performance of *Tosca*, located in the private dining room named for the soprano), a friendly and relaxing atmosphere, and wonderful food. As the gala grand opening postcard proclaimed, *Jonathan, A Restaurant* was *A Matter of Taste*. Restaurant Jonathan became one of the centers of gay café society along Rampart Street during the mid-1980s Golden Age of gay Carnival.

Recalled local artist Douglas Bourgeois, "I worked there when it first opened. I was there for Erté's ninetieth birthday bash, because I remember some of his original gouache paintings on display for a one-day-only exhibit. These were fantastic—more mind-blowing than the prints—and looked like they were painted with insect hairs! The interior of the restaurant was pretty extraordinary—the hand-painted elevator door, the fantastic mural in the entry, the amazing two-story etched glass panel, the dark lacquered walls, and period deco light fixtures and architectural details. I remember waiting on Lily Tomlin, Lillian Hellman, Tennessee Williams, Polly Bergen, and Eubie Blake."

New Orleans architect Jack Cosner partnered with Jim Maxcy, owner of the Coffee Pot restaurant, to renovate the building. Michael Morris, whose family had made its money in oil and hotels in Dallas, settled in New Orleans in 1975 and ultimately replaced Maxcy as Cosner's business partner. By the late 1980s, Morris had become sole owner of the restaurant, and it closed by the end of the decade.

The story behind the restaurant's name was and remains mysterious. Seth Jonathan was apparently a brilliant and handsome grifter from Hattiesburg, Mississippi, and his name had already appeared on the menu at the Coffee Pot, which served Eggs Jonathan, a poached egg dish. Maxcy probably introduced Jonathan to Cosner and his lover, Jay Schwab. Within a week, Jonathan had relieved them of several thousand dollars in cash and heirloom jewelry and then vanished. They then chose to immortalize this charmer and lover by selecting his name for their oh-so-chic restaurant.

Tom Fitzmorris and Max Singer, Restaurant Jonathan menu, 1976. Courtesy of the New Orleans Public Library, Louisiana Division, City Archives.

Restaurant Jonathan's Erté Dining Room. Photograph by Jaime Ardiles-Arce. Courtesy of Tulane University, Louisiana Research Collection, Howard-Tilton Memorial Library, New Orleans.

Marti's Restaurant (1041 Dumaine Street—1971)

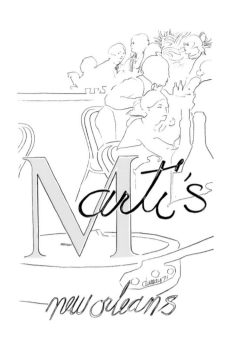

Marti's Restaurant, interior featuring one of two murals of City Park rescued from the DeSoto Hotel, 1920s. Photograph by Tom Fitzmorris. Courtesy of Tom Fitzmorris.

George Dureau, Marti's Restaurant menu, 1971. Courtesy of the New Orleans Public Library, Louisiana Division, City Archives.

The Finale Bar and Restaurant (1041 Royal Street—1960s)
The Finale II Bar (642 North Rampart Street—late 1970s)

Page 10, IMPACT, February, 1979

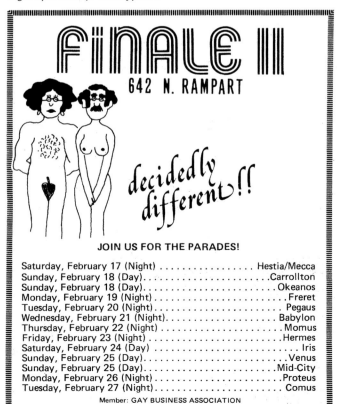

Finale II Bar advertisement, late 1970s. Courtesy of the Louisiana State Museum, New Orleans, Accession No. 2016.018.02a.

The building at Royal and Ursulines belonged to Dave and Doris DiVincente. George Wilson and Nick Donovan, early members of the Krewes of Petronius and Olympus, managed the bar for them in the mid-1960s, and Dave and Doris ran the upstairs restaurant. Gay krewes, especially Petronius and Amon-Ra, held many of their functions there. The space was cramped, and for krewe events, the stage was usually restaurant tables lashed together, while seating was haphazard and very close.

The bar was never as popular as Lafitte's but was often full when a band would play for Sunday dances. Donovan at times locked the doors so that men could dance together uninterrupted. Daisy Mae held court here almost every night, and her entourage became La Krewe Mystic de Désimé. Recalled George Wilson, "After Roland Dobson started Apollo, Daisy decided that if Roland could [start his own krewe], so could he. I think he tried to have the ball in the Superdome!" Continued Lou Bernard, "Daisy Mae got into trouble for trying to book the Superdome with a bad check, and the police ran him outta town. Only in Nawlins, dawlin'."

By the early 1980s, the Finale moved to its Rampart Street location and renamed itself the Finale II. The bar became the center for an ersatz Carnival krewe, the Kitty Kat Kocktail Klub, which was organized enough to have at least one ball.

Second Skin Leather (521 St. Philip Street and 818 No. Rampart—1980s)

Ed Cox, Second Skin Leather advertisement, 1984.
Courtesy of Ed Cox.

Brady's (700 North Rampart Street—1980s)

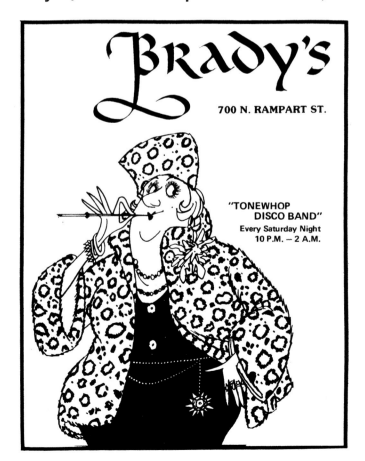

Brady's advertisement, 1980s. The bar was originally
owned by Alice Brady and was one of the first lesbi-
an-friendly mixed bars in the French Quarter. The ad
depicts Brady as Gertrude Stein. Courtesy of Tulane
University, Louisiana Research Collection, Howard-Tilton Memorial Library, New Orleans.

Ms. Kitty's (740 Burgundy Street—1980s)

Ms. Kitty's advertisement, 1980s. Owned by Kitty Blackwell, Ms. Kitty's welcomed both lesbians and gay men, and Blackwell became a supporter of the Krewe of Ishtar. Courtesy of Tulane University, Louisiana Research Collection, Howard-Tilton Memorial Library, New Orleans.

Charlene's (940 Elysian Fields Avenue–1980s)

Charlene's advertisement, 1980s. Courtesy of the Louisiana State Museum, New Orleans, Accession No. 2016.018.02a.

Charlene Schneider opened her bar in the Faubourg Marigny in 1977, giving women a place to socialize and dance. She often had live music by female entertainers such as Melissa Etheridge and Tim Williams and Her Band of Gold. "If you went in to see Charlene, you naturally got her slant on the day's current events, local and international, and a good dose of political science in the bargain, plus lots of gossip because Charlene lived to dish," said Jon Newlin, a longtime friend. "She was a grand old gal."

Diane's (700 North Rampart Street—1970s)
Diane's Cocktail Lounge (2317 Jefferson Highway—1980s)

Join us after the balls and continue the celebration . . .

Hours:
Monday - Friday 4:00-4:00
Saturday & Sunday 6:30-4:00

DIANE'S
COCKTAIL LOUNGE
2317 JEFFERSON HIGHWAY   833-9213
"Get in on the Good Times"

Hail To King David III
from
DIANE'S

Diane's advertisement, 1980s. Courtesy of the Louisiana State Museum, New Orleans, Accession No. 1995.010.078.

Diane DiMiceli took over Brady's Bar on Rampart Street after Alice Brady personally asked DiMiceli to do so. She renamed the bar Diane's and in the early 1980s moved it to a location along Jefferson Highway in Jefferson Parish, making it one of the first lesbian bars to open outside the French Quarter. Rosemary Pino's Blue Odyssey and other lesbian bars soon followed. Always a supporter of the gay community, DiMiceli helped out her lesbian clientele in times of need. In addition, she formed the Krewe of Ishtar and hosted fund-raisers and parties for other gay krewes. All of Metairie's gay bars had closed by the beginning of the twenty-first century, and no lesbian bars now exist in the city proper. A diner now stands on the site of the old Diane's Cocktail Lounge.

Pino's Club 621 (621 Elysian Fields Avenue—1980s)

Pino's Club 621 advertisement, 1980s. Courtesy of Howard Philips Smith.

Rosemary "Mama" Pino and her longtime partner, Margie Normand, operated several gay bars in New Orleans and Metairie, including Pino's Club 621 on Elysian Fields and the Blue Odyssey in Metairie. A staunch advocate of gay rights, Pino was also a founding member of the Krewe of Ishtar. She and Sue Martino, Kitty Blackwell, Diane DiMiceli, and Charlene Schneider elevated the profile of lesbians at a time when being gay meant mostly a life in the closet. Her enthusiasm for gay Carnival and her all-inclusive philosophy endeared her to other gay krewes, especially the Krewe of Polyphemus, which named her an honorary member. She died in a retirement home that flooded during Hurricane Katrina.

Lucille's & Friend Bar (626 St. Phillip Street—1980s)

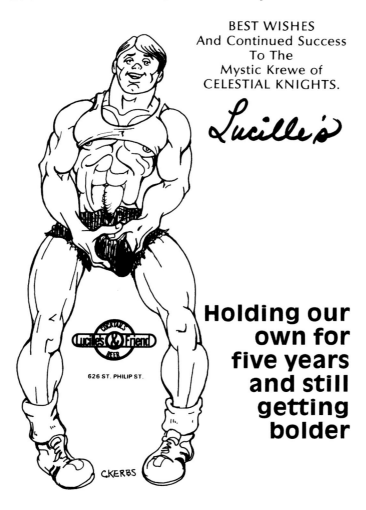

Charles Kerbs, Lucille's & Friend Bar advertisement, 1980s. Courtesy of the Louisiana State Museum, New Orleans, Accession No. 2014.005.25.

Lou Bernard, a member of the Krewe of Olympus, opened Lucille's and Friend in 1979. *Lucille* was Bernard's "drag name," while the *friend* was his longtime partner, Nick Donovan, also a member of Olympus.. According to Bernard, Lucille's was "the delight of theater crowd in the French Quarter."

TT's Bar (820 North Rampart Street—1980s)

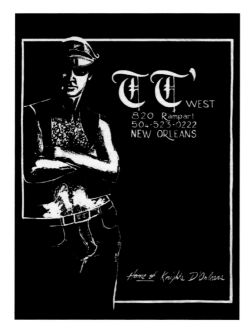

W. T. Bell, TT's Bar advertisement, 1970s. Courtesy of the Louisiana State Museum, New Orleans, Accession No. 2016.018.02a.

Though Rampart Street became home to a glittering gay café society during the late 1970s and early 1980s, some seedy bars remained from its past life. TT's Bar, opened by Clifford Rednour and Ron Smith, was a small hole-in-the-wall bar with a pool table, and it hosted the Knights d'Orléans motorcycle club from time to time. Patrons who frequented the more chic bars earlier in the evening often found themselves at TT's in the wee hours of the morning, downing one last cocktail while contemplating a visit to the infamous backroom before heading home.

Menefee's (1123 North Rampart Street—1980s)

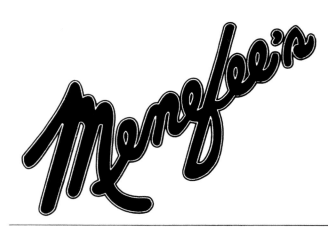

Earl Woodard, Menefee's logo, early 1980s. Courtesy of Howard Philips Smith.

Earl Woodard, original artwork for the staircase mural at Menefee's, early 1980s.
Courtesy of the Louisiana State Museum, New Orleans, Accession No. 2012.052.

Mississippi River Bottom Saloon & Company Store (515 St. Phillip Street—1980s)

515 St. Phillip St.
New Orleans, La.
566-0665

Mississippi River Bottom Saloon & Company Store advertisement, 1980s. Courtesy of Howard Philips Smith.

Andy Boudreaux opened the Mississippi River Bottom Salon and Company Store in the early 1980s, and it became popular after Lou Bernard opened Lucille's up the street. Recalled Bernard, "We were part of the other triangle away from Bourbon Street, which included the Golden Lantern, my bar, and the Bottom. Every weekend we had our regulars who would complete this circuit as a matter of course. Everyone found their friends out and about, and Andy was always around for the party. He was a hard worker with his produce company and supplied all the gay restaurants and bars with provisions. He would step in at times to help out the gay community. I don't think we all could have survived without him or his bar." Many others spoke highly of Boudreaux, including Diane DiMiceli, who said, "Andy was so much a part of our community. He came to my rescue many times, and that's a story repeated time and time again. He was an unsung hero, that's for sure. He worked behind the scenes with little or no recognition, but he came through when need be."

The Mint (504 Esplanade Avenue at Decatur Street—1990s)

The Mint advertisement, 1990s. Courtesy of Howard Philips Smith.

The Mint was a popular bar and cabaret theater at the corner of Decatur and Esplanade Boulevard, across from the New Orleans Mint, now the Louisiana State Museum. Krewes often held meetings and get-togethers there, and it hosted Becky Allen and Ricky Graham's raunchy vaudevillian act, which featured Allen's rendition of "Naughty Nefertiti!"

Jewel's Tavern (1207 Decatur Street—1970s and 1980s)

Jewel's Tavern advertisement, 1980s. Courtesy of Howard Philips Smith.

Jewel's Tavern became the center of a culture shift in New Orleans from the old-school flamboyance of the queen to the new hypermasculinity of the clone. David Jolly and Jack White, former bartenders at the Golden Lantern, transformed an old sailor bar, known for its rough men and hard liquor, into a true gay temple. Above the bar, almost unnoticed, hung a soiled painting of the SS *Jewel*.

Phoenix Bar (941 Elysian Fields Avenue—1981)

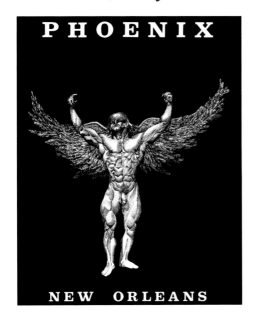

Phoenix Bar poster, 1980s. Courtesy of the International Leather Archives, Chicago.

Charles Kerbs (Matt), mural, Phoenix Bar, 1985. Photograph by Larry Graham. Courtesy of the Clint Taylor.

The Phoenix Bar was the first legitimate leather bar in New Orleans, opened by Jamie Temple in the early 1980s. It's clientele came from members of leather clubs, such as deSade & Men and the Knights d'Orléans. The Lords of Leather, a gay leather krewe, adopted the bar as its official home early on.

The Apple Barrel Restaurant (1940 Dauphine Street—1977)

Earl Woodard, Apple Barrel Restaurant advertisement, 1980s. Courtesy of Howard Philips Smith.

The Apple Barrel, known affectionately as La Cage aux Pommes, was a small restaurant that became a second home to many of the outcasts who lived in the Faubourg Marigny and French Quarter during the late 1970s and early 1980s. Miss Delores, a much-beloved character, cooked up a mean filé gumbo and fried okra, even when she was in one of her moods.

The Fatted Calf (727 St. Peter Street—1970s and 1980s)

The Fatted Calf restaurant menu, 1980s. Courtesy of the New Orleans Public Library, Louisiana Division, City Archives.

The Fatted Calf was a curious French Quarter restaurant serving up cocktails and attitude. Nothing fancy, but queens congregated there, mostly to be seen.

Nothing is falser than people's preconceptions and ready-made opinions; nothing is sillier than their sham morality.

—Petronius Arbiter, the *Satyricon*

The Muse Unveiled

Clio, the Muse of History, is a selective and hateful creature, rarely allowing a voice to her most fantastical stories. Her spotlight shines on a relatively small portion of a vastly expansive and intricately complex picture, with ever-changing perspectives and boundaries, seemingly at random and without focus. But from time to time, Clio adjusts her beam to include more and more of what lies hidden in the dark or, more succinctly, inside the cruel closet. An ancient Egyptian banquet scene painted in a tomb almost forty-five hundred years ago shows two men standing together. Officially designated as the "overseers of the manicurists of the palace of the king," they appear in several scenes, always side by side, in positions usually reserved for a husband and wife. They represent the first gay couple in history. Another Egyptian relief depicts two men showing their affection, poised right before a kiss. It was originally captioned as a god bestowing the breath of life—yet another example of the many intentional misreadings of history.

Egyptian relief, ca. 2,000 BCE. Courtesy of Howard Philips Smith.

Once the Muse has been unveiled and her secrets revealed, she becomes a source of immense inspiration and dramatic revelation. But the jagged edges and razor-sharp claws of gay culture have slowly been blunted, filed back by the great wheel of assimilation into the folds of a larger society. What had lain in the dark, beaten down and crushed, has come out in plain view. Now we see the brightness of a future filled with promise and equality, with a great wave of acceptance and a legitimate place next to other minorities. The 1969 Stonewall Riots started an atomic chain reaction that still reverberates across the landscape today. But the 1970s saw the emergence of the clone cliché and the seekers of sexual liberation above all else, a bold experiment that eventually became a source of lingering shame and discomfort, especially within the gay community. Members of this very community picketed William Friedkin's movie, *Cruising* (1980), which depicted the hard-core leather scene in Manhattan, on the grounds that it offered a poor representation of gay culture. But in *Beyond Shame: Reclaiming the Abandoned History of Radical Gay Sexuality* (2004), Patrick Moore countered that gay sexual exploration was a form of art that transcended the supposed disgrace, a fact of gay history that should be embraced rather than dismissed.

The Impact of AIDS

The bold experiment came to an end with the emergence of a global epidemic that primarily targeted gay men. Confronted with the indifference of government leaders and politicians, clergy and the general population in the face of a disease that only struck Others, the fearless members of ACT-UP took matters into their own hands, fighting back to save their own lives.

AIDS decimated the krewes, sapping the color and vigor and perhaps even the life force from gay Carnival and leaving it numb and ashen gray. In the words of Michael Hickerson, a prominent leader within the gay krewes, "The lifeblood was gone. So many of our brothers were dying and along with [them] our beloved gay Carnival. Its Golden Age had come to an end, perhaps never to return." But the krewes gave New Orleans an advantage that other cities lacked: they provided an organization, a structure to the gay community, and they were the first group to spring into action, channeling their resources to push back against the deadly virus.

Ironically, therefore, death brought what had been a narrow—though vibrant—subculture out into the open. The closet was no longer possible for many stricken with the disease. With visibility came a shift toward acceptance, and gay cultural expression, formed and tempered in the crucible of derision, violence, and contempt, merged back into mainstream society. Gay men and women gained legal and social rights. Unique expression, exaggerated gestures, and provocative behavior suddenly seemed retro, unneeded, part of another time, another world; the spirit that revealed itself in over-the-top tableau balls, extravagant costumes, and opulent themes simply dissipated.

This general trend toward societal acceptance of homosexuality has of course brought many benefits to the gay community, but it has also had its costs. Assimilation is essentially a reductive process—regaining any sort of equilibrium requires something to be lost. The immovable force that transformed gay Carnival into something fantastic and unique may have lost its creative spark. The well of outrageousness may have run dry.

Effervescence

Founded in 1979 by Harry Hay, who had previously formed the groundbreaking Mattachine Society, the Radical Faerie movement began as an antiassimilation group that rejected the mere imitation of heterocentric society in favor of more pagan, environmental, and community-based ideals. Faerie groups have formed all over the world and have gone beyond rigid gender roles and embraced all forms of flamboyance, and New Orleans is no exception. Even *Arthur Hardy's Mardi Gras*

Guide advertises the annual Radical Faerie St. Brigid Ball, a costumed extravaganza where the Irish saint and pagan mythical figure is celebrated and an empress is crowned. The group continues the grand traditions and camp sensibilities of the outrageous gay culture of the 1950s–80s. Perhaps the current crop of gay krewes needs only to tap into the Radical Faeries' Queer energy and exuberance—the same sort of effervescence that initially created gay Carnival.

The Mysteries of Drag

Before the Stonewall revolution, gay men and lesbians practiced wearing gender-opposite clothing. In *Morocco* (1930), Marlene Dietrich shocked audiences when she wore a man's tuxedo. Gay men especially were adept at portraying themselves as women, mostly for amusement, but these endeavors more often than not also contained a note of seriousness. George Chauncey wrote that Harlem drag balls in the 1920s "enhanced the solidarity of the gay world and symbolized the continuing centrality of gender inversion to gay culture." This inversion dominated the early gay balls in New Orleans, where almost every costume was either camp or ultrafeminine drag. These balls united gay men, who became swept up in the Carnival season, and became a source of fierce competition and pride. The balls later grew into more lavish and exotic tableaux, not necessarily concentrating on drag. In fact, gay men began to distance themselves from drag in the late 1970s, a trend that continues today with the hypermasculine and muscular gym devotees found across the country. However, gay Carnival is enjoying a rebirth, with a variety of themes and tableaux that echo the Golden Age of the 1980s. And drag is front and center in this renaissance. Drag queens appear to dominate the krewes, and gay culture is again embracing drag, though not as a farce but as a real form of artistic expression. There is also recognition that drag has played a crucial role in gay culture: after all, the revolution at the Stonewall Inn was started by the drag queens who threw the first bricks at the police and demanded equality.

The Excitement of Discovery

When Alvin Payne, who later became Queen Petronius XXII, arrived in New Orleans from Beaumont, Texas, in the early 1960s, he felt like a wide-eyed explorer discovering a new world—a completely realized gay world. He and many others

Shrove Tuesday revelers, 1969. Courtesy of the Louisiana State Museum, New Orleans, Accession Nos. 2016.025.19.92, 2016.026.19.25.

reveled in its newness and mystery, the gay spirit bubbling out of the closet. As we stand on the brink of assimilation and civil equality, we risk blandness. Gay krewes today must orient themselves away from mediocrity and conformity and strike out with a brave new vision if they wish to take gay Carnival in New Orleans into the future.

As Candy says in Tennessee Williams's *And Tell Sad Tales of the Death of Queens*, "Just imagine this country without queens in it. It would be absolutely barbaric. Look at the homes of normal married couples. No originality: modern mixed with period, everything bunched around a big TV set in the parlor. Mediocrity is the passion among them. Conformity. Convention. Now I know the faults of queens, nobody knows the faults of queens better than I do." When Candy's gentleman caller then asks, "Are you queer?" She can only respond, "Baby, are you kidding!"

EPILOGUE

Carnival in New Orleans has always been about the street. The hidden balls, sequestered away in auditoriums and lodges, grand opera houses and theaters, eventually ended up in the street for all to see, especially on the last day of celebration, Shrove Tuesday. Participants seemed to have an almost primal urge to costume and exhibit the outlandish in public. The laws accommodated this obsession, but only on Mardi Gras, permitting a single day of merriment. Even the first krewes in the nineteenth century paraded down the streets with strange costumes and surreal floats before retreating into the privacy of their *bals masqués*. In fact, the Mistick Krewe of Comus was arguably formed as a direct result of the out-of-hand shenanigans prevalent during early Carnival celebrations.

The streets of New Orleans remain alive with Carnival through such efforts as the splendid array of costumes deployed by the Société de Ste. Anne early on the morning of Shrove Tuesday and the massive crush of the annual Bourbon Street Awards. Perhaps this is the real essence of Mardi Gras—the fleshly presence on display and in the open before the farewell to such carnal desires during the long haul of Lent. This spirit permeates the Vieux Carré for the rest of the year as well and has already manifested itself in the guise of yet another celebration, the Grand March of Southern Decadence, which takes place at the end of the long, sweltering summer, the mirror image of Carnival. And after the quiet cold of winter, the cycle begins again on the Feast of Epiphany, when pleasure and celebration return. Gay Carnival in New Orleans lingers, bides its time, and continues despite the odds, out in the streets, unbridled and liberated.

Circus costumes, Shrove Tuesday, 1982. A circus-themed Carnival costume party in the French Quarter hosted by Earl Woodard and Spencer Lindsay of the Krewe of Olympus, spilled out into the street: (*left to right*) Steve Biel, Paul Whittle, and David Peltier. Photograph ©Nell Campbell.

John Dodt and other members of the Whistler's Mothers group costume, awaiting their turn at the Bourbon Street Awards, Shrove Tuesday, 1992. Photograph ©Nell Campbell.

Ron Ellis and the Supremettes, Shrove Tuesday, early 1980s. Ellis was a member of the Krewe of Amon-Ra and each year his group would parade in the French Quarter in a new set of group costumes. Photographs ©Nell Campbell.

Members of the Krewe of Olympus wearing costumes from the *Desert Song* ball in front of Lucille's and Friend Bar, Shrove Tuesday, 1987. Photographs ©Nell Campbell.

Costumed revelers from a private white party en route to the Bourbon Street Awards, Shrove Tuesday, 1985. Photographs ©Nell Campbell.

ACKNOWLEDGMENTS

This book could not have been compiled and written without the participants, curators, and archivists who had the foresight to preserve invitations, programs, admit cards, posters, photographs, doubloons, and meeting notes and minutes relating to the history of gay Carnival. In particular, significant collections of research materials are held at the Historic New Orleans Collection, Williams Research Center, New Orleans; the Jack Robinson Archive, Memphis; the Louisiana Research Collection, Tulane University, New Orleans; the Louisiana State Museum, New Orleans; Loyola University, Special Collections, New Orleans; the New Orleans Public Library and Louisiana and Special Collections, University of New Orleans.

In addition, the following gay Carnival krewes made significant contributions to this book: Krewe of Amon-Ra; Krewe of Armeinius; Lords of Leather, A Mystic Mardi Gras Krewe; Krewe of Mwindo; Krewe of Narcissus; Krewe of Petronius; and Mystic Krewe of Satyricon.

Since I lived in New Orleans in the late 1970s and early 1980s, I have interviewed numerous people who were directly involved with the gay krewes. I attended many of the balls chronicled here, and I spent many evenings with Tommy Griffin, who shared his vast knowledge of Carnival and the city's history. My conversations with krewe members at the original Apple Barrel Restaurant on Dauphine Street, inspired me to write this book. I had planned to re-create this innocently exciting time of gay celebration in a work of historical fiction, but the research that went into discovering the breadth of gay Carnival history forced its way to the front of the line.

Early versions of portions of this work have previously been published elsewhere: "In the Kingdom of Queens," *New Orleans Magazine*, January 2014; "The Golden Celebration: The Krewe of Petronius" (2011), "The Lost Krewe of Ganymede" (2014), and "The Krewe of Amon-Ra" (2015), all in *Arthur Hardy's Mardi Gras Guide*.

I thank the following people for their important contributions: Thomas Adams, John Alexander, Lou Bernard, Alan Bernstein, Don Bury, Nell Campbell, Albert Carey, Ed Cox, Ray Cronk, William Crotty, Daniel de Beau-Maltbie, Clay Delery, Barrett DeLong-Church, Diane DiMiceli, John Dodt, Mickey Gil, Jerry Gilley, Larry Graham, Tommy Griffin, Cleveland J. Guillot Jr., Arthur Hardy, Vance Philip Hedderel, Tracy Hendrix, Roy (Rowena) Hermann, Michael Hickerson, Jeffrey Johnson, Benjamin Jones, James Keyes, Tex Knight, Zachary Krevitt, Errol Laborde, Karen Leathem, Jim Lestelle, Spencer Lindsay, James McAllister, Charles Maniaci, Gary Martin, Michael Meads, Rip Naquin and Marsha Delain, Gabe Nassar, Jon Newlin, Ed (Blanche) Norton, Bruce Orgeron, Pat O'Rourke, Mitchell Osborne, Danny Ourso, Ken Owen, David Parker, Peter Patout, George Patterson, Alvin Payne, David Peltier, Frank Perez, Earl Perry, Buddy Rasmussen, Carl Ricketts, Christel Robbins, Marsha Robert, George Roth, Glenn Sanford, Henri Schindler, Wally Sherwood, Garrett Stearns, Wendell Stipelcovich, Don Stratton, Jack Sullivan, Claude Summers, Russell Talluto, Clint Taylor, Jamie Temple, Jake Aaron Thomas, Johnny Townsend, Mark Tullos, Nick Weber, Danny Wilson, George Wilson, Earl Woodard, William Woolley, and John S. Zeringue III. I apologize to anyone whose name I have inadvertently omitted from this already long list.

Special thanks go to Mike Moreau (Opal Masters) and Darwin Reed, who not only preserved so much of this history but also allowed me access to their incredible collection. Henri Schindler inspired my love of Carnival and shared his knowledge of history, design, art, aesthetics, and eccentricity. His research in traditional Carnival not only informed and shaped this compendium of gay Carnival but also set a standard of professionalism and design aesthetic that I have tried to reach.

My research would not have been possible without the expertise and knowledge of the following: Priscilla Lawrence, Eric Seiferth, Rebecca Smith, and Sally Stussi of the Historic New Orleans Collection, Williams Research Center; Lee Miller and Sean Benjamin of the Tulane Louisiana Research Collection; Irene Wainwright of the New Orleans Public Library; and James Warren Hodges and Connie Phelps of Louisiana and Special Collections, University of New Orleans. Emily Oppenheimer and Dan Oppenheimer of the Jack Robinson Archive not only shared their knowledge of this amazing photographer but also allowed unlimited access to the archive and provided a particular source of encouragement. The LGBT+ Archives Project of Louisiana and the J. B. Harter Foundation Trust supported this work with grants.

Wayne Phillips at the Louisiana State Museum is another devotee of Carnival as well as a dear friend. I am grateful for the materials he has collected, his help, his tireless support, and his critical feedback. This history could not have been assembled without his contributions and observations.

Heartfelt thanks go to Craig Gill and his team at the University Press of Mississippi. His unfailing support and encouragement have kept this project alive. Thus I must commend Emily Bandy, Todd Lape, and Shane Gong Stewart for their professionalism and expertise. I will also be eternally grateful for such an expert copy editor in Ellen Goldlust.

Mike Bonnet, my husband and partner for more than twenty years, has lived with this project, sometimes without choice, continually offering valuable insight and criticism. Plus he took care of our herd of cats when I traveled for research.

Finally, I acknowledge Elmo Avet. My family briefly lived on Canal Street when I was four years old, and while visiting an antique shop on Royal Street, I encountered a strange gentleman who made an enormous impression on me. Many years later, I realized that he was Elmo Avet. I had been in the presence of true Carnival royalty.

BAKERS UNION HALL A medium-sized banquet hall at 2001 Burgundy Street in the Faubourg Marigny that was the site of many gay balls and fundraisers. The Lords of Leather held their first ball there in 1984, and Petronius for years had its fall fund-raiser, the Satyricon, there. Previously known as Sir Thomas Hall.

BALL QUEEN A member of a gay krewe whose sole focus in life is gay Carnival and the gay balls. For example, "Oh, don't ask Errol to go to dinner anytime soon. She's a ball queen and has to apply another fifty layers of sequins to her costume before Carnival."

BEADS Plastic necklaces and trinkets thrown from Carnival floats to the public as gifts from the gods. Also a term used by gay men to indicate a slight being righted by a verbal attack. For example, "That bitch better watch out. I could easily read her beads at splits notice."

CAMP According to Susan Sontag's "Notes on Camp," "A sensibility that revels in artifice, stylization, theatricalization, irony, playfulness, and exaggeration rather than content." In *Queer Street*, James McCourt wrote, "Camp is a vision of the world in terms of style—but a particular kind of style. It is the love of the exaggerated, the off, of things-being-what-they-are-not." However defined, the idea of camp is essential to gay balls, and certain costumes have been designated as the "Queen of Camp."

CARNIVAL Also known as Mardi Gras. Originally transported from Europe, especially France, and tied inextricably to the Catholic calendar of religious events. The Carnival season begins on Epiphany (January 6), the day when the Three Wise Men (Three Kings) bestowed gifts on the Christ child. The season ends on Shrove Tuesday (Mardi Gras or Fat Tuesday), the day before Ash Wednesday, which marks the start of the Lenten season. Because the Catholic Church calculates the date for Easter Sunday using a lunar calendar and then counts back to find the date for Shrove Tuesday, Carnival season may end any time between early February and mid-March.

DEBUTRAMPS Young women (debutantes) made their official entrée into society at straight balls. Early gay balls adapted the practice for men in drag or costume and renamed them debutramps.

DRAG The origin of the term is obscure at best but was probably a slang word once used on the theatrical stage. Drag became defined as wearing the opposite gender's clothing, but it especially refers to gay men dressed as women and was the foundation and cornerstone of gay Carnival. For example, "Mary, you are such a drag when you attempt to do terror drag."

FRENCH QUARTER Also known as Vieux Carré. The oldest section of the city of New Orleans, originally laid out by Bienville and Pauger and now filled with bars, hotels, restaurants, and shops. Locals call this area the Quarter or Quarters. For example, "She used to stay in the Quarters before she and her lover moved to the Marigny." For many decades, the area was the center of the city's gay community.

GRAND MARCH Procession at the end of a tableau ball where all the costumes appear on stage for the finale.

KING CAKE Known as the Galette des Rois in French. Traditional cake that is ubiquitous during the Carnival season and was brought to the New World by the French, who still bake a rather small and simple galette with puff pastry and almond paste. In France, the cake is only seen on Epiphany and contains a large bean. Whoever gets the bean in the slice of cake becomes the king or queen of the party. The New Orleans King Cake is a large donut-shaped ultrasweet pastry with thick purple, gold, and green icing, reflecting the traditional colors of Carnival. A plastic Baby Jesus is baked into the cake. Whoever gets the slice containing Jesus must throw the next King Cake party, leading to a never-ending succession of parties from Epiphany through Fat Tuesday.

KREWE A private Mardi Gras organization. The first such organization, the Mistick Krewe of Comus, used the Old English term for group (krewe) to cloak themselves in mystery as they paraded through the streets to celebrate the Carnival season.

LORD OF MISRULE Originally appointed during Christmastide to lead the revelries of the Feast of Fools. The first Carnival krewe was the Mistick Krewe of Comus, derived from John Milton's *Comus*. Milton designated Comus as the Lord of Misrule, and King Comus in New Orleans rules over the Carnival season. Also known as the captain of the Lords of Leather and the Mistik Krewe du Rue Royale Revelers.

MARDI GRAS Literally Fat Tuesday. The last day of the Carnival season, when costumes and masking are permitted in the streets and the Mistick Krewes of Comus and Rex hold their parades and balls. Also known as Shrove Tuesday. May also refer to the entire Carnival season.

QUEENS Krewes traditionally honor a male "king" and female "queen" at each year's ball. In gay krewes, however, the queen outranks the king, and men and women can serve in either role. In the realm of gay Carnival, a Queen is a rather fluid and ambiguous term, which may simply refer to a gay man. For example, "That butch queen standing at the bar used to be the queen of Amon-Ra."

SAINT BERNARD CIVIC CENTER Also known as the Saint Bernard Civic Auditorium; later the Saint Bernard Cultural Center and the Frederick J. Sigur Center. Located in Chalmette, downriver from New Orleans, this large auditorium was home to almost all the gay balls during the Golden Age of gay Carnival in the early and mid-1980s. Despite the venue's location in ultraconservative St. Bernard Parish, local police made backdoor deals in which they agreed to protect the gay krewes.

STATE CHARTER An official state document required of all legitimate Carnival krewe organizations. Gay krewes used this process and loophole to obtain legal state charters. For example, the Krewe of Petronius's state charter proclaimed that they are "henceforth required to promote and carry out the spirit of Mardi Gras; to celebrate the Mardi Gras in any and every way, manner, shape and form possible; to hold Carnival balls; and to hold parties, dances and social gatherings throughout the year, for a total of 99 years."

TABLEAU Shortened form of tableau vivant; plural tableaux. A scene, usually presented on a stage by silent and costumed participants. For example, "The Krewe of Ganymede was known for its brilliant tableaux and artful staging."

"96 Are Booked after Jeff Raid." *New Orleans Times-Picayune*, February 26, 1962.

"97 Arrested at a Lewd Stag Party." *New Orleans Times-Picayune*, March 31, 1962.

Adler, Constance. "Best of New Orleans." *Gambit*, February 25, 2003.

Aldrich, Robert. *Gay Lives*. New York: Thames and Hudson, 2012.

Alexander, John, interview by author, 2000.

Ambush Magazine, February 1985, March 1985.

Anderson, Ed. "No New Clues Turn Up in Six Weekend Killings." *New Orleans Times-Picayune*, January 17, 1972.

"Antique Dealer Taken by Death." *New Orleans Times-Picayune*, December 8, 1969.

Around the Clock: The Gay New Orleans Weekly, February 17, 1984, April 19, 1985.

Ball, Mildred Piteous. "Costumers Work to Dress Royalty, Rex Requires Months on Job." *New Orleans Times-Picayune*, February 8, 1970.

———. "For the Fun of It." *New Orleans Times-Picayune*, Dixie Section, March 1, 1981.

Bartlett, Thomasine, Michael Mizell-Nelson, and David Wolf. "Club My-O-My: New Orleans Vintage Drag." http://www.neworleanshistorical.org/items/show/367.

Batson, Roberts. "Magic Masking." *Impact Magazine*, January 18, 2002.

Bernard, Lou, interview by author, 2015–16.

Blake, Christopher Stanislas. *The Fair, Fair Ladies of Chartres Street*. New Orleans: Beale, 1965.

Bloom, Scott, interview by author, 2015.

Bogie, John Henry, interview by author, 2012.

Bonnefoy, Yves. *Mythologies*. Chicago: University of Chicago Press, 1991.

Bruce of Los Angeles. *The Male Figure: Mardi Gras Special—Carnival in New Orleans*. Promotional brochure, vol. 16, 1960.

Bury, Don, interview by author, 2016.

Calder, Chad. "Petronius, City's Oldest Active Gay Krewe, Cancels 2015 Ball." *New Orleans Advocate*, February 4, 2015.

Carey, Albert, interview by author, 2007–9.

"Carnival Club Directory." *New Orleans Times-Picayune*, October 4, 1987.

Carpenter, Donald H. *Man of a Million Fragments: The True Story of Clay Shaw*. Nashville: Carpenter, 2014.

"Celestial Knights." *New Orleans Magazine*, February 1979.

Chauncey, George. *Gay New York: Gender, Urban Culture, and the Making of the Gay Male World, 1890–1940*. New York: Basic Books, 1995.

Clark, Richard. "City of Desire: A History of Same-Sex Desire in New Orleans, 1917–1977." Ph.D. diss., Tulane University, 2009.

Conaway, Jim. "Helen Hayes Sees Passing of Dirty Talk in Theater." *New Orleans Times-Picayune*, April 24, 1966.

Cortez, Harriett Davis. "Birds of a Feather Flock Together." *New Orleans Times-Picayune*, January 27, 1980.

Costello, Brian J. *Carnival in Louisiana: Celebrating Mardi Gras from the French Quarter to the Red River*. Baton Rouge: Louisiana State University Press, 2017.

Covert, Martin. "Jonathan's Enjoys Local Support." *New Orleans Times-Picayune*, November 1, 1981.

Cox, Ed, interview by author, 2014–15.

Cronk, Ray, and Alvin Payne, interview by author, 2003–11, 2016.

Crotty, William, interview by author, 2003–16.

"Daisy Mae." *Contact Magazine*, March 1977.

Dawson, Victoria. "Mask-Maker to the Stars Made a Crisp About-Face." *New Orleans Times-Picayune*, February 4, 1989.

de Beau-Maltbie, Daniel, interview by author, 2014, 2016.

D'Emilio, John. *Sexual Politics, Sexual Communities: The Making of a Homosexual Minority in the United States, 1940–1950*. Chicago and London: University of Chicago Press, 1983.

Denmark, Phyllis. "The Big Diva." *Ambush Magazine*, February 15–28, 2005.

Dennis, Patrick. *Little Me: The Intimate Memoirs of That Great Star of Stage, Screen and Television, Belle Poitrine*. New York: Dutton, 1961.

DiMiceli, Diane, interview by author, 2015–16.

Dixie-Roto Magazine, *New Orleans Times-Picayune*, Sunday supplement, February 5, 1967.

duArte, Jack. "Jonathan's Is Adventure in Interior Decor, Food." *New Orleans Times-Picayune*, February 13, 1987.

"Edward R. Cox." StageClick.com, www.stageclick.com/person/2973.aspx.

Elli, Scott S. *Madame Vieux Carré: The French Quarter in the Twentieth Century*. Jackson: University Press of Mississippi, 2010.

Erté. *Erté at Ninety: The Complete Graphics*. Ed. Marshall Lee. New York: Dutton, 1982.

Fitzmorris, Tom. "Jonathan." nomenu.com, July 19, 2012.

Flake, Carol. *New Orleans: Behind the Masks of America's Most Exotic City*. New York: Grove, 1994.

Gagnard, Frank. "Designing Man Back for Ballet." *New Orleans Times-Picayune*, May 6, 1976.

———. "Enter Gypsy." *New Orleans Times-Picayune*, July 23, 1967.

Gallatin, A. E. *Aubrey Beardsley's Drawings*. London: Wieners, 1903.

Garbarino, Steve. "Artist George Dureau Left His Mark on the French Quarter Like Few Others." *New Orleans Advocate*, April 15, 2014.

Gil, Mickey, and George Patterson, interview by author, 2007, 2008.

Gilley, Jerry, interview by author, 2014–15.

Guillard, Betty. "It's A Ball: The Krewe of Armeinius." *New Orleans Times-Picayune*, Lagniappe Section, January 26, 1983.

Guillot, Cleveland, Jr., and Luis Conde, interview by author, 2015.

Hardy, Arthur. *Arthur Hardy's Mardi Gras in New Orleans: An Illustrated History*. Metairie, La.: Hardy, 2001.

Harris, Daniel. *The Rise and Fall of Gay Culture*. New York: Hyperion, 1997.

Harrity, Christopher. "New Orleans Photographer and Artist George Dureau Has Died." TheAdvocate.com, April 9, 2014.

Hedderel, Vance Philip, interview by author, 2016.

Hickerson, Michael, interview by author, 2012, 2015–16.

Hill, Jeffrey. "Gay Mardi Gras from Debutramps to Lords of Leather: A Brief History." noladefender.com, February 25, 2012.

"History of the Gay Krewes." *Impact Magazine*, February 1978.

"A History of the Gay Krewes." Carnival Supplement, *Impact Magazine*, March 1979.

Huber, Leonard V. *Mardi Gras: A Pictorial History of Carnival in New Orleans*. Gretna, La.: Pelican, 1977.

Impact Magazine. February 1979.

"In the News, Segment 1." *Ambush Magazine 2000*, March 7–20, 1997.

Jackson, Jill. "Louisiana Man Is Chef in Los Angeles." *New Orleans Times-Picayune*, November 1, 1962.

———. "Set Is Exciting between Takes." *New Orleans Times-Picayune*, April 24, 1969.

Jennings, Christopher. "GoNOLA Guide to Gay Mardi Gras." gonola.com, January 21, 2015.

Johnson, David K. *The Lavender Scare: The Cold War Persecution of Gays and Lesbians in the Federal Government.* Chicago: University of Chicago Press, 2004.

Johnson, E. Patrick. *Sweet Tea: Black Gay Men of the South.* Chapel Hill: University of North Carolina Press, 2011.

Jones, Benjamin, and William Walters, interview by author, 2014.

"Jon Lee Poché Obituary." *New Orleans Times-Picayune*, January 21, 1987.

Keyes, James, interview by author, 2009.

Kirkwood, James. *American Grotesque: An Account of the Clay Shaw–Jim Garrison Affair in the City of New Orleans.* New York: Simon and Schuster, 1968.

"La Krewe Mystique de Désimé." *Hays Daily News*, February 17, 1977.

Krewe of Armeinius. *La Plume—If You Build It They Will Come—The Architecture Ball Program*, 2015.

"Krewe of Perseus." *The Rooster*, April 6, 1988.

Krewe of Stars website, www.kreweofstars.com.

Laborde, Errol. "Restaurant Jonathan, Star Gazing through Etched Glass." *New Orleans Magazine*, September 1980.

Laborde, Peggy Scott, and Tom Fitzmorris. *Lost Restaurants of New Orleans and the Recipes That Made Them Famous.* Gretna, La.: Pelican, 2012.

LaCour, Arthur B. *New Orleans Masquerade: Chronicles of Carnival.* Gretna, La.: Pelican, 1952.

Lambert, Patricia. *False Witness: The Real Story of Jim Garrison's Investigation and Oliver Stone's Film JFK.* New York: Evans, 2000.

Langer, Cassandra. "The Mythical Realm of Richmond Barthé." *Gay and Lesbian Review*, July 1, 2009.

Last Call New Orleans Dyke Bar History Project. lastcallnola.org, December 2015.

Lord, Catherine, and Richard Meyer. *Art and Queer Culture.* London: Phaidon, 2013.

Mack, Carl, interview by author, 2016.

"Man Booked in Two Murders." *New Orleans Times-Picayune*, January 16, 1972.

Maniaci, Charles, interview by author, 2016.

Martin, Gary, interview by author, 2015.

Matt. *'Rasslers, 'Ranglers, and Rough Guys: The Erotic Art of Matt.* Ed. Joseph W. Bean. San Francisco: Brush Creek Media, 1997.

McCourt, James. *Queer Street: The Rise and Fall of An American Culture, 1945–1985.* New York: Norton, 2003.

Mitchell, Patricia B. "Marti's Restaurant." *Community Standard Monthly Awards Magazine* (New Orleans), December 1974.

Mitchell, Reid. *All on a Mardi Gras Day.* Cambridge: Harvard University Press, 1995.

Moore, Patrick. *Beyond Shame: Reclaiming the Abandoned History of Radical Gay Sexuality.* Boston: Beacon, 2004.

Moreau, Mike, and Darwin Reed, interview by author, 2015–16.

Naquin, Rip. "Paparazzi." *Ambush Magazine*, February 23–March 15, 2001.

Naquin, Rip, and Marsha Delain. "New Orleans Loses Philanthropist Andy Boudreaux." *Ambush Magazine*, May 15–28, 1998.

Nassar, Gabe, interview by author, 2015.

Newlin, Jon, interview by author, 1990s.

Newlin, Jon. "Madame John Dodt's Legacy, No. 27." *Ambush Magazine*, November 13–26, 1998.

"New Orleans Witch Hunt" *ONE Magazine*, September 1958.

Nitschke, I. E. Bill. Trial of Clay Shaw deposition. July 31, 1978.

Oppenheimer, Dan, and Claude Summers. "Jack Robinson." glbtq.com May 5, 2015.

Oppenheimer, Emily, and Dan Oppenheimer, interview by author, Jack Robinson Archive, 2014–15.

Orgeron, J. Bruce, Jr., interview by author, 2015.

Osborne, Mitchel L., and Errol Laborde. *Mardi Gras! A Celebration.* New Orleans: Picayune, 1982.

Ourso, Daniel, interview by author, 2015.

Owen, Ken, interview by author, 2007–15.

Patterson, George, interview by author, 2007, 2016.

Peltier, David, interview by author, 2011–15.

Perez, Frank. "Alice Brady." *Ambush Magazine*, June 3–16, 2014.

———. "Amon-Ra: 50 Years of Balls." *Ambush Magazine*, February 10–23, 2015.

———. "Mike Moreau." *Ambush Magazine*, October 22–November 4, 2013.

———. "The Gay Bashing Murder of Fernando Rios." *Ambush Magazine*, November 6–19, 2012.

Perez, Frank, and Jeffrey Palmquist. *In Exile: The History and Lore Surrounding New Orleans Gay Culture and Its Oldest Gay Bar*. Hurlford, Scot.: LL, 2012.

———, eds. *My Gay New Orleans: 28 Personal Reminisces on LGBT & Life in New Orleans*. Bedford, Tex.: LL, 2016.

Phillips, Wayne, interview by author, 2000–2016.

Pits, Stella. "Restaurant Jonathan—Deco Is Its Middle Name." *New Orleans Times-Picayune*, December 29, 1978.

Pope, John. "Artist and Ex-Restauranteur Marti Shambra Dies of AIDS." *New Orleans Times-Picayune*, September 15, 1988.

———. "Charlene Schneider, Gay-Rights Champion." *New Orleans Times-Picayune*, December 7, 2006.

———. "Mickey Gil, Captain of Two Gay Carnival Krewes, Dies at 73." *New Orleans Times-Picayune*, March 3, 2010.

Powell, Troy, interview by author, 2016.

Quinn, Sally. "The Diversity of Mardi Gras." *Washington Post*, March 6, 1973.

Read, Katy. "Carnival at Its Spiciest—In the Shadow of AIDS, a Gay Krewe Sparkles." *New Orleans Times-Picayune*, February 20, 1993.

Rechy, John. *City of Night*. New York: Grove, 1963.

Reggio, Tony. "Mardi Gras Royalty." *Ambush Magazine*, February 15–28, 2011.

"Remembering Matt" (Charles Kerbs Obituary). Tom of Finland Foundation website, fall 2002.

"Restaurant Jonathan." *Interior Design*, July 1977.

Ricketts, Carl, interview by author, 2015.

Rizzuto, Errol, interview by author, 2016.

Robbins, Christel, interview by author, 2015.

Robert, Marsha, interview by author, 2016.

Robinson, Jack. *Jack Robinson: On Show: Portraits, 1958–1972*. Bath: Palazzo, 2011.

"Rosemary 'Mama' Pino Obituary." *New Orleans Times-Picayune*, December 18, 2005.

Roth, George, interview by author, 2016.

Saxon, Lyle. *Fabulous New Orleans*. New Orleans: Crager, 1928.

Schindler, Henri, interview by author, 2016.

———. *Mardi Gras New Orleans*. New York: Flammarion, 2001.

———. *Mardi Gras Treasures: Invitations of the Golden Age*. Gretna, La.: Pelican, 2000.

Sears, James T. *Rebels, Rubyfruit, and Rhinestones: Queering Space in the Stonewall South*. New Brunswick, N.J.: Rutgers University Press, 2001.

Sherwood, Wally. "Sherwood's Forest." *Ambush Magazine*, February 1985, March 1985, May 1985, February 22–March 7, 2002, April 19–May 2, 2002.

Simmons, David Lee. "Mystic Krewe of Satyricon's 14th Bal Masque Celebrates Bal des Beaux-Arts." davidleesimmons.com, January 23, 2016.

———. "Mystic Krewe of Satyricon 'Makes Scents' of Mardi Gras with 'Bal des Parfums' on Friday." *New Orleans Times-Picayune*, January 31, 2015.

"Snap Paparazzi, Radical Faeries." *Ambush Magazine*, February 15–18, 2011.

State of Louisiana v. Mark A. Jenkins (trial transcript), No. 98-KA-1603. 1996.

"Stewart Gahn Obituary—Dignity Memorial—Lake Lawn Metairie." lakelawn.tributes.com, April 2014.

Stipelcovich, Wendell, interview by author, 2014–16.

Straayer, Chris. *Deviant Eyes, Deviant Bodies: Sexual Re-Orientation in Film and Video*. New York: Columbia University Press, 1996.

Stratton, Don, interview by author, 2015.

Sullener, Elizabeth. "Gay Carnival." *New Orleans Times-Picayune*, February 13, 1983.

Tallant, Robert. *Mardi Gras*. Garden City, N.Y.: Doubleday, 1949.

Talluto, Russell, interview by author, 2011, 2016.

Thompson, Mark, ed. *The Fire in Moonlight: Stories from the Radical Faeries, 1975–2010*. Maple Shade, N.J.: White Crane, 2011.

Toole, John Kennedy. *A Confederacy of Dunces*. Baton Rouge: Louisiana State University Press, 1980.

Townsend, Johnny, interview by author, 2001

———. *Let the Faggots Burn: The UpStairs Lounge Fire*. St. Petersburg, Fla.: BookLocker, 2011.

Tressner, William B., Jr. *Queens of the Quarter*. San Diego: Publishers Export, 1968.

Tucker, Kelly. "Don We Now Our Gay Apparel." *New Orleans Times-Picayune*, January 25, 1980.

Vandeventer, Gary, interview by author, 2015.

White, Edmund. *States of Desire: Travels in Gay America*. New York: Dutton, 1980.

Wilkerson-Freeman, Sarah. "Shrove Tuesday at Miss Dixie's: Jack Robinson's Mardi Gras Photographs, 1952–1955." *Southern Cultures* 12.1 (Spring 2006).

Williams, Henry Lionel, and Ottalie K. Williams. *America's Small Houses: The Personal Homes of Designers and Collectors*. New York: Barnes, 1964.

Williams, Tennessee. *Mister Paradise and Other One-Act Plays*. New York: New Directions, 2005.

———. *Notebooks*. Ed. Margaret Bradham Thornton. New Haven: Yale University Press, 2006.

———. *Selected Letters of Tennessee Williams*. Vol. 1, 1920–1945. Ed. Albert J. Devlin and Nancy M. Tischler. New York: New Directions, 2000.

Wilson, George, interview by author, 2016.

Woodard, Earl, and Spencer Lindsay, interview by author, 2011.

Woolley, William, interview by author, 2002–4, 2016.

Young, Perry. *The Mistick Krewe: Chronicles of Comus and His Kin*. New Orleans: Carnival Press, 1931.

Zeringue, John S., III, interview by author, 2015–16.

INDEX